# FIRE ON THE ANDES

# FIRE ON THE ANDES

CARLETON BEALS

ILLUSTRATIONS
BY
JOSE SABOGAL

PHILADELPHIA
J. B. LIPPINCOTT COMPANY
LONDON
1934

# CONTENTS

[ 5 ]

# CONTENTS

## PART IV
## LINES OF BATTLE

# PART I

*CHILDREN OF THE SUN*

# I
## LAND DIVIDED

### 1

LIKE ancient Gaul, Perú is divided into three parts—three parts far more divided than those of ancient Gaul.

### 2 WHITE COAST

West of the great Andes ridge, from the Ecuadorean jungles south for fifteen hundred miles along the Pacific, stretches a rainless coastal plain some fifty miles in width, largely desert

except where rivers move through to the sea. In most of this narrow strip man's foothold is still painfully uncertain.

Midway along the coast, one beautiful, modern, if rather ineffective, city, Lima (founded by Pizarro in 1534 to replace lofty Cuzco as capital), nestles in the green Rimac Valley. But go either way a few miles, for instance to the Pachacámac ruins—where four centuries ago Hernando Pizarro and Miguel de Estete broke through the emerald and coral door of the great temple—on to the fishing village of Pucusana

9

and down to Ica: there one travels through bone-dry country over rolling powdered sands which drift up to the very
crest of gigantic hills, utterly barren; a desolate scene, broken
only by delusive mirages of magic seas, and peopled only by
fantastic congeries of hills. "Some . . . seem disfigured faces,
others menacing fists, others the backs of gigantic sleeping
animals." Now and then a few lost fluffy clouds drift over
the dead landscape forlornly.

At times the wind lifts up great cylinders of sand that beat
furiously against far horizons. Giant whorls charge on for
hundreds of miles. Plantless dunes move inland like writhing
naked white bodies.

At noon the sands are dazzling silver; the half-buried hills
are bald as glistening billiard balls; but as the sun lags westward, the round wind-smoothed contours—so lascivious and
sterile—gather purple shadows. At early dawn, or sometimes
in the late afternoon, thin mist drifts from valley or sea, and
hills and sands strike up symphonies of delicate tints from
silver and blue to rusty ochre—like the colors of an Indian
blanket.

Red is the sand around Mollendo, "as though a hundred
lions had poured out their blood there." Every afternoon the
Sun makes its red sacrifice—"like an old-time Herod beheading John the Baptist. . . . Red hills scratch their backs
against the sky like shaggy stationary buffalos." And the tiny
port itself on its dismal hill "with its white houses is like a
flock of lonely sheep, the church-tower standing up like a
solemn herder."

In winter—May to November—a dense metallic fog hangs
fifteen hundred feet over the leaden sea and, near shore,
throws a hard, dull, gray light, forlorn as the void. For a few
brief weeks only, along the sea-fronting hills, low-growing
moss-like rock-plants spread meager patches like some frightful skin eruption.

Not until the *Ceja de la Costa*—"Eyebrow of the Coast"

—thousands of feet up at the base of the Andes, where the hills become blue triangular mountains, sharp rocks stabbing the sky, does some rain fall; a thin grass mantles the customarily harsh slopes; a few hardier shrubs and trees grow perennially.

Yet most of this lugubrious coast, except toward the north, has an even delightful climate, balmy, caressing as a woman's hand, almost opiating. Though so near the equator, it is cooled by the Humboldt current which sweeps icy cold out of the Antarctic, making the region habitable—wherever there is water for irrigation—just as in opposite manner the north Atlantic is made habitable by the warm Gulf Stream. But north, the hot Del Niño current boils out of the Guayaquil Gulf and edges down the coast. Tumbes and Lambayeque are sweltering places. When this current sweeps further south —as it does about every quarter century—it alters the climate, causes terrific tropical rains, which wash away whole villages not constructed for such a catastrophe and bring strange epidemics. Then the desert blooms briefly like a rose garden.

Through this barren world of desert and death, along wide valleys hemmed in by bright red bluffs, flow tranquil rivers —thirty such have sources high enough in the Andes to ensure continuous flow.

Rice, sugar, cotton and corn fields, fruit and nut orchards, diagonal maguey rows, spread green carpets. On the outer slopes the low twisted algarroba and tall buoyant balsa trees grow wild; and in marshy spots, haunt of mosquitoes and fever, the *toquilla,* and other riparian reeds, from which Panamá hats, houses, beds and fishing boats are made. These valleys are green islands surrounded by yellow meaningless immensity.

The Mochicas, and others, probably before Christ, began the painful conquest of the desert. They pushed a great elevated road through the sandy wilderness, which later the Chimús and finally the Inca emperors, improved with sign posts, *tambo* inns, storehouses.

In all the coast valleys, the early folk built huge aqueducts circling around the upper foothills to provide water for every available inch. A fifty-mile remnant of one in the Chicama Valley required the moving of five million tons of earth.

All this magnificent effort was abandoned by the Spaniards; the desert reclaimed its own, as it has to this day save for a few short railways and bumpy roads. The conquerors further reduced the area of cultivation by stripping higher levels of all trees, thus decreasing river flow.

They were not even able to re-colonize the coast completely. To work on the large semi-feudal estates forced Indian labor, later negro slaves, were brought in; during the Republic, Chinese coolies and Japs—a racial hodgepodge, which further sets the area apart from other Peruvian regions.

### 3  CONDORLAND

Cutting the country in twain is the Sierra, the lofty Andes, with their three mighty ranges, their great upland plateaus, enormous precipices and vast valleys—haunt of the condor, flocks of wool-bearing alpacas, swift-footed herds of white-fleeced vicuña, tinkling llamas—red ribbons on their ears, gay tassels on their pack-saddles. The Quechua, Colla and Aimará towns range from 7,500 to over 14,000 feet—"the fortress of a race of quartz men."

On each snow-clad peak of this tortuous, tilted land still lives the spirit of the mountains, the *achachila* symbolized by a cross on large heaps of stones—to which every passer-by contributes and before which most kneel down. "Only on the crest of the Andes," writes the poet, "can one talk with

God . . . they are God's cathedral. . . . The Andes hear the neighborly song of the stars, the music of the infinite and the concert of long silences." The Andes "tie the world to the sky."

Better said, the Andes are the wrath of God, a gift to man that is almost punishment. The Indians say those shaggy heights are "giants trotting with hungry jaws."

At some altitudes one runs the dangers of terrible diseases, *verruga*, a fever, usually fatal, which bursts out in frightful pus; *uta*, which eats away throat, mouth and nose.

The weather is usually brutal, like the claws of a condor in the vitals, a martyrdom of ice, lightning, thunder, tempests and fierce efforts to breathe.

In the sere dry summer—May to November—the sun is paler than in winter; cold blasts sweep through the vast canyons. In winter—December to April—cold rains drive down day after day in torrents; in the higher villages often turn to snow. The great ravines with their violent storms are like abysmal coughing lungs. On over the dead plains, the weary traveler, gasping for oxygen, is shaken in his saddle; and at night can only take refuge in the lee of some rock, usually without the comfort of even a fire, for these crags produce few trees, and the supply of dung, which the natives laboriously collect and dry for months, is too scant to permit its use for aught but cooking.

During those months the snow-line creeps lower and lower. In their inadequate dwellings the people crouch shivering, fingers numb with cold, but eternally weaving alpaca and merino wool into beautiful rugs, blankets, hats, garments.

Somehow, during the rainy season—for when the sun does come out it is warm—plants contrive to grow. The highlanders raise crops more diversified than those of the Mexican Indian: potatoes, yams, oca, corn, wheat, legumes, cucumbers, onions, even sugar-cane below nine thousand feet.

They toil in the lofty mines of Cerro de Pasco, Puno and Huancavelica.

They labor in harsh serfdom for a few cents a day on the great valley estates.

The Andes are their mother; and their mother, these later centuries, has treated them ill. The hand of the conqueror still rests heavy upon them.

Travel up that astonishing railroad—built by that mad crook and genius Henry Meiggs—from Lima along the Rimac gorge, from sea-level up to 16,000 feet, and observe the rock garden terraces along the steep slopes from valley floor to sky, built by the Quechua and other folk under Inca rule, perhaps even long before the Incas—an unbelievable record of patient industry. Today only crumbling walls remain, the slopes are sere and bare; in the narrow bottoms of the upper Rimac now huddle merely a few straw shacks, homes of a people miserable in poverty.

Go on through the mining industry, where for fifty miles around the foreign-owned smelters, sulphur and arsenic fumes have killed every spear of vegetation in a region once fertile. No wonder the San Mateo Indians smashed the Proaño plant at Tamboraque, only to be mowed down by federal troops.

In the broad upland valleys stretch enormous haciendas, where the Children of the Sun toil in debt slavery for a few cents a day. Just as in the sixteenth century, they are rounded up in veritable chain-gangs for mine, hacienda and public highways. If they run away, they are *prófugos*, escaped convicts, to be hunted down like animals and returned, if not killed, to the hacienda, cost of capture added to their mountain-high debt, often passed on to their sons. Or the army-conscriptors comb through the villages, taking off the most physically fit, load them, tightly-packed like cattle, into trucks and trains, uniform them, and for three years expose them to the civilized life of booze, prostitutes and disease.

For contrast, push into the higher, more precipitous valleys, where centuries ago the ancient race took refuge. Patiently, sturdily, it has carved new terraces along the cliffs, clear to the crest of vast remote mountains—potatoes up to nearly fourteen thousand feet. All the way from Sapallanga, under its bower of eucalypti, along the Mantaro gorge down to Huanta, dreaming under cool arcades among fruit orchards, the countryside, at least during the rainy season—as in parts of Italy—is cultivated like a garden; scarcely a foot of arable land, however steep, is not planted—marvellous industry in the face of great odds.

For despite such handicaps, these people go staunchly forth, wad of lime-mixed coca-leaves in their cheeks, to toil. To an ox or burro or human shoulders, they hitch a strong iron-tipped stake with a cross-bar. They stand on the arms of this inverted cross and thus crudely and laboriously break up the soil for sowing. When the crop comes in, they weed their field meticulously; they make the most of their parsimonious land.

## 4 GREEN HELL

East of the Andes lies the low jungle country, criss-crossed by valleys, plains and low hills, called by the Peruvians, "The Mountain," less frequently "The Forest."

Already up in the highlands some of the jungle streams are powerful torrents fed by perpetually melting snows. In "The Mountain," still over two thousand miles from their Atlantic destination, they are majestic rivers. The Amazón and Ucayali, for instance, are navigable a thousand miles in Perú up from the frontier of Brazil. They move slowly and calmly through enormous jungle walls, for it is mostly low, hot country: Iquitos, several thousand miles up the Amazón, is only 350 feet above sea-level.

The eastern rivers flow through a great fan-shaped region nearly a third of all Perú, a region filled with swamps and impenetrable forests. The poet states that there "the rough oak learns to love the languid orchid," and "the evening star in the purple sky, half-seen, through the snarl of branches, makes the universe seem doubly remote." Certainly it is all a lush green wilderness—tonalities more verdant than in our northern woods, never knowing autumn colors. For over this region the rain falls incessantly twelve months in the year.

But for all the bright images of the poet, twelve months of tropic rain create horror and disease. Equatorial heat and torrential storms produce the rank vegetation, the frightful swamps which make human survival so tragic and give the whole region the name "Green Hell." Here flourish deadly diseases, carried by swarms of mosquitoes, sand-flies and other voracious insects—malaria, beri beri, typhoid, leprosy, horrible skin ailments. The Peruvian jungle is something more than—as the poet again remarks—"the cathedral of sorrow, where unknown Gods speak in hushed tones, promising eternal life to the gigantic trees, already ancient when the first tribes appeared."

16

For in it is the terrible *mariquita* tree, which, like women of ill-fame, sends forth a ravishing perfume few can resist but leaves the flesh inflamed, soon to break out in unbearable itch, then in frightful ulcers which leave welts and hard scars, like the slice of a lash. There is the *pringamora,* another inflamant of the skin; the *caruje,* which seems like a rainbow bubble but contains only flesh-rotting caustic.

The trees seem deformed, tied up in queer knots, captive in vast nets of *bejucas,* or crushed, twisted, sucked dry by the octopus *matapalo,* which flings its tentacles about the mightiest trunks. Here are trees, like men, devoured by horrible leprous diseases. Here are poisonous hot vapours and rotting odors; purple fungus and great bursting toadstools; flowers with exaggerated sexual apparati, palpitating obscenely, flinging drunken aphrodisiacal perfume that drugs the senses.

Here troop millions of devastating ants, here are great swollen toads, huge serpents, hairy spiders, slimy salamanders and ridiculous screaming monkeys.

And yet there is a gleaming fascination. The trees beckon. The heat, the strange odors, the queer sights, cause nervous tension, a constant illusion of something desirable yet evil, perverse, dangerous; at night strange fires flicker—the *ignis fatuus,* siren-like, leading lost souls to doom. At other times one is seized with an overwhelming desire to escape, but those who flee thoughtlessly merely lose their way and often their reason.

Only a peculiar type of being can survive—at least until modern science has made further strides toward controlling climatic and health conditions and has discovered new types of prophylaxis.

The so-called centers of civilization Moyobamba, Yurimaguas, Saposoa—grass-grown plazas, church, school and fly-specked stores—are pathetic refuges where men drag out a lethargic existence under the terrific sun, where the rain comes down in torrents on tile roofs, where everything turns to rust, to mould, to powder. Insects bore into the hardest furniture, within a few months eat the pages of books, perforate the finest cigars.

Lazy Iquitos, the most modern—for it went through a rubber-boom that well-nigh paved its streets with gold—however much it reflects colorful mongrel frontier life, once more is running down at the heels, is growing shabby and degenerate.

The more élite residents have imported grand pianos from across the sea, clear up the Amazón; these instruments stand idle, their strings corroded, worthless, symbols of leisure-class snobbery. Radio and phonograph deteriorate. The former, unless of exceedingly excellent make, is almost useless because the waves from coast broadcasting stations are mostly cut off by the Andes, are lost in the tangle of ravines and Green Hell heat. The conch-shell and the wooden syrinxes of the Indians reassert their plaintive melodies.

The great Napo, Yavari and Putumayo river regions remain largely unexplored, haunts of migratory Indians: some, ferocious headhunters; others, docile and non-combative. Customarily, most of them, except those few who have learned to enter more civilized centers, never wear more than a gee string.

The jungle, largely abandoned to a primitive state since the beginning of human residence there, has deficient economic development. The eastern departments send forth a few tropical raw products—rubber, woods, quina, coffee, fruits, cotton; but these must be carried over thousands of miles of river before they can even reach the sea, or else be taken mule-back across the lofty Cordillera.

The previous century, when President Piérola wished to put down a revolt in the Green Hell region, he had to send a war vessel through the Straits of Magellan and up the Amazón, nearly 8,000 miles in all. The Iquitos area, except by air, is not much more accessible to Lima even today.

Aside from providing a few meagre revenues, more than consumed by the plethora of officials, who prefer risking an insalubrious climate to doing real work, and army posts of a nation jealous over useless frontiers, the Green Hell has no important connection with the national economy.

It is a vague land of mystery and danger for coastlanders, almost entirely disconnected from the rest of Perú.

<h1 style="text-align:center">5</h1>

The Spaniards overran all of the vast region known as Perú: coast, Andes, and Green Hell. The priests, those early years, went everywhere. But the Spaniards never really conquered more than the coast. The vast Andean heights dismayed them. In the Green Hell fever and death ate into their ranks. The poisoned arrows of ferocious naked tribes, who still roam unmolested, mowed them down. Though within a few decades the conquerors smelled out the major mineral deposits and busily exploited them with forced labor, aside from the mines, their hold on the Andean region was ever precarious, that on the Green Hell largely nonexistent.

The three regions are still almost mutually exclusive. Each region lacks communications, even within its own limits, to weld it together. Though communications are normally easier longitudinally than east to west, these since Inca times have been almost wholly ignored, except slightly on the coast. Such means of transport as have been promoted since pre-Spanish times have answered the needs of international exploitation rather than harmonious national development.

At two points the coast has tapped the Sierra with railways constructed up into eternal snows at great cost and difficulty. Elsewhere are found only a few execrable roads, extremely dangerous to traverse.

To this day, though both Sierra and Green Hell have been

more extensively dominated politically, the same failure of the coast to utilize its dictatorship properly to exploit resources still persists. The coast civilization, still colonial, European, feudal, fanatically religious, knows little of the highlands or jungles beyond. A trip into the Sierras, with its danger for lowlander of acute *saroche,* or mountain sickness, its constant menace to health, the difficulty of respiration, the nervous gasping nights and lingering days of exhaustion—a trip with such penalties is looked upon by the softer *costeños* as almost a supreme adventure. Those who safely return are awesomely examined as venturesome explorers. And the big-nosed, big-lunged highlanders who come down to the coast soon get pneumonia or tuberculosis.

Professor Wilheim Sievers [1] divides Perú's area: Sierra, 63 percent, jungles, 28 percent, coast, 9 percent. He estimates —no census has been taken since 1876!—that of the total population of almost six millions, 73 percent lives in the Sierra, 22 percent on the coast, and 5 percent in the jungle. Thus most of Perú's area and population is in the Sierra dedicated to rural pursuits; the coast is urban; the jungle is merely a sparse primitive trading region.

Thus actually Perú is divided, so far as important economic and political phenomena are concerned, into only two important economic parts, antagonistic highland and coast, a duality which (except during the period of the Inca empire) has existed since the dawn of history, and which is still the secret of political turmoil and national frustration. Until this duality is reconciled, Perú can know no enduring peace, can achieve no real affirmation of its national life.

In the olden days, the Chavín peoples pushed down to the coast: the coast Chimú and Nazca folk pushed up into the Andes, planting great terraced fortresses. Their encroachment was limited by the rise of the great Tiahuanaco civilization spreading north from Bolivia. In the Inca days the

---

[1] *Geografía de Bolivia y Perú,* 221.

21

feathered warriors of Viracocha and Pachacutec Yupanqui spread the rainbow symbol of their power over the lowlands and were rapidly achieving a satisfactory reconciliation of divergent interests. The effort was ruptured by the Spanish Conquest. Since then the duality, accompanied by antagonism, has persisted.

At present snobbish arrogant Lima, city of pious hypocrisy and gay follies, rules Perú. Its more direct control is over the great coast estates and the new coat industry, where bourgeois aristocrats face proletarian misery; but it also exploits the Sierra in its own interest.

The coast, though drawn into the current of foreign trade of modern industry, of class struggles between capital and labor, remains psychologically far behind the modern era in which it to some extent functions. Its psychology is only slightly bourgeois, mostly colonial, fanatic, reactionary, dictatorial. Its people are corroded with chicanery and vices, pomp and false show. It is living the epoch of Porfirio Díaz in Mexico.

Psychologically and in habit, the coast is mostly half in the fifteenth century, half in the nineteenth century, but a bare fraction of its inhabitants in the twentieth century.

The highlands live from the tenth to the sixteenth century; the jungle, save for its nineteenth-century trading settlements, lives in the prehistoric centuries.

But these are glib classifications; the vital forces of Perú, and these are the ones which must be recognized and given scope, are in the Sierra; there are most of Perú's people, most of its area, most of its wealth. The Sierra will have to make the twentieth century an epoch of its own meaning.

"Mountainism," declares the Ayacucho magazine *Antara* (November, 1933), "the regional, characteristic and typical contributions of mountainism are on the way to forming a credo, an ideology in the new sensibility of Latin America.

. . . Indo-America is gestating a cultural cycle with the in-
eluctable force of its historic destiny."

The Peruvian Andes are the hard-tangled knot of the
South American Sierras. Just as the Rocky Mountains—
which march through the United States in one main direction—split up into cross ridges and become a twisted upheaval south of the Anahuac Valley in Mexico, so the Andes
—which are austere ridges in Colombia and Ecuador, and
again in Chile—in Perú split up into three major extremely
lofty heights, between them a chaos of ravines. The Andes
are the mountain knot of the South American chain; there
also is the river knot, the source of the Amazón and dozens of
other great streams. These flow in confused contortions in
every direction before straightening out for their long run
to the sea.

And just as mountains and rivers are knotted up, so are
men, races and societies. In the Peruvian Andes are the hard
twisted knot of ethnic, social and political problems of Perú,
and Perú is the hard unravelled knot of South America. No
genius has yet arisen great enough to untangle that knot, to
solve its major problems. Here is the uncut umbilical cord
of South America's future.

Here a new world is being born.

## 6

Go to thatched-roof Acostambo with its eternally roaring
river, sharp cow-dotted fields cut against the mountain skyline; to Chanchas, on red and green hills, far vistas of other
villages on every spur; to lofty Ocuviri, where vicuña herds
plunge through crags in a cloud of dusty snow; to the perfumed plaza of Ixcuchaca, village of the bridge of high
towers, of oleanders and white peaches and thousands of
trilling birds; Cuenca with its fences of dried shrubs, its
adobe and stone walls with gnarled growing cactus, a place

redolent with square-stemmed wild mint, bright with yellow flowers and morning-glories; Hayacachi, a bower of green and gold, tangled roses smothering spiked maguey plants, and high above all, a thin church tower; Viques, red prickly pear blossoms among the rocks, a town so lofty that the false pepper trees, native to Perú, are but shrubs, the air so vibrantly clear that the maguey plants are purple against red earth; Pilchaca, a study in yellow, where compositae dot the fields and Swedish broom everywhere throws sulphur-colored glory; Incaquasi, eternal mist on crags; Pucará of stout adobe walls and freshly tiled roofs; Colquemarca, with its browsing herds of insolently indifferent llamas; Huanchaca of the fisher-folk, thatched roofs beside a smoky sea; brown-walled Magdalena de Cao, struggling in the coils of great estates—everywhere the tidings are the same, the people are stirring.

More and more conscious of their rights, not much longer will they be hounded into debt slavery. Ere long the great land-barons, whose acres stretch along the more fertile plains, whose methods, often more backward than those of the Indians, contribute so little to advancing national economy, will suffer the fate of every absentee ruling class that refuses to heed the handwriting. The Children of the Sun, turning to ancient faiths and to new slogans from over the sea, are clamoring for justice. The tide is rising.

The land of Quechuas, Mochicas, Collas. Here is the real Perú. Here are the real Peruvians. Only when finally they reach for light will Perú, the nation, be born, not before. Then a new cycle of history will have begun for South America and the New World.

## II

# EMPIRE OF THE SUN

### I

PERHAPS 25,000 years ago, Oriental, Polynesian, possibly even African, emigration into the New World began. On Easter Island, far off the Chilean coast, huge carved monoliths, it is claimed, record eastward migration.

Probably four thousand years or more ago an archaic culture of common origin and characteristics had spread over much of the American continents.

Two or three thousand years ago in present Peruvian Ancash province, high up beyond the Maritime Cordillera, the mysterious people of Chavín were carving stones into Maya-like glyphs, jaguars and other symbolic figures. A great obelisk depicted a duo-sexed dragon-shaped monster richly adorned; ravenous serpents and plants, puma-head genital, fertility plant outflowing; on the other side, female organs.

The Chavín folk came into the coast to Cupisnique, perhaps elsewhere. From their settlements in the north, and from that other long-vanished city to the south, Paracas, new influences spread in widening circles among the coast cultures.

By 100 B.C. and down to 500 A.D., the Mochicas and other coast peoples had reached the golden art-age, producing notable ceramics and metal work.

They were modelling and painting terra cotta ware with vivid hunting and fishing scenes, scorpion warriors fighting body to body, priestly rites, birth travail, fanged gods, and chiefs in litters, exuberant sexual acts mistakenly called pornographic, portraits depicting astonishment, fear, tenderness, mother-love, despair, anger. They were making bird-handle copper-knives, golden blow-guns; they were setting emeralds and mounting gold and silver beads and bangles. Already they had built roads over which they dispatched swift runners. Hill aqueducts watered the valleys.

Their great terraced fortresses and temples, their step-shaped houses—with bas-relief walls, massive-roof combs, shady verandas and patios—supported by twisted algarroba trunks and fronted by charming gardens, rose on a hundred hills. An active imaginative people.

Father Miguel Cabello de Balboa tells the story of the founding of another great dynasty, north of the Mochicas:

To Lambayeque from the north on a great fleet of balsa rafts came Naimlap, valorous Father of Families, with his wife Ceterni, and many concubines, to found the inland city Chot about the temple of the green-stone idol Yampallac. Forty in number were Naimlap's chief officials: Pita Zofi was the trumpeter on conch-shells; Ninacola cared for the litter and throne; Fonga Sidge scattered shell-dust before his majesty's feet; Ninagintue looked after our lord's drink; Occhocalco was the royal banqueter; Xam Muchec was the keeper of the royal face-paints; Llapochilluli made the royal shirts, bird-feather tunics and bat-skin capes; Ollopcopoc supervised his master's bathing.

Naimlap, when he died—the priests reported—took wings and flew away. His successor Cium sealed himself up in a tomb to die that he might be ever considered immortal and divine. Our Twelfth Lord—Fempellec—last of the dynasty —consorted with the devil in the form of a beautiful woman, thus bringing on the land a calamitous rain followed by drouth, famine and disease; the priests and people flung him, bound hand and foot, into the deep sea.

2

The northern coast civilizations were welded by the Chimú folk—who proudly claimed descent from four stars—into one great confederation, all the way from Guayaquil to the Pativilca Valley (where stood the outpost fortress Parmunca).

The most famous Chimú city was Chan Chan (near present Trujillo), a vast place half a league across, with perhaps 200,000 inhabitants, filled with triple-walled fortresses, painted bird-and-fish bas-reliefs, gardens, reservoirs, aqueducts. It was fronted by a long sea-wall holding wide cultivated meadows.

South of present Lima, in the shadow of the high Andes, rose impressive Pachacámac, its major shrine aloft over the Pacific and green valleys of yellow-blossoming cotton, center of a vast region where all the people of the kingdom built their special shrines for worship and came on extended pilgrimages for a thousand miles. Unlike Chan Chan, which went to pieces after being conquered by Pachacutec Yupanqui, Pachacámac became even more holy and flourishing under the Empire. The creator god "Pachacámac" of the coast, "he who gave soul to the universe," rivaled Incan Viracocha—"great Ocean without beginning or end, white Ocean, calm and beautiful, God omnipotent."

Piously the Chimús buried their dead with knees drawn up under the chin; worshipped the Moon, for she made the crops grow and lifted the sea, made thunder and lightning, chastised thieves. In her Sian Huaca temple five-year-old children were sacrificed to her on heaps of colored cotton; offerings were made of chicha and fruits.

3

South of the coastal plain around Ica and elsewhere rose the Nazca civilization.

In this rainless region the dwellers practiced dry-farming, utilizing the night dews and burying two sardines with each seed as fertilizer. They prospered. Long before the Incas, they were loading their llamas with corn for the markets, making plump vases imitating elaborately robed figures with turbaned heads and bird-eyed faces; they were painting frescoes of spotted wild-cat demons, bird demons, centipede demons, puma demons, and were carving many-headed gods to take care of so many demons. They were an industrious, soul-troubled race.

4

Ten to fourteen thousand feet up in the highlands of Bolivia and Puno was developing the early Tiahuanaco culture. On the shores of Lake Chuquivitu (Chicuito), under the dead zinc-colored sky in a gray valley sodden with stagnant icy waters, this people built a great stone city with vast patios and halls and huge stone roofs, combed with carving to look like thatch—a city dedicated to Viracocha, Creator of the Universe. His likeness is in the great monolithic Calasaya gateway, a large square bas-relief figure—puma-fringed head-dress, elaborate tunic with puma-head girdle—the famous weeping God of Tiahuanaco: from large eyesockets big tears course down volcanic cheeks. His four-digit hands hold only objects, spears and a spear-thrower. Such was Viracocha.

Everywhere in their great city were gigantic statues, "so natural," according to Father Diego de Alcobasa, "they seemed to be alive," some drinking, others sitting, others walking the stream that flowed by the walls; and everywhere statues of women, babies on their laps or on their backs—

in dozens of different postures: the Tiahuanacos believed in fecundity, precious in such a toilsome latitude.

They set their flimsy *totora*-reed boats with matting sails afloat on Lake Titicaca—a thousand years now they have sailed—and went silently and patiently about their business under the ægis of the mighty snow-clad heights of Sorata, Huayna Potosí and Illamú, peaks which bite into the pale sky with glistening white teeth. A land of majesty, cold and cruel.

In the second era they built up the massive walls of Sacsahuamán and mighty terraces, artistic as well as utilitarian, to hold the soil for crops; carved bulky figures, stone friezes of marching warriors; made heavy though beautiful pottery. They were a ponderous, sure-footed, conservative people, rough-hewn from the Andean crags.

5

Thus out of the shadowy records of earlier centuries, the spiral of Peruvian civilization ascends. The legends—for the story as here presented is over-simplified—are like an intricate tangle of multicolored silken threads; only for the later centuries have quarreling archaeologists and historians been able to sort out the bright strands into intelligible pattern. The rise and fall of multiple kingdoms pass like a vague but vivid pageant, like those richly clad potentates—only shadowy names now—who once rode by on golden litters, proud in their bright garments and shining adornments.

But ever the spiral ascends. Throughout the centuries there is a constant shuttle of influence and domination from coast to highlands, highlands to coast—knowledge borrowed, improved upon. Laboriously men were learning to build ever better, to create, to establish a functioning social organism based on ever-greater popular justice; they were also evolving beautiful myths by which to live.

On an island in Lake Titicaca, the Sun created a man and a woman, the Inca Manco Cápac, and his sister wife, Coya (Queen) Mama Ocllo. He bade them set forth to found their kingdom at the spot the golden staff, with which he had provided them, should, on being struck into the earth, bury itself from sight.

Others—for there are many versions—report that eight brothers and sisters, four incestuous pairs, clad in shining raiment spangled with gold, went forth from the Tavern of the Dawn. Three pairs turned to stone, but the mightiest of them, Manco Cápac, who traveled furthest, sank the golden staff in Cuzco—"navel of the world"—and there in that densely wooded valley, he and Mama Ocllo rounded up the miserable dispersed inhabitants and founded the capital of his new realm.

He taught the multitude new ways of agriculture. Mama Ocllo instructed the women in domestic art.

A long unbroken dynasty was thus established. Until the coming of the Spaniards, the Incas, "the big-eared monarchs," ruled over Tahuantinsuyo—"the four quarters of the world,"—an ever-widening region extending all through the Andean highlands, along the desolate coast, and east into the upper Amazón jungles, ultimately from the Ancas Mayu (Blue River) in Colombia down through Ecuador and Perú to Bolivia, Chile, and much of Argentina.

Cuzco became a magnificent stone city of temples and palaces. According to Prescott, the decorations of Coricancho, temple of the Sun, probably surpassed those of any building in the Old World. Timber bridges paved with hewn stone slabs crossed the rivers running through the city; ample squares and plazas beautified it. As the predilect metropolis of the Sun God, every fountain, pathway and wall, said the ancient chronicler Ondergado, was regarded as a holy mystery.

Into it flowed the wealth of the empire. There converged the cultural and social currents of coast, jungle and height. Its buildings, in the styles of the numerous provinces, each reflecting a new extension of Inca power, caused chronicler Garcilaso to explain: "If one observed well those wards and houses of so many and such diverse nations, one could behold and embrace the whole Empire at once as in a mirror or in a cosmographic painting."

Into it flowed the currents of the empire; from it flowed the Incan administrative efforts to improve the rural regions—the great irrigation projects, roads, the building of new cities.

The other Inca cities, as well as the capital, bore the definite *cachet* of the civilization of the time. Not funereal as in Egypt, not spiritual as in Greece, not seeking depth and height like the Gothic, they were the expression of a solemn, ritualistic, but not lugubrious people, victors over material obstacles but not subtle, not disturbed by subjective mysteries, rather imbued with a sense of profound permanency —submissive, scrupulous, tending toward uniformity. They were in such a difficult region, they could not afford too much diversity.

7

The greatest of the Incas, Viracocha (Foam-on-the-Water), reached the throne in a dark hour by deposing his own father who had cravenly fled the capital when invading Pocras swarmed armed at the gates of the city. Whipping together a small force, Viracocha chastised the Pocras ferociously, reëstablished Inca authority, proceeded then to round out the borders of the empire and reorganize it on the broad basis of power and equity.

In both war and peace were the Incas effective; their military organization showed the same skill and respect for order as their stable institutions. On pain of death all soldiers were forbidden to commit any trespass on the property of inhabitants in the line of march. The rulers were not easily incited to war; they first exhausted every means of persuasion; nor did they hasten to push out the imperial frontier until previous conquests had been well assimilated.

Not that military pride was lacking. Cabello de Balboa tells of Viracocha's triumphal ceremonial entry into Coricancha—a philosophic symbolization of victory: "First of all the most valiant captains entered . . . with their arms and liveries, a sightly parade. . . . Soldiers of less renown . . . hauled along numerous bound prisoners. After these . . . the wives and daughters of the captives, singing funeral songs . . . bewailing their calamities. . . . Then . . . the common people, laden down with . . . spoils and dragging the weapons of their foes after them on the ground. . . . Then came a squadron . . . lances aloft, an enemy's head impaled upon each point . . . hair hanging loose and dishevelled . . . another squadron . . . of the nobility . . . bore the Emperor . . . upon a golden litter . . . austere of countenance . . . those eyes of a cruel tiger with which he killed and terrified the world. . . . [In] the rearguard . . . marched men of great importance, accompanied by . . . light-armed fighters who made a million movements with bodies and legs to simulate thereby the ardour and courage with which they had battled their enemies. . . . They marched around the empty square . . . all prisoners were ordered to lie face-down upon the earth. Then [the Emperor] leading the way, they walked over them, planting their feet upon the necks of the prostrate . . . and singing a verse . . . 'My enemies I tread upon.' . . . the image of the Sun was besought to consider Himself honoured . . . and always to give them similar victories."

Yet rebel peoples, once conquered and accepting Inca rule,

were well treated and rapidly amalgamated, made an integral part of the empire, given all its advantages. Extermination, mere tribute, military power, were not primary aims of conquest, but rather the erection of a great orderly realm. "We must spare our enemies or it will be our loss," so Sarmiento

quotes an Inca prince, "since they and all that belongs to them must soon be ours." There was no too great interference with local custom, indeed each province was legally required to conserve its traditional dress. After conquest, settlers were exchanged (the *mitmae* system of colonization devised by Huayna Cápac) as a means of weakening old patriotisms, thus mingling peoples of different customs and making the empire more homogenous, ever with an eye to correcting economic stress and overpopulation. Around

Cajamarca, for instance, though customs vary only slightly, modern linguistic analysis reveals Colla, Aimará, Quechua, and other ethnic groups far-removed from their homeland. The settlers were always sent to new regions of comparable altitude and climate and given well-irrigated fertile lands; they were treated with paternal benevolence; their lot bettered. Inca temples and schools in an amazingly short time disseminated the religion of the Sun and the Quechua language, to this day the prevailing speech from Ecuador to Bolivia and northern Argentina.

The Inca state rapidly rose to a perfected socialization enjoyed by few human aggregations—a vast rural communism coupled with social insurance which prevented all unemployment and material misery. As Prescott summarizes [1]: "Thus by degrees, and without violence, arose the great fabric of the Peruvian empire, composed of numerous independent and even hostile tribes, yet, under the influence of a common religion, common language and common government, knit together as one nation, animated by a spirit of love for its institutions and devoted loyalty to its sovereign."

Ancient Perú was more prosperous, with a larger population (Means estimates from sixteen to thirty-two million) with more guarantees for decent livelihood, with a more integrated system of communications, with more advanced agriculture (except on parts of the coast) than exists today centuries later. If many European mechanical contrivances were lacking, nevertheless, by any comparative standard, neither the Spaniards nor the governments of the Republic have justified their right to rule.

8

Details of the evolution of this communal agrarianism and its relation to the state—the best study is Valcarcel's

[1] I, 82.

*From the Ayullu to the Empire*—have come down to us. The simplest unit—a few households combined into the *ayullu,* or kinship tribe, under the leadership, in times of war or danger, of an elected *sinchi,* or chief. The hamlet of roughly built houses clustered about a *pucará,* or fortified hilltop, and was surrounded by farming and pasturage land held in common but periodically redistributed among heads of families.

In more advanced states several *ayullana* were united under the rule of a hereditary ruler or *curaca.* Gradually two or more curaca-kingdoms (embracing several large populous valleys) united into one entity, either federative or else resembling feudal Europe. Examples: the Colla confederacy in the Titicaca basin, the Chanca confederacy in Andahuallas, the Chincha confederacy on the coast. From such compound states grew up the great coastal kingdoms, the imposing, intricately organized Chimú and Nazca régimes. But through all political vicissitudes the backbone of the social system remained the communal *ayullu.* This continued the even tenor of its ways, safeguarded the simple routine of social and religious life regardless of prosperity, depression, political chaos, war, tyrannical or democratic systems, and continued to be the basic unit (as it does to this day) after the Inca empire forged the whole Andean region into one efficient state.

By that time all land was divided into three portions: one for the Sun, *i.e.,* the State religion; one for officials and the Incas (any one related to the head Inca or Emperor); and one for the *ayullu,* the last always sufficient comfortably to maintain the people. Agricultural methods were well advanced. There was adequate use of fertilizer from the guano islands (the death penalty awaited any one who approached them or disturbed the birds). Some of the *ayullana,* especially in larger centers, in addition to general agricultural activities, became each the repository of special cultivation or trades. Some cultivated only quinúa or made salt; others, only chile; others, corn or oca. The ancient Quechuas had better cooked, more diversified food than the average highlander today.

Each newly married couple, besides receiving gifts of everyday and holiday clothes and other objects from the imperial storehouses, was granted a *tupu* of land (about seventy square meters) sufficient for house and garden, of which they enjoyed, not the ownership, but the usufruct. As soon as children arrived, another *tupu* was granted for each boy, half a *tupu* for each girl. When a boy married, the father handed over to him his *tupu;* but the daughter's half *tupu* remained with the father or reverted to the commons. Widows, invalids and orphans also received lands, which were kept under cultivation by the rest of the villagers.

The people were further protected against want by great warehouses throughout the Empire, in which the produce of the Church and Inca lands, not needed at court or in the temples, was stored to be distributed in case of famine. Frequently to supplement the usual diet of *charqui,* or jerked meat, the Inca distributed fresh meat from the vast royal herds quartered in every part of the country. The wool, also kept in the royal storehouses, was given out according to need along with yarns to be woven for the Incas. The Spaniards found these warehouses, out of which their armies lived wastrelly for a long time, choked with corn, utensils of gold, silver and copper, munitions of war—every conceivable product of the country. Strict game and animal preservation laws, which the Spaniards ignored, also protected future supplies. The seven lean years were fully provided for and never occurred, a lesson in humanitarian forethought and constructive national welfare that few nations—certainly not the United States—have learned to this day. "No government," declares Acosta, "was ever better suited to the genius of the people, and no people could have appeared more contented with their lot or more devoted to their government."

The agrarian system, the carefully planned political structure, the social foresight, the public works, all betokened great administrative efficiency and demanded accurate information. The Incas gathered elaborate statistics, recorded by knotted multicolored cords, known as *quipús,* kept in extensive archives by a special class of skilled officials, the *Quipú Camayus.*

"He who attempts to count the stars, not knowing how to count the marks and knots of the *quipús* ought to be held in derision," was an adage of Emperor Pachacutec, a practical man who added some 250,000 square miles to the empire.

Modern Perú has not taken a census in nearly sixty years; its general statistics are inaccurate and incomplete—worthless.

Under the Incas all births and deaths were carefully recorded, and at intervals surveys were made of the products and resources of the country—knowledge used to plan development, proportion work, and build public works—a distribution of effort thoughtfully carried out to occasion no disproportionate burden on any individual or community. Besides the regular bureaucratic organization, a corps of special imperial inspectors was maintained, and a most elaborate group of secret informants. Russia did not originate State-planning or the O.G.P.U.

## 9

Communal traditions permitted the Incas to assemble great aggregations of man power for public works, still the marvel of all who behold them. The Cuzco fortress required twenty thousand men over a period of fifty years. Great stones, some thirty-eight by eighteen by six feet, were brought from quarries twelve to forty-five miles distant without mechanical assistance or beasts of burden, across rivers and gigantic ravines—stones so carefully worked that once put in place without cement, not a knife blade could be wedged between them.

Inca Viracocha was particularly interested in irrigation; it increased productivity, and was practical pro-Inca propaganda among newly conquered peoples. A canal in Condesuyne ran for nearly four hundred miles. In the conquered Chancas region one great canal, twelve feet deep, twelve feet wide, was carried one hundred and fifty miles semicircularly from the mountain summit at beautiful springs near Parcy along the lofty eastern slopes of the Maritime Cordillera just above river headwaters. Provided with minor aqueducts, controlled by sluices, it opened up an extensive new region. Some canals pierced through stone—tunnels as smoothly bored as a bumblebee's nest; others crossed ravines and marshes. These canals were well-superintended, the water equitably distributed.

Vestiges of remarkable canal systems, Incan and from a thousand years before the Incas, are seen particularly in the Departments of Piura, Ica, Ancash, Lima, Arequipa. In Tumbes (now one of Perú's most backward departments) about 340,000 acres were artificially cultivated only to be abandoned by the Spaniards and never reclaimed to this day. Elsewhere—at Nazca for instance—some few ancient aqueducts are still in use. The Quechuas also made agricultural use of hill and mountain slopes, however steep, by elaborate terraces, often of massive stone construction. Most of these have disappeared save where the communal system survives. The Incas knew how to utilize nearly all possible cultivable areas of the empire.

The Inca subjects and their predecessors were adepts in the arts of grading, causeways, terrace-making, tunneling, bridge-building. They constructed or reconstructed many great highways; through the Sierra from Quito south far into Argentina and Chile (2,000 miles); along the desert coast; from height to sea and jungle. Desert viaducts were built many feet above the shifting sands, often by driving huge piles into the ground. In the upper mountains these highways often crossed enormous chasms by means of suspended fibre bridges, some over two hundred feet in length. The cables, some more than two feet in diameter, were strung from strong stone towers on either bank. The modern traveler through the Cordillera crosses many of these ancient bridges still in use, though in most cases steel cables have replaced fibre support. The traveler swings above waters foaming a thousand feet below. Many roads passed through eternal stone; galleries were cut for miles through living rock; precipices were scaled, ravines of frightful depth were filled up with solid masonry. One can still see, after all these ages, where the waters have eaten away parts, leaving huge extended arches. The super-cautious Humboldt remarked over a century ago: "The roads of the Incas were among the most useful and stupendous works ever executed by man." Means points out that the Empire had better communications than any in Europe from Rome's downfall to the modern industrial revolution. In present-day Perú there is no modern road comparable in length or importance to the Incas' main highway.

Main roads were marked with distance stones. Conveniently located were storehouses, and at twelve-mile intervals, *tampa cuna (tambos)*, or inns, for the convenience of travelers and armies. At the more important of these, duplicate royal gold and silver dishes were kept for the Emperor's personal use. Stationed at regular intervals on all roads were *chasquis*, royal couriers (their authority established by a crimson thread from the imperial fillet). These royal messengers were known long before the Incas. Mochican pottery, placed at before Christ, reveals frieze-like paintings of Chasquis, running swiftly, clad only in a special headdress

39

and decorated loin-cloth, legs and arms specially striped, accompanied by symbols of speed (the hundred-footed centipede, flying birds)—among the most beautiful decorative representations in all Peruvian art.

Messages could be relayed often more rapidly than today. The Inca was in constant contact with every part of his domain; and when resident in Cuzco—11,500 feet above the sea and forty-eight hours distant from the coast by modern train—received from the previous day's catch, fresh *corbina* fish on his breakfast table, just as did Moctezuma in Mexico.

10

The Quechua folk were, above all, a practical, not a philosophical, people. But what they lacked in theory they made up for in science and poetry, unfortunately frequently mixed beyond recognition. They lived by simple beautiful allegories and practical applied science and much superstition.

Their doctors, the *hampi-camayoc*, "remedy-keepers," though they used more Christian Science hocus-pocus than real science, were skilled in medicinal plants and chemical substances; their surgeons could trephine broken skulls; their dentists could fill teeth with gold; their astronomers measured the solar movements at *inti-huana*—"Place where the Sun is tied"—eight tall towers on opposite rims of the Cuzco basin.

The imperial court, as Garcilaso records, achieved considerable brilliance, refinement and luxury; and any inventory of the material splendor enjoyed by the Inca's eye as he sat on his concave throne of solid gold would record great technical advance in metal-working, weaving and other arts. And as the Inca emperors proceeded over the realm or waged new conflicts under the imperial Rainbow banner, these products must have greatly impressed the more backward peoples just as they have the archaeologists who have since disinterred old bones.

Despite this upper-class show, despite sharp caste distinctions—the Incas even spoke a special language—and though punishments were severe (death for theft, adultery, murder, blasphemy, rebellion, especially severe punishments for removal of landmarks, stealing water, incendiarism and idleness) the rulers were ever permeated by a great spirit of social obligation.

On the basis of a great organized effort and a fine sense of social equality, the Quechuas lived an integrated life which had its two poles in the soil and the sun, a constant interplay of force and fecundity. About this dual concept swung their agrarian system, the facts of their daily life and their religious festivals. The Mamapacha Earth cult was vast and ancestral; the Sun cult revolved around the concept of the ultimate source of all life and beauty. They were a people of faith, and no magnificence was too great for their temples, always adorned extravagantly with gold and silver, which had æsthetic rather than commercial value.

Some minor tribes in very early proto-Chimú times probably practiced human sacrifice, but the Quechuas, unlike the Aztecs, had no sanguinary gods. The favorite Inca offering was the llama, which also served for auguries. At critical junctures in imperial affairs, a black llama from the sacred herds of the Sun was specially sacrificed. Four men sat on it, while a priest clad in elaborate embroidered and befeathered robes slashed open its left side to drag out the heart, lungs and gullet; if still palpitating the omen was good.

Religious festivals dovetailed with various seasonal activities of soil cultivation. The month of Chahuar Huarquiz (July-August) was devoted to festivals in connection with the cleaning of irrigation ditches and plowing. The following month fifteen brown llamas were sacrificed; and a white

llama with gold ornaments was led through fields simultan-
eously sprinkled with corn chicha.

At the great Raymi Sun festival, dawn was greeted by a
magnificent procession, and as the first yellow rays struck
the turrets and towers, shouts of reverent joy broke forth
from the multitude and the wild wail of strange instruments
playing *yaravi* triumph songs, which became ever louder

until the Sun rode full and bright above the Eastern mountain range.

At the great Coya Raymi festival in Cuzco, dedicated to
the Moon cult, all provincial outsiders (those not considered
descendants of the Moon), all physical defectives, and all
dogs were chased out of the city. For it was an idealistic
ceremony of a people seeking good, desirous of perfection
on earth, with a religion social, practical, mystic but not dogmatically metaphysical.

The nobility and people repaired to holy Coricancha. In
the square a gigantic golden urn was set up to receive chicha
libations, and four hundred warriors brought out Creator
God Viracocha and Thunder God Chuqui-Illapa from the
Puca-Mana temple. After proper preparations the multitude
burst into loud cries: "O sickness, disasters, misfortunes, and
perils, go forth from the land." The cry was reëchoed
through the city; and the warriors, divided into four groups,

ran forth in the four cardinal directions, crying, "Go forth all evils! Go forth . . ." The cry echoed through all the empire in ever-widening circles under the calm argentine rays of the Andean moon—"Go forth all evils. . . ."

This was the active slogan of Incan life, the basis of their social philosophy.

# III

## GOD—GOLD—GLORY

### I

SEPTEMBER 25, 1513, from a mountaintop in Panamá, Vasco Núñez de Balboa saw the Pacific Ocean. Four days later he was striding into it, brandishing sword and banner, taking possession of a vast deal of salt-water in the name of his Catholic Majesty.

Indian chiefs told him of "Pirú"—gold in fabulous quantities, new worlds to conquer. Had not Núñez been murdered shortly after by bloody Governor Pedro Arias de Avila, perhaps the bones of the discoverer of the Pacific Ocean instead of those of one of his men, bastard swineherd Pizarro, might now be resting in state in a marble room in Lima's cathedral as the honored conqueror of Perú. Francisco Pizarro, a gloomy, unrelenting man, had survived the frightful Ojeda expedition, now that of Núñez de Balboa. All he was to win was a little malarial land near Panamá. Fortune still beckoned from afar. Perú became his one great chance!

But it was November, 1524, nearly ten years later—he was then fifty—before he could gather together an expedition. His partner, Diego de Almagro, another illiterate adventurer, followed in a smaller ship. Both together mustered only 112 men. Glittering gold was the lodestar.

Battered by storms, attacked by hostile Indians, reduced to a starvation diet of seaweed, poisonous berries and bitter palmfruits, they lost thirty men and got only as far south as the San Juan River, Colombia. At Puerto Quemado Almagro lost an eye from a javelin.

44

Half-wrecked, but with some gold, they crept back to Panamá.

The two promoters persisted. Priest Fernando de Luque, also interested in the project, wheedled a new half-hearted authorization from Governor Pedrarias—no assistance but a juicy share of future profits; Judge Gaspar de Espinosa put up the then considerable sum of 20,000 pesos. March 10, 1526, the Corporation of Discoverers of Pirú was formally organized by an agreement oozing with religious phraseology suggestive of the fiery cross soon to be carried over the Andes.

November of that year a second expedition—two ships, piloted by Bartolomé Ruiz de Estrada, 160 men and a few horses—battled storms all down the coast.

Pizarro attacked an Indian village, seized a quantity of gold ornaments. Elated, at the San Juan River, he moved his forces ashore, in the face of a host of shore-lined Indian warriors, and pitched permanent camp in soggy jungle.

Almagro went back for reinforcements.

Ruiz explored on south across the Equator. A large two-masted native balsa with cotton sail and deck cabins netted him several captives to be taught to become interpreters, gold and silver ornaments, some beautiful woolen goods. He returned to San Juan.

Those in Pizarro's unhealthy camp had lived on chance wild potatoes, coconuts and acrid mangrove fruits. The frightful marshes swarmed with unpleasant chattering monkeys, slimy reptiles, great alligators, and clouds of insects so vicious that often the troopers buried their bodies up to their faces in the sand. Many had died from starvation, disease, poisoned arrows.

But Pizarro, after Almagro came in with eighty new recruits and plentiful supplies, took the expedition on south through harsh storms. A populous coast afforded numerous fights and adventures.

At Tacamez, a town of 2,000 inhabitants on the famed Ecuadorian River of Emeralds, the inhabitants were richly adorned with gold and precious stones. But 10,000 hostile warriors, displaying a gold mask as their battle ensign, almost annihilated the landing party. Only the kicking legs of a fallen horse so astonished the natives that they opened a lane for escape.

At this native show of force faint-hearted ones among the explorers wished to return at once.

Almagro proposed that he again go back to Panamá for reinforcements, that again Pizarro pitch camp and wait.

The two commanders quarreled violently, laid hold of their swords. Ruiz and Treasurer Ribera pacified them.

The expedition limped back to Gallo Island, and here, while Almagro, and later Ruiz, went to Panamá, Pizarro waited, his men half-starved, sick, mutinous at being abandoned to their fate amid swarming enemies on this dismal barren island in an unknown sea on the rim of the world.

In a ball of native wool for the wife of the new Governor of Panamá, Pedro de los Ríos, one disgruntled trooper, smuggled through a warning:

> Look out, Señor Governor,
> For the drover while he's near;
> Since he goes home to get the sheep
> For the butcher who stays here.

The Governor, alarmed, held Almagro and Ruiz, and sent Pedro Tafur with two ships and provisions to rescue the men and order Pizarro back.

Pizarro saw his men, now clad only in rags, half-starved from a diet of crabs and shellfish, rheumatic from the incessant rains, preparing to leave him.

Boldly with his sword he scratched a line on the thin soil and stepped across it north to south, bidding those of his men not fools or cowards to follow him and conquer fame and wealth: "There [south] lies toil, hunger, nakedness, drenching storms, desertion and death. . . . There lies Perú with its riches; here [north] is Panamá and its poverty. Choose each man what best becomes a brave Castilian. . . ."

Thirteen courageous spirits took the fateful step, defying the Governor's orders; and, shipless, fed only by hope, remained behind on a lonely rock of misery.

These Thirteen of Fame finally rafted their way seventy-five miles north to the more hospitable Gorgona Island where they prayed and chanted the evening hymn to the Virgin.

Governor Ruiz, still obdurate, finally sent another small ship to rescue the foolhardy Pizarro. The latter merely utilized it to continue on south.

He reached beautiful Guayaquil Gulf, continued coasting under the towering white crests of Chimborazo and Cotopaxi to the Islands of Santa Clara and Puna. After some weeks along a sandy strand glistening with white houses, he reached Tumbes.

He had discovered Perú!

2

The Indians swarmed out in balsas from the stone and plaster city, showered food upon the adventurers—bananas, plantains, yuca, corn, sweet potatoes, pineapples, coconuts, game, fish, llamas—"little camels," the surprised Spaniards called this curious animal.

An Inca noble came aboard, gorged, drank wine, and accepted the present of an iron hatchet.

Alonzo de Molina, accompanied by a negro, returned the visit, taking swine and poultry as gifts. The natives were amazed by Alonzo's dress, white complexion and golden beard; by the negro's black skin—they actually tried to rub off the color. And they wanted to know what the cock said when he crowed.

Molina reported back all the wonders of the city, fortress and local gold-filled Sun-temple.

All too marvellous! Pizarro, skeptical, sent the Greek, Pedro de Candia, ashore with men to corroborate. An exhibition of musketry fire caused many of the frightened Indians to fall on their faces. A native menagerie jaguar tried its teeth unsuccessfully on Candia's armour. Marvellous for the natives!

Candia's tidings were equally glowing: the temple, tapestried with gold and silver plates; a garden with gold and silver imitations of fruits and vegetables.

Gold and glory were at hand. The expedition gave thanks to God!

After coasting south as far as Chincha, Pizarro returned to Panamá, with some evidences of sought-for wealth.

But gold and glory had to wait. Funds were lacking, and Governor Ríos flatly refused to permit another expedition for the sake of "a few gold and silver toys and Indian sheep."

The only chance was to appeal directly to the Crown. Untutored but handsome Pizarro, the partners agreed hesitatingly, should go to Spain. He, better than any one else, could paint a vivid picture of the promised land.

Pizarro, though on his arrival in Spain thrown into prison for debt, was soon released, and with his Indians, gold and silver objects, woolen cloths and llamas aroused the King's astonished interest and eager cupidity. Charles V was even moved to tears by Pizarro's recital of hardships. Royal support was easily won.

After exasperating red tape, the coveted Capitulación, through the Queen's personal intervention, was granted, but despite Charles' tears, not one red penny to outfit an expedition; everything read—when and if Perú should have been conquered.

When and if Perú should have been conquered, Pizarro—who did handsomely by himself in futures—would receive an annual stipend of 725,000 maravedís, annual expense money 1,000 ducats, a grant of two hundred leagues down the coast from Tenumpuela (Santiago) to Chincha, the right to build four fortresses and to make further land grants to others. The ex-swineherd, as "Servitor of God our Father" and the Queen, was made an hidalgo, Governor, Captain General, Adelantado and Alguacil Mayor of Perú, and, despite his illegitimacy, was allowed to use his father's coat of arms and wear the habit of Santiago.

Almagro was made merely hidalgo and Commandant of Tumbes, and given a beggarly when-and-if salary of 100,000 maravedís, 200,000 for expenses. Luque was granted the Bishopric of Tumbes and titled Protector of the Indians of Perú, salary a thousand ducats. Ruiz was made Grand Pilot of the Southern Seas, 75,000 maravedís. The Thirteen of Fame were all made hidalgos, and raised to municipal dignitaries—in project.

Pizarro gained some backing, much of it from his relative Hernán Cortés; but owing to the tales of previous terrible hardships, he could not even assemble the 150 men necessary under the Capitulación, so, before the royal inspectors could stop him, he slipped out of Sevilla harbour, his three ships undermanned.

In Panamá he faced his associates' recriminations at his duplicity and the shabby way he had taken care of their interests. "How could you allow me to be thus dishonored in the eyes of the world by so paltry a compensation? . . ." cried Almagro.

Pizarro swore that all arrangements had been forced upon him unwillingly, that Luque and Almagro should share everything equally, made other promises. The break was temporarily patched up—"a thin scar . . . healed over the wound . . . [still] deep and rankling within."

After Mass and sacrament on St. John's day, Pizarro sailed January 1531 from Panamá in three small vessels with a Dominican friar Vicente de Valverde, less than two hundred men, only twenty-seven horses—as fantastic and ill-prepared an expedition as ever set forth on madcap adventure.

They beat their way to Ecuadorian St. Matthew Bay, landed, marched along the shore, painfully traversing rivers and jungles. In Coaque they fell on a town sword in hand, "for if we had advised them of our approach," remarked Pedro Pizarro, "we should never have found such store of gold and precious stones."

Pizarro received an emerald as big as a pigeon's egg. Some of his followers were so ignorant that they hammered their share of the precious stones into smaller pieces.

While his vessels took 20,000 castellanos gold back to Panamá, Pizarro continued his painful march along the jungle coast, through marshes and across great rivers. Then the desert—they waded through drifting sands under sun so glaring it made their clanking armour too hot to be touched. Many fell before an unknown disease of repugnant blood-filled warts.

But at last, reinforced by two vessels and a hundred men and horses, they reached the bellicose island of Puna (where years later Valverde would be killed by natives) in the Gulf of Guayaquil. Here, thanks to St. Michael and his legions, seen hovering high in the air above the Christians, they drove off thousands of attacking natives into the forests.

The army was transported over to Tumbes. Pizarro found the city largely deserted, half destroyed, the natives hostile. Abandoning his former mild curiosity, he mastered the place by cruelty and terrorism. To encourage his men, disheartened at the failure to find promised easy loot, Pizarro faked a scroll, said to have come from several perished Spaniards previously left behind at this point: "Know whoever you may be that may chance to set foot in this country that it contains more gold and silver than there is iron in Biscay."

Fifty miles south, at well-watered Tangaralá, he and Val-

verde founded the first Spanish city in Perú—San Miguel.
Lands and Indians were allotted to those who chose to remain—"it being evident," remarks Xerez [1] "that the colonists
could not support themselves without the services of Indians,
the ecclesiastics and leaders . . . agreed that a repartimiento
of the natives would serve the cause of religion and greatly
further their spiritual welfare."

Thus was established the coast base for the audacious conquest of the mighty Inca empire.

### 3

September 24, 1532, five months after landing at Tumbes,
Pizarro—already in full communication with Emperor Atahualpa—set out with about a hundred and seventy men
toward Cajamarca (second city of the Empire) and Cuzco,
both in the high Sierra.

The little band followed the desolate coast, the desert of
Zarán, crossed the picturesque irrigated fields of Piura, Lambayeque, and Chiclayo, reached the foothills—"the Eyebrow
of the Coast"—then followed through the upper Saña or
Leche River into ever harsher country.

"Let those who are afraid go back," Pizarro told his men.
Nine returned.

In Zarán the Spaniards were supplied with fresh meat, and
were brought gifts of cloth and powdered goose-flesh.

In Cajas they saw warriors, royal weavers, also Indians
hanging by the feet for having violated Vestal Virgins.

In Huancabamba they admired a palace, fortress, aqueducts.

Beyond Motupe they hewed down trunks to cross a mighty
river.

Further on they saw the magnificent Inca highway,
bridges, inns.

[1] iii, 187.

Above them now rose the stupendous Andes, rock upon rock, forests, terraces, high barren ridges and, far aloft in the heavens, glistening snow.

Unwittingly they chose the steepest, most difficult route. A bold attack would have destroyed them. Once they came upon a mighty stone fortress, fortunately abandoned.

They mounted ever higher through narrow ravines, great stone gorges, along precipices and narrow ledges over vast abysses, on into the desolate freezing upper solitudes. The only vegetation was the dried yellow *pajonal* grass, encircling the snow-covered peaks—in the rays of the afternoon sun like silver and pearls in a ringed setting of gold. Higher they went, on into the haunt of the vicuña and the wheeling condor which hovered over them lugubriously with doleful cries—on and up into the unknown.

Ahead was an empire. Ahead was the gold they sought, souls to be converted.

November 15, 1532, after nearly two months of bitter hardships, first unbearable heat, then biting cold, the little host descended into a richly cultivated oval plain five miles from Cajamarca. Its stone bulwarks loomed ahead of them— impressive, mysterious.

To one side, on the mountain slopes, they could see a vast white cloud of glistening tents—their hearts sank at sight of so great a camp—the army of Atahualpa, 40,000 men.

But they continued bravely ahead over a well-made road, banners streaming in battle array, and at the hour of vespers, entered the city, unopposed.

The place entirely abandoned save for a few soldiers, the conquerors' feet rang over the empty stones between gigantic stone walls and hollow patios. The prospect was lugubrious. The sun, dipping quickly in this high southern world without twilight, was blotted out by rain and hail, leaving them in a night of strange alarms in a forlorn alien city.

The crucial moment of the expedition was at hand. Atahualpa and Pizarro the swineherd were face to face. The odds seemed all in favor of the former.

4

Curious coincidence—Atahualpa, like Pizarro, was illegitimate.

About 1528 Inca Huayna Cápac—ill and aging, a long distinguished reign behind him, also a majestic and complicated love-life, faced dire troubles. In various provinces rebellion was lifting its ugly head; a terrible plague was sweeping the realm; the very stars, according to the soothsayers, showed unusual disturbances. Comets, earthquakes, the moon girdled by rings of many-colored fire, thunderbolts, one of which consumed a royal palace, hawks chasing and killing eagles—such were some of the evil omens of the day.

Auguries, told over the palpitating livers and hearts of vivisected llamas, all indicated inescapable evils.

And while at his sumptuous Tumipampa palace in the southern Ecuadorian highlands, Huayna Cápac received news of the fulfillment of mournful prognostications—Pizarro and his adventurers had made their first appearance at Tumbes.

Gloomily Huayna Cápac prepared to deliver his scepter into more capable hands—those of two beloved sons: legitimate Prince Cusi Hualpa (better known as Huáscar, offspring of his sister-wife Mama Rahua Ocllo) was given the Cuzco half of the empire; and Atahualpa (son by a beautiful concubine, daughter of the last independent Scyri of Quito) was given the northern part including Ecuador—a division reminiscent of the Byzantine epoch of the Roman empire. Thereby Huayna Cápac weakened the kingdom, brought on a bloody war. By the time of Pizarro's final expedition, Atahualpa, after furious battles at the foot of lofty Chimborazo and in the plains of Cuzco, had just wrenched away Huáscar's portion and had thrown his half-brother into prison. Atahualpa butchered the Inca nobility and established himself as iron ruler of all Tahuantinsuyo.

5

Pizarro, on entering Cajamarca, at once despatched—under Hernando de Soto and Hernando Pizarro—thirty-four horsemen, galloping over causeway and plain with clangor of trumpets and arms, to interview Atahualpa.

Surrounded by nobles seated on his golden *tiana*, the Emperor received the envoys from behind a thin gauze curtain held by two native ladies. Ordering the curtain dropped, either out of courtesy or curiosity, he maintained, according to Pedro Pizarro, mysterious imperial reticence; according to other writers, he sharply upbraided the Spaniards for their behavior along the road.

The almost youthful emperor was pleasantly plump, with a handsome grave countenance, a charming smile, but fierce, rather bloodshot eyes.

The Spaniards staged an exhibition of horsemanship. Soto made his small but fiery and well-trained horse gallop, prance and curvet, sweeping its head so close over the Inca that flecks of foam fell on the royal raiment. The Inca preserved his imperial calm, but several courtiers fell back in fright, a pusillanimity that cost them their lives; they were ordered executed that same night. After beautiful, if dusky, girls had served the Spaniards frothy chicha from golden goblets, the Inca dismissed his visitors, promising to dine in their quarters in Cajamarca the following day.

That Friday night, November 15, 1532, from their plaza bivouac the little band of Spaniards, in blackest despondency, watched the countless fires in the Inca's camp—"nothing less than a starry sky."

The God of battles was called upon to save them. Pizarro eloquently cheered up his dejected men, later held council with his officers. So desperate was their situation only the boldest of strokes could save them. As Cortés had done in Mexico, Pizarro determined to boldly seize the Emperor's person.

Next day, near sundown, at the head of a few thousand troops, the Inca appeared, drums beating, trumpets and flutes wailing. Servitors carefully swept the highway. Soldiers in varied uniforms, some checkered red and white, and bearing massive star-headed clubs of copper, silver and gold, sang triumphant war-songs—to the Spaniards, "yells of Hell's own demons." The richly uniformed Cañari guard protected the royal litter, carried by trained bearers in azure costumes,

men carefully chosen from two specially honored cities of
the realm. Ears distended by huge disks and pendants, about
his neck enormous emeralds, on his head the gold-adorned
imperial fillet, Atahualpa—seated on his golden throne under
a canopy of gorgeous tropical feathers and plates of gold and
silver, the Lord of Chincha at his feet—rode onwards in
silence, on into the empty square of Cajamarca. Behind him
his troops were spread over the broad meadows as far as the
eye could reach.

The Spaniards, on orders, were lurking within the buildings; acording to an Indian spy, who had brought back word
to Atahualpa, they were cowering like women, so frightened they were urinating copiously.

At last, in the center of the square, the Inca broke his
majestic silence. "Where, then, are the strangers?"

Friar Valverde scuffled forward, breviary in one hand,
uplifted crucifix in the other, and thereby broke an empire
in twain. For all Atahualpa's pomp, his contempt for Valverde's religious symbols, the monarch little realized that
the power of the Cross, sustained by gunpowder, steel
armor, cavalry and greed for gold, was more powerful than
the great Viracocha, father of all the pagan gods, of all the
world, the universe.

It may seem an inappropriate moment for Valverde to
have explained verbosely all the mysteries of the Trinity,
the creation of man, his fall and redemption by Jesus Christ,
the crucifixion and ascension when the Saviour left Apostle
Peter as earthly Vicegerent, how through a succession of
good wise apostles, the representation passed on to the Popes
who held power over all earth's potentates. But this gibberish must have increased the Emperor's confusion regarding
the incomprehensible bold creatures from over the sea. For
the Spaniards—not any freer from rabbit-foot superstitions
than was Atahualpa—Valverde's sermonizing probably stimulated more hope than would have any purely political par-

ley. Those rude adventurers, faced by the vast array of Quechuan soldiery, undoubtedly trusted less in the power of their strong right arms than in that uplifted crucifix. More than courage, science or surprise, holy magic was the real factor.

Valverde finally invited the Incan monarch to embrace the true faith and bend the knee to Charles V.

The Emperor's eyes flashed fire, his dark brow grew darker. He would be no man's tributary. "I am greater than any prince on earth . . . the Pope—must be mad to talk of giving away countries which do not belong to him." He ridiculed the strange concept of the Trinity—three Gods and one God and therefore four. "Your own God, as you say, was put to death by the very men whom he created. But mine," he concluded, pointing to the Sun, unfortunately just then sinking in glory behind the lofty mountains, "my God still lives in the heavens and looks down on his children."

As his authority for his brazen demands, Valverde showed the Inca his breviary. Atahualpa could make nothing of the lumpish brass-clasp object and tossed it vehemently aside. "Tell your comrades they shall give an account to me of their doings in my land . . . of all the evil they have done."

The friar snatched up his sacred volume and scampered off to Pizarro. "While we stand here wasting our breath with this dog, so full of pride, the fields are filling with Indians. Set on at once; I absolve you."

The sacrilege to the breviary served as an excuse for surprise attack—"Santiago and at them!" Horses galloping, pikes ramming forward, steel armour, swords and trappings flashing in the sunset light, guns barking, sulphur fumes rising in clouds, a handful of adventurers rolled a proud empire into the mire of the Cajamarca plaza.

Valverde rushed hither and yon shouting absolution. The bewildered Inca was tumbled from his splendid litter, a perfect Humpty Dumpty. His sacred imperial *llautu* was snatched from his brows by soldier-chronicler Estete. He was almost stripped of his glittering apparel before Pizarro, at the cost of a wound from one of his own frenzied men, rescued him—and led him into captivity. The carnage continued; hundreds of unarmed or lightly armed native warriors were hacked to pieces or trampled into slime by the horses.

Thus Christianity proved its superiority to the pagan faith Atahualpa refused to betray.

## 6

Pizarro had struck at the fountain-head of power. A dumb but realistic consciousness, born of fierce desire to conquer and a desperate situation, had given him the key to the control of the empire, had revealed the weakness of its too great perfection and centralization of authority—Atahualpa had boasted not even the birds ventured to fly contrary to his will. He was the one central pillar of the Incaic political structure.

The Emperor in captivity permitted mock imperial importance, maintained court and royal guard, received his vassals, gave joy to his many women in private. He ate off golden service, wore his imperial insigniae and glorious raiment, never twice donning the same garment. Once when food specked his clothes, he rose precipitantly from the table to change to a fresh bat-skin robe which aroused the amazed admiration of the rude Spanish soldiers. He learned to speak Spanish, to play well dice and chess, and endured prolonged proselytizing harangues from chatter-box Valverde.

But even with these privileges his confinement was humiliating. Official Indian interpreter Felipillo, with complete immunity, seduced one of his concubines. Soon, too, he discovered the ignorant boorish character of Pizarro. Intrigued by Spanish writing, the Inca asked one of his captors to ink on his finger-nail the word "God." He was delighted to find everyone knew what it said. But when he showed it to Pizarro, the illiterate commander remained dumb and embarrassed, and never forgave Atahualpa's scornful glance.

The Emperor soon learned that aside from converting souls, the only vital interest of the Spaniards was gold. He offered to fill a big room thirty-five by eighteen feet, as high as he could reach—about nine feet—with the precious metal, and a smaller room thrice over with silver, in return for his freedom. Pitiful hope.

But the Spaniards who feared the treasures of the empire would all be concealed before they could reach the leading temples, their avarice whetted by the thought of so much tangible treasure, drew up a formal contract with the Inca. Runners carrying the orders for the collection immediately set out over the vast empire.

Ere long bearers came in with heavy loads; llamas staggered down from a hundred shrines to add to the store—cups and plates of gold, goblets and ewers of gold, wheels of gold, tiles of gold, huge slabs of gold. From the royal gardens at Yucay were torn out from among the true foliage all the gold and silver imitations—a great golden stalk of Indian corn in replica, an ear of pure gold, half disclosed among broad leaves of silver and the light tassels of the same metal floating gracefully from its top; a golden fountain sending up golden spray.

With each new consignment the conquerors' eyes bulged with surprise and greater greed. A bitter dispute arose between the first comers and reinforcements from Perú (led by Almagro, who had hurried on to Cajamarca on hearing of the gold pouring in) over the proper division of the spoils —the old quarrel—dark omen for Perú's future peace.

Pizarro even upbraided Atahualpa because the shipments did not come in fast enough. Hernando Pizarro was sent out reconnoitering for more treasure, first to Huamachuco, then to Pachacámac on the coast, then back to Jauja—a terrific trip in which his men to get over the crags had to resort to shoeing their horses with silver. Another mission, with imperial safe-conduct, also went ahead to Cuzco, where the members lorded it over the natives, seized whatever they wanted and raped the Vestal Virgins. But they brought back two hundred *cargas* of gold.

When melted up, and this did not include the silver, there was in all over a million and a quarter pesos, the equivalent today of at least fifteen million dollars, a booty (excepting nineteenth- and twentieth-century war-indemnities) unequalled in all history.

Pizarro at once invoked the assistance of heaven in distributing the treasure equitably. Almagro and Luque were ignored except for promises. For himself Pizarro took all the silver, also the Inca's throne and supporting slab, valued at nearly $700,000. Even so each cavalier received close to the equivalent of $100,000. In all due holiness the new Church of San Francisco was beneficently endowed with $30,000.

Gold and silver for the Quechua inhabitants had no monetary value; but those metals did have holy importance: gold was the "tears wept by the Sun"; silver was the sacred metal of the Moon. The looting represented a major profanation of the Inca world.

Despite his heaps of treasure, Atahualpa was not released; he was done to death. Twelve fantastic charges: first, he had usurped Huáscar's rightful sovereignty over Cuzco where the Spaniards would next be going; then, while in Spanish custody, he had sent secret orders to have his brother assassinated; he had squandered public revenues! He had plotted against the Spaniards. He had—and here enters Valverde's resentment that the Inca had steadfastly repulsed all his voluble proselytizing—violated Catholic morality by polygamy, incestuous marriage, adultery, idolatry. Historian Fernández de Oviedo indignantly denounces the "badly contrived document, devised by a factious and unprincipled priest, a clumsy conscienceless notary, and others of like stamp . . . concerned in this villainy." [2]

"What have I done, or my children, that I should meet such a fate?" Atahualpa cried to Pizarro. "And from your hands, too, you who have met with friendship and kindness from my people and with whom I have shared my treasures, who has received nothing but benefits from my hands!"

August 29, 1533, the Inca, in clanking chains, was led out of prison toward his doom. When bound to the stake, faggots piled high about him, he was promised by the ever insistent Valverde, that if he would merely accept baptism, he would receive kindly strangling instead of being burned alive.

He accepted the Christian faith, confessed, was named Juan. Whether Valverde gained a soul or merely mutilated bones, only God, St. Peter and the angels know.

Afterwards, nervous from their bloody deed, De Soto (who had wished to protect the Emperor), Pizarro (skulking mournfully under a huge felt hat slouched low over his eyes), Riquelme, the treasurer, and Valverde, scratching at his black robe, squabbled bitterly over who exactly was responsible for the murder.

Atahualpa's funeral, solemnly attended by his murderers, singing the credo for his soul, was held in San Francisco Church. During the ceremonies, his sisters and concubines, who the day before had to be held back from the stake where they intended throwing themselves into the flames, now killed themselves with loud lamentations.

## 7

An empire beheaded, the last unifying force gone, the social and political fabric crumbled, anarchy resulted.

[2] *Hist. gen. . . . de las Indias*, III, 8, 22.

The populace lost all restraint. Spanish greed, in an hour of general fear, had spread like wildfire to the Indians—a universal panic due to a universal catastrophe. Feuds broke into life. Towns were burnt. Palaces and temples were plundered, treasure scattered or hidden.

Many *curacas* declared themselves independent. Rumiñahui, with a previous reputation for treachery, murdered Atahualpa's kindred to seize the Quito throne. Generals Quizquiz and Tito Atauchi were leading enormous armies.

Pizarro hastened with his own hands to crown Inca Toparpa, Atahualpa's brother, as rightful emperor.

In a dark hour, September, 1533, with only five hundred Spaniards and a few Indian allies, Pizarro set forth for Cuzco over the royal highway. To impress the populace, Toparpa and General Chalcuchímac were borne forward on rich litters.

They passed through desolation. Inns and storehouses abandoned, fields ruined, towns smoking—sad contrast to the peaceful industrious scenes previously observed.

In Tocto Pizarro was attacked by Tito Atauchi with six thousand men.

In Jauja, set in wide irrigated meadows, he and Valverde knocked over the native idols and founded a Spanish colony. Inca Toparpa suddenly died, apparently poisoned. General Chalcuchímac was blamed, condemned to death. Spurning Valverde's efforts at conversion he threw himself into the flames, shouting "Pachacámac! Pachacámac!" name of his creator God.

In Bilcas, Soto was attacked, lost a number of men.

Near Cuzco, Manco, brother of Huáscar, came in with a brilliant delegation of "Big Ears" or Incas, to demand the imperial throne. The deal was made.

Still nearer Cuzco, in the Vilcacunca ravine, the invaders were attacked bloodily by Quizquiz' forces.

Still nearer, on the open plain, the Spaniards saw the thou-

sands of bleaching bones from the battle by which Atahualpa had defeated his half-brother Huáscar to become emperor.

November 15, 1533, a year after seizing Cajamarca, Pizarro's forces filed between the massive stone buildings of historic Cuzco—into the main square.

There, through torture and other pressure, he raked in,
despite all the treasure previously collected or concealed,
some 500,000 pesos ($7,500,000) and 215,000 marcos; he
stripped the jewels and gold from the imperial mummies in
the Temple of the Sun and looted the imperial storehouses.
The invaders found many twelve-inch planks of solid silver,
twenty feet long and three inches thick. In a near-by cavern,
they found gold vases embossed with serpents, locusts and
other animals, four golden llamas, life-sized gold and silver
female statues. Cavalryman Leguzano received the golden
image of the Sun from holy Coricancha—which he gambled
away in a single night, giving rise to an enduring Spanish
proverb: "He gambles away the sun before it rises."

Quizquiz was murdered by his own followers.

Rumiñahui, defeated by Commander Benalcázar, who had
moved up from Tangaralá, also perished.

Pedro de Alvarado, of Mexican Sun-God fame, arrived
with forces from Guatemala, crossed the snow-clad Andes
at the most terrific incredible points—leaving behind a trail
of cast-off equipment and gold, and a fourth of his men
and nearly 2,000 Indian allies dead—to dispute possession of
Ecuador. Almagro and Pizarro bought him off for 100,000
pesos cash.

In Cuzco Pizarro with the aid of Valverde, soon to be
named Bishop of Cuzco, personally crowned Manco II puppet emperor, with Mass, waving of Spanish flags, the drinking of chicha from golden goblets, and altogether much
pomp. Coricancha was transformed into the spacious Santo
Domingo convent, and by March, 1534, Pizarro had founded

a local Spanish government and had allotted lands to settlers.

January 18, 1535, he laid the first stone of Lima, city of Kings, planned as the future capital.

## 8

Anarchy and more anarchy.

From Quito to Charcas armies marched and battled.

Almagro and Pizarro quarreled. Almagro seized Cuzco.

Again Pizarro diverted him with honied words. They attended a solemn Mass together. Almagro blinked his one eye, went off across the terrible Atacama desert to seek gold and glory in Chile.

Manco II fled from Cuzco, raised revolt among the royal Cañaris. Hernando Pizarro, then governor of Cuzco, captured him.

Released on promising to bring in a huge gold statue, Manco hurried to the Yucay valley and organized general uprising. Forty thousand native troops, attacking Francisco Pizarro in Lima, with cries, "Embark, bearded ones!" swarmed into the very streets of the city, but after many weeks were driven off their high vantage ground on San Cristóbal hill, defeated.

Manco in person attacked Cuzco with 200,000 warriors, seized the powerful Sacsahuamán fortress, burnt most of the city down in a fire that converted it into a glowing oven and left the Spaniards with singed beards and soot-covered faces. He reduced the Spaniards to the main plaza and the ancient palace of Inca Viracocha. For months the siege continued. The Spaniards faced starvation. Every expedition sent by Francisco Pizarro was hacked to pieces and the bearded heads of the captured rolled into the Cuzco square to brighten the days of the defenders.

Finally, largely through the help of the Virgin and St. James, the Spaniards drove the Indians off. Gigantic General

Cahuide, rather than surrender Sacsahuamán, wrapped his head in his cape and plunged from the precipice to death on the rocks. Manco retired to the bulky square-windowed Ollantaytambo fortress, where he successfully resisted all attacks.

Almagro, returning—with a record of having burned thirty Indian chiefs alive—from Chile, where he had found no gold, only hardship and death, held parleys with Manco. Again he seized Cuzco, taking Hernando and Gonzalo Pizarro prisoners. Approaching Pizarro forces were defeated in Abancay.

Francisco Pizarro, again using honied words, induced Almagro to release Hernando (Gonzalo had already escaped), pending submission of the dispute to the Crown.

Orgóñez, Almagro's chief officer, said testily: "He who cannot keep his word in Castile, less will keep it in the Indies." Now, all the Pizarros broke their word, moved swift to destroy Almagro.

The forthcoming battle, which Almagro, aged and sick, watched from a stretcher, went to Hernando Pizarro. Taken prisoner, Almagro was executed with pious words and broken pledges. His follower Pedro de Lerma was assassinated in his cell while lying sick. Orgóñez was stabbed on surrender, his head piked up in Cuzco's plaza.

Manco II kept hostilizing the Spaniards. For thirty years he successfully maintained headquarters in the Vilcapampa mountain region, finally was killed by the refugee Spaniard Núñez de Vela in a quarrel over a game of *bolas*. On one occasion, Gonzalo Pizarro had one of Manco's young and beautiful wives stripped naked publicly, beaten by rods, shot to death with arrows. She never whimpered.

Hernando Pizarro went back to Spain loaded with presents for the king. Expecting to be honored, he was thrust into prison for nearly twenty-five years—a mere bagatelle, for he lived to be a hundred.

Gonzalo Pizarro became Governor of Quito and explored the Napo and Amazón, with fantastic adventures and unbelievable hardships.

Francisco Pizarro was assassinated in Lima, by the Mozo, the half-breed son of Almagro, at the head of a band of bitter conspirators. Throat stabbed, the mighty Conquistador fell bleeding, made the sign of the cross with his own blood, kissed it and died.

The Mozo took charge of the government; the populace crying, "The tyrant is dead!" sacked the houses of Pizarro and his friends.

Pizarro's followers rose in arms.

The Almagristas quarreled among themselves but fought the Pizarristas.

Special Crown envoy and new governor, Vaca de Castro, deposed Almagro junior, marched south from Cuzco, his forces also quarreling.

The Mozo took the field of battle, his men still quarreling —Commander García de Alvarado murdered Commander Cristóbal de Sotelo in his quarters. The Mozo lost, was captured at Chupas hard by Ayacucho and beheaded—after receiving last unction.

The first Viceroy, so-titled, Blasco Núñez de Vela, was received with great pomp under a holy canopy. He imprisoned Vaca de Castro and sought to enforce the Las Casas Crown edicts bettering the lot of the Indians, but this only swept most of the country into revolt behind Gonzalo Pizarro. In a quarrel Blasco Núñez knifed popular *Factor* Suárez de Carbajal and though he tried to conceal the body by burying it in the cathedral, this served as an excuse for the Oidores, whose privileges had been menaced, to seize him, try him in the cathedral atrium and out him under permanent arrest.

Carbajal, advance guard for Pizarro, long under arms,

entered Lima and hung three prominent cavaliers, letting them choose their own tree-branches out of consideration for their high rank.

Pizarro entered soon after in great pomp, a thousand soldiers shooting arquebuses, amid music, trumpets, church bells and a Te Deum, and was named governor.

Diego Ceteno revolted in Charcas, declaring himself Viceroy. Whipped, he hid in a cave.

Blasco Núñez escaped with the connivance of the commander of the vessel taking him back to Spain, raised an army in Ecuador. Wounded and taken prisoner, he was snatched away from the priest confessing him by the brother of murdered Suárez de Carbajal who had his throat slashed by a negro slave. Blasco's head was carried triumphantly upon a pike clear to Quito; there Juan de la Torre cut off the long white beard to make a plume for his hat.

Gonzalo Pizarro, having well-earned the title "the Demon of the Andes," now ruled supreme from Quito to Chile, with a large fleet dominating the Pacific. Rumor has it he planned to found an independent kingdom.

Inquisition Sacerdote Pedro de la Gasca, with no other weapons than robe and breviary, was sent out by the Crown to restore royal authority. Soon he won over the fleet and many of Gonzalo's followers.

Gonzalo obliged the Audiencia to condemn Gasca to death, sentence to be executed when and if caught, and October 20, 1547, defeated the Crown forces in Centeno. But surveying the bloody field, Gonzalo exclaimed, "Jesus! Jesus! What a victory!"

On the eve of a second battle at Jaquijuana, some leagues from Cuzco, Gonzalo's forces began to desert in droves. The game was up.

> "The wind blows the hair off my head, mother;
> Two at a time it blows them away,"

chanted his General Francisco de Carbajal.

"Let us die like Christians," remarked Pizarro.

"No, let us die like Romans," cried Carbajal.

Whereupon they charged in bloody combat and died each in his own way.

Pizarro was beheaded after Christian confession.

Carbajal was ordered dragged by horses, hung and quartered. "Quite enough if I'm killed," he replied indifferently. On being dragged, not by horses, but in a basket by mules, he let out a roar of laughter and sang insolently:

> "Ho, cradles for babies,
> And a cradle for the old man, too."

Bearing his eighty-four years bravely, he went to his sentence luxuriously attired—in the best Roman style.

In the 'fifties, the large landowners revolted against pro-Indian edicts of the Council of the Indies. "Who tries to take away the slaves and towns granted me by his master, look out . . . for his life," said wall-lettering.

Hinojoso, Corregidor of Plata, promoted insurrection in Charcas, was assassinated by subordinate Sebastián Castilla, who was assassinated by another subordinate, Vasco Godínez, who was captured and hung by Marshal Alvarado.

Francisco Hernández Girón, follower of Gonzalo Pizarro, revolted, won a victory, then was defeated, captured, had his head piked up in Lima's main plaza.

Everywhere, in addition to these more historical events, quarrelsome soldiers, banded in ruthless forays, looted, fought, raped and murdered.

The Conquistadores made good mince-meat of themselves and of thousands of bewildered Indians. Cities old and new were wrecked and abandoned.

Thus most of the visible wealth of Perú was plundered or destroyed—gold and silver and jewels stolen, bridges demolished, irrigation systems shattered, the imperial warehouses gutted. The roadside inns were abandoned and tumbled over, the roads fell into ruin, the enormous royal llama herds scattered, killed or eaten, thus further depriving the conquered of food and the warm fleece that protected them against the cold. No greater gang of vandals ever descended upon a civilization or so completely wrecked it in so short a time.

After fifty tragic years, the long period of anarchy was drawing to a close.

### 9

The change is first noted in the arrival of Andrés Hurtado de Mendoza, the great Viceroy of Mexico, who appeared with his wife, the Marquesa, and a suite of 120 poor relatives. Lima took on a courtly, etiquette-ridden aspect, rendered gracious by urbanity and hospitality, traits which still distinguish its artificial society.

But not until the arrival in 1569 of Count Oropesa, Francisco de Toledo, Perú's greatest colonial governor, was the colony put upon a truly organized basis and the Inquisition introduced as a governing instrument.

Soon after, Inca Tupac-Amaru, last resisting Emperor, was brought into Cuzco, a rope around his neck, and beheaded before the Viceroy's eyes.

By that time the Spaniards were settling down to the more arduous but systematic effort of seeking out the mineral sources of Incan wealth. Mines were opening up; the great estates had been parcelled out and to some extent put in operation; society was taking on a definite structure.

Anarchy, the marching and countermarching of armies, had, in brutal fashion, mixed races and cultures, a process greatly halted now that hard caste lines were drawn. In the new scheme the Spaniards enjoyed all the real privileges. Next in the social scale came the Creoles or Chapetones— Spaniards born in the New World. The mestizos or cholos of mixed blood enjoyed only scant rights and opportunities, but gradually carved out a rôle as intermediaries between the Spanish authorities and the subject race. Underneath the pyramid, bearing all its weight, were the conquered Indians, parcelled out like slaves, dragged off in chains to work mines and haciendas, used as pack animals. Within less than a century, the vast native population had been reduced to less than two million souls; negro slaves had to be imported to work the coast plantations. Pizarro himself, in his original Capitulación, got the first license—to import fifty, one-third of them to be females. Wrote Cieza de León in his *Guerra de las Salinas*,[3] telling of the "great evils and violences . . ." the taking of women and properties: that which made one "weep even more was the manner in which the Indians had to carry loads, chained to each other by their necks: And as they had to cross deep sands and their loads increased and the sun was big and there was no tree to give them shade, nor spring to get water, the poor Indians grew exhausted; and instead of being allowed to rest, were given heavy beat-

[3] 58-9.

ings, called lazy pigs . . . so maltreated many fell on the ground and . . . in order not to have to stop to unfasten the chain to get them loose, their heads were cut off with little fear of God. . . ."

And he concludes:

"Once in these valleys there were great numbers of people and because of the evil treatment they have received from governments and past captains, they have been reduced so much that now many of those valleys are uninhabited and so deserted there is nothing to be seen but ruined buildings and the sepulchres of the dead and the rivers that flow through those valleys."

Philip II's royal Cedula to the Peruvian Archbishop (May 27, 1582) recited even worse abuses: "In some parts a third are missing . . . they are treated worse than slaves . . . bought and sold . . . murdered by flogging . . . women die and break under their heavy loads . . . and give birth in the fields . . . bitten by poisonous insects . . . many hang themselves . . . others starve themselves to death and others take poisonous herbs . . . mothers kill their new-born babes . . . to free them from toil . . . said Indians have a great hate for the word Christian. . . ."

Francisco de Chávez killed all the babies of one village. Indians, for sport, were often dragged by their hair tied to horses' tails, or were hunted down with bloodhounds. Women were raped at will. What exploitation and cruelty did not accomplish was completed by the great pests of 1546, 1589, 1597, 1700 and 1719.

But Lima became more courtly, wealthy and pious.

On the basis of mineral wealth and despotic centralization in Lima, due to its overseas connections with Spain and the Orient, a false and briefly glittering colonial culture developed, a splendid viceregal court, private opulence, showy residences and four-in-hand coaches. European masters were copied for the temples; an Italian-influenced literature, imi-

tating the involved rhetorician of Spain—obscure Góngora
—but preoccupied with theology and scholasticism, betrayed
the inevitable omniscience of servile minds.

The Church had pallid Rosa of Lima beatified, accumulated vast properties, founded religious hospitals and schools,
grew corrupt and vicious. All the Viceroys were holy men.
Pedro Fernández de Castro was wont to visit the hospitals,
kneel down and kiss the feet of the sick. Often he swept out
the churches.

Quinine was discovered; the Marqués of Mancera introduced chocolate into Europe. Into Perú were introduced
wheat, barley, grapes, olives, oranges, limes, apples, quinces,
peaches, plums, melons, cucumbers, squash, sugar-cane, vegetables, new flowers, horses, mules, donkeys, cows, sheep, rabbits, and negroes; but the Spaniards destroyed more agriculture than they ever promoted.

For two and a half centuries viceroy followed viceroy with
minor eventfulness and increasing pomp, show and dicta-
torialness. They were received under arcs of solid silver; they
travelled with 24 mulatto lackeys, 24 pages, three footmen
and six outriders in boots and spurs, all in red, silver and
blue livery. Artillery salutes, troop reviews and bull-fights
honored them. The Court was sumptuous and formal.

Their power was almost omnipotent. The early democratic
features of the first cities were emasculated. When the
Cabildo elected Gaviel de Castilla and Juan de la Pesa as new
Alcaldes of Lima, Viceroy Santiesteban remarked: "You
have elected two excellent Alcaldes: Gaviel de Castilla and
Josephe Castella de Mendoza." Not a protest was heard;
Juan de la Pesa cooled his heels jobless.

Aside from forays of English and Dutch corsairs—the
great Real Felipe fort was built in Callao to hold them off—
and occasional Indian uprisings (more and more serious
toward the close of the eighteenth century, invariably put
down bloodily by mass executions), the rigid system of

colonial rule, with its hard trade restrictions, its tight barriers against new intellectual currents, rolled smoothly enough through the decades in an atmosphere of political and ecclesiastical intrigue. The most exciting events were probably those frequent spats between Archbishop and Viceroy over jurisdiction and special privileges, social etiquette and precedence, feuds carried on with slightly more ferociousness than that of a Dolly Gann.

Doña Ana Fernández de Velasco y Avendano, a lady of noble Spanish blood, wife of Marshal Alonzo de Alvarado, was a terrible shrew, and her overweening pride, despite her good blood, made bad blood wherever she went. The sight of any woman less nobly born than she using a cushion in church or occupying a better place at Mass—her favorite battle ground was the House of God—drove her quite mad. In the Cuzco cathedral she obliged her servants to knife an honorable widow who had taken the place the haughty termagant wanted. Fury incarnate, she caused the widow's mother to be shorn, the dress of the widow's sister to be slashed, and the bones of the dead husband to be disinterred and scattered. In these Christian-like outrages Marshal Alvarado complacently sided with his wife. Chief Justice Cianaca publicly and severely reprimanded him, whereupon Alvarado's servants gravely insulted Cianaca. He in turn condemned Alvarado to death. The marshal was saved only by the personal intervention of Governor Gasca.

# IV
# POINT COUNTERPOINT

## I

$A$LL historical testimony coincides—the Incaic people, laborious, disciplined, lived in simple material well-being, pantheistic security and artistic creativeness. No great civilization ever developed from such meager resources in the face of such enormous obstacles. Social coöperation is the one clue to its development—age-old communal agrarianism drawn into centralized efficiency by the severe Incaic paternalism.

The Spanish conquerors, obeying a pious but empty formula of mass conversion to Catholicism, anarchically looted the empire, destroyed—without being able to reconstruct or for nearly a century to replace it—all this formidable socialized machinery of production.

To the Spaniards, the Indians lacking Christianity, alphabet, money, iron, the wheel, gunpowder, monogamy, many plants and animals, seemed barbarous. To the Indians, the Spaniards, for their wanton destruction of irrigation canals, roads, terraces, temples, cities, granaries; for their greed, cruelty, lascivity, even for their military superiority, seemed equally barbarous.[1]

Little by little, upon the shattered residues of a semi-Socialist economy, the Crown emissaries—once the autonomist spirit of the early Conquistadores had been exhausted or suppressed—erected a pseudo-feudal system, more arbitrary, less organic than that which Spain in her own house was fighting tooth and nail to extirpate.

[1] Cf. Basadre, *Perú*, 13.

74

J. S.

This anachronism was necessary. The Conquest was primarily a military and ecclesiastic, not basically economic and political, enterprise; Spain had to rule with a handful of bureaucrats, missionaries and "get-rich-quick Wallingfords."

Spain sent out no home-seeking pioneers—the Dominican, Franciscan and Jesuit friars most closely approximated this category—but rather viceroys, courtesans, adventurers, clerics, Inquisitors, theological doctors, and soldiers. Never in Perú, much less than in Mexico, was there real colonization. The Spaniards, also the mestizos or cholos, were too few, even if of the right type, adequately to develop the country's resources; they not only destroyed native ability to do so, but so reduced population by excessive toil and wholesale massacres (not to mention measles and smallpox) that increasingly negro slaves had to be imported; feudal society became further corrupted by a slave society.

After the first looting years, the favored recipients of slave-labor usufruct were not military adventurers but the Crown, the mine-owners, the large *encomenderos*, the bureaucracy and the Church. Principal post-Conquest activity was gold and silver mining, plus some large-estate agriculture. Mining created small Creole cities in the Andes; a small highlands Creole agricultural- and trading-class arose to supply resultant needs.[2]

But most immigrants settled along the coast, especially in Lima, there living in luxury and libertinage—symptoms of ruthless exploitation of hinterland mines. Lima, international depot with a shallow glittering culture, ruled despotically. Thus no truly integrated economy, utilizing coördinated

[2] In some cases, however, these cities temporarily achieved considerable size. Potosí, site of mines originally owned by Gonzalo Pizarro, reached 150,000 inhabitants—became "a monstrous earthbody, with silver soul, opening its mouth to swallow human beings," where adventurous Basques, Extremadureñans, Andalusians, and Creoles, battled bloodily and drunkenly. The place erupted wealth. It spent eight million pesos on Charles V's coronation, six millions on Philip III's funeral, and from its discovery until 1783, produced 821 million duros, a sum in excess of the entire monetary circulation of Europe, and which, in today's values, would total billions of dollars.

mass energies, ever arose to replace the Inca structure. Rural Perú declined to petty village self-sufficiency with none of the humanitarian or scientific supports of the Incaic system, a local isolation, inadequacy and resultant poverty which persists to this day.

The eighteenth century of the Bourbons saw changes: the break-down of commercial exclusivism and arbitrary caste lines; enormous contraband activities; experimental, more liberal, trade legislation; Church corruption and inefficiency; expulsion of the Jesuits; decline of the Inquisition; new French free-thought influences, rationalism, buddings of scientific investigation; sanitation; rise of a small Creole bourgeoisie cleaving the old rigid Spanish ecclesiastical aristocracy; looser sex-ties, prostitution, high-class courtesans—the famous divine Perricholi, who netted a Viceroy.

Early viceroys had been relatives of the Crown, of aristocrats or high prelates; but the later O'Higgins was an ex-storekeeper. Titles and posts were now bought by the new traders. The ecclesiastical cock-sure but servile writer Peralta Barnuevo gave way to the heterodox semi-rationalists Baquijano, Carrillo and Rodríguez de Mendoza. The printing presses, previously used only for tracts, turned out newspapers. The elaborate rhetoric of Góngora changed to prosaic Frenchified realism. Flamboyant Churrigueresque capitulated to classic severity, imposed by architect Matías Maestro.

The previous century was that of miracles, saints, the Inquisition. But the Bourbon century witnessed the expulsion of the Jesuits, mundane licentiousness in the convents, the last *auto-da-fé* and the trial of Inquisitioners for fraud.

The Spanish colonial system was breaking up under the blows of modern industrialism, represented especially by England. Mining, Perú's main industry, was growing less important; agriculture, trade, economic self-sufficiency loomed larger.

Spain made frantic efforts to reorganize the colonies on a

more enduring political and economic basis, but she lacked the technique to meet new world trends—she could not even introduce new inventions and machinery into her mines. And not only were her own trade, industry and agriculture declining, but these efforts struck at too many vested interests. Spain had acquired feudal hardening of the arteries. Her efforts at renovation, inadequate at best, came too late.

## 2

The small trading-class had grown stronger—a Peruvian Creole bourgeoisie, with some cholo infiltrations. New ideas, new political beliefs.

Also, the great 1780 Indian revolt of Tupac Amarú indicated that other social and racial tendencies were likewise in ferment. Independence was at hand.

If Bolívar, San Martín and other brilliant non-Peruvian leaders imparted to the Hispanic American independence struggle a romantic heroic aspect, it also represented the desire of the new bourgeoisie to break Spanish exclusivism, to abolish the trade acts and institute *laissez faire* industrial expansion and free trading. But the Creole landlords who likewise came into the movement had no such freakish ideas! Since the new bourgeois class was so weak and since the Indian unrest had no real coördination, although masses of Indians were swept into the fight, independence signified merely an upper class split—Creoles versus Spaniards; emancipation was "entirely an urban force, not rural; bourgeois and Creole, not indigenous." Both sides merely wished to use the Indian masses for their own ends. Thus the Spaniards took in tow a native cacique of royal descent and threatened San Martín they would proclaim a new Inca empire. And after independence San Martín and Creole aristocrats as early as 1821 sought to establish a monarchy, an attitude in which they were backed by churchman José Ignacio Moreno, and which some of them have clung to until the present century. All the old caste lines remained despite the fact that Pérez de Tudela insisted that in Perú "there is heterogeneity of colors, but not of desires and sentiments. The soul is equal in all."

Thus, the weakness of the new state, geographical separatism and lack of communications, the antagonism of border nations, the plethora of greedy militarists and politicians, the civic ignorance of the masses, the natural unruliness after centuries of subjection—all the sharp racial and caste divisions prevented any real unification.

But the bourgeoisie were strong enough to secure a liberal constitution with democratic trimmings, but little related to the real social, cultural and racial facts of the country— a borrowed system that could not be enforced, which therefore became merely a deluding slogan, a barren bone of military contention. The aristocratic landholding class remained in the ascendancy, and the colonial system was able at the advent of the Republic to say with Mark Twain, "The news of my death is slightly exaggerated."

The military chiefs, after independence, formed a powerful privileged caste, gave Perú the heritage of a vast army, a tradition of militarism and the heeled boot. The Army, utilizing masses ignorant of the causes for which they sacrificed their lives, became the Great Elector. Typical of the military mentality is the anecdote of Castilla; when robbers entered his house, he came dashing out, shouting, "Hey, this is the government," a vulgar version of "I am the state." Whatever the deep causes of disorder, the surface battle was ever based upon greed, power, vanity, popular applause, only now and then, patriotism. As elsewhere, these amazing Peruvian military personalities were brutal, ignorant and devoid of intelligible justification. In general the militarists helped maintain the new hybrid bourgeois-feudal system.

Civilians in political affairs, part of the new but ever rapacious bureaucracy—during the earlier period known usually as *Válidos* or *Censores*—were mere sycophants of the militarists, intriguing trouble-makers who prepared the psychological and philosophical pretexts for new armed attempts. Poets prostituted their talents by lauding the most successful iron heel, as José Joaquín de Mora who wrote a hysterical poem on Santa Cruz' victory in Yanacocha. Thus Perú also received the blessings, which it still has, of a greedy unrestrained bureaucracy mouthing cheap patriotic slogans. Gunpowder nationalists.

Liberty became in reality a liberty of military chieftains to lord it and liberty of Creole landlords to steal lands.

The old caste system continued, in most respects worse than before, merely minus Spaniards, minus Crown bureaucracy. Crown protective legislation, thanks to new theories regarding mankind's universal equality, was destroyed; the Indians remained "the vile clay with which the social edifice was built," still uneducated, agriculture unimproved. However much the highlands provided revolutionary man-power and vain hopes, Lima and the coast, with all its outmoded hierarchy, its large landholding class and the Church (elements which soon sidetracked or absorbed the newer bourgeoisie) ruled.

Thus, underneath all this upheaval, the century of independence was basically a stale-mate struggle between two cultures, native and colonial, one legally recognized, the other tacitly ignored. That struggle had been held in abeyance, or at times intelligently directed, during colonial rule. Now, though the odds were ever on the side of the Creole feudalists, it prevented any constructive effort, undermined all efforts really to found a nation.

## 3

If Spanish American independence ideas came from France, *i.e.*, the Encyclopædists and the revolution, the practical trade and industrial afflatus came from England. The United States merely looked on with jealous eyes; we kept a finger in the pie in Mexico, prevented Cuba's—for us

premature—independence, and wherever possible put a spoke into England's imperialistic activities in Central America. England saw in New World independence, not a propagation of dangerous ideas as did other European powers, but a death-blow to hated Spanish imperial rivalry and a vast new market previously closed. The economic interests of the freed Spanish colonies and those of England were reciprocal. Raw products complemented finished products. Mr. Canning, therefore, was quick to espouse Hispanic American liberty; British capital hastened to finance the new Republics.

Argentina, Chile and Brazil were soon re-colonized, Euro-peanized. For geographical and other reasons, the rest of the countries swung back to a dark brutal feudalism. Perú, especially, sank into the lethargy of ecclesiastical, militaristic, landlord, and racial exploitation which strangled every new effort. Facing west upon the Pacific, she found her normal trade relations, not with Europe, but with the Orient, and thus, parting company with her sister republics, she enjoyed a long period of Oriental influence; Japanese and Chinese immigrants came in, supplanting negro and Indian slaves; a flourishing trade grew up. But Japan and China, as compared to England, could provide no modern machinery and industrial technique—only rice, camphor, precious woods, silks and art objects for the feudal aristocracy.

## 4

From 1842 on British capital hurried into Perú to obtain guano and saltpetre. These fertilizers took the place of gold and silver as products of easy exploitation and quick revenue —glorious prosperity for the Lima *nouveaux riches,* money to squander for the government. For several decades Lima's upper classes lived wastrelly. Work and better wages made part of the coast proletariat more contented. But this facile lucrative activity, this hasty skimming off of the cream, blinded Perú's rulers to the need of a more balanced, enduring economy; everything except guano and foreign loans were ignored. Rural Perú rotted more than ever. Once more sensible integration of the Peruvian nation was delayed.

A new wealthier bourgeois group was formed, mixed as usual with feudal aristocracy, which instead of looking to Perú, turned to the outside world for sustenance—financial and cultural; it impounded Perú's future to England; it aped French thought.

But actually contemporary Liberal-capitalist ideas had little real effectiveness, made little impression upon the country or upon the State. Never organized into effective channels, Peruvian liberalism, based upon *laissez faire* economy, vague democratic rights, anti-militarism, anti-centralization, was intermittent, very heterogeneous. Because of lack of civic consciousness and mass education, because of the continued predominance of feudalism, Peruvian Liberalism was overly proclerical and leaned too much on the militarists whom it opposed and who invariably betrayed its aims. The Liberals sought only legal and governmental reforms, never faced basic economic problems. In general, their ideas, like their goods, were brought into Lima from the outside, an aping of capitalist mentality without capitalist organization. Its few effective moments were the Progresista Club of 1849-51, the abolition of slavery and Indian tribute in the 1854 revolution, the earlier program of President Nicolás de Piérola. Aside from this—as in the case of Leguía—the feudal aristocracy ever quickly absorbed bourgeois elements, suppressed their normal ideology.

Furthermore the guano-saltpetre era ended abruptly—too soon to establish the Liberal coast bourgeoisie firmly in power. Conflict with Chile and the loss of Tacna and Arica ruined Perú's entire guano prosperity and precipitated the country into a disastrous abyss. Foreign credit was ruined. Previous long neglect of all other economic activities, the selfish failure of the rulers to promote any rounded development, was now bitterly felt by all classes.

Power again reverted to military chieftains. Perú was swept by anarchic civil war. But spiritually and socially the militarists were, as always everywhere, incapable of promoting economic recovery; rule soon returned to the coast feudal-bourgeois group. Reformer Piérola, heading the Democratic Party (made up of bourgeoisie, aristocrats and ecclesiastics), came into power with generous but empty catchwords: "public good," "free citizen," "patriotism," "duty," "law." Desperate efforts were made to bring the country out of chaos.

The solution, despite popular antagonism, was found in British aid. New financial dickerings. New and larger British investments. New foreign banks and corporations functioned. The Andean Oroyo-Guancayo railroad was finally finished, opening up traffic with the rich upland department of Junín, making possible new exploitation of mineral wealth. And in 1893 the great Peruvian Corporation was formed, by which British bondholders exchanged paper debts for railroads, mines and tropical estates. British hegemony over Perú was re-ratified. Soon cricket was being played on the greens of Callao and Lima.

Slowly the country recovered. The old feudal plutocracy, allied with British capital, was again in the saddle. Modern industry, though still half-strangled by the iron circle of feudalism, gradually permeated various parts of the country.

The opening of the Panamá canal, shortening the distance to the United States and Europe, and the World War, hastened the process of reestablishing a colonialism subjected to alien capital; but shifted the emphasis from British pounds to American dollars.

5

Only four forces have ruled Perú since the overthrow of Tahuantinsuyo: the feudal *caciquismo* of the Sierra, the coast feudal plutocracy, military bureaucracy and ecclesiasticism. With these foreign capital has made its alliance. Thus despite modern capitalist trends, the ancient feudal class, camouflaged as "republican bourgeoisie," has conserved its positions. The new development has been the creation of the inevitable proletarian class, which has closed proselytism in the cities to the military caste.

But Perú, despite imperialism, remains essentially a self-sustaining agricultural country; only 11.5 percent of the population lives in cities. The mass of the population is tied to the land, dependent upon the soil for a livelihood. But the old feudalism survives. The old colonialism survives. International trade and capital have merely buttressed up the traditional benighted ruling classes.

On the other side of the scales, the modern world and its ideas are battering at the gates, not merely foreign dollars, but all the manifold currents of Bolshevism, Fascism, the collectivist trends of our times. And the old village communalism survives. Therein lies a long-standing struggle, soon to become more acute.

"Perú," remarked Mariátegui, "must choose between the Indian and the *gamonal*," the large landholder. That is the basic conflict. Involved with it is the geographic, economic, racial and cultural duality of coast and highlands—a vast problem of social amalgamation, the problem of Peruvian nationality. Perú can have no intelligent economic development, no enduring prosperity, and no peace, until the agrarian and regional problems are solved, the people liberated, and an organic planned system of production put into operation. Perú until that time will fail to achieve nationhood.

## CHRONOLOGY

*Pre-Spanish*

4000 B.C. (?)–100 B.C.

Northern Andes: Chavín culture.
Southern Andes: Pre-Tiahuanaco culture.
Coast and Jungles: Archaic and migratory cultures.

100 B.C.–500 A.D.

Highlands: Tiahuanaco I culture.
Northern Coast: Mochican culture: Chimú conquest culture.
Southern Coast: Pre-Nazca culture.

500 A.D.–600 A.D.

Coast wars with highlands.

600 A.D.–1,000 A.D.

Tiahuanaco II empire, coast and highlands.

1000 A.D.–1400 A.D.
> North Coast: Late Chimú culture.
> South Coast: Late Nazca culture.
> Highlands: Tiahuanaco decline; rise of early Incas.

1400–1533. Inca empire.

*Colonial Period*

1513. Núñez de Balboa discovers the Pacific.
1524. November. Pizarro's first southward expedition.
1526. November. Pizarro's second expedition.
1532. Pizarro discovers Perú.
——. November 15. Pizarro captures Cajamarca.
1533. August 29. Atahualpa garroted.
——. November 15. Pizarro captures Cuzco.
1536. Great Manco revolt. Seven months' siege of Cuzco.
1533–1552. Anarchy. Civil War.
1570. Establishment of the Inquisition.
1666–67. Laycacota mine revolt.
1742–43. Juan Santos Indian revolt in the Chanchamayo.
1780. Tupac Amarú Indian revolt.

*Independence Period*

1812–14. First independence revolts.
1814–15. Pumacahua Indian revolt.
1820. Liberator San Martín invades Perú.
1821. July 28. Declaration of Independence.
1824. December 9. Battle of Ayacucho. Capture of Viceroy de la Serna.
1824–36. Dictatorships and civil wars.
1836–39. Santa Cruz founds the Perú-Bolivian Confederation.
1836–42. Civil wars and dictatorships.
1842–1879. Guano prosperity period. British capital dominant.
> 1845–51—1855–62 Castilla Dictatorship.

|  |  |
|---|---|
|  | 1855. Castilla liberates black slaves. |
| 1866. War with Spain. | 1866. Indian revolt of Huancané. |
| 1879–1883. War of the Pacific | |

86

with Chile. Loss of Tacna Arica. Economic collapse.

1883–95. Military governments.

1893–1934. Rise to power of Piérola and reactionary bourgeois feudalists—the "Civilistas."

1893–1914. New British capital invasion.

1893. Founding of Peruvian Corporation.

1919–1930. Leguía dictatorship supported by American loans.

1930. August. Sánchez Cerro (Spanish - Indian - Negro Sergeant Major) revolution. (Middle-class Army alliance plus lesser bureaucratic Civilistas.)

1932–34. Leticia controversy.

1933. Assassination Sánchez Cerro.

1934. Military Civilista government of Benavides.

1884. Great Huarás Indian revolts under Atusparia and Uchcu Pedro.

1909-20. Rise of student movement.

1912. General strike in Lima.

1920-23. Fusion of student and labor movements.

1926. Student-labor strikes.

1926–30. Student and labor agitation. Indian uprisings. Pro-Indian organizations.

1930–34. Rise of Aprista movement (middle-class, student, proletariat, led by Haya de la Torre).

1932. Trujillo Aprista revolt. Colonel Jiménez revolt. (Army, proletariat.)

1930–34. Emergence of small Communist movement: Lima, Arequipa and Cuzco. Indian and peasant revolts.

1934. Lima. Unsuccessful general strike. General Strike Southern railways.

# PART II
*PEOPLE*

# V

# ROULETTE

I ARISTOCRATS

IN that noble hall great crystal chandeliers threw diamond-bright light; tapestry wall-paper depicted the life of the Italian aristocracy. But the patterned hardwood floors were burned by countless cigarette stubs; the one-time elegance of that ancestral salon had grown shabby; it had acquired the vulgar, slightly frazzled make-up of a lascivious woman betrayed by many cheap amours. For there, in the late decades of the past century, the Lima élite assembled to play roulette.

Perú was rapidly recovering from the disastrous Chile war. New capital was flowing in, new mines opening up. The large coast haciendas of rice, cotton, and sugar were booming. Prices were rising, money plentiful.

Even labor shortage existed. For though Andean Indians were rounded up by force, soon they sickened and died in the hot lowlands. For many years now, Chinese had increasingly filled the void left after the stopping of the African slave trade.

Money was easy come, easy go. The garnering of wealth in Perú has always been a gamble. Once garnered it is gambled in more obvious ways.

The gathering in that noble hall was select. Many men wore evening clothes. High-class décolleté courtesans drifted in and out of the polished bar.

Between conversations and rounds of cognac or *pisco*, the game went steadily on.

The chips stacked up. A red chip was called a "Chinaman"—it was worth five hundred *soles*. A green-black chip

91

was a "zambo," worth a hundred *soles*. A blue chip was an "Inca," worth only fifty *soles*.

Human lives converted into chips!

2

This is the story of the patron of a very modern gambling house—Count Montesinos de Valverde, an elegant gentleman with waxed moustaches, who knows all the niceties of social etiquette, but who has never learned not to spit on the floor.

He is the son of an army colonel, who had enriched himself by padded army rolls and false fines as Prefect of Jauja.

The present Count had started his career by participating in a frustrated revolutionary attempt in Arequipa. Out of nervous inexperience, he displayed incredible bravery which cost him a serious wound, capture and imprisonment in Lima, but gave him a reputation for fearlessness, much needed in a country where power is usually achieved by a bold stroke.

Pardoned, he at once founded the Liberal Conservative Radical Party, composed of job-seekers, to conspire against the government.

An incoming administration, to silence his opposition, offered him the Ministry of Finance.

He accepted, betraying some of his followers, giving fat sinecures to others. Still a young man, he was convinced the road to the Presidency was now open. But to arrive there, much money was needed. Through juicy contracts with British and American capitalists and other manipulations, patronage of gambling establishments and police rake-offs, particularly from the red-light district, he soon amassed a considerable fortune, most of which he deposited in a London bank.

He learned to live in luxury and properly to appreciate

fine food, drink and art. For his mistress he took the beautiful daughter of an ambitious office-holder, who thus received promotion—a common Peruvian practice. At first his relations with Clarita, for whom he soon conceived an overwhelming passion, were entirely clandestine, but gradually she lost her conventional shame; he set her up in the most luxurious establishment in all Lima.

His operations became so scandalous he was dismissed. Once more he became a plotter. Now he had powerful enemies, but also powerful partisans, especially as he donated heavily to the "cause." He founded a newspaper, which ate up large sums but which devoted its columns chiefly to his eulogy. Several score men were ardently attracted to the noble principles he espoused, because of his beautiful mistress; her ménage was the rendezvous for all the plotting.

Even military men began drifting in to the more social reunions. In time a few were admitted into the inner circle of anti-government machinations.

Once Montesinos came in just as young, handsome General Cárdenas was leaving. Clarita, all in a glow, threw her arms around her protector, telling him the general (just named commandant of the important northern department of Piura) had pledged himself to strike for their cause when the moment should come.

Montesinos was a bit worried lest she might have been indiscreet, especially as the government was now watching him uneasily. But he trusted her judgment greatly. Cárdenas would be a big asset, particularly now matters were coming to a head. Soon, the conspirators knew, they must strike or be lost. Plans were laid. A quick *coup* was projected. The President would be seized, a provisional dictatorship established until elections would put Montesinos into the Presidency.

Some weeks later, Montesinos caught his mistress and young General Cárdenas *in flagrante*. Quietly he closed the door on the pair, but rushed out through the streets, striding along hatless, like a madman. One minute, out of his head with jealousy, he determined to kill the general, to kill Clarita; the next he was eaten up with passion for her. A thousand furious incoherent ideas flickered through his brain.

Late that evening he returned somewhat exhausted, therefore calmer. No guests were in the house. He half expected to find Clarita gone.

But she was waiting for him, pale and frightened. All tenderness, she tried to placate him. Terrible the charm of her, but he thrust her violently aside.

He paced to and fro.

She pled. She loved only him. In a hundred different ways, she swore her undying affection, told him how proud she was of him, how much she wanted him to succeed. Her every thought had been for him to achieve the goal at which he aimed. She had taken the foolish step with the general merely to win him over completely to their cause.

He was moved.

She sensed his emotion. If he desired her to do so, she hastened to tell him, she would go away forever—anything to help him.

Her words sent a pang through him. He could not bear to lose her.

She knew, by his expression, she had won. She crept back into his arms. He forgave her.

But he continued eaten up by jealous fears. To how many of his followers, he now wondered, had his beautiful Clarita delivered her charms—all for the sake of the cause?

The general, frightened at having been discovered, betrayed the revolutionary plans to the government.

A few days later the police took Count Montesinos de Valverde prisoner in the house of his mistress, led him off in pyjamas—a salacious morsel that made all Lima chuckle.

To the Count's dismay, he now realized his fortune was almost dissipated. Completely confident of success, of soon being able to put his hands back into the honey-jar of public wealth, he had taken little account of the rapid depletion of his reserves. He had thrown everything away. Without money, now, caught red-handed in disgrace, he could not hold his group together. In fact none of his so-called partisans stood by him; very few even visited him in prison.

Clarita came several times, then failed him.

After six months' imprisonment, he was deported into penniless exile.

By that time Clarita had become the mistress of a former admirer.

Montesino's only regret now was that he had not strangled her white neck before he was arrested.

### 3

The Marqués Cabello de la Espada, descendant of one of the first colonial families, was a gay young blade. Though noted

for extravagant dress and amorous conquests, a wise cynicism ever kept his dissipations within bounds. By astute combinations with government officials, he constantly added to
the vast landed patrimony of his ancestors. He was officially
assisted in driving off Indians from their ancient communal
lands or was given chances to bid in bankrupt property at
a song. He had a finger in various tobacco, guano and other
monopolies.

He married late, adding not only beauty to his household
but doubling his great holdings.

Thus, despite early escapades, he became far wealthier
than when he had begun teething on his silver spoon.

His wife, a fanatically pious woman, brought up the children, Aurora, Josefina and Guillermo, strictly in the faith.

Aurora was a small hysterical girl with huge soulful black
eyes and a tendency toward epilepsy. Although the oldest
daughter, hence bound to be the recipient of much worldly
goods, her flighty ways daunted the most calculating suitors.
She finally fell violently in love with a young chap of very
good family, but soon made the relation so hysterical he also
became alarmed. Of weak character, not knowing how to
break off with her, secretly he married another woman.
Aurora already had her wedding togs ready when she heard
of it.

She took the news quietly, but burned her wedding dress,
his pictures, everything he had given her. That same week
she hurled a heavy vase at the head of her French teacher
and went into a fit. They took her off to an asylum violently
insane.

Guillermo proved a reckless wretch who spent money like
water and early acquired all the vices. He began using opium,
then morphine. Parental threats proved useless; after violent
rows, his father threw him out of the house for good.

Tall, lily-white, chaste Josefina, most balanced of the lot, daunted most suitors by her extreme piety and austerity; also, extremely selfish, she never gave a tip and never more than a penny to a beggar and that only because it was her Christian duty. She had the cold biting character of her father, minus his early vices.

Her mother died when she was eighteen, her father when she was twenty-one. Before he died, he had established a small trust fund for the insane Aurora and put all his other property in Josefina's name. Guillermo was left without a single penny.

Guillermo appeared in a shabby state at the funeral, received the news of his disinheritance sullenly, demanded funds from Josefina which she refused. Thereafter when he called at the house, she absolutely declined to see him, knowing he had probably come for money; and money and God were the two things she prized most in life.

He went from bad to worse. The Chinese, who for a time provided him with opiates free because of his family connections, finally cut off his supply. Miserable in the coils of his vice, he pawned, borrowed, committed every sort of chantage, finally began to lose his reason.

Today he wanders the streets of Lima in a torn suit, face unshaven, begging alms with nervous twisting hands.

Once he found himself whining up to a beautiful woman just stepping out of a limousine. It was his sister, his lovely chaste sister.

She swept past him without a flicker of recognition.

So ended the noble family of Cabello de la Espada.


### 4 GOD

Every night above Lima on the high crest of San Cristóbal hill blazes an electric cross visible for many miles in the populous valley of Rimac. The illuminating of this cross, donated by a canny English company, is paid for out of the Lima city tax funds.

When this cross first flamed in the clear southland heavens, the nuns in the numerous Lima convents, believing it a visitation from God, were lifted to unheard of religious ecstasies. In their lifelong search for religious verity, those good ladies (set apart in white hoods to be supported in righteousness by the community) read no newspapers or modern books, hence, so completely were they swept away, by the divine symbol, from their daily routine of petty intermural feuds and resigned piety that their excesses of prayer and chanting led them to the brink of orgiastic revivalism and flagellation.

The ecclesiastical authorities hastened to assure them that though the ages of miracles might not have vanished, this particular blazing cross was not any superior evasion of nature's laws, but merely God's spirit working sacredly through English commercialism to stimulate the devoutness of the city fathers.

5

Quite some generations ago, Señora Florencia de Mora died, leaving her large Chuyugal estate, so it is said, to the Indians. As was the custom those days the will was duly filed with the ecclesiastical authorities. The Indians for many years continued peaceful, cultivating their lands.

The Bishop of Trujillo, grown fat, administering the worldly goods of the convents of Santa Clara and Carmen, buying and selling property for them, collecting rents, decided that Chuyugal really belonged to the Church.

He informed the Indians that investigation of the records (and few are clear in Perú) showed the Church to be the rightful owner; henceforth they would have to pay 3,000 *soles* rental.

The argument grew hectic. The Indians took the matter

to the courts. The last will and testament of Señora Mora mysteriously disappeared. With the assistance of a pious cabinet minister, Fermín Málaga de Santolalla, the Church's right to collect rents was upheld.

The Indians, having exhausted every legal recourse, refused to pay, rioted, and were put down by the army. The leading rebels were thrown off the estate, losing all their worldly possessions; the others were locked up nightly in the hacienda church and taken out each morning to toil.

The Indians thereupon joined the July, 1932, Aprista revolt. On its failure, some twenty were brought down to Chan Chan and shot by the army.

Recently the good Bishop made a valuable contribution to sociological principles, an extensive pastoral letter (*El Comercio*, Lima, March 18, 1934) in which he attacked socialism, divorce, public schools and lack of religion:

"Of the classes of society that of the worker, the most numerous, should most preoccupy us. It is reached only by the false prophecies of those calling themselves defenders of the people, the impious and socialistic newspaper, the revolutionary book. When Religion ruled in their hearts, strikes, threats, despotisms, and lockouts were unknown, a holy Cross nestled in the paternal arms of rich and poor, and all were united in the common center: the Faith.

"The working classes go in search of liberty and from the arms of the common Father of the poor, the divine Worker of Nazareth, they fall into the arms of the most shameful slavery; they go in search of fraternity, forgetting as Rousseau said, that they were Christians before becoming revolutionaries, and they find only hates, rancor, and selfishness; they go in search of light and science, and find only darkness, errors. They abandon the Church of Jesus Christ because they have been told that the Church cannot give them well-being and fall into the most lamentable miseries. The working class is sick and suffers because its heart is poisoned."

The good bishop still collects the rents for the Church from the Chuyugal estate.

## 6

Jorge Rivas, an Indian, died leaving only an elderly sister, too poor even to pay for the burial. Father Diego refused to permit interment until the fee was paid—if the sister could not, then let the neighbors take up a collection. Bad precedents could not be established. The neighbors refused to act. The priest became more stubborn. The body in that warm coast climate soon began to gather worms, filling the whole neighborhood with an unendurable stench.

Raymond Carson, Adventist missionary, finally placed the necessary sum in the hands of one of the villagers for the priest.

Jorge was buried, but the priest brooded over Carson's act, conceived of it as a special insult coming from the sacerdote of a heretical faith making inroads into the faithful.

Every month Carson made a trip up to the villages along the Eyebrow of the Coast. Some days before Carson's departure, the priest hoisted his portly and gouty body onto a horse and groaningly set forth to a hill village utterly devout, beyond cavil Catholic.

Ere the week was out, Carson came riding toward it. Suddenly rocks whizzed through the air. A mob of Indians, armed with sticks, stones, and knives rushed at him. In the brush on a little knoll, he thought he detected a black robe.

Before he could take account of his danger, a stone laid him low. His horse's throat was slashed. He was left unconscious in the middle of the road. Late that afternoon, a muleteer threw him across one of his animals and took him back to the coast.

Shortly after, another mob burned down the Adventist school.

7

"In Ferreñafe . . . we penetrated into the broad temple.
. . . All Saints' Day. . . . Every altar had many lit candles
. . . even the floor was covered with such an infinity of
them it was difficult to get by. We saw, seated on a chair at
the foot of the last altar on the left . . . an old priest of
beatific countenance, . . . at his side, on the floor . . . a
sort of urn of white metal, perhaps silver, full of holy water.
. . . On the altar was a small box and beside it some bills
. . . and at the . . . priest's feet, a multitude of women all
wearing mantles. While he mumbled some Latin phrases, the
beads of the rosary flowed through his hands; not to count
the paternosters and ave marias, but so he would not lose
track of the *reales* which he had charged for the responses,
to take some soul out of Purgatory . . . which did not last
two minutes. Finished with those whose money he had received, he put it into the box and began with others of the
multitude . . . humbly . . . holding forth in their coppery
and dirty paws bills of various denominations dirtier than
their hands. And so he kept on all day and all evening, he
who has such power on earth to liberate from torment those
souls that suffer and purge their sins. Probably with this
practice, Purgatory will remain emptier, leaving room for
new guests, but certainly the faithful are left with their
pockets empty while those of the priest grow full. And this
has been repeated since the beginning of the Conquest and
will continue for centuries upon centuries." [1]

## 8 WITCHCRAFT

José Salcamayhua, though merely a leaser on a large hacienda,
was the most potent sorcerer in the countryside. Unfortun-

[1] Bachman, 116.

ately, so it was believed, he used his dark arts mostly for evil purposes.

One day he went down to the nearby Salas to be best man at a wedding. Previously he had served the bride well, providing her magic potions to conquer the love of her betrothed.

A typhoid epidemic was sweeping away whole families. The Salas authorities arrested Salcamayhua, accusing him of being the cause of so much sickness. They planned to assassinate him in his cell.

But friends immediately informed the wealthy hacienda owner with whom Salcamayhua was a favorite; the hacendado at once demanded his release, which was reluctantly promised.

The authorities, torn between their fear of the powerful hacendado and their fear of the black arts of Salcamayhua, finally succumbed to superstition; that night, the district governor, the mayor, the municipal councilman, the judge slipped into jail; one and all they fell upon Salcamayhua, sliced his skin with their nails and began sucking at his veins —for that is the only manner to prevent a sorcerer from doing evil.

## 9

An old bearded man, almost in rags, a short black cloak, like an emasculated priest's robe—he walked bent with a cane and cross. He was a "Blesser," a *Santiguador*, whose holy words had power to cleanse those struck with the evil eye, especially babies, of their infirmities.

Half in Spanish, half in unintelligible Latin, he bent over a sick child in the arms of a buxom young Indian woman. Bringing his cross close to the infant, but just out of reach of its hands, three times he crossed himself, three times he blessed the child and intoned hypnotically under his breath: "The Father is Life, the Son is Glory, the Holy Virgin succors you. Over the head of Saint Peter, three times, I say:

Jesus, Jesus, Jesus . . . Like three virgin founts, I send the Holy Pity to this creature—Jesus, Jesus, Jesus. For when the name of Mary is mentioned, the child is freed of sickness. Christ was born, Christ died, and Christ was resurrected— these are truths. The Healthy Eye of the Father heals; the Healthy Eye of the Son heals; the Healthy Eye of the All Powerful heals." Again he made the sign of the cross three times. "*Votis meam santigen tiris benedictus gloriæ espiritu. Amen.*"

The next morning the house of the Indian girl had a black cross over the door.

## 10

Señora Josefina Navarro, an Indian *chola* and a widow, the owner of a small store in Arequipa, noticed her trade falling off alarmingly; finally it stopped entirely. She inquired of one of her erstwhile clients why he did not buy any more.

He had come several times only to find the door locked. Like most little stores, it had been open from early morning until late at night.

Only witchcraft could explain such a matter. Hearing strange sounds that night at the window Señora Josefina hurried, considerably frightened, to consult a sorceress.

She was advised to keep a shotgun beside her and when she heard the mysterious sounds again to fire in their direction. She hired a young man to handle the gun and fire at a signal from her.

The following night a swishing sound was heard. The young man fired. A moan followed, but all he saw were two Castilian rabbits dancing.

The following morning news spread of the death of Valdeño, husband of a shop-keeper across the street. He had been shot through the heart by shot-gun slugs.

From that day on Widow Navarro's sales increased, her old clients came back. But some weeks later, strange noises were again heard—like the scratching of a hen with chicks. The sorceress advised the widow to have the young man fill a terra cotta jar with earth from any tracks found near the window. The boy reported that the tracks were those of a mountain-lion.

The sorceress mixed the earth with mustard and garlic until it was one gray texture, mumbled charms over it.

A few days later, Valdeño's widow, taken ill with rheumatic pains, was obliged to close her shop. Soon she broke out in horrible ulcers, in a few months died.

Since then Señora Navarro has had all the business of the locality.

## II SCIENCE

In the highlands of Piura in far northern Perú are the famous curative springs and rock-hollowed pools of Guaringas.

Anciently these pools, said to have been baths of the Inca, were created in curious fashion. The dwellers of a nearby highland village where it scarcely ever rained, and drouth made farming difficult, heard there was a great lake to the west, so vast no man could see its further shore. Wuari, ancient god, set out with two great terra cotta urns, promising to bring back plenty of water.

He travelled and travelled, finally came to the Pacific Ocean where he filled his urns. But the road back was steep and difficult. Many times he stumbled, spilling water here and there, starting little streams. Finally he fell and broke one of the urns. The water rushed back toward the sea; thus the Piura River and its tributaries were formed. He finally arrived near home and poured his other urn into the rocky basins, forming the famous curative lagoons, slightly salty and sulphurous, which have remained there to this day.

In the vicinity now live renowned native medicine-men (*curanderos*), who utilize the ponds for healing the sick. The Indians come from all along the coast clear from Chimbote in Ancash, from Moche near Trujillo, and from the mountain regions of La Libertad and Cajamarca; they journey long weeks across desert sands and up into the crags to take the cure.

For weeks they attend the mysterious night sessions of the *curanderos* in which spirits are invoked, until at last they are ready to enter the water. Their old clothes must be left on the bank; on their emerging, new ones donned.

Neither they nor any one else can touch the discarded apparel. Deposited there for hundreds of years, it lies about in great mouldy heaps.

## 12

Gabriel de Castilla is a great archæologist. Also a good politician, for more than twenty years he has conserved numerous public posts. Some have dared whisper he is a better politician than an archæologist.

As a politician of Perú's ruling caste, he has the predatory instincts of that class. These extend to archæology as a private kingdom into which other students should not venture. All the ancient artifacts are his personal possession, to dispose of at will. He even begrudges those few objects which remain in the museum.

Undoubtedly he knows more about Peruvian archæology than any other living Peruvian. He has been hailed at home and abroad for his discoveries and books. Yet to achieve this pinnacle he has largely utilized the paid patient investigations of others; he has merely provided the grandiloquent summaries. Whenever his fame has threatened to wane, he has suddenly discovered, with a big fanfare, some new archæological site, usually a site known since the time of the earliest Spaniards, but long abandoned. Señor Castilla thereupon collects heaps of ancient *huacas,* equipment, metal work, some of which he gives to the museum, the rest of which he appropriates. Photographs and articles are published in the papers.

The news of his discovery goes out on the wire to all corners of the world.

But this is not for the good name of Perú or for science. In Perú archæology is one of the most lucrative professions. Not only does it provide juicy political posts, but its artifacts, labelled in a proper scientific manner, command fabulous prices abroad. Despite the fact that there are laws restricting the improper export of such articles, as Castilla has at various times been head of the National Museum and other bureaus which give export permits, he has been able to sell large quantities of ceramics, jewelry, dresses, mummies, statues, in Argentina, New York, London, and other European cities, at gratifying prices.

After these many years of his paternal care, the National Museum of Perú does not have a representative collection of gold and silver artifacts, or of ceramics, or of anything else. It is a shabby stable where a few dusty objects are kept without being properly classified for the intelligence of the ordinary visitor. New York, Berlin and other cities have better Inca collections than Lima; Señor Castilla himself has a better personal collection than that in the National Museum.

Also he has a thoroughly miser-like spirit about his vast erudition. One cannot discuss archæology with him; he replies in diplomatic generalities; real information, like a beautiful woman, is something to be guarded from the vulgar. He does not appreciate the value of give-and-take discussion to clarify moot points. This instinct, which conflicts with true scientific approach, has prevented Castilla from making any really great discoveries or conclusions. Despite his knowledge being superior to that of any one else in the field, this miserliness has filled the pages of his books with egregious errors.

"Why don't you write more, Señor Castilla?"

"One should be cautious about what one writes, especially in the newspapers so one will not be attacked. I write just enough to establish my reputation."

The rest of his knowledge Castilla carefully seals up in his own bosom and study. It will not pass on to posterity.

Of late he has fallen under a cloud. Despite the numerous obstacles he has put in their way, new archæologists with real scientific interests have developed. Public charges, aired in Congress, have been brought for Castilla's theft of museum articles and for spoliation of ruins. Castilla considers it beneath him to answer them. "I discovered all these articles. Who are these fools to say what I shall do with them?"

This is the general Peruvian politician's attitude about Perú. "It belongs to me; who shall question what I do with what is mine?"

## 13 MACHINES AND INDIANS

Señor Proaño, one of the powerful institutions of Perú, has many ramified interests, is on the board of directors of banks and other corporations. The new mining development of Tamboraque, halfway up to Oroyo in the Andes, was due to his initiative. Shafts were sunk, an expensive smelter established, aerial tramways for carrying ore were built—a complicated ore of gold, silver, copper and other metals. Smoke began belching. Arsenic and sulphur fumes rolled through the canyons for miles, sereing crops, choking lungs.

The worst sufferers were the Indians of nearby San Mateo village. The rarefied air became harder to breathe, crops withered, chickens grew sickly. They took their complaints to the Tamboraque manager, to the government, to the courts. Nobody heeded them. What are the life and happiness of a few village Indians compared to a great industrial development patriotically furthering the fatherland? Besides, proper smoke consumers cost money.

Bitterness accumulated. Last year when an old man died, the villagers, thoroughly convinced the cause was the acrid fumes, demanded that the company buy a coffin and pay for his burial. The mine officials refused. Violence resulted.

The Indians mobbed the works. A thorough job of demolishing. The aerial tramway was ripped out, machinery smashed, buildings set on fire. Now a heap of blackened ruins and twisted rusting iron greets the traveler through those canyons.

All the press told the public was that some foolish Indians lost their heads because a mining company refused to buy a coffin. To commit such an outrage over a mere coffin! The whims of the strange mountain creatures could never be fathomed!

"You simply can't teach the Indians progress," is the customary comment. "They hate machinery; they hate working in factories; they are interested only in living in their century-old squalor and cultivating all the vices."

The government took swift action. Troops descended on San Mateo. Numbers of villagers were killed.

Net result: no mine, no coffin, no progress, no peace. At any rate, dead men have no further grievances.

## 14 CRICKET

The veranda and bar of the Lima Cricket Club pavilion looks out upon the broad green which spreads over valuable centrally located property donated to the English members by Dictator Leguía—a title which subsequent governments have not relished.

Cricket is a civilized game which helps remind Britishers they are Britishers, however surrounded by evil Latin ways, helps uphold traditions against the corroding influences of an inferior foreign environment.

A game which only an old race could evolve, it requires skill, exercise not too hurried, and gentlemanly finesse. Bowling is a very artificial overhand throw, as if the player felt that the normal use of his muscles was a bit ordinary. The goals are so set that no very energetic running is required. Rather the trick is not to bat swift and hard, but to slither the ball off in some odd direction. The batters do not hurry out to position. When an out is made, the next man leisurely buckles on his shin-protectors, while the fielders patiently chat. It is a civilized game.

In no better place than the Lima Cricket Club could the farewell banquet have been tendered to the departing British executive of one of the most powerful American firms in Perú, a man who lived there twenty-five years, for to the club he had given both time and money generously.

Though somewhat obese, he formally batted the first ball of that day's game, a match with a native team from Callao. Presented with a handsome silver case, he rose to give heart-felt thanks.

He pled with those British white collar boys, did that great executive, to remain loyal to cricket, to cling to their grounds and forestall threatened dispossession, to keep the club going at all costs. It prevented clerks from the home-country fall-ing into careless habits.

"There are not so many of us here now these days of de-pression, but in promoting cricket you are promoting the interests of your country, helping to safeguard its valuable properties here. Teach the Peruvians to play the game. Many years ago we English were the only ones who played it, then a few high-class Peruvians educated in England; now as you see here today, it has spread to the common people. That is a good thing, a healthy thing. It helps keep the minds of the common people off Socialism and Bolshevism and all the new radical ideas menacing Perú."

Shortly, at tea-time, after the British players and foreign guests had received their cups and cakes, the Callao team of natives, negroes, zambos, Indians and cholos, filed up for their share of the repast.

After all one must make some concessions to keep the hearts of the people pure.

## 15 RUBBER

We found him, an old sick man, tossing with fever on the banks of a lost river. His legs were full of ulcers. In the ulcers were white worms. Worms and he still lived!

He got better. He talked.

"I have been a *cauchero* (rubber gatherer), and I am a *cauchero*. I have lived in poisonous swamps in the solitude of hill-jungles with my gangs of malarial workers, hacking at the bark of trees that give white blood—like that of goddesses.

"A thousand leagues from the home where I was born, from my fathers, my brothers, my lovely sisters.

"At times, on striking my axe into the living trunk, I have felt the desire to strike it against my own hand. Who created this frightful inequality between reality and insatiable soul?

"I have been a *cauchero*, I am a *cauchero*. I belong to my boss body and soul. He can sell me with my debt. We are always in debt. We never escape. And if I had a son—he is long since lost—the debt would be inherited by him. If our fellows do not rob or murder us, we are badly cheated on the rubber we do bring in. If we fail to bring in enough, we are whipped. If we object we are shot, at least flogged. Women are treated the same. Lucky is he who can kill and rob his fellow worker and escape with the extra rubber. But that, too, is dangerous. Only the rivers are transitable. The jungles are closed to all but the hardiest. Escaping men who forget to blaze a return trail are usually lost. And the return trail leads back to slavery.

"While we bleed the trees, the water-leeches cling to our legs in the swamp and bleed us. That is why I have ulcers and white worms. And the mosquitoes. And the *tambocha* ant—

poisonous as a scorpion—comes by millions, sometimes traps human beings, leaving only their bones. Once, for two days, I stood buried to my neck in a swampy lagoon, eaten alive by mosquitoes, till a troop of ants went past. If you have ever heard that long rustle and hum of approaching armies of *tambochas*, you will want to run in panic and hide your body in the bowels of the earth.

"The jungle transforms a man, brings out his most inhuman instincts. Cruelty, like a twisted thorn, digs into the kindest souls. Greed burns like a fever. Hope of riches warps the noblest. The smell of rubber produces the madness for millions. The peon sweats and toils, hoping some day to go forth and spend money like water, to enjoy white women and get drunk months at a time. Of a thousand slaves rotting away, not one in a thousand realizes his dream.

"Those brutal enough, become gang bosses and collect the rubber at the crack of the lash.

"I have been a *cauchero*, and I am a *cauchero*. I have had hands at my throat, choking me—for rubber. I have killed for rubber. And here I am, white worms in my legs.

"When women are wanted for the soldiers or the bosses, or to content the *caucheros* they are seized from the Indians; every Indian is required to bring all his womenfolk to be looked over; at ten years of age they are dragged off—to become mothers, knowing nothing of the meaning of maternity.

"But the only reality, and this soon tracks down every dream and ambition, is the terrible beri-beri fever.

"Lost and alone in the jungle, many die. In their dying convulsions, they grasp the trunk that gives forth white milk, glue their fevered lips to the open cut to calm the fever, for lack of water, with liquid rubber. They rot there like long-fallen leaves, eaten by rats and ants—the only millions that arrive when they die and long before they die." [2]

[2] Cf. José Eustacio Rivera, *La Voragine*.

## 16 JUNGLE

Little Indian Mapiripana is the female genus of the jungle solitude, guardian of springs and lagoons. She lives in the very heart of the forests, sending forth fog, sending down water into rivers that flow majestic to the sea. Thanks to her, the Orinoco and the Amazón have tributaries.

The natives fear her, the animals stampede in fright. She allows men to hunt only provided they make no noise. That is why loin-loth Indians with bow and arrow survive, why white men with Winchesters die.

To know if she has passed, seek out the wet clay; she leaves a single footprint, heel forward as though walking backwards.

At night she is heard screaming in the depths or on moon-lit banks. She travels over the waves on a conch-shell drawn by sweet-water dolphins, who keep perfect time to her singing music.

A missionary once came to these regions, who stayed drunk on palm-tree liquor and slept in the sand with pre-puberty girls. As he had come to put superstition to flight, he vowed he would boldly wait for Mapiripana on the banks of a river, then would wrap the cord of his robe about her and burn, her alive.

Sure enough, in the flood of moonlight, he saw a woman, beautiful and young, dressed only in silver webs.

With sensual desire he followed her. She escaped into the shadows. He called her anxiously. The treacherous echo be-fooled him. Thus he kept going deeper into the marshes until he came to a cave.

There she kept him captive many years. She sucked the blood from his lips, left him pale as a ghost. She became preg-nant and gave birth to a bat and an owl. The missionary, filled with horror at having engendered such creatures, fled from the cavern.

But his own sons pursued him and gave him no peace; he

could not even sleep. The bat sucked his blood; the light of the owl's eyes, like green glass lanterns, burned brightness through his closed lids.

He continued, hungry, weak, emaciated, eating only fruit and palm pith. On and on he stumbled, finally found a canoe on a river. But Mapiripana so filled the water with boiling eddies and tumbling boulders that he was obliged to seek shore. He was defeated.

Guided by the owl, he returned to the cave. He was met by Mapiripana, smiling, and he fell on his knees, pleading to be defended from his own progeny.

"Who can free a man from his own remorse?" was the reply.

From then on he delivered himself entirely to prayer. He died there in the cave, prematurely old and emaciated in the arms of fever, on a bed of leaves and rushes. He died agitating the air with his hands as though trying to give breath to his soul. And when he expired, there remained fluttering in the cave an enormous azure-winged butterfly—last vision of all those who die of fevers in these zones.

## 17 SOLDIERS

Prefect Tomás Alcántara of Laguna in the Green Hell region was a colonel who had been through many bloody civil disorders. A small heavy-set fellow with stubby pompadour hair, stubby moustache and stubby hands, like most of the interior prefects, somewhat dark of skin, he was a cholo, a man of mixed blood.

To reach Laguna was a difficult trip of many days horseback across the lofty mountains, the swamps and jungles. It took a communiqué from Lima a month to arrive. So he was practically king in his domain. Usually he never had time to await instructions from the capital, or at least such was his excuse.

He had had a sharp dispute with Colonel García (on the non-active list). Word conveniently came to Alcántara that on the Colonel's property all employees, old military companions, went armed. Undoubtedly García was planning revolt.

When the Colonel and an aide came into town to transact business, the Prefect had him seized and thrust into the little adobe jail. Friends at once began moving heaven and earth to get García out. Runners were sent to the nearest telegraph station to send messages to the supreme government. A prominent wealthy hacendado of the region registered his vigorous protests with the Prefect.

The Prefect found himself in a dilemma. His duty and the law required him to send the prisoner on to Lima, with full details. But Alcántara had no documentary proof that the Colonel was really planning revolt—only those rumors that float around, usually bearing out the ancient maxim, "Where there is smoke, there must be fire." He further realized that the President of the Republic had to carry out the laws, or at least make a semblance of doing so. The Colonel would be held in Lima for some time, then the chances were he would be released with a warning. He would come back to make trouble, embittered against the Prefect, would probably attempt to have him assassinated. The Prefect's authority in the eyes of the community would be weakened.

Convinced in his own mind that the Colonel was guilty, that night Alcántara had him and his aide taken out of jail and shot in the back on the edge of a swamp a mile out of town.

There was a scandal, threatened investigation. The Prefect reported that the Colonel had escaped from jail, aided by friends, that he had been killed by parties unknown. The central government, since the murdered Colonel was of the opposing party, archived the protests of the Colonel's friends and forgot about the matter.

Among those most horrified was a local priest. But to him the Prefect's wife said haughtily: "The Colonel was a wicked man. My husband was merely God's instrument."

"God is always on the side of authority," said the priest with resignation.

## 18 STUDENTS

Edmundo Bocanegro was a brilliant law student about to graduate when the university strike to reform the curricula and throw out politician professors occurred. Edmundo, a tall handsome young fellow, was quite a leader.

Promptly he was seized by the authorities and jailed for several months without trial. He went on a hunger strike. After fifteen days he was taken, in a weakened condition, in a train of military prisoners, mostly hardened criminals, to the military colony in the terrible Madre de Dios region of the Green Hell.

There, ball and chain on his leg, he was put building a road. The unaccustomed climate, the bad food and harsh toil, soon undermined his health. Taken down with malaria, scarcely able to stagger, nevertheless he was still driven under the lash to his task.

When finally he fell unconscious, he was lashed again and again, left bleeding.

He lay there, flies and ants crawling over him, until sundown, then was carried back to camp and tossed upon a straw mat. He passed many days in delirium. His companions in misery brought him food and water; aside from that he had no attention.

Despite everything he improved. One morning he became fully conscious. Though sore from lying so long on such a hard bed, he felt clean well-being in his body. Feebly, but happy, he whistled an old love song. He would live. He would fool them all.

It was a very brief moment of expansion. Presently he began to shudder. A cataleptic ague shook his body. He wanted to scream, to move, to get up, but his muscles grew rigid, his very hair stiffened. Ice crept through his veins; it penetrated through his finger and toe nails, crept up his body inch by inch like water melting sugar. His very heart turned into a cold glass casque; white blows beat on his eyelids.

He screamed, but realized his screams were in his own brain, mental echoes beating in his skull. He struggled to move his body and must have gone into convulsions. A guard came running and struck him over the head with the blunt end of his lash. Lead crashed in his skull. The bones seemed to smash and fall about his brain like the clatter of a glass skylight, like tinkling coins tossed on an empty pavement.

They gave him up for dead and were about to throw him into a hastily dug trench, when he revived again and screamed that he was alive.

In the meantime, the report of his illness had reached the authorities in Lima.

Bocanegro was of a good family. The government did not wish to assume the responsibilities for the scandal of his death in the colony.

He was ordered returned immediately to Lima, and liberated, a bag of bones.

He is no longer a danger for any government, his health and spirit were forever broken. He will never again lead any righteous cause. In the midst of excited conversation, he suddenly grows quiet, morose; his friends shake their heads sadly.

# VI

## POLITICIAN

### I

The Marqués of Rivevalle, his Excellency Señor Don Amador Guerrero de Riestra y Espinoza has modeled his brain and his acts to conform to the careers of those remarkable urbanized feudal aristocrats who held sway in Europe from the decline of the Middle Ages up through the early rise of the modern state. Perú, yet to become a modern state, still affords a partial theatre for such a type—cultured, unprincipled, extravagant, cynical.

For the Marqués, Perú, the Republic, is no reality. Democracy, which he despises, does not exist; his world is the suave upper class of Lima, which if not intrinsically of such worth as similar European groups, at least is capable of maintaining, with occasional slips, the outward trappings of the Old World refinement. The Marqués, from long residence in Europe and his literary tastes, something of an aristocrat in the courtly sense, stands out as a sort of super-aristocrat in provincial but snobbish Lima.

He accepts the Industrial Revolution, scarcely begun in his country, rather sadly; he hates its libertarian and Protestant implications. Emotionally and politically he is a staunch supporter of the Catholic Church; and whatever emotional life he may have over and beyond his hard realistic will to power, consists in prolonged hot baths of mysticism in dim chapels of black carved altars and incense blackened paintings. The modern world, except for its manifold luxuries, does not enter into his scheme of life; he abhors its rationalism, fears its science, and hates its demagoguery, though being himself one of the most adept of old-school demagogues.

His home, a palace in the Miraflores suburb of Lima, has—except for its exterior—an almost ecclesiastical appearance, a distinctly medieval atmosphere. Its dark woods, its cloistered air, its old oils and carved religious objects suggest a lost æsthete mooning sweetly over delicate things. But the Marqués' medievalism is no soft resignation; he believes in it with the bright faith of a Loyola, with all the bitter passion of the Counter-Reformation crusaders. Boldly he carries this hoary viewpoint into public affairs. Effectively; for now, at the age of fifty-five, a wiry, fierce but witty little man with a high squeaky voice, he not only holds an important cabinet post, but is the real power behind the throne.

Even with much wealth behind him it took him many years to forge a personality. Involved in his present ambition to succeed politically, his unconscious resentment at his past indecisions, his failure to achieve matrimonial normality, his early childhood training distorted his whole life.

Despite his æsthetic inclinations, he has much of the character of a screaming monk.

2

He is the only male descendant of a prominent Spanish family, dating back three and a half centuries to early colonial rule. His forebears were nobles, honored by the Crown, rewarded for their exploits of valor and loyalty, with vast haciendas and encomiendas of Indians to be converted to the Catholic faith; they were appointed as viceroys, bishops, army officers. Hence the Riestra y Espinoza properties, instead of diminishing through the generations, constantly swelled in size.

It is doubtful if the present Marqués can tell exactly how great is his domain. He has haciendas in nearly all the coast

river valleys, from ancient Tumbes down to ancient Moquegua; they dot the rich foothills; they stretch up to the bleakest snow-clad peaks of the Andes where range vast herds of llamas, alpacas and vicuñas. In recent years, thanks to his good relations with the fallen dictator Leguía, he obtained, for practically nothing, vast stretches of land along the Tigre River in the jungle, potentially rich in rubber, petroleum and tropical products. He has had a finger in guano and other concessions and monopolies. An entire marble-faced building in the center of Lima bears the sign:

ADMINISTRATION OF THE PROPERTIES OF GUERRERO DE
RIESTRA Y ESPINOZA, INC.

When he was six, his parents died in a railroad accident in France, where the family for generations had spent most of its time and money. He himself was raised in beautiful Lima, City of Kings, by a grandmother and two maiden aunts, all fanatically religious. They doted over him. On religious festivals they dressed him up sweetly in the Franciscan habit; they looked after his morals with extreme care. He was always such a well-mannered little fellow.

In due time he was sent to a Jesuit school for his first letters. Later he was sent to a Catholic preparatory school in England. There he passed through adolescence into late teens. The school had been carefully chosen. The amount of religious instruction was considerable; the conduct of the boys was carefully guarded. It was perhaps there that his early upbringing, the narrow company of doting religious old ladies, produced in him certain effeminate traits that have made him remain a bachelor all his life.

Later, due to these idiosyncrasies, he suffered some disagreeable rebuffs, which increased his resentment against humans and gave him an acute consciousness of being different. He hid his discomfiture under a mask of superciliousness, an air in any event proper to the great family of Guerrero de Riestra y Espinoza.

Sedentary habits had made him studious. He wrote a little verse, published in a de luxe edition at his own expense. Later he became interested in politics and social phenomena. He dug into the new somewhat ominous field of French revolutionary doctrines cautiously. At first some of the ideas, so contrary to his religious upbringing, shocked him disagreeably; but gradually he became convinced that life could not be contained within cloistered walls.

He spent two years in Paris. There his soul flowered. He tasted Bohemian life, circulated in an atmosphere of painters and writers and gloried in new bold ideas. For a time at least openly, whatever may have been his inner convictions, he became a Liberal, almost an anti-clerical, talked of free love, pagan life, democracy, the rights of man.

This was his one brief period of attempted emancipation from youthful dogmas and training. It had other consequences. He was only uncomfortable in this fascinating setting when his companions boasted of amorous conquests. He essayed several courtships of semi-chaste ladies of the Quarter, always eager for new affairs. But too timid, not sure of himself, in each instance he retreated precipitately and unsuccessful. Bordels nauseated him. He finally took refuge in companions of quite a different stripe whose literary guides and mentors of conduct were Gide and Proust.

He was still talking the lingo of liberalism and free living when he went back to Lima.


3

But Lima is not Paris. Its narrow criteria regarding society and human conduct—though he clung to a few Bohemian friends—frowned upon any doctrines later than the time of

Dante. All his wealthy aristocratic circle was steeped in ideas
of feudalism; it despised the Indians, talked slightingly even
of people of mixed blood, however white their skin, however
great their fortunes. The rights of man were an absurdity.
Life, society, the universe, was an immutable hierarchy over
which the Trinity and the landlord class presided eternally
in unalterable majesty.

Gradually he abandoned politics, abandoned his seemingly
bold yet, by any modern criterion, slightly stale ideas,
frowned now upon free living not conforming to set
standards.

He took refuge in æsthetics, collected beautiful art. In
the beginning, interested in art products of his own country,
even the beautiful handicrafts of the despised Indians; gradually the pseudo-European tastes of his group predominated.
If he purchased anything from Perú, it was now always of
the colonial period, usually some religious carving or illus-
tration.

His idea was to write. He turned out a history of Perú,
a hesitant hodge-podge, basically conservative, but here and
there tinged with some of the broader ideas he had garnered
in Paris. This, though not voluminous, gained for him a certain literary reputation; people said he had promise; he would,
once he really emancipated himself, become a forceful writer.

They did not know that his brief urge for personal emancipation had already evaporated. He himself was afraid to
face the findings of his own mind; more and more he became
the correct gentleman, the æsthete. Instead of ideas, he talked
brilliantly of the history of æsthetics, of the findings of
philosophy—he pawed over all the dust-heap facts of the
past. He was undoubtedly a very informed man. And in the
usually vapid teas of gracious and meaningless Lima society,
he was ever the center of a palpitating throng of beautiful
females.

Perhaps they were not merely intrigued by his culture and

polished manners, but also by those vague rumors that he had no real interest in feminine companionship; but more likely because he was extremely wealthy and handsome.

He almost married one tall beautiful creature who satisfied his æsthetic tastes. Physically and for her carriage and her dress, she was something to be prized, would grace his house, would stand so well and artistically beside that beautiful long Virgin of Guadalupe he had recently acquired in a local art store. They arrived at some furtive intimacies.

These merely cast him into a terrific despondency. He had no desire to kiss her. That seemed a bit messy to him. It would be nice to touch her, to caress her, but as one might caress a horse or a statue. He extricated himself gracefully from his half-way compromised position. After that, gossipy tongues began to talk more and more.

Certain sly winks worried him. He must protect himself. He promptly acquired three splendid mistresses, the cream of Lima's courtesans, and established them in sumptuous residences, bought them auto cars, jewelry, everything they could possibly wish. He flaunted them in public places, enjoying the hypocrisy—secret wry humor mixed with pride. His real personal life was led furtively with a few select companions schooled in his own perversions.

His sudden interest in mistresses gave Lima society plenty to whisper about. Matrimonially he became more desirable, and mothers with marriageable daughters—who might despite his wealth have somewhat hesitated—redoubled their efforts to bring him into the net.

But more than ever, he was polished, aloof, impeccable, baffling. For him the rôle became almost enjoyable. He gathered increasing pleasure in being a man of mystery, gained contempt for those he was fooling, those gossiping about him.

The years rolled by, ten, fifteen, twenty of them. He was still unmarried. Occasionally he rid himself of some mistress who became troublesome or who, unable to bear his chaste state, committed indiscretions, and provided himself with a new one. They were just like the marble façade of the new Miraflores palace he was building—nothing more in his life.

He continued studious; he conversed with knowledge larded with malicious wit; he knew every one worth knowing who ever came to Lima. He took occasional trips abroad; but the rush and hurry of modern life in other countries annoyed him. He enjoyed the cloistered peace, the eternal spring, the luxurious ease of his own capital.

"He is the first of the Guerrero de Riestra y Espinozas to live in Perú," was the comment.

4

He was past forty-five when he began to become aware of the utter void in which he had been living. He felt himself to be, if different from others, also superior, a man marked for a remarkable destiny, who strangely had never had a destiny. His dark hatred of mankind increased. More than ever he resented his early training, without realizing that he was now completely dominated by it.

For the moment his only solution was more ostentation. He abandoned his automobile on Sundays, and rolled down to Mass in a magnificent carriage, footmen in yellow livery. He went over to Spain and paid fifty thousand dollars for a title, and on the doors of his carriages and his calling-cards blossomed the five-point crown of the Marqués de Rivevalle. This struck him as quite proper even in Republican Perú of the twentieth century bourgeoning into modern prosperity by extravagant foreign loans.

Unexpectedly he was called to the cabinet, and this seemed fitting tribute, an honor for which he had not scrambled like the politicians of the day, something which had come to him because of his essential aristocratic worth.

In that post he found ample opportunity to exercise his

scheming talents. He pulled political factions this way and that, toyed with political enemies as a cat toys with a mouse. Soon he became head of the cabinet.

The bitterest onslaughts never made him lose his temper; his sense of personal superiority was too great for him to be

scathed. Against those who attacked him openly or secretly he used a compound of benevolence, trickery and force, invariably disconcerting. He was not vindictive—that would have been ungentlemanly; but he enjoyed cruelty, if refined in its processes, and also he enjoyed its more unrefined results.

Soon he became firmly convinced his talents would enable him to manœuvre himself into the presidency. This also was apparent to the opposition, and the hue and cry against him deepened.

This antagonism took more definite shape when he began tampering with the university, ousting Liberal and long-established professors, putting in ecclesiastics and politicians. He proceeded then to modify the curricula, cutting out modern courses, trying to conserve its traditions as a hoary theological institution.

The student body revolted, issued proclamations, declared a strike. Groups of workers threatened a general strike to support them. This was demagoguery in its worst form. The students put out a pasquinade, ridiculing him savagely; his effeminate manners, his squeaky voice, his foolish title, his ostentation. It was cleverly done and really got under his skin. A cold fury such as he had never known took hold of him.

Definitely, arbitrarily, he closed down the university. "It will never reopen while I'm running things," he boasted. "Let them go to the Catholic University; that is much better for Perú anyway."

5

Perhaps he lost his head. Offending student leaders were thrust into jail; a manifestation was ridden down in the streets with cavalry—five dead, fourteen wounded. The jailed students went on a hunger strike. It lasted fifteen days, then most of them were shipped off to the Loreto jungles to die of fever and hard toil. One, said to have written the offending pasquinade, was held in a special dungeon.

There the Marqués appeared, immaculate in tall silk hat, bow tie, Oxford morning coat, pin-stripes and pearl-gray gloves, and smoking a cigar.

As he settled in the cushions of his carriage, to attend the Empire Day reception at the British legation, he felt a rich glow of satisfaction far deeper than he had ever enjoyed during his æsthete days when he had come across a particularly beautiful piece of statuary.

But soon after, the Marqués' very sincerity caused his political downfall. When Congress, with a queer streak of liberalism, recently passed a to him immoral law and the

Church went on a twenty-four hour strike, the Marqués valiantly resigned. Strangely enough his resignation was accepted. The law stuck. And if he was powerful, others more powerful were glad to make him the goat for popular hatred of the government's oppressive tactics.

# VII

# BLACK SARA

Tall lean Sara had slim features more European than African. Under the smooth ash-brown skin on her cheek-bones a Nordic glow came to ripe orange. Her leanness was not that of an American or English female—perhaps the buttocks were slightly more rounded, the bones hung differently, for the most angular African woman hints at curves, alien grace. Something hypnotic in Sara's movements, lean though she was, suggested voluptuousness, almost license.

From Sara and her neighbors in the little adobe shacks of the hot coast town of Pampas Grande, I picked up something of her past.

All feared her. Despite occasional superhuman cunning, she was a bit deranged mentally. She was a witch, did evil things, separated husband and wife, caused strange maladies and torments. They warned me not to chat at her door.

The tales merely aroused my amused interest. Once in the market I bought her a basket of figs, arranged in leaves with artistic Indian skill. She was as happy as though I had brought her pearls and diamonds.

At times, it seemed to me, this strange creature was anxious to attract me. At the late afternoon hour when I strolled through her neighborhood, she was dressed in bright clothes; her long black hair, tending to coarse kinkiness around the temples, was caught with silk ribbon and flower into some sort of coiffure other than its usual wild disorder. Her favorite color, yellow, made her a subject for a painter—a queer blending of tones into an original satisfying harmony.

Her neighbors warned me she often had convulsions—for them, another symptom of witchcraft. She was, I took it, an epileptic.

A bad start in life. Her father a negro, her mother a chola of Spanish-Indian blood, had both been alcoholic. Even at the age of seven, she had already contracted tuberculosis, which explained her present thinness, though the disease had

been stayed by the hot dry coast climate. Naïve descriptions of a neighbor crone—her best friend—led me to put my findings into more technical terms: Sara, from earliest years had suffered from psychopathic neurosis and precocious epilepsy, ailments that with the years had deepened their tracks in her system.

In school, even before puberty, she had displayed a mystic aloofness interrupted with prankish rebellion. For her teachers she was difficult, wayward, obstinate—an enigma. Her fellow pupils, afraid of her moods, her rapt absent-mindedness, her freakish tempers, shunned her. In violent irresponsible fury she stamped and tore at her enemies with cruel nails, even teeth, then fell into frothing convulsions. Her parents neglected her entirely; often she came to school in rags. Occasionally some teacher tried to instruct her in cleanliness and morality. But she hated them, and she hated the other students.

She developed early. At nine, beginning to be interested in males, she paid what pitiful attention she could to her personal appearance.

Her way to school lay through a cactus lane past a much-feared cabin, where lived a *brujo*, or sorcerer, by the name of Borja, a cunning man nearly forty. Exercising an uncanny hold over the more ignorant villagers, he sat in his stout little cabin, in the midst of his garden, animals, and strange objects of his practice, like an evil spider, drawing every superstitious soul into his net.

It was rumored he had great stacks of gold buried under the floor of his hut, but his treasure was as safe as in the Bank of England itself—no man would have dared touch it.

Borja's victims, knowing doom had been decreed against them, usually took to their beds, sometimes even died out of pure fear. Or Borja would cause houses to burn down, or crops to be lost, or animals to die or be stolen. For a price, he would protect his clients against sickness and injury. Equally could his dark magic provoke hate or love; many a despairing sweetheart slipped through his door to recover the lost object of affections or to destroy a hated rival.

Proud Don Clemente, the most powerful member of the community, the *curaca*, or boss, quite free of base superstitions, tried to run Borja out of the village. But Borja made a doll with a puckered snout just like Clemente's. After hocus-pocus and cabalistic language over burning coca, he stuck a needle in the effigy's knee joint.

Strangely, that very afternoon Clemente was seen limping —an inflammation in his knee.

Ten days later Borja stuck another needle in the effigy's

thigh. Sure enough Clemente came down with paralysis in his left leg.

It was nearly a month before he could hobble about; by that time he had heard of Borja's efforts. Thoroughly frightened, he sent a messenger to the medicine-man with hints of a truce, possibly mutual alliance in running village affairs.

Borja would deal with Clemente only personally. The Curaca hobbled painfully up the cactus lane. They had a long conference. Another bowl of coca was burned, some more hocus-pocus, the pulling out of needles from knee and thigh, other rites, then the solemn cremation and holy burial of the effigy. Clemente received a stone talisman to wear about his neck.

Sure enough, from that day on he improved. Ever after, until he was struck by lightning, he enjoyed perfect health.

The witch doctor took a curious interest in Sara, used to talk with her whenever she went to and from school.

He was intrigued by the uncanny fire in her black eyes. And he attracted her. She used to search his face with long questioning looks, realizing, child though she was, that as an exercizer of uncanny powers he was mysteriously set apart from the rest.

At times he calmed her down, sent her on her way in that rapt aloof mood of hers that so annoyed and frightened her playmates. At other times, he made her high-strung, almost hysterical. Whether these were normal cycles of her ailment or whether ascribable to Borja's influences, hard to tell.

As she grew older, he gave her strangely carved pebbles and other odd objects, from which her playmates, even her teachers, recoiled, recognizing them as having come from the witch-doctor. Sara found that these talismans were more potent in working her will than any use of teeth and nails.

Her teachers solemnly warned her not to go near Borja. Their councils were in vain. He soon had more control over her than had any other human being.

When she became nine, he saw her quickened interest in boys, her childish efforts at personal adornment. At ten puberty overtook her, and because he had power over her and because she hated her moralizing teachers, she let him do what he wanted with her. After several months she went to dwell in his house.

For five years they lived together. He taught her his magic arts. Strange stories got around about how she danced naked in the garden under the moon, to the sound of struck metals and queer burning incense, then would fall in convulsions, while the witch-doctor made passes over her body. Other stories of what he did are too terrible to mention.

But apparently the pair was happy, and at the age of fifteen she was as proficient in the black arts as her master.

Unexpectedly he died of pneumonia.

## 2

Restless, no longer could Sara remain quietly in the little cabin. In a distraught state, she wandered about, through the town, over the hills.

One day she disappeared entirely. From fifteen to twenty she drifted from place to place, carrying her little bag of mystic objects, performing miraculous cures and superstitious rites which provided her easy livelihood. She spent her money liberally for whatever pleased her. She took to drinking, and though lovers were not common, she delivered herself to more than one, either in an orgy of drunkenness or pre-convulsion emotion, but remained with none.

On the coast near Yunga, David Dávila, an industrious young Indian of twenty-eight, a chauffeur, owner of several cars making trips to adjacent towns, fell desperately in love with her. He had had a bit of schooling and, utterly free from superstition, he had no belief whatsoever in her dark practices.

Perhaps his scorn for her black arts, in which she herself believed so implicitly, put her in awe of him, created affection. They became lovers, finally lived together.

Despite her infirmities and mode of life, she must have been unusually handsome then, at her fullest flush of physical development, probably enjoying better health than before or since. Her wildness, lithe ways, independence, must have made her appealing. Even now in Pampas Grande, I could appreciate from her bearing, her occasional hectic manner, that once she might have been exceedingly attractive and baffling.

Her new relation was not the happiest arrangement. A silent duel began between her lover and herself. She wished to bring him within the spell of her dark arts, to make him believe. He laughed at her. She hated him but loved him passionately. He pitied her and loved her passionately. He was sane, stronger than she, his will greater. She broke under the conflict.

In his very arms, she went into the worst convulsion of her life. He dashed out for a doctor. For weeks, months, she lay at death's door. Something besides her health had snapped in her. Tuberculosis, in abeyance, lifted its head and began to make ravages. She coughed violently. But slowly her health mended.

Then one day he came home to find her nude, clothes torn off, hair awry, snatched out in handfuls, in her hand a wooden "devil" image and in the other a broom, which she was brandishing as she danced and frothed with wild glances and laughter.

He had destroyed, as fast as she made them, all her appurtenances of the dark art. For a time she had desisted. He had thought he had cured her, had convinced her.

But the fear of her helpless state without magic, her hatred of his domination, had again gotten the better of her. When she could no longer stand it, apparently, secretly she had made the devil image, and the pre-epileptic frenzy of her

133

nude dance, her torrents of incoherent language, were efforts to exorcise the devil, to gain power over it, to feel herself again able to control the forces of darkness and direct them toward her own ends.

With great difficulty the image and the broom were wrenched away from her. She was put, in the last stages of her convulsion, frothing terribly, to bed, fell into a torpor.

During her second sickness she was in a pitiful state. At times she wept and cried for the arms of David. At times she spurned him, ferociously ordered him out of her sight. She mumbled that she was dominated by the devil, that there was no salvation for her, that she would die.

But she got well. It was a shock to her that she had done so without the customary gibberish and ritual. It worried her. She was morose, doubtful. They were not happy at all after that.

One day she disappeared, went down to Pampas Grande alone.

Now, evidently, grown quieter, she did not entirely depend upon her black arts for a living. When her health was good, she liked doing other things. When the fits came upon her, she became more convinced of the potency of her dark superstitions. A contradiction and terrible doubt had entered into her that she herself could not explain. She was not happy.

### 3

One day, without mentioning my intentions to Sara—our acquaintance had been but a passing doorway conversation—I took a trip down the Casma River.

When I returned, ten days later, it occurred to me to walk down toward Sara's place.

The door was closed, and the step, which she always kept cleanly swept, was cluttered with dust and rubbish.

I sought the old crone, of all the neighbors most intimate with Sara.

"For three days she has been up the *barranca*," said the crone. "I am afraid she is sick. I am too old to go see. No one else will go; they are afraid. Why did you go away, Señor? Where have you been? You are to blame."

"*I!*"

"You. She liked you. Suddenly you did not come. She is very easily upset. She went off. Only you can bring her back."

The thing sounded fantastic.

"Which way did she go?"

"Up the *barranca*, up the right side near the fork, there is a cave. Sometimes she goes there. You must see."

"But it is getting dark."

"And if she is ill?"

With much trepidation I set out. The little street dwindled away to a tight lane of adobe walls and hedges, then to a track filled with boulders and animal excrement. Presently it plunged down into the steep *barranca*.

Quite dark now. I could scarcely pick my way. My doubts at this solitary expedition became greater.

Somehow, now and then grasping a prickly shrub, I scrambled down into the ravine, thick with trees. For half an hour I stumbled on, trying to distinguish some of the landmarks the crone had told me about. I was to follow the trail along the *barranca*, take a left fork up again to a little ridge, keep on until it dipped. Then, if lucky, I would see an almost trackless way to cross over to the other side, down a very steep wall, and up through a tangle of vines and chaparral to the cave. Perhaps I would see a light.

Fortunately, as I began going up the trail to the summit, a glow appeared in the southeast; presently I topped the ridge to meet the rim of an orange moon—ineffably beautiful across the desert sands stretching away to the bald sky-tossed Andes.

Again the trail dipped. I saw a figure over in the shadows of the opposite wall. I halloed across. The figure kept on without answering. Again I called. No response.

The figure topped the ridge. A woman. It was Sara.

She began running, once slipped, almost plunged off the cliff. Only a few tatters fluttered from her almost naked body; her long hair was streaming wildly. In her hands, she brandished several objects I could not distinguish.

Again I shouted.

For answer—an unearthly scream, then laughter, several more shrieks.

I scrambled down into the ravine to get across somehow. "She is mad," I told myself. "What can I do with her alone? She will not listen to reason. I can't hit her on the head and subdue her. If I try to control her, we might both plunge into the ravine. Or in her present superhuman strength, she might even kill me."

But I kept on going. It seemed a sort of duty.

I plunged on down, tearing my clothes, scratching my hands. My breath came in gasps.

Still she kept running along the ridge—a Grecian silhouette against the pale light, dancing, cavorting, hair streaming—an uncanny spectacle.

I paused, shouted again.

Laughter and screams and still wilder movements.

I continued plunging down and down.

Presently she began descending the ravine further up. I altered my course slightly, finally reached the rocky bottom choked with vegetation and huge boulders. I stopped and listened.

A queer noise came from further up the ravine. Again I shouted. Again wild laughter and screams.

I plunged ahead, trying to get over the great boulders and through the thickets, an almost impossible task.

The shrieks became more distant. How could she get

through the undergrowth, naked, at such a rate? Undoubtedly she was quite insensible to the pain, her feet hardened, her nerves opiated, intent only on her madness.

I struggled on. She was going much faster than I. Again, far up in the moonlight, I saw her tattered figure racing on, her arms waving over her head, hair streaming. She disappeared over a ridge. Her shrieks became fainter and fainter, far cries drifting through the dark, but a faint lost echo in the ravine.

I was weary, my clothes torn, my hands bleeding. I could no longer hear her. No answer came to my shouts, only the rolling echo of my own call, then the cry of a night bird, then silence.

### 4

Hours later, about midnight, I was back in Pampas. What should I do?

I finally aroused the local authorities.

They hemmed and hawed. It was Sara. She was mad. They could do nothing. They would not be able to follow her. If she didn't fall over a cliff, ultimately she would be all right. Tomorrow they might take a look, not tonight.

Aside from natural laziness, I could see they were really quite frightened.

There was nothing else for me to do.

### 5

I hurried home to Don Pancho's where I was staying.

My imagination was playing me terrible pranks. I saw Sara leaping madly against the faint moonlit skyline, falling into a convulsion, dropping over a cliff, her body bruised, mangled, to be eaten by the buzzards and animals.

I assembled my belongings, woke Pancho up. "Get me a horse."

"Now!"

"Now."

"Tonight!"

"This very minute."

"But—"

"I must leave within half an hour for Huarás—"

We lit a carbide lamp, dragged a saddle from an outhouse, fumbled with straps and buckles.

Soon I was saddled and on my way—alone in the dark.

My route lay near the ravine where Sara had disappeared. I would salve my conscience by one more reconnoitre. But I prayed I should not meet her. I did not. There was no answer to my repeated shouts. A dark presentiment of tragedy settled over me.

I reached Huarás in the blazing sun at eleven the next day. Weary beyond words I slept a long siesta, went to bed early.

## 6

About three weeks later, in Trujillo, I picked up a local paper.

An item from the interior. Pampas Grande. The nude body of a black witch named Sara had been found mangled on the stones under a cliff. "The world is well rid of such characters who feed upon people's superstitions," concluded the item with naïve provincial editorializing.

But I can still see her leaping across the rocks. Without being the least superstitious, I know she was close to some mystery of life hidden to saner persons, and in that achievement she may have flung herself over the precipice. For I do not believe her death was entirely accidental.

# VIII

## PUNISHING SAN LORENZO

### 1

THIS story of Huancabamba—one of the first native cities visited by Pizarro's troops—was told me by my good friend José Eulogio Garrido one twilight in his roomy house in Moche. Later he read me a fine poem he had written about it.

Born in Huancabamba in the high sierras of Piura, northern Perú, Garrido knows every foot of that region; it is woven into the texture of his life, precious details others might not notice.

I cannot hope to recapture the moving sequence, the fine rhythm, or half the quick images of the tale as told by him —to have its full effect it really should be related either in Spanish or Quechua.

### 2

It is still the dry season in Huancabamba. The rains should have started two months previously. Already it is January, but the sky is clear, a high clear blue, a stone blue, quiet, one texture, impenetrable.

Now and then, like large ships across a windless sea, drift enormous coagulated white clouds. They peek over the crest of some peak, then slowly sink from sight again.

The Huanca River scarcely murmurs; the stones in it are scarcely covered; it is a mere trickle.

The Lungulo River is dry—only a few pools surrounded by strips of green.

The land is yellow, hungry. The flanks of the hills—stonier than ever. The roads are thick with white dust.

139

February. The sky still clear, clear blue up there, all blue stone, all stone stillness.

No longer are the clouds moving ships; they are square blocks, huge white blocks of cotton quartz. They make the blue sky bluer; and they laugh in rocky ruction at the anguish and ill-humor of the hillsides.

The Huanca River is dying now without even the strength to complain. The Lungulo River has crossed its arms and stretched out its legs under a brown coffin.

The land is yellow, knotted up in impotence.

The Pariacaca and Gutiligún mountains frown menacingly.

The roads—more dust.

The fields of the people plead for mercy—each morning, each afternoon.

At night huge fires on the crest of the Cordillera tell of the prayers and curses of the Indians. . . .

## 3

Towards the end of the month, down the dusty road trot three Indians wrapped in ponchos, heads bent. Slowly, looking neither right nor left at anybody, they cross the bridge and enter the town.

They reach the priest's house, take off their hats. They scarcely lift their eyes from the floor. They twirl their hats slowly in their brown hands. They wait a long time. . . .

"Good day may God give you, Señor priest."

"Good day."

The sombreros continue revolving in copper fingers.

"What do you want?"

At last the oldest one, nose and cheek-bones rough-hewn, plucks up enough courage to speak. He crushes his sombrero, dirty from dust and former rains. "We have come, Father . . . to see how much you would charge us . . . for . . .

for a little Mass to Taitito San Lorenzo . . . the old saint—not the new one—to . . . to make rain."

Another Indian, younger, more musical of voice, crushes his sombrero agitatedly, and speaks up, "Our fields are completely dry, Father. . . . We haven't even any water to drink now, Father. . . ."

The third Indian, whose wide staring eyes make him seem a bit stupid: "Just yesterday my little cow died, Father. . . . And this morning the sheep of my Taita Pascual woke up stiff . . . Father. . . ."

The large eyebrows of the priest lifted. "Do you want the Mass chanted or recited?"

"Sung it should be, for . . ."

"A chanted Mass will cost you eight pesos. . . ."

A deep silence except for the slight noise of brown hands on sombreros. . . . "Father, please see that . . . that we are very poor. . . . Especially now. . . . Couldn't you make a little reduction?"

"It can't be for less. . . . Or unless you bring me a pig and a sheep."

"And merely spoken, how much?"

"Four pesos."

"Ay, Father, that is very dear for us. . . . We will give you two pesos . . . we can't give more. . . . The good Father himself can see that we have lost our crops. . . ."

"Four pesos. . . . You heard me. . . . Let's not talk more about it. . . ." The priest, in robe and striped hat, stood up.

The Indians, completely crushed, turned slowly away. . . . "Father . . ."

"I told you . . . four pesos. . . . Get out. . . . Bring me the four pesos and it's a bargain. . . ."

The Indians went away, their heads lower than before, eyes more hidden. They went dragging themselves over the tiled corridor floor. . . .

141

They came back to the curatage late in the afternoon with the four pesos obtained on the promise of several loads of potatoes and beans at the next harvest, God willing. . . .

The priest promised to come, at bottom angry he had not demanded six pesos.

On the day of the Mass the roads to town were filled with clouds of Indians—from Quispampa, Cabeza and Cajas.

San Lorenzo, *the new saint, not the old one,* dressed up in fiesta clothes, looked down from above the altar at the massed Indians among their candles. With glassy stare, he let them burn incense to him. . . .

"Ah . . . the other Saint is the miraculous one . . ." a Macuca Indian woman said from the folds of her *reboso* shawl.

"Yes, it is the old San Lorenzo who brings rain, every one knows that," replied her common-law husband, an Indian with a pointed skull.

"Why didn't they bring out the other one?" she complained.

And while the priest masticated Latin that no one understood, all the Indians murmured hopelessly: "This Saint on the altar isn't the one that brings rain. . . . The one that brings rain is the old one, which is in the Sacristy. . . ." Every one regretted the lost candles, now burned half way down. . . .

The Mass ended. And the Indians, eyes lowered, arms hanging loose, slowly went out from the church, all of them, with all their wives and children. Outside they did not even look at the sky which continued to be blue stone.

With weary steps they went their ways, to their huts, fireless now, more miserable than ever.

## 4

The days passed, the sky still an immobile turquoise.

Another day just the same.

Another day just the same.

March came finally. But the sky was still clear.

Blue up there; bluer, bluer than ever, hard stone without dimensions.

The clouds, in immense white spirals, slept out the hot siesta on the crest of the mountains; they lay there motionless. Their whiteness made the blue more sapphire, infinite. At times they seemed to wish to free themselves from the clutches of the mountains, but could not break away.

The Huanca River gives its death-rattle. Mount Gutiligún, which does not know how to pray, watches it die, watches it with silent pity.

The Lungulo River, its vertebræ dispersed, is as stony as Mount Pariacaca. And Pariacaca merely yawns and yawns and yawns, and between yawns looks menacingly at Gutiligún.

The land, thirsty, shrinks and shrinks more and more in eternal crunching.

The roads and fields are dust, dust, only dust. . . .

The Sun makes its daily trips harshly, omnipotent, supreme.

The people look at the cemetery for long minutes, hopelessly.

The church bell is hoarse from so much ringing.

At night, when the cloud spirals sink down behind the mountains, the huge fires burn. . . .

But the sky stays clear. . . . One morning the anguish of the people demands prayers. . . . The priest comes forth morosely in his brown cape with his book of Latin phrases. . . .

> *Sancte Petrus*
> > *Ora pro nobis.*

*Sancte Paulo*
> *Ora pro nobis.*

But the clouds grow more stony, they sleep more; the sky becomes more glassy.

5

One morning strange news runs through the village like a shower of sparks, burning all lips.

"The church has been open since before dawn!"

"The Sacristy open since dawn!"

"The San Lorenzo of the Sacristy is no longer in his corner."

An old woman reported that "between dark and dawn" she had seen several Indians, carrying a bundle, running toward the Lungulo River.

The priest ordered the bells rung. "What was the village up to?"

Everybody was running about. Groups of excited people. Questions no one answered.

And in the meantime San Lorenzo, the old San Lorenzo, black, half naked, tied to a maguey plant, is out in the red Pampa, among a tumult of Indians who shout prayers and blasphemies.

Above, the sky is blue and still.

Above the mountains—the white still clouds.

The running to and fro of Indians continues. The noise of the Indians strikes the metallic flanks of Pariacaca, and re-echoes like an apocalyptic trumpet.

Above, the sky is blue and still.

Suddenly the clouds, as though whipped by the wind, start moving . . . then fall back heavily again upon the peaks.

The Indians, who had begun to hope, become furious. . . .

Scattered voices. . . .

"To the fire. . . . To the fire . . ."

144

The running ceases. . . . Some untie San Lorenzo; others start building a fire with dry maguey leaves.

Again the clouds move. The sound of the wind can be heard . . . nearer now. . . . The Indians wait hopefully . . . but . . . again . . . the clouds are quiet, still. . . .

Desperate hands seize San Lorenzo, rip off his shirt, bring him close to the fire. . . .

Indian women cry out in fright, sobbing. . . .

"No . . . no. . . . Don't do that. Let San Lorenzo go. . . ."

It is too late. They bring San Lorenzo's feet close to the flames. . . .

A distant sound beats through the air . . .

The Indians look up astonished.

The wind comes rushing.

More noise, closer, louder.

The clouds, which had seemed of stone, spread their huge sails. The wind drives them like herds, covering over the sky. . . .

Another sound, closer. . . . Thunder! Thunder!

The clouds make a gray canopy from Pariacaca to Gutiligún, and the canopy seems heavy, freighted, ready to burst asunder. Drops of rain.

The Indians pull San Lorenzo's feet, completely charred now, from the fire. They are frightened, terribly frightened. . . .

Amid claps of thunder, rain begins. . . .

And the rain puts out the fire and heals the feet of San Lorenzo. The saint smiles like a martyr.

The Indians, amid triumphal shouts, carry San Lorenzo running—the Holy Patron who has made it rain . . . at last . . . at last. . . .

"Didn't I say it was the old San Lorenzo . . . who . . . brings rain," said the old Indian woman, smiling amid tears, like a sky at the end of winter time.

And it rains and rains and rains. . . .

Memory of the heavy blue stone is wiped out.

The Huanca and Lungulo rivers are reborn, Gutiligún rumbles and rumbles and spits spume upon the valley, a duet of thunder and wind.

Pariacaca washes away old scars and relaxes his customary frown.

The church bell rings and rings happily—as on a flowery Easter.

And when March goes out, the Sun looks down one afternoon to paint the rocks and fields green and fill the valleys with beautiful flowers.

San Lorenzo is brought out again down the maguey lane, all dressed up in the green branches and red *retama* flowers, all the first flowers of the canyons.

The Indians carry him on their shoulders, their black eyes dancing and smiling. Ample puffed-out sea-blue woolen shirts are festooned with brilliant borders; red *lliclla* scarves are pinned with maguey spines over happy breasts. With burnished copper arms, men and women come dancing along the maguey lane; they make joyous arabesques in the air with colored kerchiefs, wave them like fantastic birds—just come, one might imagine, from remote magic forests.

And the flute and the "music box" follow them—their singing carries in its deep rejoicing the whole epiphany of the Andes.

# IX

## MEDICINE-MAN

### I

CURVA and Charazani in Bolivia are cantons peopled almost
entirely by those skilled in magic and herbs (according to
Spanish-speaking people *curanderos,* according to the Quechua tongue *Colla huayas*). They perhaps congregated there
shortly after the seizure of Cuzco by the Spaniards. Another
center is Lambayeque on the northern Peruvian coast.

Their mysterious arts, jealously guarded, have been handed
down in certain families through generations from the days
of the wise Incan *Kollana.* The Callahuaya customs differ
from those of all the Indians who inhabit the same region.

They travel all through the highlands, clear to Colombia
and to Argentina, in some places down to the coast, practicing their profession.

The Indians prefer them to white physicians. They have
more confidence in one speaking their own tongue than in the
white man, ever their betrayer—besides, the fee is usually less.
They take the sick to white doctors only when every other
resource has failed. Naturally the patient usually dies. The
white doctor is blamed; the prestige of the *curandero* is aug-
mented.

Tata Sabaya was a medicine-man from Curva. He was
early initiated into the mysteries of curing and magical control over good and evil by his uncle, a famous *curandero.* He
learned the properties of various herbs and minerals, even of
certain useful remedies of the energetic firm of Bayer, and of
patent medicines in free almanacs.

When but a boy of fourteen he accompanied his uncle on one of his shorter trips through southern Perú.

Some years later Tata, though still in his teens, was himself achieving fame for his own marvellous cures. Already, besides the secret tongue known only to the Callahuayas, he spoke three languages: Spanish, Aimará, and Quechua. As time went on he would learn other native languages such as Puiquina, a great professional asset.

No Callahuaya set out on his professional travels until getting married. Tata fell in love with a girl of his own village—Joaquina of the plump smiling face. She had good sturdy legs beneath her bright knee-length skirt, below which coquettishly showed her lace drawers, the typical costume of the locale.

His courtship followed the routine customs. He announced his attentions by boldly walking up to Joaquina and pinching her sharply. At least a girl remembered you while she nursed her bruise. After sufficient attentions of a more amiable sort and the giving of presents, he took away a bracelet from her by force. At a fiesta he got her intoxicated and carried her around on his shoulder like a sack of meal—all part of the usual procedure. After that he calmly took her home with him. No one could be formally married until after a period of mutual probation.

Joaquina proved more than an industrious housewife, otherwise she would have been returned to her parents with proper payment and the achievement of permanent family enmity. But Joaquina even showed great aptitude in mixing various concoctions.

As Tata was well-satisfied, she also, they were duly married by the priest. Their parents brought them gifts: wood, potato flour, beer, liquor, all sorts of produce.

The third night after the wedding, a big celebration was held in the home of the godparents—a lively affair, much dancing, drinking and fighting. At midnight the godfather presented the new husband with a whip—instructing him always to exercise his authority over his wife and children. The whip was a "symbol of force, reason and justice to be used as circumstances should demand." He told Joaquina she had been "born for sorrow and suffering and should ever bow

J.S.

down as a sign of submission, respect and resignation before her husband."

Thereupon, in front of all, Tata gave her a good beating. She wept and screamed, until finally the godfather ordered the spectacle to cease. Every one then danced, and Joaquina seemed as joyous and happy as the rest.

## 2

Shortly after, four days before carnival, lands were distributed, and Tata was finally put in possession of a plot of ground already granted the pair by the elders.

Some days previous, the wisest of the sorcerers, old Ciro, was put alone in a room having a black cloth table with four candles and a bottle of fiery *aguardiente*. The sorcerer carried on incantations in the Callahuaya tongue. From a bag of live rabbits, he chose four. Secretly in the high hours of a dark night, he buried these alive on the four cardinal points of the land—a ceremonial process bound to bring good weather, good crops and keep away pests.

The day of the distribution a cavalcade set out, headed by the Corregidor (appointed mayor), who was ceremoniously fitted with silver spurs and who for this little trouble was rewarded with a *chajjracoco,* a purse of approximately three hundred dollars. Every one came with his best animal, mule, horse or burro, adorned with silver and ribbons.

Tata put on his best poncho for the occasion. His broad peasant's hat with a pink silk kerchief gave him the aspect of an Argentine *gaucho,* the type all good Callahuayas try to imitate, even to accenting their Spanish.

Every one got drunk in the fields, including the Corregidor. After they came back, for three days and nights they danced the *cintakcaniris* and drank copiously.

### 3

Some months later Tata prepared to set out on his first independent trip. He made a special expedition to the Camata valleys, richest in curative herbs and roots. Many weeks were then spent in preparation: some roots were painted bright colors; others were dried and powdered; bones and hard seeds were carved, stones polished, to sell as supernatural amulets—especially good in love affairs—charms known as *huarmimunachi.*

A send-off fiesta. Much liquor was drunk. Wishes were given him that his black arts and cures might have every success.

He left precisely at midnight, as every good sorcerer should do. Joaquina accompanied him the first two leagues, weeping, then returned home to wait patiently for his return, which might be anywhere from one to ten years, for he went with no fixed direction or destination.

Tata, like all other good Callahuayas, set forth dressed in odd blue-striped trousers with dots on the lower legs; a large wide poncho striped horizontally red and white, a Panamá hat; over his shoulders, a large square bright-colored bag containing the implements of his profession: herbs, roots, bark, seeds, charms, whatnot, all mixed in promiscuously together. Several burros were loaded with provisions and additional medicinal supplies.

Tata travelled clear to the north of Perú. Everywhere he enjoyed unusual facilities, generally received hospitality free; at most he would pay by some act of healing or some superstitious rite to ward off evil from the household.

When any one gets sick, the Indians believe the soul is trying to leave the body attracted by the sickness. To prevent this, friends assemble at midnight and single-file before the house, begging the sickness to go away but not take the ill person's soul. They plead with sweet words, offering to treat the Sickness well; they bring the evil spirit offerings of bread, food and drink for his journey elsewhere—nothing so different from the prayers in any religion when a loved one is stricken. But these are poor expedients provided a bona fide Callahuaya is at hand to take care of the case.

And in any event, the Indians, afraid of Tata's arts, hesitated to show him any disrespect; usually they put all they had at his disposal. Often he received valuable gifts even when he rendered no services—for one who could drive evil away quite likely could also bring it down upon the head of his enemies.

### 4

So much awesome attention gradually turned his head, made him proud and arrogant. Not content with being a mere *curandero,* desirous of being above every one, he became vain and touchy. More and more he demanded and imposed exaggerated respect. He dressed ever more elegantly, now in the finest casimere trousers, held by a bright belt adorned with foreign coins. His horse had a silver bridle.

As time went on Tata became ever cleverer in informing himself about people in the various villages ahead—those who had infirmities, who were most wealthy.

Near Chavín he made a very big fee. He learned of a daughter, ill with pneumonia, in the home of the wealthiest landowner, who though an *hacendado,* was a dark-skinned and superstitious cholo. Secretly near the cholo's house, Tata buried a toad with needles stuck in its chest.

He then presented himself casually, pretending unawareness of domestic happenings. The cholo literally fell upon his neck.

But no, Tata had to be pushing on; he could not stay to cure the man's daughter. Impossible. He was urgently called elsewhere.

Not until the alarmed cholo had pleaded many times and raised his fee to unprecedented proportions, would Tata accept the case.

Thereupon Tata got out his bag. He put a wad of coca leaves in the patient's breast, inquired about her habits and associates, possible enemies. So—he laid a black kerchief on the floor which he sprinkled with the coca leaves. He examined the manner in which they fell, then went out, looked at the sky long and intently. After muttering cabalistic phrases, he declared that the sick person was bewitched in some animal.

"But don't be alarmed. I will discover the spot where the bewitchment has been perpetrated."

After new hocus-pocus, juggling of words and objects, and accompanied by those in the house, he went straight to the place where he had buried the toad and drew it out. Angrily he yanked out the needles with which it was pierced.

"Now we can save your daughter."

Rapidly he prepared hot herb drinks and plasters; and through these, with the Christian Science previously practiced—or else in spite of such things—the daughter improved. Within a few days she could sit up.

The cholo was overjoyed. Though a close-fisted man, he paid his fee gladly without haggling, and added handsome gifts beside. The girl herself dropped a golden jeweled necklace into Tata's hand.

5

One day in his travels, Tata met a fellow-villager and heard unpleasant stories about Joaquina. She had become gay and giddy.

Tata had been away two years. It was growing near Easter, the customary time to return—for though the Callahuaya shuns the Church, he loves its Easter festivals. Suddenly now he conceived a deep nostalgia for Curva, a burning desire to return at once. His worldly goods had increased. He had four handsome mules loaded with valuable possessions.

He traveled fast across the plateaus, through all that great tangle of mountains, ravines and precipices. When near Curva, he again received tidings of his wife's flighty conduct.

Joaquina had heard of his unexpected return and was waiting for him at the river ford a league and a half from the town, with beer and an abundant repast.

To accept these gifts would be a declaration that he was quite satisfied with her conduct during his absence. Instead, gravely and bitterly he refused them.

Joaquina began to weep. She pled, fell on her knees, seized him by the legs, imploring pardon.

He had really planned, at this juncture, to give in, to pardon her. She had been good to him before he left; one should not trust idle gossip. But somehow—he had not been without feminine attention on his travels—she now seemed a bit dumpy and stupid. He remained obdurate. Overweening pride hardened his heart grimly. He shook her off without a word, mounted his mule, rode on alone.

The beer and food were left behind. Joaquina, sobbing, dragged her way back with faltering steps.

There was only one thing the spurned wife of a Callahuaya could do. She did it.

She went straight to the Karka cliff near the town plaza and hurled herself into the abyss.

### 6

A dark humor then fell upon Tata. He was unbearable, sullen, quarreled bitterly with one of his neighbors. One night, both slightly drunk, they whipped out knives and fought a long duel, keen blades flashing in the orchard moonlight.

Tata seriously wounded his opponent.

With this as a pretext, the Corregidor at once seized all the rich goods Tata had garnered from his two years' travel.

# X

# THE SHE-DEVIL OF THE HUALLAGA

I

THE jungles east of the Andes.

We had left Tarapoto's mildewed roofs, had struggled down to Picota, across a tributary on a tilting balsa to reed-walled Juanjui, hemmed in by lofty rank vegetation, pine-apples, bananas, sapotes, palms. With Mateo, a mestizo guide, and two Jíbaro Indian carriers, I was on my way up the broad Huallaga River.

Mateo, loyal soul and queer, looked like a composite of every race in Perú. A fungus disease, known as *Ccara*, had painted almost his entire body black, brown, yellow, pink—broad bands and odd-shaped spots resembling fabulous monsters, an awesome batique of color.

The authorities, every one, had shaken their heads ominously over our trip. The German expedition, the American traveler, had gone into the jungle and disappeared, lost, murdered, abandoned by their guides and porters to mosquitoes or wild animals—no one knew. Most ascribed their death to the famous She-Devil of the Huallaga, famed for her black arts and cruel deeds.

I suggested quite probably that previous travelers had merely neglected to send back word—no, the German, certainly, had been murdered, his goods stolen.

But such things happen in Chicago. I was carrying only necessary supplies and a few Indian gewgaws. One always hears such tales. I was determined to make the trip.

Far from easy going. The map showed three obstructing rivers. We had already crossed about twenty, would ultimately cross more than one hundred and fifty. Some we could ford, from ankles up to our necks. For some we had to fell trees. Several required building rafts. Often we had to hack through jungle wall, an exhausting, hot process. Dangerous swamps. Tricky terraine. Malarial mosquitoes, sandflies, and other disease-carrying insects plagued us unmercifully.

The uncomplaining Indians rarely spoke even to each other—this was their life, their world. They merely trotted tirelessly forward, in silence, heavy burdens held by broad straps across their foreheads, arms crossed, sharp curved machete ready to hack away obstacles or to strike swiftly at deadly serpents. They went naked. Their nightgown-like shirts, now wrapped around their loins, were put on only when they entered settlements; and between Juanjui and Pachisa—allowing for river-twistings and detours, nearly two hundred miles—were only occasional clusters of Indian huts.

Though naked, the Indians streamed perspiration. Mateo and myself, despite swarms of insects, the bites of which often left ugly swellings, went stripped to the waist, and we also perspired profusely, even when tropic deluges almost swept us from our footing.

Hour after hour—only the swish of leaves, the pad-pad of the Indians on the soft humid ground, every man's thought bent on the dull routine of going forward. At other times the jungle was in an uproar from our passing—screeching birds or chattering monkeys. One troop followed us grimacing, hurling down fruits and sticks, bridging twenty-foot gaps by a long swing and fling of their bodies.

During noonday heat, we invariably rested on dry ground. The Indians then eased their burdens, slipping their foreheads out of their straps.

We would munch on toasted corn and jerked meat. After a time the Indians would squat down, adjust their head straps, give a heave, grunt, take a few wobbly steps until they balanced their loads, then go trotting on in silence.

This lost world was ineffably beautiful, lonely, terrifying. The Will concentrated starkly to go on, finish the trip, get back to civilization, to comfort; at the same time, a subtle disintegration, a supreme indifference bordering on an almost luxurious contentment, as one sank into the passionate embrace of the heat, so that little really mattered; better to drift along forever on a warm current of oblivion. Thoughts, in no logical sequence, glinted through the brain like light flashing on some rare jewel, gorgeous images of beauty, promiscuities, fantastic realms, distorted memories, vague aspirations—then the terror of persistent rain, the downpour, endless, rotting the world away. But always the jungle's queer glamor, once known intimately, ever unforgettable. The jungle, as painter Rousseau knew so well, is a female tiger with cruel claws sheathed in velvet.

## 2

Late one morning we came upon a little thatched *choza*. Hoping to change our monotonous diet, we asked food from the old Indian woman. Dressed in wrapped skirts, torso nude save for a kerchief hung triangularly only half concealing her large dangling breasts, she merely shrugged hopelessly at our request—no food, only a little parched corn.

Several hundred yards further on, we passed a neatly cleared hill with a stout dwelling—amazing in this wilderness! Still more amazing—in the doorway stood an attractive young woman clad in a red dress of European origin and a broad straw Panamá. Such a being, apparently civilized, in the depths of the Green Hell! Inexplicable!

She waved to us to stop.

A queer expression came over the customarily stolid faces of my Indians. With no sign to me, only a furtive glance one to the other, they trotted on more rapidly than usual.

"Surely she can give us food," I suggested to Mateo.

He shook his head dourly, and without explanation, trotted along after the Indians.

Nothing for me to do but catch up with him. "But—"

"Come on," he hissed in fright, breathing hard.

I trotted along by his side, waiting for him to comment. But his lips were sealed—tight. Both he and the Indians were anxious to be on their way.

After nearly a mile, a sound caused me to look around.

The girl in red was struggling to catch up with us.

She waved. "Hello!" she called.

Presently she was by my side, a mocking smile illuminating her tanned face. About twenty-five, body supple, features uncommonly handsome, apparently she had considerable European blood mixed with Indian. Around her neck was a gold and jade necklace, long earrings to match; her dress was of good well-tailored material, but she was barefoot. Even so she carried herself like a queen—an air of derision, complete self-assurance.

Mateo returned her greeting with a grunt. He hastened to leave us, joined the Indians. I called on them to slow up, wait for us.

"My house is a mile further on," the girl said simply to us. "You must all stop, and I shall get you something to eat and drink."

Queer looks passed between the Indians; Mateo's hands were positively trembling.

He half grunted something. He and the Indians moved ahead again, but did not let us out of sight.

She asked me where I was from, where going, what I carried in my cases.

It was growing hotter. Although the country here was more open, travelling was difficult.

Near noon we reached her place, much like the previous

one, on high dry ground. Trees shaded the yard and thickly thatched roof.

The Indians hurried on past.

"Rest here," she commanded; "there are only marshes ahead. I will prepare some food, and we will go swimming."

At my orders, reluctantly the Indians came back to the clearing. Mateo's face more than ever revealed fright.

"What in God's name is the matter with you?" I demanded, provoked. "She is only a woman and apparently alone."

"Please, my chief, don't stop here." His teeth fairly chattered. "*She's* the She-Devil of the Huallaga. She killed the American and the German. The dress she's wearing is part of the German's goods. He was taking four trunks down the river, over to Saposoa—trading. Her Indians drowned him in the river, took away all his things. She's a devil; she knows black magic; she will ruin us."

"Nonsense!" I replied. "When we spread out the things, she'll see we have nothing worth stealing."

"Everything is of value to these people. Go on, I beg you."

I laughed him off. "This is the hottest day we've had. I simply must have a swim. Pitch tent here."

Sullenly the Indians put up tent, unfolded my cot.

"We shall merely eat here," I told Mateo. "After siesta we'll go on."

"But don't go swimming with her. She's a wonderful swimmer. She'll drag you down or some of her men will be hidden on the bank. She's a demon."

I felt his fears childish; still a warning was a warning.

### 3

Matilda, for that was her name, prepared what in that part of the world was an excellent meal—soup, rice, peppery stew, fried plantains, coffee. Mateo and the Indians she served out of doors. For me she set a little Peruvian walnut table, but did not offer to sit down with me.

She hovered over me, asking many questions about my trip, our plans. She gave me good pointers about the best routes. She was puzzled that I was merely a sight-seer with apparently no definite purpose. "You must find it hard. We who live here can stand the climate; it is not so easy for outsiders."

Some day, she said, she would go out and see the world. She had never set eyes on a stone building, a railroad train or an ocean vessel. She had heard tales about Lima's splendor. It must be very beautiful and wonderful beyond the sierra.

Presently I went to my tent for a siesta under the mosquito netting. Mateo posted himself at the entrance belligerently.

I woke up with a start, weighted with the heaviness of noon-time sleep in the tropics, perspiring profusely, sticky, uncomfortable.

"Mateo, I'm going for a swim."

"Don't."

"I've simply got to have a swim. But I'll go alone."

He nodded resignedly.

"You still think it dangerous?"

"Be careful, be very careful," he said in a low set tone.

"All right. Then you follow me through the woods. Stay out of sight but keep an eye on me."

At the river edge, I carefully piled my clothes on a high bank of gnarled roots and boulders and on top of them put a large stone easily visible from the stream.

The water was cool, refreshing. I splashed about nearly ten minutes.

Matilda appeared on the bank. "Why didn't you tell me?" she called.

With utterly no false modesty, she stripped off her dress, her only garment, carefully removed her earrings and necklace, and dived into the stream. She came up bubbling and laughing, then struck out toward me.

A sound in the brush. It couldn't be Mateo; he was further down. Perhaps some animal. I suddenly recalled the utter terror of him and the less expressive Indians.

Grasping a branch, I swung out on the shore.

"Where are you going?" she cried. "Just as I get here, you go off."

With a little wave of my hand, I began dressing, then struck off through the jungle toward the cabin.

In a minute she was beside me, hair dripping, earrings and necklace in her hands.

She was vexed. "Why do you go away?"

"Because I don't want to swim anymore."

Without further comment, she walked along beside me, adjusting her earrings as she went, a puzzled slightly angry expression on her face.

The Indians were not at my tent. "Where are they?" I demanded of Mateo.

He shrugged, as if to say, "I told you so."

"Up at the house," replied Matilda. "I gave them chicha."

Getting them drunk—not so good. "Send them down," I told Mateo.

He looked at me imploringly, hesitating.

"Come," said Matilda to him. "You too must have some beer."

To my surprise he obeyed her without objection.

"Hurry back," I told him. "We must get going."

"Why don't you rest here today and get a good start in the morning?" suggested Matilda pleadingly. "I'll fix up some supper for you."

"I'll see." I didn't like the way she had pulled my men off.

I stalked on into my tent alone.

It was nice here in this clearing, very few insects. For days now we had been going steadily, resting very little. The meal, the swim, the short rest, made me little relish proceeding. It was fairly late now. Would we find a better camping place?

The will to go on completely left me. A strange irresolution seized me, the very sort of irresolution that always comes over one in the Green Hell when one stops to think or tries to reach a decision through any other means than habit, will, or instinct. I sat on my cot, languidly fanning myself. "Go or stay? . . ." Go, I finally decided. "I must get Mateo and the Indians. We will go on." I was saying this over and over again. But instead I just sat. Mateo and the Indians did not return.

### 4

Suddenly—cooler now—Matilda appeared, a splash of red in the doorway of the tent.

"Your men tell me you have music."

I remembered. A mouth-organ I had traded off a Chinaman in a store in Chachapoyas for a pair of native sandals he had admired. Never able to reproduce a tune, it was a queer choice. But as we went along the trail, I had distracted myself from the insects and the heat by making sounds on it. I had to do my own composing, but had achieved a certain proficiency, or so it seemed to me, in contrast to the wailing sounds of native bamboo-flute music.

So—my men really called my sounds music. I laughed, got out the harmonica.

Matilda took it in her hands, slightly disappointed; she had never seen one before in her life.

She handed it back. "Play it."

I put my best effort into the attempt.

She was enchanted, and presently leapt up from the case on which she had been sitting and began dancing. Around and round and round she whirled.

Whenever I stopped for breath, she cried, "Go on! Go on!"

Ever more rapidly and wildly she whirled, completely intoxicated by the rhythm of her own body—pure joy, abandon.

My lips were dry. I could play no more. My own efforts seemed to have cost me more energy than all her mad dancing.

"Play! Play!" she pleaded.

I could not.

She sank down beside me on the couch, panting only slightly, a sure even rise and fall of her full breasts.

She turned the mouth-organ over in her hand curiously, almost reverently, as though she would like to draw forth from it by mere will eternal music so that she might dance on forever.

"Try it," I suggested.

Tentatively and very low, she blew into it, running her mouth along its length to test each sound. Presently, with that uncanny instinct of these people, she had the knack of it, and was converting its sounds into music more understandable than mine had been.

"Oh," she cried, her eyes shining. "It is a marvelous music." She threw her arms about me with pure happiness.

Again she tested it, grew surer of the sounds.

"Ah, how I would like to have this!"

"You can have it."

"No." A bewildered look came over her face. "It is very marvelous. Why, this would cost my whole house!"

I thought of life's strange contradictions. Here was a woman, who, through astuteness or some queer magnetism, had thrown fear into a whole region, a Lorelei who did evil things to chance travelers. The She-Devil of the Huallaga had become a legend for leagues about, famous for her black arts, yet she was enthralled by a little gewgaw modern civilization had evolved to amuse corner grocery stores.

Queer, those differences in values wherever the industrial age meets the backward rural community: the latter is still imbued with ideas of utility, æsthetic appreciation; ancient customs have greater importance than either time or labor content. To send a chunky letter by air mail recently had cost me nearly a dollar; for that same amount of money I had secured a beautiful native blanket which, in addition to the years of grazing of some alpaca, the shearing and carding of the wool and the dyeing process, had probably required at least two months' patient labor. For a harmonica, I was offered a house, by a woman skilled in the black arts, able to manipulate the mysterious forces of good and evil, of life and death, of health or sickness, of love and hate!

"I give it to you. I want nothing."

She looked at me startled. It almost fell from her limp hand. "You give me *this!* But why?—"

"Because you want it. Because it gives you happiness."

"And you?"

"I am a very poor music-maker."

"You give it to me?" she repeated incredulously.

"It is nothing. I am glad to give it to you."

"Oh!" She danced up and down, threw her arms around me, kissed me full on the lips. "I am so happy."

She began playing it and dancing again with even more abandon than before. She was not dancing for me, but for the vital forces that surged within her, for her unaware kinship with all of life, for some self-completion her lonely existence denied her. There was in her gyrations not the least hint of sex-awareness or exhibitionist vanity.

She was as simple in her present emotional state as the water that flowed in the river, as the wind over the tall *caoba* trees.

And yet the human soul is complex. Even this untutored little savage was terrifically complex—in part, the mixture of races that lifted her out of Indian and Spanish traditions, making her entirely a law unto herself. I wondered at the tales of robbery and murder. If those stories were true—which I could hardly believe—her motive must be something far different from mere greed for worldly goods. Such deeds could have their source only in this same fount of vital energy revealed by her dancing, in some desire for power and achievement which mere victory over jungle terrors could not provide; perhaps, too, resentment.

Her father, possibly some chance European traveler, not Spanish but Nordic, had satisfied a whim and passed on. The fruit of his whim was the beautiful dancing creature before me. Perhaps, feeling herself different, superior yet inadequate, feeling that she could have belonged to another world closed to her, unconsciously she wished to vent spite on those who came out of that strange desirable world, spite at her foreign father who had abandoned her here.

She danced on and on. The shadows grew long, but still she played and danced. She danced until her red dress, wet from perspiration, clung snugly to her shapely body, which seemed like a glowing coal, consuming itself steadily with sure fire. Still glowing, as dusk fell upon the world, she sank down, happy, on the cot beside me.

Tired now, wanting not so much soul and body outlet as a refuge, a harbor, a place safe from jungle menace and storms, from the dangerous dark which was wrapping us around, she was human again, a woman, not some blind force of movement and creation.

Without a word she crept softly into my arms, with a sigh of contentment. This, too, I realized, was as natural and inevitable for her as everything else. She lay still for a while, then her lips sought mine.

5

We were on the road before dawn. The white mist was lifting over the marshes. Morning birds were trilling. The dense leaves were dripping.

But already it was hot, not the hammering cruel heat that

strikes over the world after the sun rises, but a damp bandage-like warmth, the day already half stale before it begins.

The Jíbaro Indians were trotting on ahead of us. Mateo was by my side.

"It was the music that saved us," he said, wrinkling up his painted face lugubriously. His tone implied I had been more lucky than intelligent.

## POPULATION CHART

COAST

### Lima and other Cities
Creole Aristocrats.
Ecclesiastical authorities.
Creole militarists.
Creole and Cholo professionals.
Creole and Cholo bureaucracy.
American and British corporation heads and employees.
Cholo, Chinese and Japanese tradesmen.
Cholo and zambo proletariat.
Indian peddlers.
Indian and negro soldiers.

### Towns and Villages
Cholo bureaucracy.
Cholo, Japanese, Chinese and Indian traders.
Cholo priests.
Cholo professionals.
Indian medicine-men.
Indian and Japanese peasants.
Indian fishermen.
Indian and negro soldiers.

### Large Estates
Creole, Foreign and Cholo owners, administrators and technicians.
Cholo bureaucrats.
Cholo majordomos.

Cholo priests.

Negro, Chinese, Japanese and Indian *yanacona* or serfs.

### HIGHLANDS

*Cajamarca, Huancayo, Arequipa, Cuzco and other cities.*

Creole and Cholo landholders.

Creole and Cholo bishops and priests.

Cholo and Indian bureaucrats.

Creole and Cholo army officers.

Cholo professionals.

Cholo, Japanese and Indian tradesmen.

Cholo and Indian craftsmen.

Cholo and Indian ranchers.

Indian medicine-men.

Indian serfs and communal landholders.

Indian soldiers.

*Villages and Countryside*

Cholo and Indian bureaucrats.

Cholo majordomos on estates.

Cholo priests.

Indian *yanacona*.

Indian medicine-men.

Indian blessers.

Indian communal landholders and ranchers.

Indian craftsmen.

Cholo and Indian traders.

Indian herders.

*Mines*

Creole and foreign owners and officials.

Cholo majordomos.

Cholo and Indian proletariat.

### THE JUNGLE

*Iquitos and other settlements*

Cholo bureaucrats.

Cholo professionals.

Creole and Cholo army officers.
Cholo priests.
Indian medicine-men.
Cholo, Japanese and Indian tradesmen.
Cholo and Indian rivermen.
Cholo, Indian and Japanese ranchers.
Indian soldiers.

*The Interior*

Cholo, Indian and Japanese tradesmen.
Cholo, Indian and Japanese ranchers.
Cholo and Indian rivermen.
Cholo priests.
Indian medicine-men.
Indian soldiers.
Indians: communal agriculturists, semi-settled soil cultivators, nomadic primitive tribes, head-hunters, cannibals.

# PART III
## KNOTS ON THE CORD

# XI

# LIMA: CITY OF KINGS

I

THIRTY years ago prosaic writers described Lima as triangular. But "Tunante" called it "heart-shaped"—the encircling Rimac River made it "actually a heart of flowers, bound together by a silver ribbon."

Since then, streets and houses have sprawled out across the Rimac and in many other directions. New paved avenues to Callao and the bathing beaches—Miraflores, Chorrillas, Magdalena, San Miguel, Ancón, Herradura—have attracted fashionable modern dwellings. Elsewhere small factories and workingmen's quarters have broken the silver ribbon. The flowers of nineteenth-century quaintly provincial Lima of picturesque venders and frequent lively fiestas have been scattered and have withered.

Already, towards the end of the last century, old Lima which Prada called ugly—"from the phallic towers of Santo Domingo and La Merced to the façades of the Palaces and other public buildings"—was being "buried under progressive embellishment . . . like tombs smothered under roses, jasmines and daisies." Nearly everything today considered magnificent did not exist. The stately Plaza de San Martín, the Paseo Colón, were then but meagerly building up; now they are right in the city, already outdated, a florid Europeanized architecture ludicrously non-Peruvian.

Lima's great expansion came under Dictator Leguía; our generous golden dollars were used by a small government clique mostly to beautify the capital at a fantastic cost be-

171

yond the country's capacity. Every stone in the still-unfin-
ished Plaza de San Martín—in the exaggerated saying—cost
its weight in gold. But if ever Lima deserved the name, "City
of Kings," it has been since the World War. Streets were
paved, a water-supply developed; old government buildings
had their faces lifted. A company, in which the Dictator
lushly participated and to which his government donated the
valuable urban ground, erected the sumptuous Hotel Bolívar,
a huge marble sarcophagus in atrocious taste. The race-track,
markets, military casino, palaces, bank buildings, museums,
barracks, the military and naval schools, a dozen beautiful
parks, sixteen avenues, a cemetery and a school complete the
list of Leguía's notable eleven-year promotions, which suddenly made Lima over into one of Latin America's show-
metropolises.

Indeed it is the only city of Perú; elsewhere—except for
Trujillo, which is an agrarian-proletarian place—are only
small rural towns, largely of peasants, close to the soil, their
animals, and their markets. From any main square can be
seen the open fields. But Lima has metropolitan habits and
psychology.

Lima is a false diamond in a rough setting. The city has
developed largely because of typical Latin extravagance and
love of pompous show rather than from vital forces spring-
ing from the country at large.

Hence these new developments, however modern, are quite
in line with Lima's long traditions, its artificial character, its
colonial physiognomy, its centuries of reactionary government ever devoid of national vision. Both in structure and
spirit, the city is further removed from Perú than ever.

It is selfish, arrogant, isolated.

"Lima was founded near the sea so it could look toward
Spain; ever since, it has grown used to looking away from
Perú; it is the bride of the sailors of the seven seas."

"What does it know about us?" demand the people of imperial Cuzco, proud and hostile.[1]

"We languish in backward neglect," wails a paper of Pacasmayo, northern port. "Lima absorbs everything; its bureaucrats fatten on the country; it piles marble block on marble block, but we receive nothing for our roads, our schools, our sanitation."

So far as the real Perú is concerned, Lima is a hot-house flower, a non-native species from the conservatory, germinated and pampered under the white crystals of Spain; its perfume has been the incense of the Counter-Reformation; its bright petals were flushed colonialism, priestly and feudal rule. As Belaunde has said, Lima is a little island "of grace, courtly life and ironical spirit in the great tragedy of the geographic contrasts and historical sorrows that constitute the country."

Lima, despite its advantages, has always been a soap-bubble city, its slight economic significance ever falsely inflated. Its bureaucratic influence is inflated. Its social snobbishness is inflated. Its gracious urbane society, striving for elegant sophistication, yet utterly lacking sophistication, though knowing etiquette and amorous intrigue, is essentially bigoted, egoistic, bound by narrow outworn beliefs—it is a "City of Kings" in a Republic.

2

Pizarro founded Lima January 18, 1535, with less than a hundred men on twenty-seven checkerboard squares. The choice of the coast site for a capital in that soft climate, "where it does not rain, nor snow, nor hail," provided a counterpoise to traditional indigenous Cuzco, then too much of a storm center. At first Pizarro had contemplated making lofty Jauja the capital (which would have changed Perú's whole history), but almost inevitably, ties with the mother

[1] Saenz, 26.

country drew him back to the coast. If subsequently Lima was exposed to piratical attacks, it came to serve conquest exploitation admirably; trade with Panamá and the extraction of minerals, silver in Potosí and Cerro de Pasco, and mercury from Huancavelica.

After the first fifty years of anarchy, for two centuries, from 1600 to July 28, 1822, when the Republic was born, Lima with only slight modifications maintained an unaltered aspect, buildings alike, customs stagnant, but self-assured.

The new façades were false, as all of Lima is slightly false, humble adobe artfully concealed by freakish magnificence. Surrounding Indian ranches were invaded, adobe walls torn down and (since Lima lacks a quarry) better adobe walls were reinforced by thick beams; only in rare instances were the portals of real stone or brick.

But the entrances were ample and hospitable. Multiple salons and alcoves, sumptuous tiled chapels, gardens filled with flowers and fountains, flat roofs with typical outlook towers, featured the better homes. Lima society belles peered forth from the semi-concubinal atmosphere of beautiful carved Oriental balconies, latticed like a seraglio, with sighs for romance to alter life's tedium.

The cultural center and court of all South America, colonial Lima, despite stale ecclesiasticism, had a tradition of learning; and an austere aristocratic air was imparted by the viceregal court, the Audiencia, the municipal Cabildo, the Archbishopric, the Dominican University (San Marcos), founded May 12, 1551, institutions supported by wealthy aristocratic families. Each profession wore its typical dress— an air of dignified medievalism.

The rude campaign days of the Conquest forgotten, Lima became a city of blue-bloods. To no other New World country were sent so many nobles—one grand duke, fifty-eight marquéses, forty-five counts, not to mention knights and hidalgos. All—exempt from the common laws—enjoyed special privileges.

The depot of all South American commercial life—the merchandise of Europe, China and New Spain was shunted there to dodge the English, Dutch and French bucaneers. Lima had an international life, more important than its relations, aside from bureaucratic matters, with Perú. Its residents consumed lavishly—a city of concentrated rich consumers.

"O Lima!" . . . exclaimed a contemporary writer. "How many shape gold and silver in the shops of Milan and Sevilla, how many work linen in France, how many loads of wool are carded in England and Ireland; how many weave labyrinthine rolls of gold cloth and Flanders lace; how much delicate glass from Barcelona and Venice; how many Belgian and Roman engravers work metal sheets and presses; how many carpets are designed in Cairo and filigrees in China—tributes you garner in the universal fair of Portobello."

In contrast, the Indians and slaves were locked up at night, as in ghettoes, in a ward across the river known as the Cercado. The city salved its conscience by multiple works of piety, hospitals and asylums; there was even a *gimnasio*—San Juan de Penitencia—to gather in the half-breed children of the Conquistadores.

### 3

The Limeñan, however urbane in other things, is not urbane, as is the Cuban, in his religion; he remains not only fervently Catholic but has absorbed into his faith the superstitions of the ignorant masses he exploits. Believing unshakably in Adam and Eve, in all the miraculous myths, in witchcraft, he runs to pray and buys innocuous pills stamped with the image of the Virgin of Perpetual Aid rather than call the doctor. Distinguished families, whatever the illness, use reliquaries of holy earth taken from the sepulchres of Martín de Porres, Juan Marius and Santa Rosa; they cure eye infections by rubbing them with the blessed image of the Virgin of Carmen.

Such fanaticism has endured from the days of Pizarro's first invocations on founding the city. In 1841—according to Manuel González de la Rosa—Lima still had an ecclesiastic, monk or nun, for every four-and-a-half families. "What is Lima?" asked Prada in 1903. "A Dead Sea in which churches and monasteries poke up like islands without water or vegetation. . . . Thus a population that embraces more than a hundred edifices destined to the worship and teaching of religion does not possess a single municipal school worthy of a civilized people." (Leguía later constructed one modern school building; its curriculum is still medieval.)

Colonial Lima, as modern Lima, took its religion in great surges of orgiastic frenzy, a reaction to rigid etiquette. Church images were and are paraded through the streets on the slightest provocation to cure all the city's ills.

Phillip III, as a result of a long polemic with the Dominicans over the Immaculate Conception, ordered all sermons to begin: "Praised be the most Holy Sacrament and the Virgin conceived without original sin."

Pious Perú, until then untroubled by niceties of dogma, at once took the official position. San Marcos University students were suddenly required to swear to defend the Immaculate Conception. Processions, ringing of bells, public fiestas, fireworks, celebrated the myth. December 8, 1654, after Mass and panegyric in the cathedral, the authorities voted that this doctrine be defended by the Viceroy, the Ecclesiastic and Secular Cabildos and the Audiencia. A plaza mass-meeting acclaimed the Immaculate Virgin patroness of the city.

Shortly after, the Dominican Prior prefaced his cathedral sermon with merely: "Praised be the most Holy Sacrament." The faithful clamorously continued, "And the Virgin conceived without original sin." Immediately they formed a procession and that night a mob of 10,000 persons trudged about with burning candles, singing: "The Virgin conceived without original sin." The bells of all the churches except Santo Domingo rang out.

The following night all the commercial employees marched with blue banners singing: "Mary conceived without original sin." It was planned to roughhouse the Dominicans, but when the procession passed their church at two o'clock that morning, all the members of the order dutifully came out with lifted crosses and flaring candles.

Every night processions, weeks of orgiastic faith and slobbery emotions.

Again a Dominican father in a cathedral sermon omitted the sacred phrase. Clerics, cannons, everybody, leapt up and extending their arms toward the pulpit, shrieked: "And the Virgin, our Lady, conceived without the stain of original sin." They pulled the friar down by force, almost tore him limb from limb.

Again processions: "Mary conceived without original sin." Night after night the city was in a senseless uproar until March. Then the death of the Provincial of Santo Domingo and the election of one more conformist ended the controversy that had kept Lima frothing for over ten years. July 19, 1664, litanies to the Virgin were sung in the Dominican Church. The people embraced each other in delirious joy. In the exuberant commemorative procession of July 30, the Dominicans chanted, the processionaires roared back:

> "Mary conceived—
> Remedying our evils—
> Purer than the sun of day
> Without original sin."

October 20, 1687, earthquakes well-nigh destroyed Lima and Callao. Only twenty-five houses were left standing. Over a thousand people lost their lives. The quakes continued till December 2, then a terrible rainstorm, melting the remaining adobe walls, completed the desolation. Women swooned from the stench of unburied bodies. People confessed in screams. Others seared their eyes and mouth with flames. The Papal Legate had himself lashed naked through the streets: "This is the just penalty the King of Heaven orders executed on this vile sinner." For three days and nights a shrieking, flagellating mob carried the image of Our Lord of Miracles through the streets. Naturally the dire calamities ceased.

The three-day procession of Our Lord of Miracles from the Church of Nazarene is still an orgy of fanaticism. Vast masses of people, from the poorest *barrios* up to the élite of Magdalena, many barefoot, many on their knees, frenziedly follow the image through the streets.

These outbursts are animal reaction to the city's smug polished normalcy. Carnival—in Spain and many Latin countries, a beautiful and enjoyable diversion prior to Lent—in Lima is brutal slapstick. Instead of flowers, buckets of water; eggs full of colored water, which stains clothes, are hurled recklessly; people are doused with cheap perfumed talcum powder, until every one assumes the aspect of animated dough, and the city smells like a second-rate brothel.

Symptoms of a psychological state. Except for a small group of lucid intellectuals, by and large Lima's inhabitants, mentally unaffected by modern science, live either in cynical compliance with religious forms or in ignorant superstition. Max Radiguet, who visited Perú early in the nineteenth century, remarked that "if Limeñans believe in Mass, they also believe in money." But aside from those who utilize religion as a hypocritical varnish, practically all, believing in ritual without morality, feed upon necromancy and fetishism. Any extended conversation in any Lima home soon turns to weird tales of ghosts, enchantments, fortune-telling, black magic, bedevilment, witchcraft, and in a few bolder instances to spiritualism, telepathy, spirit-rapping, and astrology—all passionately believed. Lima lacks an Indian tradition, but pagan superstitions have oozed up through faith in miracles and direct saintly intervention in petty affairs to color the Lima mind with a muddy tinge of supernaturalism.

## 4

After independence, Lima continued old colonialism, as aloof from Perú as though a revolution had never occurred. Pancho Fierro's drawings, the elegant scenes depicted by Segura, his conversations of personages on the Rimac Bridge or in the Gold Ball café; Pardo's dignified pages with their musty atmosphere of old-style carpeted salon; the chronicles of Fuentes—all evidence records a European metropolis slightly provincial with the same old colonial social notes.

True enough, their life broken by constant political disorder, the good aristocrats time and again had to bar their doors against revolutionary hordes. In the scramble, once even negro León Escobar, roaring with laughter, swept into the city at the head of negro troopers to be President for twenty-four hours. The next day Indians came in under Vivas.

International trade and other relations cut off, it became ever more difficult for Lima life to retain foreign criteria. After a time, the city almost promised to fuse itself with the national consciousness, to become an organic part of the national life. More and more, the hinterland bent Lima's trim aloofness to a more genial typical atmosphere.

Forty years ago it was a pleasant provincial place, soft, glowing, semi-Andalusian; it loved its typical dances, its promenades, balcony conversations, café *tertulias*. Indian and negro activities enlivened the city: the flower-vender; the Indian, head-balanced ice-cream freezer; makers of soft tropical fruit drinks in terra cotta vats; sidewalk restaurants;

sellers of chili sauces and tamales from vats over open charcoal fires, of chicha from tall urns balanced on turbaned
heads above copper faces; tradesmen of fruit and of flowers
wrapped in chirimoya leaves; milkmaids sideways on donkeys,
boys with ambulating show-cases of bread and sweets; big-
earringed fish mongers "—*Chancayano, muy bueno* . . .";
venders of matches, cheeses and lottery tickets (the last specially dressed in long coat and black top hat) ; the blanketed
hawker of fiesta candles; the rambling puppet shows; and
finally the old night-watch *sereno,* with his square lantern
and iron-tipped staff, gave the city unique color, the flavor of
coast, jungle and Andes. Lima was more a national focus
when international communications were poor than today,
improved.

Nearly all this has disappeared. In the older city, beyond
what was formerly called the "Seven Gerinjas," one still finds
old buildings, little mussy shops, a queer conglomerate of
people, the "riff-raff" who seem to belong no longer either
to Lima or Perú, but live in some twilight world precariously
perched on some vague economic ledge. The Victoria ward,
home of prostitutes, proletariat, and invading provincial
lower middle-class mestizos, is another hybrid world of old-
fashioned "Creole" *fondas.* On Manco Cápac street is a typical Arequipan restaurant, tables flowing out from pink and
blue calcimined rooms into the tree-shaded patio, where the
*aji,* or chili condiment, is plucked fresh from the vines. From
a queer assortment of chipped bargain-counter dishes and
terra cotta ware, one may gorge on sizzling hot soups and
stews, *antecuchos* (calves' hearts on bamboo spits) and
frothy chicha. Now and then the *marinela* is danced to guitar
and other music—a queer hodge-podge of lilting Indian-
negro-and-Creole melody, slightly decadent, modernistic.
Except for a small radius about the central market, the only
former activity remaining for poorer Limeños, besides carry-

ing trunks and being servants, is selling lottery tickets—in rags now instead of top hats.

All other petty retail lines, even in the market, have been absorbed by canny Japs and Chinese, more adaptable to Limeñan psychology and needs than the native Peruvian.

The Indian who ventures into Lima's confines, unless Europeanized in dress and thought, suffers sharp ridicule, finds all economic doors closed. In Lima, the Indian and Indianized cholo, comprising eighty percent of the population, are pariahs, must stay away. In times past, they were promptly seized and shipped off to mine, hacienda and army—a memory never forgotten. Now competition, foreign customs, citified psychology, impose Lima's criteria upon every one. Hence the Indians, too poor to travel much, mostly remain in the remote highlands. Lima thus lacks Peruvian tradition. Saenz remarks: "A Perú without Indians loses its historical significance"; Lima is without national roots.

Lima, ethnically cut off, tries valiantly to be European, which merely means that however much it becomes physically beautified, it remains weakly colonial. Basadre writes: "The New World is full of imitation. Not without reason is it the continent of the monkey and the parrot." This particularly applies to Lima, scarcely at all to the hinterland. Lima's tendency toward Europeanization, despite much propaganda about the noble Quechuas, despite Indophile intellectuals, has again grown stronger—partly due to the inrush of foreign capital—during the twentieth century. Not that proper cultural borrowing is ever to be condemned. But the light gay Limeñan borrows from a Europe and an America he poorly understands for a Perú he understands less. He borrows, not with national vision, but with instincts of parvenu wealth, ostentation, snobbishness, contempt for his native land.

Artificial aping. As far as possible he utilizes only foreign products, takes up horse racing, cricket and football, copies dress and customs, yesterday French and English, today American, but obdurately refuses to accept the social concepts and technique which made those products possible in other countries. He still governs his city pretentiously with an appointed Council of Notables.

It is scarcely surprising that recent embellishments show no vital creative originality, have only the empty beauty of a past era, or else are atrocious imitations of the flabbiest French and Italian architecture. Their hollowness will become at once apparent as soon as Perú becomes Perú; when a proper valuation will have been put upon Inca motifs and forms, which dovetail so well with severe modern concrete and steel. Even the new homes of Lima are sad bourgeois imitations of California bungalows, without their comfort. Lima's creative efforts (save those of a small group of well-rooted artists) are like spun museum glass, pretty, curious and insignificant. Lima is still dawdling in the Porfirio Díaz epoch in Mexico; its outward show is a playing to the galleries, enslavement to foreign criteria, stubborn resistance to native ideas and forces.

True, incipient industrialism has created a proletarian movement that on occasion, as the general strike of 1912, successfully shocks, without endangering, Lima's smugness.

The Lima proletariat, if not so removed from inner Perú as Lima's upper classes, nevertheless does not think in the same terms as, say, the proletarian of Trujillo, where foreign estates impinging upon the city make the problem more obviously feudal and imperialistic, not disguised with liberal modernity as in Lima. Inevitably, because of Lima's separatist character, the Lima worker is a proletarian separatist. Factory smoke is not yet an important feature of Lima's life.

Lima has merely entered upon a new kind of colonialism. Foreign capital, rapid rail, steamship and air communications, once more bringing Lima closer to the outside world

than to Perú, have helped the feudal landholding class rein-
trench itself with all its privileges and decadent ideas.

The agents of this class are the jostling politicians. Into
Lima flock the semi-primitive provincial bosses, congressmen,
bureaucratic employees. Soon they learn to wear proper
clothes and acquire pomposity. They return to their consti-
tuents only during election days; the rest of the time they
intrigue, secure jobs for friends, promote petty graft projects, and carouse. They soon grow obese, for as Cabello de
Carbonera sets forth, "*To banquet,* is a verb, undoubtedly
accepted for the exclusive use of ambitious candidates. In
Lima we public men must be like public women: eat as many
times and as much as is necessary to seduce a friend."

To back up this tribe is a more than usually servile gang
of newspapermen and writers. Lima's leading periodical *El
Comercio* gives as little news as falsely as it can. No large
paper in a capital of comparable size in all Latin America is
so inadequate, with such ridiculous format, or so vicious,
lying and insensitive to popular currents. Owned by the
aristocratic Miro Quesadas, it is the typical output of a class
without intellectual curiosity depending for survival upon
popular ignorance.

5

"Lima's expansion," remarked Mariátegui, "is a symptom of
exploitation." Its rapid development is not supported "geographically or economically—only politically."

Though to this slight exaggeration economist Emilio
Romero takes violent exception,[2] its site could not have been
better chosen to isolate it from the interior—perhaps this
was desired by Pizarro. Though its climate is excellent and it
has a natural economic relation to the fairly rich Rimac and
Carabayllo valleys—somewhat as Trujillo (population 24,-
000) has to the much richer Chicama and Moche valleys—

[2] *El Decentralismo,* 125 ff. *Geografía,* 503.

it is not well-located for exporting national products, or for distributing foreign goods. It does not focus national productive energies.

Yet nearby Callao is today Perú's major port. Being the capital and largest city, Lima has at great cost artificially rounded out economic hegemony, by sheer stubbornness has opened up parts of the interior. From Lima, direct ascent of the Andes was well-nigh impossible. But though the persistence of Yankee adventurer Henry Meiggs was built the world's loftiest railroad, but rates are necessarily high and oxygen has to be used liberally on fainting passengers. Though this road taps the Cerro de Pasco, Junín and Huancavelica mines and the tropical Chanchamayo valley, it does not penetrate the richest sierra or jungle regions. If finally extended to Iquitos as planned, it will haul produce out of the Loreto Amazón basin over the most paradoxical route. Southern Perú and northern Perú—which offer the greatest possibilities for future development—have no economic relation to Lima.

Nor can Lima become a likely industrial center. Some textile factories have been built, but any important textile development will more likely occur closer to the live-stock regions of cheap labor, easy transportation, and abundant water power.

Artificially bloated Lima remains essentially isolated, parasitical, unsound economically and geographically. Its present governmental domination rests upon a defiance of geography and distance, upon a feudal-caste system, a mercenary conscript army, a technic of exploitation and a glittering foreign culture—all doomed to extinction. The extravagant efforts of Leguía to beautify it beyond rhyme or reason, its topheavy development, its failure to merge its destinies with those of Perú, make its future doubtful. From it will never come the vital forces for the remaking of the real Perú.

No coast capital can ever achieve the cultural and eco-

nomic rôle that Cuzco had for the self-sufficient Inca empire.
Perhaps in a world of international exchange this is no longer
desirable. The evil of Lima lies in its trying to assume an
octopus economic rôle, in its consistent effort to keep from
becoming Peruvian yet to dominate politically and economically all local life. For Prada, Lima was a vast focus of prostitution—female, political, and religious—like a huge swamp
infecting the Republic. Lima's evil lies in its harsh centralization, its false ideals and backward social psychology, its
wrong-headed leadership—as one writer puts the matter: its
lack of "clean hands and lucid brains."

And yet it must be finally admitted, there is something
admirable in Lima's effort to surmount all natural obstacles,
to maintain its superior predominance, to be a proud repository of foreign influence and to forge a personality independent of the country of which it is the capital.

Founded primarily as a foreign army camp, then become
an aristocratic colony alien in spirit, it still pathetically plays
an outworn rôle. It is the bride of the sailors of the seven seas,
but, like most polyandrous ladies, it knows nothing intrinsically important about the real life of its long-absent spouses,
and of Perú, its true love forever spurned, even less.

# XII

# TRUJILLO: LANDLORD CEMETERY

I

Chan Chan, near Trujillo, is a vast conglomeration of crumbling adobe walls, which in its heyday, perhaps 1200 A.D., probably harbored several hundred thousand people. It

and Pachacámac, near modern Lima, were the two great pre-Inca Chimú coast metropolises.

Between Trujillo and Moche, close to the mountains, are the much older bulky Moon and Sun pyramids; deep under the high drifting sands, where even before the Christian era went Mochican irrigation ditches, are still found Perú's finest ceramics. There, Father Calancha claimed, was discovered a

gold sacerdote in mitre, woolen robe, ear-spreaders, and sur-
plice; there he saw moulded figures of bearded men with
forked tongues.

But Chimú consolidation of the north coast made Chan
Chan the new center, though quite possibly it stretched clear
to the distant Mochican hill city. Chan Chan's former importance in a great economic zone is still evident. In far sands
from Chimbote to Chicama are found signposts of the old
roads; near Paiján, from the sea to Hacienda Salamanca, a
great wall; near Pampuesto and Ascope, vast aqueduct remains; ruins of a dozen towns—Fachén, Rosario, Chiquitoy,
El Brujo; the castles of Virú, the fortress of Cartavio.

Chan Chan ruled supreme until Inca Yupanqui's 50,000
warriors subjugated the coast and the bulk of its unappeas-
able inhabitants were sent as colonists to other parts of the
empire. The Spaniards found the place nearly abandoned.

Yet Chan Chan's history embraces the entire Christian era,
perhaps longer. It is still the scene of vivid events.

I made two trips to Chan Chan, one in the company of a
specialist, Señor José Eulogio Garrido, director of Trujillo's
conservative daily *La Industria,* to learn about its ancient
splendors; the other, with Apra revolutionists, to learn about
its modern tragedy.

At first glance merely a chaos of crumbling walls, the more
one penetrates into the shattered tangle, the more clear becomes the definite plan of the place. It spreads out from the
bas-relief Palace of the Great Chimú in a series of quad-
rangles with high, thick, triple walls containing fortresses,
temples, community centers, sport fields, schools, dwellings.
Aqueducts brought water from the Moche River to large
cobblestone reservoirs; adobe steps lead down to the surface.
For miles along the beach a sea wall protected irrigated meadows, now overgrown with reeds and peat-like plants.

Picking our way through these forlorn bogs, we came to
the hut of a lone fisherman—a survivor in physique and cus-

toms of the old Mochicas. The *enea*, the local reed, he uses for almost everything: walls, roof, bed and his boat, the *caballito*, "little horse"—two bundles firmly tied, cut to leave a little kneeling place in the bow and tapering up to the high curving prow. With half of a thick Ecuadorian bamboo for a paddle, he ventures out in the stormiest weather many miles from shore and hundreds of miles along the coast; a journey to far Ecuador is nothing to him.

Fish, potatoes, oca root, and chicha form his diet. He markets fish only occasionally to supply petty needs, a few yards of cotton goods, leather for sandals, a new fish-hook. Independent, unresentful, contented, he lives peacefully among the ruins of his forefathers.

On my second trip various leaders of Apra (the people's party seeking political renovation) took me to numerous crosses over dozens of crumbling *huacas*. These crosses are white with buzzard droppings—for under them lie the half-buried bodies of over a thousand people lined up and shot after the failure of the 1932 Apra revolt which shook this whole region from Trujillo clear up into the Cajamarca Sierra.

Bloody sergeant-major of Arequipa, Sánchez Cerro, had overthrown Leguía. My friend, Apra leader Victor Raul Haya de la Torre, was then held in Lima's big brick penitentiary. Sánchez Cerro was scourging the Apristas with blood and fire everywhere. His repressive tactics precipitated the three-day Trujillo revolt.

We drove out the tree-shaded country road. At the edge of town the cobbles were broken by a strip of earth—the site of Aprista trenches now covered over. "In this trench are buried half a dozen defenders."

Beyond the stadium—"APRA" painted in big letters on its roof—another trench with many crosses. "At least thirty are buried here!"

We penetrated on into the tangle of Chan Chan. There people, taken out on trucks, had been lined up alongside of ancient holes, ditches, and reservoirs and shot into their graves. Weeks passed before the townsfolk dared sneak out to cover over the bones, by then picked clean by vultures, rodents and town curs which had repaired here by hundreds to snarl over the unburied remains. For months Chan Chan was a carnal house. Its pestiferous stench rose to high heaven for miles about, even to Trujillo.

Many bones are still uncovered. Beside a chauffeur's cap, tennis shoe and rusted buckle we found a skull, cleft open by a machete blow, hair still clinging to it.

After suppressing the revolt, Sánchez Cerro soldiers ran amuck, entered homes, dragged people out on merest suspicion, hustled them to Chan Chan. Hundreds of peasants from the revolting Casa Grande and Cartavio estates were killed. In Cajabamba, the prisoners were bayoneted in their cells.

One Indian, Gregorio Piscoya—whose cross the Apristas keep eternally fresh with flowers—charged like a mad bull against his executioners. He survived two volleys, a miracle that so unnerved his aggressors he managed to disarm one of them before dropping dead.

At the foot of one of the largest huacas Colonel Jiménez and three others, who also rebelled shortly after against Sánchez Cerro's tyranny, were similarly shot.

As we jumped from wall to wall, young Enrique Tello told me of those exciting days. In the first barracks attack, the three Apra leaders had been shot down. Confusion was spreading. Tello tightened up his belt, leapt into leadership, directed rebel forces during three days of furious combat.

After defeat, many who had participated took to the hills. Most were seized on the road and shot. Tello hid right in Trujillo, then one night walked out across country to the remote Sierra. For six months he lived utterly alone off wild game and the milk of a companion cow.

Trujillo still remains ardently Aprista. Frequent pilgrimages are made to martyr graves and to niche 44 of the cemetery to which Jiménez' corpse has been transferred—the word "Hero" is scratched crudely upon the cement. The Apristas control one of the leading dailies, *El Norte,* edited by Haya de la Torre's brother and by Antenor Orrego. Pérez Treviño edits a weekly magazine. Propaganda is active. Everywhere houses are daubed with signs; even high Andean precipices have been carved with gigantic letters: APRA. Desert plants, set out on high arid sands, spell APRA. On the Argentine beach I saw a lean dog branded on the side: APRA. Propaganda enthusiasm can go no further.

From the Mochicas to the Chimú kings, from Spaniards to Republicans, from dictatorship to Apra revolt, the course of Chan Chan's history unrolls its scroll. Chan Chan, older than New York, young when London was a mudhole, already ancient when Madrid was founded, now crumbles into the cemetery of bloody tyranny.

Once light-footed runners went forth over great highways carrying royal tidings; once the tall pikes of Chimú guards held the noble gates; now its forgotten streets are prowled by a few lone fisherfolk and guarded only by vultures perched on Christian crosses.

## 2

Accustomed to comfort, paved streets, electric lights, automobiles, you probably won't like Moche.

Moche merely watches occasional autos, on the way from the pest-hole port of Salaverry to Trujillo, bump over its narrow cobbled streets, dodging ruts and open drains. Trujillo, Perú's third largest city, has feeble electric lights, several rattle-trap hotels, a few hundred automobiles, but no paved streets either. It does have a great granite statue of liberty surmounted by a gilded figure carrying a gilded torch far too big for it, bastard art perpetrated by some forgotten German artist, who these later Hitler days probably could execute a more feeling symbol of liberty.

But Moche is just Moche—unpretentious, indifferent, only a few cubbyhole stores, at first glance merely the typical nondescript Indian-mestizo town ever encountered half way between more important points. Its multi-tinted flat-roofed buildings—dark adobe rooms with high ceilings and few windows—glow somnolently in the dusty haze and fierce sun of the dry coast under a sky of pale blue silk. Fields stretch here and there, adobe fences, banana trees, corn plots; cows moo; half-starved curs bark.

Life is simple in Moche. People don't read many books, most are busy about their crops, petty sales, families, children, love affairs. Moche, quite plain-spokenly, vegetates. For two thousand years it has vegetated, a longer time than any place in the United States has had a chance to vegetate.

But I like Moche. I like it if for no other reason than that my friend Garrido lives there. Garrido, slightly lame, slightly bald, is reclusive, not easy to cultivate; his silences are long and portentous. But he is gentle, considerate, his speech wise. Besides being a practical Trujillo newspaper editor, he is a poet whose soul is partly in the high sierras where he was born, partly here in Moche, where he wanders about in blue overalls. His beautiful Andean prose poems, mostly about his native Huancabamba, are vibrant with rich remembered emotions: every flower, every rock leaps into the eye with fresh sacred affection.

Though I visit the Andes out of curiosity, I will never love them. They are too brutal, too vast, too remote. They have lifted me to frightful agony of body and soul, to grand awe, but I always want to escape quickly. Unlike the harsh mountains of Mexico or California or New England's wooded hills, they do not pull me on and on with irresistible fresh delight. But from Garrido I learned at least to understand them better, to discover even in that rugged vastness, minor delicate notes, human life there, sad yet also rich and hopeful. But perhaps, since for so many centuries the Andean people have quite forgotten the inner meaning of the Andes and of themselves, even Garrido had to go to the lowlands, to Moche, to discover them. However much this bland little town on the

open starry-sky plain differs from the stark bitter Andes, both are places of ancient Indian soil wisdom.

Garrido lives near the railway station, in a vast colonial house, surrounded by ample verandas, fronted by majestic wind-whipped palms. Enormous rooms ramble endlessly. Endlessly the sea breeze whips through those long ancient corridors.

Garrido lives there. The old wooden floors, knotted, eaten by time, are scattered with Indian rugs; few chairs, but many divans, cozy corners with Indian sashes hanging down in colorful fringes, many book cases in odd places, lofty walls covered with paintings by Sabogal, Camilo Blas and others, Perú's best artists. The big roominess, at times gloomy, forlorn, nevertheless conduces to peaceful meditation. I have sat there alone, thoughts inevitably tinged with melancholy, of something lost in life, a peace never found. In such a place as this would I have found some unshakable architecture of philosophy and conduct? Since I left Trujillo and Moche I have wanted much to know the whole history of that house. I never asked Garrido. And we both dislike writing letters.

Twilight dips over the world. Garrido lights a little lamp and reads those deeply moving poems of the far Andes, so remote, yet so near.

Garrido was one of that rare group of which Haya de la Torre was a member—students who came out of Trujillo University about fifteen years ago, most of whom have formed the nucleus of the Apra movement. But Garrido edits a Conservative newspaper, and his old comrades consider him a renegade. But not a politician or a lover of the immediate battle, his real life is in Moche. There he is patiently seeking something, seeking it in the dim boyhood past in the Andes, in the most rooted part of all Peruvian life, that which has survived more centuries than the Christian era, which had its glories in the days of Greece—the Indian community, where men live in such social cooperation that individualism seems a sickly disease.

One afternoon, laden with gifts, we walked out through sandy adobe walled lanes, crossed over half a dozen irrigation ditches bridged by fallen trunks, to the home of Don Sergio, descendant of the ancient Mochicans who built the Sun and the Moon *huacas* and did other glorious things.

Formal greetings. The cloth was promptly spread on a table under the trees and a great terra cotta vat of chicha brought out and blessed by the sign of the cross.

A very definite ritual rules chicha drinking. The host dips the half gourd into the frothy brown beer, greets his *compadre* with whom he wishes to drink, drains nature's goblet at one long draft, refills it, hands it to the chosen one. He in turn repeats the process. As a guest of honor, I received more than my share of greetings.

Plates of little crabs cooked with seaweed in rich greasy brown sauce and mellow boiled potatoes—I ate crabs till my fingers dripped from the brown sauce. Plop them whole into the mouth, shell and all, crunch on them, suck out the edible portions, then spit out the bits of shell. Hands and mouth are wiped on a big communal rag in the center of the table.

Music came—a guitar, a box to hammer on—survival of the Mozambique tom-tom, to dance the *tondero*—a Spanish-negro-Indian survival. A "captain" first danced in pantomime with his silver-topped staff as partner. Then he picked the next pair.

> *De nuevo y acomodarse,*
> *dicen los mozos de cuerda . . .*

Though I had never tried the *tondero,* I was called on first to dance with the barefoot grandmother of the house, an agile though portly lady. She carried her skirt well lifted in her right hand between index-finger and thumb, her arm and body arched; in her left hand, at the height of her shoulder, a kerchief. The man keeps his left hand behind his back, body curved graciously, hips outward to the right, the weight ever on the left foot. In his right hand he waves a loose kerchief to the compass of the movement. Backward, forward, circle around, in a series of quick stamp-jumps. The guitar twangs ever swifter; the beats come faster with an occasional guttural *"Ora!"* With tiny stamping steps, bodies vibrating, the eyes are fixed on the partner's eyes, mouths smiling; the dance quivers to a panting climax. . . .

Slowly the day melted away. The fine gold of the sun sifted in under orchard trees, glinted on bare brown skin, on white skirts and white trousers, color tones growing softer, ever softer, quietly fading.

Late twilight; we came back through the lanes, now smelling of burning brush and cooked food and cows. In the hushed odorous peace of a rural Peruvian night, we reached

Garrido's roomy dark house and told over forgotten tales in the flickering shadows of a kerosene lamp on ancient walls.

### 3

The train slipped away from Trujillo's low tinted adobe houses, left cornfields and meadows behind, and entered the barren desert—to the left, shifting dunes, sparse low vegetation; to the right, the first Andean ridges, drifting sand high up on their flanks, like white wounds on writhing monsters; here and there humped sandstone outcroppings. Red heaps suggested pre-historic ruins. We passed through a pre-Spanish wall running straight as a die from coast to mountain—perhaps for defense, perhaps for royal herds.

Topping a little rise, we slid down into irrigated land, adobe fences, long reaches of sugar-cane, only here and there a balsa, scrub acacia, or false pepper tree.

Garrido and I were on our way to Chiclín, Chicama Valley sugar plantation.

The proprietor, Señor Rafael Larco Hoyo, a plump jovial man in white under a broad Panamá hat, was at the station in his car. Rolling down a tree-shaded avenue, we reached the grange, a large quadrangle, the hacienda house, administration and social service buildings. A pretty late-colonial-style church was under construction. Larco swept his arm around the quadrangle: "Some day I hope to make all this colonial."

Since Larco runs a great colonial enterprise, such architecture is fitting. But if his estate is colonial, it is also the most modern in Perú. He, his brothers and sons, all Princeton University graduates, have built up a pseudo-humanitarian enterprise for their three thousand employees—in contrast to Casa Grande (German) and Cartavio (Grace and Company). We visited a neat company cost-price restaurant, chemical laboratory, dispensary, drug-store, nursery, swimming pool, movie house, athletic field and stadium. In a malarial region, Larco boasts that Chiclín has the lowest mortality rate in all Perú. He has also transplanted here the Sierra Indian governing system. A Council of Elders, twelve employees, one of whom carries the Indian staff of authority, enjoy special privileges, such as free movie tickets, and inspect the various social services and home conditions. All complaints must be transmitted through them. Larco has no labor trouble.

Larco was not particularly keen on showing us the blocks upon blocks of workers' homes. These have cement floors as contrasted to the dirt floors in most company houses and are not inferior to the living quarters the same class would enjoy in the cities or in home villages, but they have only two windowless rooms for whole families and are without plumbing or sanitary conveniences.

Larco's effort, though partly for show, staged for visitors' consumption, is far in advance of what the Peruvian government does for its citizens in general, but its basic purpose is to avoid labor troubles and continue traditional low wage scales. It is a paternal system. Having given benefits to their workers, the Larcos also exercise more control over their habits and thought. Thus *El Norte,* the Aprista daily, cannot circulate in Chiclín. Any Aprista worker is immediately discharged. The Larcos fear and hate the movement; so would I if I owned the Chiclín or any other estate.

The Larcos, more than any one else in Perú, have fomented charities, worthy enterprises, learning, and especially archæology. They collected, built and sold to the government its one worth-while museum. At Chiclín they have an even richer collection of Mochican artifacts. Rafael Larco has made a comprehensive survey of all the Mochican sites from Chimbote north to Pacasmayo. He has carried on the only really intensive study of one culture ever made in Perú. He has traced off the designs from hundreds of ceramics. From these and other sources, he has rediscovered the materials, plans, and decorations of the ancient houses. Another set of plates covers ancient dress and equipment. Little by little he has reconstructed a vivid comprehensive picture of a civilization two thousand years old—its customs, its economics, its social system, its religion, and above all its art—in decorative sense surpassing anything ever produced on the two American continents. "They knew all the tricks of our modernistic painters," I remarked, delighted.

Don Rafael picked up a handle vase. "Here, for instance, is a drawing of an ancient subject bending the knee before the king, kissing his hand. Today, after two thousand years," he added with pride, "the Indians still salute their superiors in the same way." His remark, meant to justify present relationships between employer and employee, hinted that he felt himself quite as important as the ancient Mochican ruler.

At the luncheon table, perfectly appointed and served, the Larcos unanimously condemned the modern painting of Perú's greatest artist—José Sabogal.

"I simply can't see anything beautiful in it," remarked Don Rafael. "Why does he paint Indians and zambos and negroes? And if he must paint them, why does he pick such ugly types? Why does he paint them in such a futuristic style? Now here"—he produced a painting by an Arequipan artist—"is a man who knows the beautiful." It was a sweetly conventional Indian rural scene, without force or significance.

"Why," was my retort, "do you condemn the very modernity and symbolism in Sabogal which you praise so highly and find so beautiful in Mochican art two thousand years old?"

When Diego Rivera and Clemente Orozco turned their backs on the dead themes of Europe and peopled their canvases with Mexican life and character, the Larco class in that country, then and since, have vociferously denounced their work as ugly. Their and Sabogal's subject matter inevitably has attacked traditional snobbish white traditions. In Sabogal's work, though not directly propagandist like the Mexican school, are social implications little relished by an owner of broad acres.

Larco's attitude is typical of the mental and artistic confusion of the class which he represents and personally far surpasses, a class living between worlds, half feudal, half modern, almost aliens in their own country. Larco is strenuously delving into Mochican culture, which he obviously likes better than modern Peruvian culture; but he tries to make his hacienda colonial. And his house furnishings are a hodge-podge of the United States and Europe. Much of the furniture is American style, France contributes naughty pictures, Toledo in Spain adds numerous inlaid Moorish cabinets —the story of such contradictions could be carried on indefinitely.

Just because of the Larcos' eminent superiority, their mental portraits serve all the better to emphasize inescapable traits of the social group to which they belong.

4

Modern Trujillo, a simple little town, in even blocks (probably thus laid out by Pizarro in 1534 on a site selected the previous year by Estete) boasts only twenty-four thousand inhabitants. Its climate is far more agreeable than Lima's; the air comes fresh and salt from the sea across Argentine beach. The tinted flat-roofed buildings have a clean, washed appearance; the clear light dances with subtle modulations; everything seems transparent, slightly glowing, a vibrant but delicate play of shade and sun and soft tones so typical of many places in Mexico.

In spirit it is still colonial, though it is without particularly noteworthy temples. Carmen has four magnificent altars, and native art has expressed itself on a series of paintings of the life of the Virgin on Ayacuchan marble. In San Agustín from time to time the Indian talent of Moche has been drawn upon to paint new frescoes, mostly execrable in taste and inspiration. The plaza cathedral, the façade of which looks like a cheap stage background with false marble streaks, has one rich painting of a Lima Archbishop.

But however colonial in aspect, Trujillo has a population more mestizan, mulatto, and zambo than that of Lima. Here —it can be seen in the simian mixture on the streets—is Chimú and Inca Perú, thinned by scornful Spanish blood, blackened by African, yellowed by Chinese. It is the melting-pot of the coast, just as Arequipa is the melting-pot of coast and sierra, and Huanuco of sierra and jungle. And due to adjacent large estates, it has a floating farm labor population which gives it a jerky tempo distinct from strictly colonial centers such as Cajamarca in the Sierra.

Despite modern proletarian influences, Trujillo is slowly decaying. Why is it that this region, today after all these centuries, can only support a dying city a tenth the size of forgotten Chan Chan?

Strangled little by little by the surrounding haciendas, its economic roots have been completely cut. The coast haciendas, largely in foreign hands (petty republics within the Republic of Perú), have very little relation to Perú, only with the outside world. Products are brought in to Casa Grande from Germany in company bottoms; Grace also uses its own steamship lines; thus though the haciendas import cheaply—usually the workers are given some benefit of low prices—nearly all commerce with adjacent towns and cities is cut off. Whatever relations these haciendas do have with Perú are largely disastrous for the latter. The owners absolutely control, often appoint, the civil authorities. Casa Grande, with its own port, Chicama, pretty well controls customs officials and payments. The coast haciendas pay very

low taxes. They run everything to suit themselves, enjoy un-
limited privileges.

Thus the great Chicama Valley estates have well-nigh
ruined not only Trujillo but Chicama, Santiago de Cao,
Magdalena de Cao, Paiján and other centers. The hacienda
lands creep closer and closer to near-by communities, blocking their expansion, destroying business and trade. Loss of
local revenues prevents the maintenance of proper schools,
good streets, sanitation. Communications cannot be built.
The haciendas are interested only in transporting to the nearest port. Public roads along the coast or on into the Sierra,
even when built at great cost with little local support, must
traverse long distances to reach any populated center, thus
reducing their economic importance and the possibility of
proper upkeep.

During the past ten years, most of Trujillo's important
businesses have gone bankrupt; wholesale houses have with-
drawn their representatives; half the people are unemployed;
crime and violence feature its daily life. Trujillo, founded
before Lima and once the flourishing center of two large
valleys and an important outlet for much of the Sierra, has
been isolated, cut off. Perú's third largest city is withering
away. Its population steadily decreases. Today it has little
reason for being more than a fifth-rate town. It is going the
way of ancient Chan Chan.

The Larcos collect dead artifacts for their private museum;
Trujillo, bitter with bloody memories, provides skulls for
future ethnologists.

It is a landlords' cemetery.

# XIII

# HUANCAYO: MARKET OF THE ANDES

I

Its black and red soil stencilled by quivering light and shade through soft shifting clouds and the thin leaves of thousands of graceful gray-green eucalypti, Huancayo, provincial capital, sits 11,000 feet above the sea at the base of the sere Andean mountains in the verdant arm of the Mantaro River. This river, an Amazón tributary already impressive at this height, plunges through rocky precipices, a gigantic rift zigzagging from a distant lofty lake near Cerro de Pasco, thence south to historic Jauja—anciently Hatun Xauxa—to Huancayo and Huanta; then northeast, it dashes down into the Green Hell to join the mighty Apurimac, still nearly a thousand miles from the Amazón. Everywhere, save where the mountain walls occasionally widen to green meadows, the Mantaro is bordered by the high bleak Cordillera, painted and terraced by nature into a thousand changing tints and fantastic formations, painted and terraced by man into red and green gardens and patchwork fields.

Huancayo, with progressive San Gerónimo—an old-time stage-change—lies on the eastern side of the river; further south are Sapallanga amid Inca ruins, the red hill-perched Pucará, scene of a bloody massacre during the War of the Pacific, and beautiful Huayucachi. On the western bank are the hamlets of Chupaca, Sicaya, Ahuac, picturesque Chongos Bajo, Chongos Alto, and in the distance, Colca. All are typical Indian towns.

Every road, during the week-end, leads to the Huancayo

market. Every road is a ribbon of festive Indians, a ribbon that curls, loops and knots with agitated bright-colored humanity. Every lane, track, byway and path is flocked by Indians—the rustle of their sandals or bare feet over the stones all night long and all day long is like a wind scuffling autumn leaves eternally.

They come running with balls of llama wool carded from a swinging distaff, fingers busy as they go. They come trotting down the ancient streets, bowed under the weight of products of the fields, pottery, handicrafts. Somewhere in the top of their burdens, slung hammock-wise in the multicolored *quipe* shoulder-capes, poke the tousled heads of their babies, jolted at each step, but eyes open wonderingly to the sky, sun or rain. The Indians come with their burros, mules, llamas, bearing wares to the plaza to sell.

With their hundred-pound loads, troops of tinkling llamas come down from the crags, sometimes as many as half a thousand, spongy hoof and pointed talon clinging to steep trails and ice. The llama's stomach, like the camel's, stores up water for months; its wool is thick and shaggy; the Andean drouth, the bitter Andean cold, hold no terrors for this docile beast. Part and parcel of the old life, not only do they carry burdens but they provide artistic motifs for blankets, pottery and jewelry.

The market. What an assortment! Brilliant-hued rugs, maize, carved fruits, pigs, ponchos, lariats, woven belts and sashes, chop-suey blankets, alfalfa, barley, potatoes, hides, silverware, vicuña and *huanaco* furs, dolls, knitted betasselled llamas, pottery, embroidered sleeve-protectors, shoes, sandals, fur slippers, baskets—everything they can grow or make to barter.

In the *Hampi-Katu*, market of medicinal herbs, are found linseed, copal, the sleep-producing *tara*, dried rose-leaves, melon seeds, *mani* for the heart, llama grease, *verdolaga* for dysentery, vanilla beans as an aphrodisiac, vanilla leaves to remove freckles, powdered *chirimoya* leaves to kill lice, alfalfa flowers for cough syrup, cotton roots to boil as a diuretic, cat nails for the verruga; *malesherbia* carnation for asthma, tuna cactus leaves to extract juice for erysipelas and

against hydrophobia—a thousand and one remedies, along with amulets—bits of condor, fox, llama, serpents, vicuña, bear, wild-cat, deer—magic rings, iron crosses, and other hocus-pocus rubbish. "What will you have? . . . Love powders? . . . This good-luck flower? . . . This magic earth for prosperous business? Or this clay sheep to protect your flocks and make them multiply? . . . This little bull?"

A motley crowd swirls. Each Sunday, a giant hand scatters heaps of human confetti over main street and adjacent plazas

—so bright and fluttering are men, women, animals and bundles milling about, a blaze of violently contrasted colors. Huancayo is the market of the Andes.

In a manner all comfortable, but incomprehensible to a Nordic, the Huancayans perch over their wares, just like birds ready for flight, yet with a solid earth-rooted sureness, too. They gossip, toss quick jests, bargain to the last centavo. Now and then a younger woman, under the intent scrutiny of male eyes, tugs and pats her scarlet velvet shawl, sometimes also a covert smile may lead to racy repartee.

Underneath her velvet shawl is another one—green; beneath that a third, intensely purple. The women's heads seem like black chicks coming out of broken painted Easter eggshells. Below a skirt of yellow flannel, caught up coquettishly at the brilliant sash, another skirt of pale mauve; beneath that, a dozen others, pooched out in a wide circle, like a Menina of Velázquez, about bare ankles—the number and quality of the skirts, more than anything else, denote social status. The women swing through the streets like painted human bells that never give forth their mellow music save in rhythm and line.

Huancayo is the market of the Andes—one of those curiously dual places often encountered at the end of railroad lines anywhere from Mexico south to Patagonia, where two civilizations meet and flow into each other, sometimes clashing, sometimes harmoniously reconciled. In one sense, Huancayo is a European outpost; in another, the center of a vast Indian region. It is a trading post, where cunning citified merchants of the machine world match wits against an old culture. Also, it is a flourishing center of ancient Incan life, indifferent to outside intrusion—at least on Sunday, market day.

During the week it is just a typical colonial town with a typical colonial administration. Though Indians, in number and culture, dominate the region, Huancayo's Spanish plaza and adjacent streets house the prosaic bureaucrats who do Lima's bidding.

To the fashionable casino resort the cholo "aristocracy"— in reality a petty trading and official bourgeoisie, with a sprinkling of better-class ranchers, all of whom vehemently deny being cholo. This group imitates Americans, Britishers and Lima Creoles; they foregather about the radio, over billiard tables, or for afternoon tea to play bridge with curious rules; they stage exhibits for local or visiting artists, most of whom in this remote spot high in the Andes puerilely imitate their French cousins, oblivious to the perennial exhibition of art which springs full-bodied from the life and toil of the mass of the people—an art quite unsensed by the casino socialities ruled by vanity of local importance, snobbery and nostril disgust for the market folk.

2

Without the Indians and their market Huancayo would be quite meaningless, for it has no other essential resources. Hence, though Huancayo's colonial aspect dominates every day except Sunday, it is the Indian, here more independent, easy-going and acustomed to intercourse, who really moulds the character of the place. Each week Huancayo drowses uneventfully waiting only for Sunday.

After market, the Indian takes his rounds of *pisco* or chicha, then huddles, family, chickens and bundles, before the favorite saint. He packs his beasts of burden and carefully tucks away his week's supply of coca leaves, and sets out for his village, sometimes close, sometimes an all-night jaunt or longer. But he goes jovially, genially greeting each fellow traveler, content with the day's sociability, belly warm from the drinks, soul uplifted by spiritual communion.

However much the Huancayan natives are puzzled by the impinging outer world, however much they dread government officials and unfathomable legal papers and courts, which ever divest them of worldly goods and often freedom, they are essentially free men and feel it; they are vital to Huancayo and know it. The famed sullen Indian taciturnity does not exist around Huancayo. His niche in the scheme of things here is too definitely carved out; he goes about his business with pride and ample assurance.

This region is less dominated by large haciendas than are some valleys. Beyond the large estates, which monopolize the

fertile bottom-lands, the Indian communal villages stretch from lower rolling country on into the mountain ravines. Every possible inch of soil is cultivated; everywhere the people are busy with handicrafts; never a step is taken anywhere without the *putchka* of wool, brown hands eternally preparing threads for weaving.

However dominated by priest, however exploited by unworthy officials, however menaced by encroaching landlords, these indigenous communities, solidly rooted in centuries of experience, have achieved an economic security and happiness denied many more civilized groups. If Huancayo seems colonial, merely a convenient market place, in surrounding villages the Indians completely dominate the scene.

True, local governments are dual; but the central officials elected or appointed in accordance with Conquest formulæ to enforce the federal laws and collect the taxes are little more than diplomatic agents, do not govern directly. They express their desires to the Council of Elders, the real authorities. Sometimes friction results; soldiers may be sent in. But the Elders invariably win out. After a false show of authority, the offending official is ultimately removed: On a small scale, the story of Ambassador Sumner Welles in Cuba.

### 3

Legend has Huancayo founded by one of the later Incas, perhaps the great Huayna Cápac. The word "Huancayo," meaning "My Stone," is said to have originated from a large rock or *huanca*—made use of by the reigning Inca on his frequent trips along the great pre-Spanish highway from Quito to Cuzco. There he rested his royal bones and made his required obeisance to the Sacred Sun. Excellent soil and pasturage caused the place to grow up gradually and naturally.

Today the principal street, the Calle Real, is a portion of the main Incan north and south highway, begun supposedly by Emperor Maita Cápac, continued by Cápac Yupanqui, and finished by Huayna Cápac. Starting from Cuzco the mighty road passed to Villaconga, traversed the rivers Apurimac, Pachachaca and Villca by magnificent suspension bridges, and along the Mantaro, via Huamanga and Huanta, reached Picoy and the bleak Acostambo highlands. Descending from the Cordillera through the long Pucará slope it stretched on to Huancayo. Northwards it passed to Cajamarca, the second imperial city. From there to Quito, one road kept on through the lofty mountains, another lay along the desert coast via Tumbes—in all a stupendous undertaking through a rugged region even today well-nigh impassable.

Once along what is now the main street of Huancayo passed in triumphal procession Incas Pachacutec, Cápac Yupanqui and Huayna Cápac in magnificent ostentation of golden litters, borne by gaudily attired attendants, surrounded by the curacas and officers of state, tunics and headdresses decorated with waving rich-colored plumes. White sandals indicated their superiority over the common herd. Hordes of warriors, each clad in the customary habit of his native district—the conquered Chachapoyas, the Ecuadorian Canarís, the Huilcas, Pocras in totemic puma skins, the Chancas, the indomitable Cajamarcans, the formidable Huancas, woolen-shirted, helmeted with vicuña skin caps—all these guarded the emperor's person. Royal trumpeters heralded the approach, servitors swept the way, hundreds of Vestals, "Daughters of the Sun," scattered flowers.

Along this highway in 1533 marched Francisco Pizarro, armour clanking, on his way to besiege Cuzco. His brother Hernando traversed it in search of the ransom gold demanded of Atahualpa. Bitter Almagro passed here several times to and from Cuzco, both during the Conquest and during subsequent battles with Pizarro.

By 1565 Felipe de Segovia Breceño de Balderbano started operating the La Mejorada hacienda, which still exists within six miles of the city. In 1570 Viceroy Toledo, during his provincial readjustment, mentioned "Guancayo" as having 56 taxable people, i.e., about 280 persons, and paying a yearly tribute of 247 pesos and 4 tomines. But not until the eighteenth century did Huancayo obtain the title of "town" with mixed Spanish, Cholo and Indian population. In neighboring Sicaya, Fray José de Castilla's large painting, dated 1736, portrays the entire Mantaro Valley, each community branded with the number of cattle and anunal tribute. Huancayo, Pampas, Jauja and Sicaya then yielded 9,000 Castilian cattle and 1,600 pesos yearly. By 1879 it became necessary to build a new cathedral to replace the old Mother Church by that time inconveniently located almost outside of town.

Thus Huancayo grew up to its present importance gradually as a convenient Spanish sierra outpost, in the rich Mantaro region, ere long surpassed previously more important places. Now it complements Lima on the one hand, the indigenous Andes on the other; it still remains important as a contact center, a meeting ground for two civilizations.

4

Perhaps as an outpost of two civilizations, sensitive to the currents of both cultures, Huancayo has ever enjoyed a greater tradition of liberty, has ever been ready to embrace new causes. Long before the rest of Perú was stirring during the independence movement, Huancayo hastened to rename its central square, Plaza Constitución—in honor of the new 1812 Spanish Magna Charta of Cádiz. Soon the ancient imperial route again echoed to marching armies.

Here Francisco Hernández Girón led the earlier army of independence to defeat in nearby Pucará and suffered execution in Lima. Later liberators Bolívar, Sucre, and Alvarez de Arenales traversed the highway with their legionaries.

Alvarez de Arenales, San Martín's Commander-in-Chief, using friendly Huancayo as a base against Royalist forces from Tarma, won a decisive victory near Jauja. Jubilant, the Huancayans nailed up an independence tablet that still exists in tarnished state on the fourth block of the Calle Real. The great San Martín knew and used the old Inca road; and Castilla, liberator of slaves, marched over it many times.

As a result of Huancayo's subsequent participation in various libertarian struggles, from 1839 to 1855, and various times from 1856-65, it became the capital of the Republic.

There, as if further to affirm its tradition of liberty, General Ramón Castilla, December 3, 1855, read his famous "Proclamation of the Abolition of Slavery." Making Huancayo his base, vigorously and successfully he prosecuted his campaign to liberate the slaves. Huancayo has shirked no duties. Its sharply dual character has made it passionate to defend causes. As the market place of the Andes, all currents flow through it.

Though not much of a town until the end of colonial rule, it continues to affirm its leading position over the central part of the Sierra. It remains the colliding place of civilizations. Beneath its gay market scene is a secret and continuous struggle.

# XIV

## HUANUCO: THREE PEAKS

### I

Huánuco, a jumping-off place on the eastern declivity of the Cordillera, does not quite belong to the Andes or to the jungles. It breathes the warm humid air of the almost unex-

plored Amazón forests, which rots away bodies, will, material objects. And it looks up to the lofty snow-clad crest—like a man trying to dig his toes into a precipice. Below it stretch the tangled reaches of the Huallaga River, twisting off into the putrid mystery of the Green Hell. Above it rise the bleak sky-jutting heights. The terrific panorama makes man pinioned there on the ledge of nowhere seem unusually insignificant.

As a matter of fact, its even climate, reasonable altitude, well-watered lands, held communally, relative freedom from *gamonalismo*, all permit languorous resignation, humbleness, and love of beauty remote from tragedy. There babies are cured of ailments by caressing them with the petals of roses, carnations, jasmines, and violets. There sweet passion is so strong that women carefully destroy the combings of their hair, for one strand in the hands of a pretender would make them powerless to resist. More often is love sought. Carmen Suárez, a young and pretty girl, visited aged witch-doctor Casiano Avila, down a side street, to have him help her get a husband. Casiano told her to bring him cards, candles, and pieces of money from the home of a happy married couple. One night in a solitary place, with these objects and mysterious aromatic herbs and flowers, Casiano started his incantations in an atmosphere of burning incense. He ground up the herbs and tossed them into a steaming bath. Disrobing the girl, he bathed her. In the corners of the cloth with which he dried her body he tied four of the coins and threw it into a busy street. She was assured on paying the witch-doctor's fee, that the man who found the coins would become her husband.

The modern Huanucan—and an almost blond cholo predominates—perhaps do not worship the three lofty peaks Marabamba, Rondos, and Paucarbamba that lord it over the town, but the Indians do. Secret shrines in the rocky crevices, kept bright with flowers, are decorated with bones, crosses and queer amulets; death awaits any profane outsider—the mountain spirit, who can either injure or befriend travelers, must ever be propitiated.

The three peaks have cast an abiding spell over the place, a spell much more embracing than that of the near jungle.

The Indians have personified these great outposts, have woven their history and deeds into the local legends—tales similar to that retold so artfully by López Albújar in his *Andean Stories*.

Each of the three Father Hills has a distinct personality.

Marabamba—perfectly geometrical, a triangular sail set in the rough sea of ridges and valleys—is both sad and beautiful; its granite flanks carry not a spear of grass, not a single human hut. No smoke spirals up from those sheer slopes; no animals cross its terrible precipices. It is doomed never to feel the grip of the plow, or be cooled by irrigation, or give birth to life—no germinating seeds can send their roots into its barren rocks.

During the hot hours, heat waves vibrate from its bare surfaces; light strikes to and fro glaringly, like a metallic echo. A fantastic flame sweeps over it. But mostly it is gray, eternally gray, as if dead and abandoned. And at night, under the moon, its barrenness looms large, portentous—an overwhelmingly melancholy spectacle.

Perhaps within those gray volcanic veins are rich deposits such as those which man converts into rails, money, jewelry, cannon, but at present it is merely one of those grandiose creations of nature to baffle and obstruct man, to test his ingenuity.

Rondos, in contrast to Marabamba's smooth majesty, is all disorder, tumult, confusion—the chaos of blind brutal force hating symmetry. Poised there in furious upheaval, it is an eternally crested wave just breaking into wild spray, but frozen in the fury of its lifted crest, doomed never to burst upon the long jungle beach below. Rondos, so fantastically shaped, seems quite unreal—like those *papier-mâché* mountains decorating toy trains, or the backdrops on the Jesus-birth scenes of homemade altars at Christmas time.

But through its sinuous folds, streams flow and fork, leap among rocky precipices with monotonous crystalline song—

like white blood gushing from the tatters of a beggar. During tempests these waters dash down torrentially, sweeping everything before them, carrying great waves of mud and huge battering boulders, with galloping uproar, into the valley.

On its slopes, among the cascades, can be seen green and gold patches of potatoes and wheat, fruit trees, cornfields, octopus-like cactus. Sheep drift slowly in and out of the rocks, the lagging herders weaving busily from arm-draped yarn; spotted cattle move cautiously or stand patiently; goats perch on the crags. Dotting the slopes everywhere are white houses with red tiled roofs, dazzlingly bright by day. At twilight, smoke curls up. At night, home-fires shine across the lonely valley—lights on an inky sea. . . . Even a church —old, tilted, rotting away—neglected by the incredulous Indians, who return to the bosom of their more ancient beliefs; soon it will fall apart.

Paucarbamba, differing from both the other two peaks, is harsh, aggressive, proud; sharp pinnacles hurl defiance at the very sky. It is like some wild animal ready to pounce upon its prey. Only here and there are patches of green; only an occasional white leaping stream flings itself into the broad valley. It is a martial mountain.

Marabamba is a seated giant; Rondos a giant lying down arms crossed; Paucarbamba, a giant standing erect, buckled and girted, ready for the fray.

Eternally these three peaks stand guard over Huánuco. They capture the snows and remake them into turbans, ruffs, collars. They stop the fury of the high sky tempests and draw to their towering crests the beating thunder and dagger-like lightning that might otherwise shatter the town.

But they are also a menace. Within them are locked tumultuous forces seeking new equilibrium, able to find it only in violent outburst. At times their entrails rumble as if trying to mutter some terrible prophecy for mankind. No one knows when they will burst asunder, vomiting fire and lava. For they seem to be moving. Such mountains are like caravans resting on the journey; some day they will continue their march, will face new battles. . . .

The sun went down majestically behind Rondos' crest. Seated on the rocks of Paucarbamba, the local poet, an old Pilco Indian, exclaimed: "Ah, the mountain is angry; he is hungry. He wants sheep, coca, bread, food. He eats like a man; he is as sweet-toothed as an infant. He wants food and sweets. When he has not eaten for a long time, when men grow careless and do not carry food and offerings to his altars, he grows angry. When he is given food, he is happy."

"But, Pilco, do the mountains really eat like men?"

"Ay, yes, *Tata*," was his reply. "They not only eat, they speak; they are gods. During the day they are silent, thinking, murmuring, or sleeping. But at night they move. That is hard on a man—to see a mountain march. But at night they march. On cloudy nights they go further, eat more, speak more."

Indeed, at night, outlines less sharp-edged, those mountains, the clouds slipping by, do seem to move. Slowly, surely they gather headway. The more one gazes the more the illusion is confirmed; they march ponderously forward— caravans silently advancing.

2

Stone, White Hair, Bearer of Flowers were three warriors from three distant kingdoms. Bearer of Flowers came from the jungle; White Hair from the sea; Stone from the crags. Bearer of Flowers was the youngest; Stone the strongest; White Hair the oldest and wisest.

They fell in love with the same woman, Cori Huayta, Golden Flower, daughter of Rumi, the powerful Curaca of the Pilca tribe.

After engendering some fifty children, all males, Pilco Rumi finally begot a girl—his one and only daughter. So fresh, so exuberant and beautiful did she become, he gave her the poetic name, Golden Flower, and placed in her all his love, all his pride.

The jewel of the realm, she was soon desired by every man and wanted by the priests for sacrifice. When she went forth in her litter to gather flowers and fruits for the Raymi festival, people looked out from their doors, men stopped in their tracks and thereafter for many days remained pensive and troubled.

Her three most persistent suitors were Stone, of the Pasco tribe, White Hair of the Huayalas; Bearer of Flowers of the Nataguas—the three most warlike peoples. Each spring equinox each of the three warriors told Pilco Rumi he wished to marry Cori Huayta. But confident in his power and the good auguries of his soothsayers, the Curaca scorned them. He believed her far too good for any living man, though he knew very well he must marry her to some one when she reached the age of eighteen—that was the unbreakable law; or, since chastity—the ancients rated fecundity as the highest good—meant sacrifice to Pachacámac, God of Creation, she must be given as a holy bride in death, a living offering to the gods. Though this seemed almost preferable to giving her to a man, the thought made him shudder.

Pilco Rumi, far from pleased with these regulations, wanted his lovely daughter longer for himself. Surely, she, the most beautiful of all creatures, was rightfully above the law. The more he thought of this, he determined to follow his own whim. He swore in the holy of holy temples she would be given to no man; none was worthy of her; nor should she be sacrificed. First, he would kill her with his own hand.

As Curaca he had to celebrate the annual marriages in the public plaza. On the eve of the ceremony when his daughter had reached the compulsory age, he called in the greatest sacerdote, Racucunca, He-of-the-Thick-Neck, and the great sorcerer Karu-Ricag, to ask them how the law might be evaded.

Karu-Ricag replied: "The wisdom of a Curaca resides in compliance with the law. He who complies best is the wisest father of his subjects."

Racucunca said: "There are only two courses: either sacrifice your daughter or deliver her to the Virgin cult of your Father, the Sun."

Pilco Rumi objected strenuously: "Golden Flower, eighteen tomorrow, has already passed the age at which a girl may enter the service of the Sun."

"For our Father," replied the priest, "all Virgins are equal; they merely must be young. And as there is no man in your whole kingdom worthy of her—"

But the soothsayer said: "A wise and valiant young man could make Cori Huayta happy."

The sacerdote, concealing his own scheming hopes, said, "Tomorrow at the hour of sacrifices, I will consult the entrails of a llama."

The Curaca remained brooding, dejected, resentful.

### 3

The fatal day! Flags whipped in the breeze on the main square. Warriors, crested with tropic feathers, performed manœuvres with gleaming pikes, shot arrows, flourished studded clubs, whirled swords. The minstrels, the *yaravicus,* stationed in three angles of the plaza, intoned their most tender love-songs to the strident sound of struck copper.

The youths paraded happily. About the great sacrificial stone destined for those not to wed man walked the future brides, tunics flowing white, jade-gold necklaces about their young throats, their temples crowned with flowers. They walked slowly, blushingly, hands clasped. Cori Huayta, still ignorant of her fate, waited the nuptial hour.

Pilco Rumi stood like a tower on the eastern side of the plaza, arms crossed, lifted nostrils dilated, mouth contracted in a stiff line, brow furrowed by a dark plan. The sun struck his face like an interrogation mark.

To himself he prayed a half-blasphemous prayer:

"Can men do more than Pachacámac? Will you, Father Sun, not strike blind him whose eyes seek to possess Cori Huayta's charms? I want her to be the joy of my old age, that in the morning when You come forth flooding your golden fructifying rays over my humble temple, Cori Huayta shall be the first to bathe in them, but that no man look upon her and desire her. Cori Huayta, O Lord, is worthy of you. Free her from the lust of men."

Calmed by this invocation, Pilco Rumi turned his contemptuous gaze full upon the clamoring multitude.

Priest Racucunca appeared. With a huge concave mirror of burnished gold he concentrated the sun's rays upon the white heap of cotton for the sacrificial fire. He lifted up his fist like a threat, spat into the air, and from his mouth came forth, like a poisoned arrow:

"Cori Huayta shall not be yours, traitor. I, as did Karu Ricag, surmised your secret thought. Before you violate the sacred laws, I myself shall kill Cori Huayta."

The multitude grew quiet. The songs ceased. The copper instruments fell dead. The dances stopped. The girls trembled.

Suddenly the concave mirror slipped out of the sacerdote's hands, fell clanging.

A warning! Ill tidings! The crowd broke into a hoarse roar. Cori Huayta's heart tightened with fear.

The priest swept his arm in a vast circle: "Enemies! Enemies! They come for our virgins. Where is Pilco Rumi? Defend us, Pilco Rumi. Pachacámac defend us."

4

Three enormous dust columns rose up on the horizon, touched the sky, advanced, swept forward, ever closer. . . .

The invaders were warlike Stone, White Hair and Bearer of Flowers. They had come on the day of marriages to seize Cori Huayta away from her father, from all young rivals, from the priests, from each other. They had come from the sea, the jungle, the crags, upon the city not of the sea, or the jungle, or the crags.

Previously they had come supplicating; now they came followed by their entire armies. For many days they had hewed their way through forests, traversing vast plains, crossing abysses, defying storms, defying heat and cold. All three arrived at the identical moment, determined not to cede anything to anybody, determined each to have Cori Huayta.

White Hair, during the march had meditated: "My age means wisdom. Wisdom beautifies the countenance. Wisdom knows how to triumph over youth in love."

And Stone: "Force impresses and attracts the weak. And woman is weak and loves strength."

And Bearer of Flowers: "Youth can do everything; it can accomplish what wisdom and strength can never achieve."

Pilco Rumi, when he saw the smoke and dust columns rising up on three sides, knew he could never repulse this simultaneous invasion.

In supreme desperation, he invoked Pachacámac anew. "Father Sun, I speak for the last time. Embrace the city, flood the valley, or kill Cori Huayta before I must commit the horrible deed myself."

Pachacámac, there above the Rainbow, responded. He hurled a mountain of snow at the feet of Bearer of Flowers, already entering the city. The snow melted into a roaring river. Bearer of Flowers was stopped.

Pachacámac hurled another snow mountain in front of

White Hair with similar result. He heaved Stone back with a terrible blast. Then, with a single glance, he converted the three warriors into three gigantesque mountains—the same ones that now guard Huánuco.

Pachacámac then looked down upon Cori Huayta, the cause of all this uproar. Frightened, she had run to her father for protection. Lovingly Pachacámac looked at her and said softly: "*Huáñucuy*—Die!" Cori Huayta expired in her father's arms.

In the face of these calamities, the people fled from the place, and at the foot of the three new mountains founded the city of Huáñucuy—"Die!" in memory of the awful voice of Pachacámac.

Now each year eagerly they wait the spring, when for a brief time Pilco Rumi's beautiful daughter again becomes the Golden Flower of the Valley. Then yellow blooms spread a quilt of flame over the Huánuco meadows and up the slopes of the silent peaks.

5

And so it is that Huánuco, midway up the Andes, belongs neither to coast plain, nor to back jungles, nor to the Sierra. It is itself. But at its gates, as though menaced by all of Perú, stand the symbols of sea, jungle and crag—the three crested mountains. All wish to descend upon Huánuco and claim it; but Pachacámac ages ago willed that it should remain apart, that it should remain Huánuco. White Foam from the sea, Stone from the crags, Poisoned Flowers from the jungle— not all of these could wrest away Huánuco's eternal spring.

For this, for Huánuco, Cori Huayta died and is eternally resurrected.

# XV

# AYACUCHO: CORNER OF DEATH

I

HEED the solemn Runa-Simi oracle: "The sacred fossilized bones were changed by great Mother Nature into precious azure-green or lapis-lazuli stones." Various early Spanish chroniclers mention the common Quechua legend that men, on dying, were converted into bright blue stones. These were then carved with the lineaments of the deceased, or into totemic animals, and worshipped as penates—*conopas*—in the homes of the descendants.

A quaint satisfying symbolism of universal unity, not only poetically and philosophically embodying all human hopes for immortality, but striking away the frail barriers between animate and inanimate, investing all tangibility with common vital source. The first men were made from stones in an ancient cave by Creator-God Viracocha, and God Thunapa reconverted men into stones when wroth at their orgiastic dancing; and God Kuntun when they neglected to pay reverence to the mountain spirit. Travelers on their way in the valley beyond Cuzco may still see at Callacoya the petrified form of a princess changed to stone in vengeance for her father's murder of her sweetheart.

Everywhere throughout the New World, turquoise, of all gems the most cerulean, symbolizing eternal mystery, the infinite, was anciently associated with the death-immortality paradox, *viz.*, the magnificent Aztec turquoise death masks —the deceased given the face of the sky itself.

Two turquoises are encountered: mineral and osseous. Subjected to certain geological conditions over long periods,

222

bones in contact with copper oxide, cinnabar, cardinal stone, lapis lazuli, or other minerals, petrify into turquoise—the Incan philosophy had basis in nature's recondite processes. The Quechua priests may even have imitated and hastened the transformation.

2

One balmy afternoon in Ayacucho—"Corner of Death"—an ancient city nine thousand feet up in the Andes, I bridged the mighty gulf between the modern materialistic world and a mysterious lost civilization. As one might cross one of those hair-raising fibre bridges the Quechuas built across awful chasms, I stepped from prosaic today into a vanished kingdom with far fantastic boundaries and a weird æsthetic and metaphysical flora. Because for me that realm, however ancient, was so utterly new, evolved from obscure alien life-ways and perfected unto itself, my customary logical processes failed before my lightning-like glimpses into that mysterious beauty and incomprehensible life-truth.

Perhaps, except for set problems, abstract thought is unrealizable. Environment, man's senses and thought—petty instruments by which he manœuvres through his particular corner of the still unintelligible universe—so dovetail with his geographical, economic and political determinants that a quick glimpse at another culture is disconcerting. Mutual interpretation is really an arduous task. One must slough off customary sensatory and mental habits, must get new eyes and new brain-grooves. The investigator must become a child learning humbly and wind his way slowly up through the sinuosities of a people's whole development; his very thought must grow up anew with theirs. Only then does an alien culture become inescapably logical; fragmentary, it appears ridiculous—a piece of jig-saw puzzle in the wrong box.

Really my experience that afternoon was much simpler than all this sounds. I merely walked down Arequipa Street,

223

past the broad Spanish Plaza de Armas, along the side of the sixteenth-century cathedral and university, its enormous stones rifled from ancient Pocra temples, down over the brow of the hill, across grass-grown cobbles and big hand-hewn flaggings to the tiled adobe house of Señor Manuel Benedicto Flores.

An assemblage of corrals and outhouses sloped to the undergrowth of the busy little Totorilla River, where Indian women bathe and wash clothes and think of babies and family.

Seated on Don Manuel's back piazza of time-worn brick balustrade, we unlocked the golden door of the past.

Don Manuel, a country gentleman, a scholar and an archæologist, unknown and unheralded in and about his native Ayacucho, has toiled at his hobby for thirty long years, content to live alone in the unknown realm he has discovered, undisputed monarch over its secrets.

He talked to me of the turquoise death-immortality cult, and gave me such astonishing tidings that my emotions were soon similar, I imagine, to those of Conquistador Miguel de Estete when he stood before the coral and turquoise door of the inner shrine of the great Pachacamac temple—observant ere wrenching it open—save that out of the entrails of the mystery I sought not gold of touch or emeralds that glitter.

Dan Manuel brought forth a series of saucers showing each step in the transformation of human bones into turquoise—not by nature, but by Inca priests. Fantastic!

"Three centuries ago," Don Manuel told me, "Ocros, later others, found human bones in subterranean ovens—*thulpas* —invariably described as crematories. Actually they were used to convert bones into turquoise."

The theory of a madman? But before my eyes were the saucers. In the two end dishes it was difficult to tell whether the fragments were bones or blue stone; in the very last, only by chipping could the osseous formation be detected.

Don Manuel spread out a chart. "Here is a diagram of large clay-buried tubular ovens I found right here in Ayacucho. These tubes, leading to the surface, were for the escape of gases; these others sucked in air to continue oxidation. In those ovens—the process was incomplete—I found all the bones and stones in these saucers."

He showed me a collection of minerals. "Here is *para*, a vermilion stone and cinnabar, both found in Huancavelica; and *binços*, a blue powder; *llacsa*, copper oxide; *huinzo*, lapis lazuli. *Carvamuqui* provided yellow. Most of these ores old chronicler Pablo Joseph de Arriaga mentions as used by the Incas."

"And this?" I pointed to three rectangular spaces on his chart.

"Stone slabs. The charred skulls were placed on one slab, the torso bones on this one, arm and leg bones here. Over them, still piping hot, were poured fermented juices, part of the hardening process, possibly some sort of chicha, made from the sapote tree—like that one towards the river —or from *aut*, or *molle*, the false pepper. The bones were then reburied to complete the process."

"And so," I exclaimed, "if you are right men were really turned into blue stones! But how was it the Spaniards never discovered this?"

"If the Inca priests hid this secret from their own people, were they likely to disclose it to the hated conqueror?"

I visualized the ancient scene: Incan sacerdotes in beautiful, embroidered robes, gold and silver adornments, feather plaques, ages ago in dim stone-carved rooms filled with dream-invoking coca incense; there, anointing dead human bodies, doubling them into terra cotta vats, and burying them in solemn procession in ancient patios, perhaps under the night sky, the Southern Cross blazing overhead, to carry out a long-forgotten alchemy in the dawn of science unborn —all the hocus-pocus of all the priestly tribe of all times and places. Yet in this case the whole rigmarole was over and beyond mere ritualistic taumaturgy.

Unlike the Germans, the Incas never divorced metaphysics from poetry; unlike Protestantism, they never divorced theology and rite from poetry. Their shin-digs involved an allegory that embraced the whole creation process, life, death, the concatenation of animate and inanimate force. We moderns preserve our ancestors in portraits and photographs, enlargements properly tinted from old snaps. The Incas, from the very bones of their ancestors, carved the lineaments of the dead, carved out the totemic animals from which the family, the *ayullu*, the tribe, was descended, instinctive endorsement of modern evolution theories. And they wore green turquoise around their necks, a sentimentalism for us a bit macabre, but dignifying the mysterious eternal procreation process.

### 3

Ayacucho's former name, Huamanga (abolished by Liberator Simon Bolívar's decree of 1825), meant "Hill of Condors," a bird allied to the buzzard. The history of Huamanga-Ayacucho is bloody. Death is woven deeply into its consciousness.

At first glance, Ayacucho is bright, full of music and dancing, but this gaiety has a hushed plaintiveness. Of course, death, for the Latin, and in a somewhat different way for the Indian, has its gay familiar aspects—that is why the Ayacuchan during the death-watch drinks hilariously and gambles furiously with llama-bone dice. Ayacucho seems more closely linked with death than life.

It is slowly decaying. Its moss-covered tiled roofs sag pathetically. Its electric lights blink more feebly than candles; its best bread is unleavened shoe-leather; it has fewer inhabitants than it had a century ago; and the valley as a whole, fewer by far than it had ten centuries ago. But then, most of rural Perú—save for brief partial recovery during the colonial period—has been decaying for centuries.

Long before Inca rule, the proud peoples of this region had built great temples and impressive aqueducts so that the valley bloomed like a garden; the massive arches of the Sutucchaca aqueduct still attest to old-time industry. They even terraced the crags, now bald and desolate, to plant their crops. But today the fields are barren, only here and there grow eucalypti (first introduced near Cerro de Pasco by an American miner), the maguey (introduced in the 'eighties by Bishop Pollo) and the native *molle*, with pencil-like leaves and brilliant clusters of red berries. Now only patches hard by the little streams are cultivated. Beyond is only harsh rock and hard-baked earth, and an occasional palm-thatched *pamacari* to protect travelers from rain and sun.

Old chronicler Cieza de León found great pre-Inca ruins here. Reginaldo de Lizárraga, another early comer, found a Chimú-style edifice only four leagues from Ayacucho. On a nearby hacienda are four huge mysterious monoliths. And Don Manuel recently discovered the famous Concho Pata ruins, long lost to archæologists. Today in Ayacucho every spade brings up artifacts, every excavation reveals ancient edifices, aqueducts, fences—an extensive cultivation betokening a concentrated population far in excess of that actually existing today.

But for an accident of history, this valley might have harbored the capital of a great empire, and the Pocra Indians, instead of the Quechuas, might have been the wielders of Andean power.

May, 1323—if we are to trust the chronology—the local Pocra chief, with a vast military array, invaded Abancay (conquered over half a century earlier by Inca Llocca) and on the plains of Surucoriti (now Zuriti) battled the advancing army of General Titu Maiti, nephew of Inca Yahuar Huaccacc. The Incan forces were completely routed. The

Pocra chieftain moved on to within a few miles of Cuzco itself.

But for the sudden emergence of a great Inca personality, historians might today be writing about the Pocran instead of the Incan empire. Viracocha, son of the ruling emperor, boldly deposed his father, whipped forces into shape, and smashed the Pocras within six miles of the gates of Cuzco.

Over 5,000 Pocras emigrated across the Cordilleras to Huánuco on the upper Huallaga. Viracocha marched in and terribly chastised the still rebellious, hanging scores of them by the bridge on the Ayacucho-Huanta road, a point ever since called Ayahuarcuna, "Place where corpses are hung." The bulk of the Pocras, he resettled at Quinúa, Huamanguilla, and other points; and recolonized the region with Huancas, Chancas, Vilcas and Collas.

As a defense against rebellious Indians, Francisco Pizarro, January 9, 1539, founded Huamanguilla, "The very noble and loyal city of San Juan de la Frontera de Huamanga," midway between Lima and Cuzco, with twenty-one Conquistadores and several thousand Indians. Among the Spaniards was Miguel de Estete, who in Cajamarca had snatched the royal fringed *mascapaycha* from the head of Inca Atahualpa. Six months later the settlement was removed to the more salutary site of the present Ayacucho.

Here El Mozo, son of Almagro, came storming in a last effort to wrench away the realm his father had helped conquer. On both sides, remarks Incan chronicler Garcilazo, all were men able to rule an empire—Pedro de Candia, one of the starving Thirteen of Fame who stepped across the line on the storm-washed Isle of Gallos, and some of Cortés' ablest lieutenants.

A bloody battle in nearby Chupas left most of the Mozo's forces dead on the field, the rest prisoners. Forty were executed in front of the cathedral—and the city's name was changed to San Juan of Victory. Two years later, the Huamangans with 2,000 native allies had to fight an invading Indian army. From then on repeated Indian uprisings occurred. As late as 1827 the Chacras attacked the city unsuccessfully; in this century native revolts have occurred. It has ever been a place of battle and death.

"Revolutions start in Arequipa," says the Peruvian adage. "When they reach Ayacucho, the matter is serious."

## 4

Cieza de León and Lizárraga, who visited Ayacucho soon after the founding, declared it had the best buildings of any city from Quito to Chile; González de la Rosa said the same in 1821. Besides a beautiful cathedral it soon had an impressive university. In 1667, Bishop Zamora y Castilla (bastard son of Charles II) brought out able professors from Spain to found San Cristóbal, which was given the same privileges as the universities of Mexico, Salamanca and Valladolid.

Religiosity and learning produced several famous poets: Diego de Aguilar y Córdova, Countess de la Vega, and Josefa Cruzet, "Josefa of the Assumption"—their verses were *aves* of devoted souls clamoring to God for protection. But this enlightenment (for Huamanga was a holy city, almost one vast convent) was soon crushed by the Inquisition. The town sank back into provincial bigotry, except that, a frontier place, it was ever torn with ecclesiastical and civil strife. Bold adventurers were with difficulty kept within the law.

One stormy night in 1617, twelve Spanish adventurers gambling behind closed doors were frightened by hard blows on the door.

"By St. Milán, he of Cogulla, the thirteenth comer brings no good!" exclaimed one of the players.

In with a rush of wind and rain came a jaunty young caballero, feathers and ribbons somewhat bedraggled but handsome in velvet, Holland lace and carmine stockings.

Tossing his purse on the table, he picked up the dice and threw aces. "The pot is mine!" He reached out his hand.

"Not yet," retorted the last thrower, and duplicated the play, except one of the dice was slightly cocked. He demanded the pot. The other players sided with him.

Whipping out his sword the newcomer struck out the light. In the wild mêlée, one gambler was stuck through the stomach. All fled to the street.

The youth valiantly cut his way through the King's guard, only to be tripped up. He was taken to jail and subsequently tried.

Everywhere, it was brought out, he had gotten into fights. A troublemaker, he had had to flee from half a dozen localities to escape punishment. The necessary gallows were erected in the plaza.

Taken to a chapel to be confessed, the intrepid adventurer seized the Host from the priest and dashed out with it, crying, "The Church calls me! The Church calls me!"

No one wished to commit sacrilege by attacking the Host, so the prisoner successfully reached Santa Clara. He knelt before the altar, safe from the civil authorities.

The Bishop, wrothful, came in person—determined to punish the sacrilege severely, which meant the cutting off of the right hand, then burning at the stake.

The youth confessed a life-long secret and, strangely enough, he was at once most considerately treated. Despite the sacrilege, the Bishop left him in the Santa Clara convent, an astonishing immoral step—setting sheep to guard a lion! The scandal grew, but the Bishop merely sent his prisoner to Lima, again to a convent, that of Bernardes de la Trinidad, until embarked for Spain.

Gradually the truth outed. The miscreant was a nun, Catalina de Erauza—now known in history as the Standard-Bearer Nun—who had escaped disguised as a boy from the

San Sebastián convent in Quipúzcoa. Reaching Perú, soon she gained fame as the best duelist in the land. She joined the royal forces, and in the battle of Valdivia in Chile bravely captured an opposing standard, winning the crown-granted title Alferez—Standard-Bearer. At Callao she helped beat off the Spillberg pirates. But after many heroic engagements, she finally had to flee from the army in disgrace for her bumptiousness.

Eventually, after the Ayacucho episode, the Pope gave her the special privilege of dressing in men's clothes; she finally went to Mexico as a member of the Viceregal guard. . . .

Women as well as men have played a heroic part in the "Corner of Death": Ventura Ccalamaqui, "She of the Bare Arms," led a mob of women to resist conscription of their husbands into the royalist armies; the beautiful Indian girl Phallchamascachi-Ttica succored the Independence troops; María de Belledo—now celebrated by an impressive statue—died before a firing squad rather than reveal insurgent secrets.

Independence brought out fierce passions. When news of Ferdinand VII's deposition by Napoleon arrived in 1809, the Ayacuchans promptly voiced hot disapproval and signed with blood: "Whereas Ferdinand VII, restorer of the nation, father of the peoples, the delight of every good Spaniard, has been despoiled of his crown," be it resolved "that the people of Huamanga, ever since learning of such an unheard-of wrong, have been given over to sorrow, amazement and indignation; that they protest before heaven and earth against such an execrable affront and swear not to recognize or ever recognize any one but Ferdinand VII as their sovereign."

Yet the following year Ayacucho had become so fervently independentist, that Viceroy La Serna's forces under bloody Carratalá murdered townfolk right and left until streets and highways stank with unburied bodies. Again Ayacucho became a place of death.

Among others Basilio Auqui, seventy-five years old, formed an independence squadron made up of his sons and seven grandchildren, and by 1814 the royalists had been driven out. The angry citizens yanked Spanish Commandant José Vicente de la Moya (who previously had threatened to open artillery fire on the incensed women led by Ventura Ccalamaqui) from his refuge in San Francisco and killed him ruthlessly. Turn-coats Tincopa and Echevarría were beheaded, their skulls stuck on pikes. Soon the Ayacuchans were chanting thanks to God for having given them Bolívar.

Most of the patriot leaders passed through Ayacucho. Bolívar, "wrapped in the cape of the rainbow, came from where the stormy Orinoco pays tribute to the God of waters," and if he did not get as far as Huamanga, gave orders for one of the crucial battles in its vicinity. Here came Sucre, "developing his hard-headed plan of combat with the determination and serene valor of a Napoleon," to fight the famous battle of December 9, 1824, on the near-by plains of Quinúa. Nine royalist divisions were routed by a handful of patriots, leaving 1,400 dead on the field and Viceroy La Serna prisoner—an engagement in which, said Santa Cruz, "the patriot sabres destroyed the Spanish cavalry, breaking the strongest link of the chain that bound Perú to Spain," a battle, said Bolívar, "that liberated five nations."

## 5

Ever since patron Saint John was first carried in solemn procession in 1539 by the new civil and ecclesiastical authorities, Ayacucho has been deeply religious, the home of miracles, fanatical fury, deep piety, ecclesiastical intrigue, Inquisitional terror, priestly corruption. It was crowded with colonial churches, convents and monasteries, still supports over thirty religious establishments.

Its favorite images are miraculous. On the cathedral altar

233

of our Lord of Burgos is the Weeping Holy Child, placed there in great reverence centuries ago.

Shoemaker Perico, obliged to take a trip to neighboring Huanta, left the image of this Holy Child to guard his house and his honor. Instead of an expected two days' absence, he spurred his horse with such fury he was back by nine the following morning. To his surprise—his good wife Casilda was wont to rise early for her domestic duties—he found the house closed. She was not there.

Furiously he seized hold of the Christ Child to punish it for its failure.

An old woman, hearing the wail of a baby and knowing her neighbors had no child, entered to find the shoemaker in a dead faint, still tightly grasping the image. Its cries had ceased, but blood was flowing from its legs, staining Perico's impious hand.

The Bishop at once had the image taken in great pomp to the cathedral. The shoemaker entered the Ocapa monastery, and as for Casilda, "she ended up in misery as do nearly all the heroines of prostitution."

No less sacred is the Jesuit Crucifix. The great snow mountain Guamaco, crowned by three peaks, long harbored iniquitous idolatry and devil consorting, headed by a local sorcerer and an Indian chief. According to bona fide information acquired by the Jesuits, the Devil, Apamuguaco, ordered them to whip and burn a Crucifix. The Crucifix refused to burn. To hide their dastardly crime, they buried it. Two years later, the Bishop investigated the impious rumor. The Christ, on being dug up, showed fresh ulcers, just like a human body. Its miraculous powers proved so great it was brought in to Ayacucho.

In dire disaster the good saints have always comforted. During the serious 1719 earthquakes, blue-robed gold-adorned Santa Barbarba was taken out in solemn procession. The Bishop, civil authorities, every one, marched from six in the morning until nine at night, barefooted, barelegged, ropes around their necks. The earthquakes ceased.

Often there were pitched battles between saintly cults. Once Spaniards and Creoles, Indians joining in on either side with right good will, fought bitterly over the possession of San Sebastián. Many were killed, including the priest carrying the Santísimo.

Though numerous disputes arose between civil and religious authorities over the Church's exorbitant assessments, though more than once the city smelled to high heaven with dead bodies, the priests refused to bury till the required fee was paid, faithful devotion saw no wrong in such abuses; the Church thrived, priests became corrupt. From the founding of the Bishopric by Pope Paul V's 1612 bull, many a bishop tried to rectify abuses, but more than one—so Bishop Olivas himself has admitted—was poisoned.

The first incumbent passed unto our Lord in sad gastronomical agony in 1618. The same fate was supposed to have overtaken Bishop Zárate, La Fuente, Matienzo and others. Seven of the Bishops of Huamanga died strangely before two years in their posts. Antonio Condorino passed away soon after taking charge. Bishop Cipriano Medina set out to visit his diocese, threatening to reform the clergy; within two leagues, he was taken with mortal spasms.

Forceful and honorable Bishop Francisco López Sánchez was found dead in his chair, a letter in his hand. Suspicion pointed to poisoning by a dissolute priest.

Bishop López had encountered this priest, bottle in hand, drunkenly dancing the *cachua,* to the tune of the *charango,* with six beautiful, if somewhat dubious, chola girls, short skirts lifted high. The priest, his robe stained and dirty, was sweeping out the turns of the hilarious dance: "*Aro! Arito!* Give me your arm, my soul—to the right . . ." "*Aro! Arito!* Give me your arm, curly head, to the left."

"To the right," roared Bishop López. "Right to the cala-
boose."

On another occasion he called in a priest nicknamed Cabbage-Head, who had slashed a sweetheart in the face. Cabbage-Head ascended the Episcopal Stairs drunk.

Furious, the Bishop kicked him in the stomach.

Catching hold of the bannister, Cabbage-Head shouted in
Quechua, "*Ahuila llaipas patalla mantacca!*" "Beautiful! My
old grandmother can hit me from above below!"

The Bishop, when he learned the meaning of the words,
swore the priest would never come out of jail "until he reforms or I die." Shortly after, the Bishop died, poisoned, some
say by red *floripondios*.

Ayacucho is still as devoted as ever. Over it day and night
ring the mellow bells from dozens of church towers. It has
more priests today than in the eighteenth century when still
prosperous with over 30,000 inhabitants. Its processions and
worship—if no longer as magnificent as in the 1564 Corpus
Christi, when the Cabildo spent 40,000 ducats just for candles—are still solemn and fervent. In the midst of its decay,
Ayacucho sits in pious conformity, scourges heretics bitterly.
Nearly all its streets bear holy names. It is *the* religious strong-
hold of the Andes. Ayacucho clings to bigoted beliefs with
the passion of a being who is lost. This is not merely piety,
it is part of Ayacucho's decay.

6

In the seventeenth century about Ayacucho were produced
annually 5,000 *arrobas* of wine. Today it is easier and
cheaper to get wine for the large coast cities from Chile. In
the old days in the Paccaiccassa ward of that city, a thousand
workers wove *tocuyo*. Now it is cheaper and more satisfactory for the coast, even for Ayacucho itself, to import
cottons and calicos, silks and linens from abroad.

The reasons why Ayacucho, along with most highland agricultural areas, has declined are patent. Modern industry, modern communications—concentrated on the coast or penetrating into the interior only where the richest mineral wealth can be readily extracted—instead of bringing places like Ayacucho into a wider national and international economic system, have driven them into isolation, into petty rural self-sufficiency. In pack-train days Ayacucho was a great communications center. Today—despite the building of a new, if very dangerous, road—it is altogether lonely in its remote valley.

A common story of economic shifts. But Ayacucho, with a little foresight, could still be important, except that Perú's officials labor, never for the Peruvian people, but for a few large landlords, a swarm of military and official bureaucrats, and for a type of international trade that retards rather than promotes the country's development.

## 7

Today Indianism contributes everything at all vital in Ayacucho. Today it is preeminently an Indian-cholo city.

Many aristocratic Creole families still live there, proud in their lost world. They dwell in fine, but uncomfortable, colonial homes without modern conveniences, but with magnificent patios. Rarely visible, they make little outward impress, save to dominate politics and support the clergy. They do nothing to further progress; their surrounding estates merely strangle the town. And the blood in their veins has grown thin and pale, their knowledge antiquated. Feeling their importance waning, they grow more unbendingly dogmatic, cling bitterly to all the medieval fetiches which once had importance, but which today have little meaning—even in enforced isolation.

Amazing the Indian power of survival! Though these Pocras and allied tribes were, next to the Chileans, the most difficult for the Incas to conquer, during the two centuries prior to the Spaniards, they had been assimilated. Yet even benevolent subjugation leaves scars. Spanish conquest further dislocated local practices, especially as the Spaniards unlike the Incas sought to extirpate old social customs. From Ayacucho and surrounding regions, Toledo sent 3,000 Indians to the Huancavelica mines—the quota had to be kept filled no matter how many died under the lash.

The best lands were wrenched away. Patiently the Indians took their protests to the Spanish tribunals; there the cases mouldered from generation to generation until at last predatory tenure was established beyond chance of repudiation.

Many native activities were prohibited, especially weaving. The Viceroys, become merchants promoting Peninsular commerce, arbitrarily allotted silks and satins to the Indians. Only when alarmed by the distinction such dress gave their racial underlings did the Spaniards suddenly forbid Indians to wear finery—no silks, velvet, Holland lace, shoes, or jewelry. Disobedience meant severe punishment; the second offense, confiscation of property; the third, beheading or burning at the Inquisition stake.

Not until June 9, 1691, were the Indians permitted to have on each ranch one loom and three spools. Gradually the native textile industry revived.

The Indians! They come down from everywhere among the surrounding crags. From Hatun Pampa across a sloping tableland, Ayacucho's tiled roofs far below them among fruit trees. From snow-clad Condorcuna, site of heroic battles, across the Cangallo pampas. From meadows between the high peaks of Acuchimay and Picota, where once were mounted independence cannon. From the lonely heights of Tutipucro, where only the *puco-puco* bird chants its monotonous cry, to the broken ravine of Punqui, where nickel glistens in kidney-shaped milky quartz crystals. From the

plain of Chupas, hard by Lambrashuaycco, site of other
heroic battles, down terrific cliffs and ravines, down through
the red brick Puca-Cruz gate.

They come singing in Quechua:

"¿*Condorchalla, condorchalla,*
*Yana raplaijo caspucho*
*Curapacc pensacapunque?*"

"Cóndor, cóndor,
Because your wings are black
Do you think you're a priest?"

At dawn one hears them scuffling like wind through trees.
They come gliding into town, with queer swish of alpaca
sandals, fur curling up around the toes; they come bent under
loads. Viewed from some balcony, they seem intent ants; one
senses their intuitive communal spirit. Not private-profit
merchants, they are performing a social rite, instinctively
fulfilling community life rhythm, imposed by the habits of
generations, imposed by the survival needs of highland harsh-
ness which welded them into well-knit group-conquest of
gigantic natural forces and impelled them from that time to
this to automatic harmonic participation in common ends—
mosaics in a beautiful pattern. Old Spanish chronicler Polo
de Ondegardo pointed out long ago: "The Indian is ineffective in individual effort; fecund in collective effort."

And so they glide swiftly through the streets, a stream
iridescent with sun-reflection, into the buzzing market with
its babel of sounds and odors and brilliant colors, its thousand and one handicrafts—stands heaped with fruit and vegetables, potatoes and yams, great stacks of woolen blankets
covered with pink birds, or colors dashed together like an
agitated rainbow. Odorous eating booths smell of pork grease,
chili, garlic and strange herbs.

The women wear fluffy and pleated blouses, bright hand-woven girdles, mountainous skirts of different colors—a new one is added each year, until they become bell-shaped; every movement of the body causes their skirts to swing like some many-petalled flower. The shoulder *liclla*, a square cloth of velvet embroidered in many colors, is held in place over the breast by a large gold or silver *tupu* brooch. Their long lustrous black tresses, usually braided, sometimes hang down over their large bosoms, less frequently are wound about the head on which perches either a Panamá or a home-made felt hat or else a triangular cloth (*chucupa*) which hangs down the neck—like the kerchief covering of the Roman campagna peasants. Babies and bundles are carried in a bright striped cloth knotted over the chest, gaping behind. In the markets, since their blouses are sleeveless, they put on, by cords tied at the shoulders, long velvet cuffs, embroidered with bright flowers and animals.

The men are colorless birds in comparison: home-woven woolen trousers and calico shirts, the latter, though, sometimes pleated, piped with a bit of lace, and often of bright hues; in any case the knotted sash is brilliant. For rainy days and nights an alpaca, or llama-wool poncho, with bright designs—flowers, birds, animals or figurines—is slipped over the head through a slit in the center; occasionally they use goat-skin coats; and the Morochuchos, a nearby group, perhaps partly mestizo, wear a jaunty spotted cap.

In various *barrios*, one discovers the native industries. Over some adobe fence, long lines of terra cotta pots, drying in the sun, wait the oven. In the Cochopata ward, chiefly devoted to weavers, Maximiliano Gutiérrez, a bright-eyed barefoot Indian with unkempt black hair, can weave on a primitive foot-loom—almost—the finest English woolens. Give him a sample of cloth, he will observe the pattern, count the number of threads, and reproduce it almost exactly. A craftsman of the old school, he prepares and dyes his own wool.

Another ward is devoted to the sculptors—enough native

talent to start a new Florence. The local alabaster is fine and white, perfect in texture.

Take the road to the cemetery. Walk out Arequipa Street, dip down the hill, across the little bridge over the Totorilla, here cut deep into the living rock, and up the winding lane through native adobe houses and orchards, workmen busy in the doorways.

This part of town is alive at almost any hour with the plaintive music of the native harp, mounted on a triangular sounding board, or the bamboo flute—the *antara*, and people singing ancient songs:

"*Anillitoypas capuhuan . . .*"

"I've got a ring
With precious stones seven;
And twelve are
My beautiful sweethearts."

"Of the tuna fruit I ate;
On their peels I slipped;
Every one I tossed away,
Not just you."

Beyond on high ground is the cemetery, surmounted by old massive sandstone statues of the saints, in bulky Barcelona style. Around the walls of small patios, each ruled over eternally by a designated saint, are tiers upon tiers of mortuary niches, each fronted by a small square marble bas-relief. Most—though in inspiration and theme conventional, largely in the Canova style, many not unworthy of Canova—are exquisitely wrought; three or four rise to real originality.

But persistence of old social and racial exploitation inhibits creative achievement. Textiles made by Indians are bought and traded by cholos; the owners of gravestone establishments are cholos; the work is done by Indian artists. Thus in all lines intrinsic native talent is subdued, tinged with death and ecclesiasticism. Yet, despite this, something so vital shines through it, that out of such latent talent some day will come a real contribution to the new Perú. If the native artists had a chance to celebrate life instead of death, the name of Ayacucho might go around the world.

All in all, Ayacucho has decayed without ever having achieved a cultural synthesis or a creative personality. The merging of forces is there, but uncompleted. Thus old habits, old ideas, old superstitions have survived. Religion. Duality has brought about a queer fanatical pagan blend with Catholicism, well seen for instance in the Coracora, the festival of the Purísima, when on Holy Wednesday they bring out the Virgin known by the good Quechua name Mama Percca. The Ayacuchans have peopled their world with strange monsters. White-haired Supay, the Quechua devil—and the Catholic sacerdotes have been obliged to use the native word—brings his Liquor of Death with his legion of black crows. He takes many forms. The *Janchanchu* takes people to a banquet of death in the abyss. The *Amaro* descends down the ravines in the form of a bull or pig to destroy houses and crops, scattering desolation and misery wherever he passes. Or he who malingers at night is likely to be met by the strange local centaur, half llama, half man, the *Ccarcacha,* who spits in the faces of all he meets.

Or one is likely to meet a *Kke Kke* flying head, or an arm or intestines that wrap themselves in death-like grip about the throat, for animism even extends to corporeal organs— the *human-tacctac* belief—that escape from their owners during sleep "to go flying," with strange humming sound and blowing an icy coldness into the air that freezes the very marrow. And even the unexplained howl of a dog brings tidings of evils and death. Or the *nina-mula*—women who have had intercourse with a priest and have been transformed into mules ridden by the devil.

They have other queer spooks to keep them company at deathwatches, marriages and fiestas. At fiesta or deathwatch, despite these strange invisible guests, there is drinking, banqueting and dancing. The performers, in close-fitting gold-spangled *jubón* jackets and feather-decked hats, leap up in the acrobatic "Scissor dance" to the sound of *quirquinchos*, harps, violins, flutes and drums; now they dance on their hands, now on their knees, now on heel and toe. Ayacucho thrums, harps and dances—in the gay way of people who have carved immortality into abiding stone, it dances its eternal rendezvous with death, and fears it not; for it is, after all, "the Corner of Death."

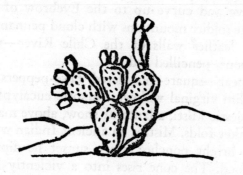

# XVI

# AREQUIPA: GATEWAY TO THE ANDES

I

AREQUIPA is a white city, kin to the white cone of Misti, slim and swift above it—a white city made "from the foam of volcanoes and flakes of snow."

One comes to it from the port of Mollendo, across sterile desert, across the Joya pampas, a great red ruby on the earth's breast; curve and curve up to the Eyebrow of the Coast, through blue soldier mountains with cloud pennants, through the seamed leather walls of the Chile River—valleys like golden ribbons, pencilled red.

Trees appear—square-shouldered, false-peppers with rash-like bark, slim virginal willows, quixotic eucalypti.

Then majestic Misti, a lance of snow, above many-colored Indian-blanket folds. Misti is an ancient Indian warrior bundled in his bright poncho; every sunset he dips his white lance in blood. The cone rises into a violently blue sky, a blue-blood sky in white gauze drawers—such are the clouds. At other times they are undulating, compact as flesh; or motionless, compact as marble.

Over the fields drifts the perfume of *albahaca* and honeysuckle.

Arequipa's white houses are "tired doves resting on the hills." When stamped by the golden kiss of the sun, the place seems to blush; its houses then are many-tinted: rose, lilac, greenish, yellow, lemon, bluish.

Over Arequipa floats the mellow sound of church bells—morning, noon, and night. Churches everywhere—cupolas on gray elephant heads. Bell-towers—the cathedral has ears like a wolf.

It needs to be alert. Last century the previous edifice was completely gutted by fire—because of "the sins of the people and the iniquities of the priests." Thirteen fires burst out on thirteen altars. Jehovah was angry. Bishop José Sebastián de Goyeneche y Barreda spoke so terrifyingly of eternal damnation that men wept who had never feared cannon. An illustrious local philosopher, who elucidated that earthquakes were due to natural causes, was all but driven out of town; Arequipans prefer to placate God's wrath rather than submit to non-personal implacable nature.

The Arequipans, making a pagan-Catholic *pot pourri*, have childish faith in the efficacy of particular saints:

St. Anthony: Secures a sweetheart.
Santa Filomena: Drives away unwelcome guests.
Santa Rita: Calms matrimonial quarrels. Drives away headaches and undesirable suitors.
Santa Lucia: Cures eye-trouble.
San José: Cures lung infections.
Santa Elena: Finds lost objects.
Santa Apolina: Cures tooth-aches.
San Andrés: Cures insanity.
San Lázaro } Cure skin diseases.
San Roque }
San Cipriano: Prevents bewitchments.
San Emigdio }
San Genaro } Protect against earthquakes.
Santa Barbara }
San Antonio Abad: Protects domestic animals.
Santa María and others: Help women in childbirth.

San Jerónimo: Brings death-bed unbelievers back to the faith (Put
    his image under the pillow).
San Pedro: Cures hernias.
Santa Magdalena: Aborts unmarried pregnant women.
Etc., Etc.

They believe implicitly that the leaves from the orange
tree of Mother Monteagudo, given out by the Santa Catalina
nuns, will cure all pains. The church sells ribbons of the Virgin to stop hemorrhages or excessive menstruation.

Arequipans have always been proud of their faith. When
the pulpit, contracted in France for the new cathedral,
arrived, its devil-figure pedestal had gone astray. "The devil
is afraid to enter Arequipa," said the citizens gleefully.

Just as they accept miraculous divine intervention, so they
listen to their priests in political matters—only the Lord's
ministers can provide true salvation of the state, not political
science or economic laws. With the aid of his frenzied Arequipans, Bishop Juan Gualberto Valdivia made and unmade
governments, Prelate Luna Pizarro headed a congress, Goyeneche took part in Santa Cruz' confederation, and other
illustrious ecclesiastics have carried God's word unadulterated
direct from golden throne to government halls.

### 3

Arequipa, composite of coast and highlands, is the synthesis
of all that is Perú. Misti looks equally upon crags and dunes,
disputes the passage of Andean tempest and shifting sands.
Just as more isolated Huánuco is a jungle-highlands hybrid,
so Arequipa, on the western Andean slope, is the crossroads
of two regions, two cultures. A depository of dual influences,
it has knit these distinct outer worlds into one pattern, into
a personality far more significant than that of Lima, to which
it is second in size. Though in a web of southern regionalism,

comprising Puno and Cuzco, Arequipa is above any regionalism; if further north, more central, it would be the ideal
capital. Arequipa is a compromise between Perú's extremes.
There, in any case, predicts Valcárcel, will be signed the
"Covenant" which will some day consolidate Perú's political
unity, harmonizing the different great regions, a refuge from
the confusing Indian-European cross-currents.

Its medium altitude, 7,600 feet, is agreeable both to low-
landers and highlanders. Coastlanders do not suffer the panting agony of greater elevations; those from the 9,000 to
14,000 feet towns do not run the risk of sea-level pneumonia.

This has affected the character of its people. Arequipa, if
sufficiently high to sap vitality periodically, is not so high as
to preclude reckless joys. Its fine but treacherous climate
makes men alternately lethargic and quick and nervous—a
constant break-up of normal currents between reason and
deed, a resultant inconsistency of conduct. The real highlanders are conservative; they have to be; economic survival demands, as the Inca empire so well testifies, methodical organized effort. Coast life is softer, more corrupt; greater leisure
allows for more joyous grace but not for deepening of character or thought; the sun-lazy coastlanders are flighty extra-
verts balanced by drowsy luxury and conservative traditions.
The Arequipans are soul-searching introverts, highly
charged with irrational conduct; they sunder their Ham-
letian doubts by desperate deeds. The greater altitudes enforce sobriety, the hot coast sun irons out the will; in Arequipa men and women brood long, love deeply and fiercely,
hate venomously and kill easily.

Like the Mexicans and unlike the Peruvians, the Arequipan
is violent and passionate; the women, more elemental, resist
sophistication. The highland wife is patrician, capably, dig-
nifiedly shouldering her obligations. The coastland wife is
lascivious, obedient and loyal. The Arequipan wife is ma-

247

ternal, tender and passionate, but often is an extremist who permits no overt slights. If necessary, she will pay her spouse back in his own coin with clandestine love and alcohol and a sad despair.

The people have the energy of the volcanoes in them. They store it up gradually until it reaches the explosive point. According to temperament, they brood with introspective luxuriousness or resentment, then react in bursts of unreasonable anger or amusement, in heroic deeds or vulgar violences. Arequipa is the "Lion of the South." It breeds quixotic revolutionary *caudillos* and Sanchos who abandon pipe and bowl in ecstatic armed loyalty. Every Arequipan has something of the mystic and the warrior. A very dual creature constantly at war with himself and the outside world, to escape inner tension he is often mercurial, quick changing as the temperature of his city which fluctuates violently from blistering noon to chilly nights—a daily cycle that starts with lucid mornings when the sun throws joyous pebbles of light against the windows, and warm milk is juiced, foaming, from cowteats at the door, and the bread comes hot and soft; the highnoon lassitude; the quick scattering afternoon rain, with its sudden breath of chilliness; then a swing back to warmth; finally the moon rising white and cold above Pichupichi—the volcanoes become groups of Vestal Virgins. Men clutch their coats tighter about them; the Indian mantles himself up to his eyes. These abrupt shifts cause the very bones to creak, the body to be brusquely and unduly strained, narrowing the margin between health and disease, between sweet reasonableness and irrationality, and from gentle piety to fanaticism, from domesticity to war, from love to hate.

These traits are reinforced by ethnic and cultural background. Arequipa is Perú's most mestizo city. Mestizo blood accentuates emotional periodicity. Belonging neither to one culture nor the other, the mestizo is still a badly rooted being, subject to extremes of conduct; he is amoral, for his group has yet to achieve a norm. Though ritualistic and conventional, his conduct ever overleaps these frail restraints.

Geographically, racially, culturally, Arequipa is a synthesis of all Perú—it best represents the Latin-American, tropic-mountain, mestizo culture norm.

Thus it has singularly Mexican characteristics. At the elevation of much of the Mexican plateau, Arequipa's character, the quality of its light, the nearness of its vibrant deep blue sky, the soft mellow tones of its buildings, the vagrancy of its zigzag streets, its mestizo attributes—all remind me of Mexico, where national fusion is so much further advanced.

Just as Popocatepetl and Ixtaccihuatl rise snow-crowned above Mexico, so Misti rises above Arequipa, a perfect and beautiful cone—except that Misti is closer, dominates the city completely. The volcano, like a good wife, has become a scape-goat for the Arequipans. If the weather is bad, they blame Misti. If the traveler feels the altitude, they blame the snow on Misti. If people douse each other and dance during carnival, it is because Misti lets them. He who becomes temperamental excuses himself, saying: "I am with snow." . . . "What do you mean?" . . . "The influence Misti exercises on the nerves." Misti, according to one writer, has taught Arequipa asceticism, piety and fanaticism.

In addition to mystic, stern super-sensitivity, offset by spontaneity, the Arequipan's inner world, enriched by the vivid light and soft color tones, is sensuous. The Arequipan, when not chained to moods or false dignity, is delightful, effusive, salty. Keenly relishing double-meaning words, he has, like the Mexican, a racy vocabulary beyond classic Castilian. His food is the most highly spiced and original of all Perú. Much of his life is spent in the little *picantería* restaurants. Guitars thrum, joyous *yaraví* are sung; the *marinela* is danced. No one gets more delight out of the world of senses; no one better enjoys food and drink; his *raja-raja* potatoes, his *liga-liga* cheese, his *rocotos* and roast pigs' heads, his *calduy-rabo*, represent gastronomical spontaneity; music, dancing, sharp-edge repartee represent amorous spontaneity, and all represent escape from his inner tautness.

J. S.

These descriptions must be qualified for differences between town and country. The rural cholo, 80 percent Spanish, 20 percent Indian, in politics is Spanish, in daily life Indian. Loving the soil, got from the Indian, he is just enough Indian to cherish old ties. Many live like peons. Petty trading is the local peasant's dream; the price of wheat his great preoccupation. Like the Italian peasant, his only ambitions are to eat and drink well and push his children into the profes-

250

sional groups, politics, law, medicine, the army, the church. Obstinate, hard-headed, of simple sentiments, his life goes like the plow, direct and deep. Rigidly religious, the fiestas of Sachacca and Cerro Colorado satisfy his emotional and artistic needs with music, food, noise and mystery. A band of *caperos* is for him sweeter than Bach. A peon cultivator and a hard petty Spanish trader, he sings the ineffable nostalgia of all the humble *Chujlla* of all the Andes, guitar chords vibrating with the thousand-year sadness of the *mitimae*, the dolorous echo of *ayullus* transported from maternal soil to new lands, plus the wailing nostalgia of Moorish Spain.

The more restless urban cholo is troubled by the modern world, by new forces of which he has nebulous knowledge. Proud, often bitter, ireful, uncertain of himself and others, though his local patriotism is ineffaceable, he resents the provincial trammels. Usually with dreams of grandeur, he "can't be a prophet in Arequipa;" "all the heads of wheat are just alike." Many go forth to seek their fortunes, often to Chile, "to triumph."

Arequipan mysticism is not other-worldly; at its worst it is base superstition; at its norm it is Catholicism taken superstitiously, at its best it is a soul malaise, though not born of spiritual or intellectual urge or abstract love of beauty or truth—in fact he doesn't like disinterested writing, analytical approach—but of a desire for self-aggrandizement, power—at bottom, false pride, touchy dignity. Because of his rich sensatory environment, he accepts Catholicism pictorially, without superior seeking, no transcendentalism. The freest thinker of Arequipa believes bigotedly in the Virgin of Chapi miracles. Everywhere gray mountains throw him back into himself; but not of the Sierras proper, he resents their implications—these lofty heights do not contribute any Gothic note to his character; rather he becomes ingrowing, narrow but intensely ambitious, not for creative achievement, but as a frustration reflex. He never asks, "Where are we going?" in a metaphysical sense. Dogmatic heavens close too tightly about him. An artistic individualist, social doctrines find no echo in him. His introspection, not intellectual, scarcely spiritual, is merely sensatory moodiness; but the vivid surrounding sense world, despite the set spiritual creeds, does make him an incipient materialist. Not our American practical materialism of wealth accumulation and new technical gewgaws, but sensuous hedonism, a desire for tangible, not necessarily man-made, pattern, a consciousness of environmental inadequacy, this at least breaks up pre-conceptions, makes for insurgency—an Arequipan is an Arequipan.

## 4

Founded seven centuries ago by a great Inca, refounded soon after the conquest, Arequipa has had a strong local patriotism.

The Arequipan recalls the shining episodes. Almagro passed through here on returning from his fruitless conquest of Chile; Gonzalo Pizarro, hard beset in Lima, made Arequipa his new base; Viceroy Toledo's momentous 1570 tour. Above all, August 15, 1540, Day of Assumption, Francisco Pizarro and Manuel García de Carbajal "spiked into the entrails of these lonely but fertile regions, the banners of Aragón," founding Villa Hermosa of Arequipa. The ex-swineherd drove his pick into the future plaza and planted the true cross on the cathedral site—"Arequipa was born with its cathedral."

Warm with such memories, the Arequipan, with a natural proclivity toward bellicosity, is ever ready to defend his local rights, is determined in his vengeance. When street-fighting starts in Lima, the inhabitants hurriedly bar doors and windows; in Arequipa, every one grabs a gun and rushes into the street, crying, "Whom are we fighting for now?" Just as he is quick to take personal offense, so he is hasty in resenting Lima's centralization.

But deep passions have ever made Arequipans even more eager to fight for personal loyalties than for place or principles. Though never Liberal—a symptom of coastal industrial development—when the Arequipans, Urquieta and Mostajo backed a Liberal program, the place stood behind them valiantly. Any hard-beset leader who found friendliness in Arequipa could count on loyalty unto death. The place has not merely produced many outstanding personalities, it has stood by them whatever the sacrifice.

In 1834 it gave itself whole-heartedly to Nieto against Bermúdez' usurpation; later it supported Santa Cruz against Salaverry, who finally met death there. It backed Vivanco through thick and thin (the women even gave their jewels), and fought desperately for his dying cause against the Liberalism of Castilla, fought from street to street, house to house. In 1865 it headed the Prado revolution in the name of national honor; that of Canseco in 1867 in the name of religion. The famous Nicolás de Piérola is one of its most illustrious sons. And probably Sergeant Major Sánchez Cerro will not be the last of its military heroes. It has produced any number of fascinating agitators.

Jacinto Ibáñez founded its first printing press, copper on wood. The Spanish authorities broke up the type. A new secret plant was also discovered and destroyed by Viceroy La Serna. Ibáñez had to hide out. A third plant was also seized but was recovered by the insurgents, who dedicated it to proclamations, independence hymns and descriptions of victories. Royalist forces retook Arequipa. Ibáñez had to flee. This time his shop was saved by the Franciscans, who changed from the literature of liberty to catechisms. The battle of Ayacucho permitted Ibáñez to return. He published *The Star of Ayacucho*, one of Perú's first newspapers.

His courage is paralleled by any number of known and

unknown heroes: Francisco Javier de Luna Pizarro, Valdivia, Domingo Gamio, the Masías, Vivanco's wife, Alvizuri, Bustamante, Manrique. Such as these fomented local pride—a spirit of undying defense and love for the soil, and ever for the true faith. "Your bells have been cannon and your cannon, bells," writes poet Alberto Guillén.

## 5

Architecturally also Arequipa reveals welding of spirit. In Cuzco, the Indian remained rebellious, aloof, hostile to the Spaniard, a chip-on-the-shoulder attitude enduring to this day, hence never contributed anything vital to the erection of the new Spanish régime. In Arequipa native talents flowed into the new Spanish purposefulness, leaving definite impress. In Cuzco—so Cossio del Pomar notes in his exhaustive work on the colonial art of that city—native artists, if they conformed to Spanish technique, expressed a subtle satire of the Conquerors; in Arequipa art was more fused. In Cuzco, the Spaniards could not escape the massive lines of the older city, which subtly influenced all their new building, but in Arequipa Indian culture exerted a more direct influence.

Future cultural synthesis, even in colonial times, was already definitely in process. The early ornate Churrigueresque in Arequipa reveals florid ease elsewhere lacking. The Jesuit church façade, executed by Indians under Spanish direction, shows marked indigenous traces—"the soul of Arequipa converted into heaven!" Argentinian architect Angel Guido finds in these heavily ornamented façades the closest approach to the true Hispanic-Indigenous architecture: "In opulent decorative designs such as these there occur numerous motifs derived from the natives' experience through the channel of their traditional art." Indian men and women, sun, moon and stars, patently related here to the ancient sun-cult: pumas, llamas, serpents, *viscachas,* and other animals, maize ears, coca leaves, cotton flowers and the holy cantut blossom. Guido mentions Indian rhythms, alternations, repetitions, antithesis and balances. Means declares these are universal principles, not Indian; but certainly their execution and assembly are definitely influenced by Indian æsthetics.

Today Arequipa's artists—unless landscapists enamored of the local panorama, such as Vasimiro Cuadros—turn naturally, as does Hector Searoing to Incan and Indian themes—*The Assault of Sacsahuamán, Coricancha, Machu Picchu.* Painting is predestined to be Arequipa's happiest contribution to Peruvian consciousness; of all places it is most appropriate to be South America's Florence. This doubles Arequipa's importance, for Perú, along with Mexico, is destined to become, once its political system is decently renovated, the outstanding exponent of pictorial art in the New World. Arequipa's luminous landscape, bright colors, precisely stencilled details are the ready-made precious backgrounds of the Italian renaissance; excess of light here provides even greater tone diversity. Rather than colorists, remarks one critic, the Arequipan painters will always be masters of the luminous. And since the beginning Arequipa has been the Academy of Paradise. The old church painting, *Our Lord of Vera Cruz,* was not, as one might suppose, brought from Spain, Lima or Quito, but was made in Arequipa by two angels sent direct from heaven for that purpose!

# XVII

## CUZCO: CITY OF THE SUN

### I

FULL of rich memories, strange imaginings, I come from the lofty City of the Sun, where ten centuries ago Manco Cápac struck the soil with his golden staff of empire—Cuzco.

City of male mountains, of old fortresses, of conquering warriors, of bold towers on uplifted crags, a city chained to the Sun with golden links.

There the Sun rules. There the Sun consorted with Mama Ocllo, sister-wife of Manco Cápac—on such myths are religions and dynasties founded; so was incestuousness concealed, and the divine right of the Incas established. Mankind loves to be ruled by lies. In Cuzco, Sun is God; the Incas were Children of the Sun by direct descent.

I prayed in the temple of the Sun and in the temple of Dawn before the gigantic altars of the Andes. I lost myself in the labyrinth of narrow zigzag streets that weave a pattern of strange life between ancient stones about the mysterious palace of the Great King. Like Aurora Cáceres, through gauzy curtains that seemed woven in the Egypt of the Pharaohs, I heard the soft sighs of damsels waiting their gallants, hopefully fingering their condor-tongue amulets of love. In a little high-walled plaza, I also found the seven witches invoking Our Lady of the Moon and hounds wailing death about a strange image. Out of a bird-cage temple, on the top of massive Tiahuanaco stones, priests came out, crucifix lifted for Corpus, scattering holy water over massed Indians rocking to a festival rhythm as ancient as Raymi, as of old greeting the dawn in a city that once had temples and gardens of gold, temples and gardens of silver—a city chained to the sun with golden links.

When Huáscar's birth was solemnly celebrated, the main plaza was marked off with a great encircling chain of solid gold—symbol of power on earth and union with the Sun. The sacred chain, to avoid all profanation, was thrown into the depths of Lake Titicaca, that inland ocean suspended in the Andean heights. Today nations merely sell their souls for gold . . . gold . . . more gold . . . ; people starve amid heaps of Midas gold. . . .

Cuzco is America's Toledo, an imperial episcopal city, Christian altars set among idolatrous altars. Santo Domingo, once the Sun temple, is like Santo Cristo de la Luz and Santa María la Blanca among older Jewish and Moorish walls; the streets twist out like those from the Zocadover. A sandaled Indian stroking a guitar in the soft night before a balcony reinvokes a Moorish sultaness imprisoned behind harem lattices—a beautiful bronze princess in gold and purple, shining with the emeralds of the cult. Only an Indian chanting a *yaraví*, but that wailing melody came, not merely out of the whining winds of the Andes, but from the soft sad dreams of Moorish Spain. . . . Strange confusions of time and place and race. . . .

Fiesta in Cuzco is like a meadow filled with blood-red flowers, a moving sea of red—pathetic beauty of bewildered hope.

From the balconies hang ancient tapestries, rugs, bright scarves, Manila silks; the people turn their houses outwards, toward the plaza, toward the city, toward the Sun.

The tide of brown folk comes waving branches with white waxen leaves that flutter loose, rise, and fall and float over the plaza like a sea of white butterflies.

Passion of Jesus! What more appropriate than the red Mucchho flower, cut by the venerating Indians only one day in the year? Like a gory sacrifice, its blood-red petals flow about Our Lord of Earthquakes; day and night candles burn at his feet. Once this image came white from Spain. Perpetual smoke has converted the lacquer into a humble brown robe; smoke and the years and the prayers of brown folk have turned it brown, have turned it Indian. The image stands in a dark corner like an Incan waiting for the light to dawn over century-prolonged slavery. This Christ, condemned to the dark like brown folk, weeps, perspires, trembles. . . . He lives, he gives, he protects. . . .

2

From Christian temples the trail leads to old mysteries and glories, to the old city, not so much that of the earliest Incas, which huddled upon a narrow strip of westward sloping land between the Huatanay and Tullumaya, noisome rivers rushing from the Sacsahuamán heights to the Cusimayu, but the late Incaic Cuzco, whose splendors Inca Roca first envisioned, which Pachacutec with thousands of workmen built up during twenty years of planning, and which in its heyday, according to Ondegardo, had 320 native shrines. To the northwest towers Sacsahuamán, crowned by its stately old fortress; to the southeast are the Pumpa Chupán (Puma Trail) fields; between the two streams lies the most venerated Cuzco. On the west stretches Huaycay Pata, the holy terrace, six hundred feet long, the very axis of the empire.

Once more through the streets pass sumptuous Incan parades and priestly processions; warriors bring corn to the feet of Mama-Sara, Mother Maize; once more arises the victory chant:

> From his skull we shall drink,
> We shall adorn ourselves with his teeth;
> His bones will serve us as flutes,
> With his skin for a drum we shall dance.

258

Plaza masses lift arms to the Sun God and dance around the golden rope in gyrations profane and sacred—an archaic voluptuousness under a shower of flowers and white butterfly leaves.

No longer is Manco Cápac's Colcampata Palace deserted, no longer in ruins. Stark and strong as of old, it is sonorous with music, shining with dalmatics. Through its stone cloisters, the favorite nobles pass languidly in their litters. Slaves, nude torsos gleaming from ancient flambeaux, prostrate themselves, foreheads on cold stones—those postures immortalized forever by olden clay-workers in rapt designs on the sides of old holy *huacas*.

Near here a lowly herder, a *llama-michec*, thanks to his personal charms and a love philtre given to him by a demon in a mountain cave, wooed away a fair damsel from Sinchi Roca himself.

The spirit of Princess Sumac Tica, obliged to commit suicide for love, comes down from the mountain heights in a rope of silver water; those crossing the stone-paved bridges kneel down to drink the white blood of a princess who once caressed pet lions and puma cubs.

Once more they drag out an adulteress to hang her by her hair from some lofty crag. She croons her lament: "Father Condor, carry me hence; Brother Falcon, guide me hence."

Once more pilgrims (come from every corner of the empire over a thousand miles of stone-carved road and swinging fibre bridges) mass in the plaza. The sacerdotes burn coca incense in twelve huge gold urns in the vast Coricancha, the Palace of Gold, and sprinkle holy water brought through golden pipes to the fountain of the five gold spouts—just as the dawn Sun leaps through the portals to strike the great golden disk studded with emeralds and precious stones; its central deified countenance stares out from a dazzle of light, polished brow a blaze of flame, and from this reflected glory light glistens on golden jewelled walls; the whole temple fills with a crackling flame.

Once more the whole city lifts up in pæans of religious praise. In the Moon chapel, the Mother of the Incas stands stately, hands clasped in silver peace—she is all silver. Three other chapels are a host of stars forming the bright court of the Sister of the Sun—Chasca, "the star with long curly hair," Venus and the Pleiades. Others honor the Sun's dread ministers of vengeance, Thunder and Lightning; in still another, people pray for peace to the Rainbow under radiant multicolored arch-spanned walls.

Everywhere gold and silver. All the holy vessels, the immense chicha-libation vases, perfume censers, holy water ewers, the very pipes, the temple reservoirs, even the agricultural instruments, and the imitation fruits, flowers and animals in the sacred orchards—all were of gold and silver. The Inca mummies, each on a gold chair, had robes heavy with gold and jewels. From the Sun temple alone the Conquerors tore out seven hundred gold wall-plates.

Has the old power vanished? Once more, Inca warriors, lances uplifted, pace the triple-walled terraces of Cyclopean Sacsahuamán; there again the old-time battle of Manco rages; the city swirls to its doom in smoke and flames; there Cahuilde hurls himself to death—a death that spelled finis to the great empire.

Now the Spanish conquerors snarl over the broken remains of the realm. Now comes Pizarro, the swineherd, with a flourish of trumpets; he wears the rich velvet suit given him by Cortés of Mexico. Now comes Roman rebel Carbajal, roaring with laughter, to execute three hundred haughty cavaliers.

Now the Inquisitors meet in black hoods in dark stone chambers smelling of torture and fanaticism and blood. Indians are flogged and sliced, and sent to the mines for refusing the true faith, for remembering the days of Inca glories. . . .

Here are the imperial baths, covered with velvet moss, the Bath of the Ñusta, hidden among trees, where once princesses laved themselves. Perhaps from those banks concealed courtesans spied upon those lush bronze bodies. Would today the great Goddess Cauillaca, adversary of profanations, turn them into stones as of old, as is told of Carirava Virachocha?

On the Sacsahuamán esplanade were held the imperial festivals; the Incas viewed them from the Suchuna, a stone throne, its steps polished by the love of centuries. Twenty-seven other stone seats of varied forms to accommodate the body in different postures descend in hierarchical order.

There in the Huracá feast quivered the sensitive puberty flesh of maidens, brought to dance and be loved in religious Sun orgies—part of the imperial training. The Prince and young Incas from eighteen to twenty years were submitted to severe physical trials, even obliged to endure lashing without a whimper; their food was restricted to innure them to rigours. Physical trials were accompanied by excessive love trials. . . . During their month of training they slept constantly with fourteen- to fifteen-year-old girls. Even when they dashed all day up and down mountains and slept where they could, in the fields, in swamps or on rocks, young girls were provided them.

The feast closed with the images of the Sun and Moon in procession and the distending of the neophytes' ears with gold disks—then a last orgy among flowers, chicha-drinking, dancing, music, love, until mind and body were dulled in a sensualism all-consuming, an apotheosis of materialism.

In huge Ollantaytambo—Mighty Palace—lived Ollantay —Military Governor of Antisuyo (one of the four main regions of the empire). Though not one of the imperial caste, at Inca Pachacutec's court he dared fall in love with Infanta Cussi Cuyllar. Their love was mutual, beyond mortal limits.

Ollantay determined to overleap the rigid rules of hierarchy and make her his wife. Supreme sacerdote Huillac Homa tried to dissuade him and betrayed him to the emperor.

The girl was promptly locked up in Acllahuasis, the Convent of the Virgins of the Sun.

The impetuous lover stormed into revolt to conquer the crown and recover his bride. Pachacutec died without ever having been able to subdue the fiery rebel.

The Princess doubly shamed the royal caste by giving birth to a child—she called him Imac Sumac, "How Beautiful."

The emperor's son, Yupanqui, on taking the throne, through the treachery of General Rumiñahui, who pretended to join the rebel, finally captured Ollantay. But instead of chastising his prisoner, Yupanqui allowed the lovers to marry with due imperial pomp.

By the river, on the way to Ollantaytambo, rises a smooth cliff with a grotesque design, a blood-red figure with open arms, known as "The Inca Bathed in Blood"—a guard of Ollantay. In Ollantaytambo are two gigantic stones (worshipped long after the Conquest) which many declare to be the two lovers set there side by side eternally.

### 3

Cuzco. Two cities. Two cities which embrace yet spurn each other.

Though the Quechuas are beaten to the dust, the Inca capital still predominates. Though ruined, its spirit rules; it is still cyclical, monumental, gigantesque. What a thirst for immensity! It is the base which holds up the glistening Spanish city like a toy, a beautiful toy with Churrigueresque fripperies, coquettish Moorish balconies, slender palace arches and jasper *zocalos*.

Both old Cuzco and less old Cuzco are of stone, stone everywhere—beautiful darkness, polished like velvet.

The same stones that parapeted the Inca warriors, which held up the Sun-gold temple and the palaces, now hold up the Christian convents, monasteries and chapels, save that now the old Chacán reservoir, holding several hundred thousand gallons of water, and all the underground canals have been destroyed and clogged, so that modern Cuzco is neither so clean nor so healthful as the Incan metropolis.

J.S.

Those ancient stones! How the Incans loved the straight line—scarcely a curve, scarcely any decorations, only now and then bas-reliefs; except that on the way to Huayna Cápac's palace, the great blocks are carved with snakes, frogs and other reptiles—ancient announcement of the Amaru-Cancha zoological gardens. Mostly those evenly carved stones reflect a government paternally severe, saturated with rigid solemnity; those huge volcanic blocks tell more of ancient psychology than many a written chronicle.

In comparison the Spanish city is parvenu, slight, nervous, beautiful. In any other setting than gigantic stones and gigantic mountains, might even be considered impressive.

Two cities, locked in deadly embrace of love and hate eternally.

Cuzco is a mute Freudian symbol.

Two other cities are locked in antagonistic embrace within the womb of Peruvian nationality, dissimilar twins warring ere parturition—Cuzco and Lima. Two opposing centers. Cuzco represents the mother culture, heritage of the Incaic centuries; Lima is the hope for adaptation to European culture. Cuzco already existed when the Conqueror arrived; Lima was founded by the Conqueror to offset a Cuzco that was feared, that is still feared; for Cuzco is the city, declares Valcárcel, that will ultimately redeem the Indian.

There were two colonialisms: that of Lima, sybaritic, refined, with strong Versailles perfume—the courtesan Pericholi its ultimate symbol; and the colonialism of Cuzco, austere, manly, laborious. One is told of in the dulcet chronicles of Ricardo Palma; the other, only hinted at here and there, has had to wait until almost this century for its chroniclers. Today, as of old, Lima is soft and feminine; Cuzco fierce and masculine.

Lima still has a futile nostalgia for the courtly viceregal days. But Cuzco harks back to its august emperors, the Children of the Sun. Lima still takes Spaniards and all foreigners to its bosom hospitably. Four centuries have never erased Cuzco's hatred of the Spaniard and the colony. Pizarro's bones could not rest there in peace.

4

The duality of Cuzco is not the inner harmonious duality of Arequipa, but of two worlds still at war, unreconciled. The colony still governs Cuzco but the deep stream is that of Indian energy and culture.

One modern house still uses the ancient Inca plumbing. Upon the firm ruins of an Inca Palace another modern house repeats ancient themes in frieze; the Incas' mummies are lined up, *macanas* in one hand, the axe of gold—symbol of Cuzco's founding and of labor—in the other. Their brows, even as of old, are crowned with gold, subjecting the proud Persian-like crest and the imperial fillet, delegated authority of the Sun. The little Indian domestics pause there to look at them, their fur-sandalled feet sunk in the lowly clay, brown hands twisted in their coarse-woven capes over which their tresses fall black as their black eyes.

Modern dwellers in dark cubbyholes have fitted flimsy doors to old stones, like Granada gypsy caves. There in the obscurity of present and past centuries, they sleep, cook, sell chicha, and speak softly the same old Sun language, unusually tender, beautifully rhetorical. In the still night of deserted streets, from behind those closed doors one hears the grinding of maize or *jora* for chicha on stones extracted from some ruin. The noise is heavy, dull, steady; it beats eternally through closed doors like ghosts knocking at the portals of the dead city of the Incas.

Indian medicine: the rabbit-like *cuy* cures with deep religious significance; its "innards" are pulled out warm and palpitating and passed over the patient's body until they come to rest on the sick spot. Herb treatment follows: *Ccocmirache* favors procreation; *cangonillo* cures stomach pains; *huañay-huañay* ("always young") is a talisman of youth that protects against age as effectively, I am assured, as Voronoff's glands; *mucchhu* is deposited on the route of religious processions; *chichirilla* for purges, *raqui-raqui* for pneumonia—not to mention at least 362 others still unclassified botanically.

And dreams. The Cuzqueñan Indian, like backward dwellers in Texas and elsewhere, has an elaborate, if unwritten, dream book. He knows the meaning of every symbol—clean water, muddy water, an ox, dog, potatoes, a horseback rider, street car, robbing, eggs, teeth and whatnot—it may be

suspected, not with much Jung and Freudian exactitude.
Who has won the victory in Cuzco?

Over the ruins of Sunturhuasi Palace, where the trapped
Spaniards defended themselves desperately against Manco II
in 1536 and were saved by heroism and Christian miracle,
was erected the Temple of Triumph. There, where the first
Cross of Conquest is preserved, is a painting of the old miracle scene—six indigenes, dressed colonial style, praying with
colonial candles—to convince those otherwise skeptical: "To
this site of Sunturhuasi descended Mary, Queen of Castile."
A portal niche tells that there was built: "In this protected
spot, years after, a church, where Mary Mother of God put
her feet, showing her power, making heaven of this site and
giving victory in the happy battle of the Conquest, surprising countless numbers of Indians, putting out the fire of
those barbarians, aiding the Spaniards, planting the faith
and converting those most idolatrous ones. . . ."

Go into Santo Domingo—the capitular salon obeys the
conformity of old Coricancha; the niches once held the idols
of conquered Tahuantinsuyo provinces; here was once the
dwelling of the Sun sacerdotes. The outer wall of Coricancha,
knit together against the storms, polished by centuries, still
stands. Something of the ancient religion seems to have seeped
through the wrinkled pores of the grave priest who guides
me.

As one climbs up and down the streets and goes deeper
into the inner mystery of the place and its people, one still
asks—as perhaps might be asked of all armed victories—
"Just who has won?" True, the Indians come into the Temple
of Triumph past the plaque which tells of their humiliation,
but they pay it no heed—an old scar forgotten in the pain of
living ulcers—to kneel before images, Catholic in name only,
for these lace-panty saints bearing faded tulle flowers, live
in the indigenous heart with the same pantheistic soil-cult
meanings as the centuries-old idols they replaced. And the

267

Christs bleeding from every pore—two-dimensional Indian Christs, no profundity, no perspective! When the catechism was translated into Quechua, Catholicism absorbed the native psychology. To call God Cápac Apu is to alter God; to call Heaven Janac Pacha is to create a new heaven. How different the Angelus sounds in the sombre temple of the Andes from that on the plains of Castile! "The Catholicism of the Sierra is Incanized Catholicism," concludes Uriel García.

Though the Indians did not, as in Arequipa, consciously help the Spaniards, did not integrate their concepts with those of those Conquerors, mass communal labor inevitably brought native influences into Spanish techique. Santo Domingo carries an Indian tower; the façade of the house of Marqués del Valleumbroso is Incaic. Even the Spanish plaza portals have a subtle New World asymmetry. San Cristóbal is dominated by the atmosphere of ancient Colcompata. In general colonial Cuzco's urban contour is determined by Incan styles and dimensions.

Painting too. *El Hallazgo de la Virgen de Belén* back of the choir cathedral is dimensionally Indian; Miguel Angel's *Infierno*, like all local copying, has gathered some uniqueness of color and composition suggestive of Indian mannerisms. Certainly the *Marriage of Captain García Loyola with Beatriz de Mendoza* veils Indian psychology.

Sculpturing also. In *La Virgen de la Almudena* and the Pulpit of San Blas the Indian world peers vaguely through the curtain of Spanish form. The Spaniards dominated best in architecture; other art forms slither off into the Indian world.

The Cathedral, founded when it was, expectedly should be Gothic. Was it the massive setting that determined it Spanish Renaissance? In other ways old traditions imposed themselves; the Children of the Sun had covered the temple walls with gold; the Conquerors, not so rich, covered the cathedral with slabs of silver.

There also the Indians go to weep their sorrows; they kiss the altar steps; they are swept in the holocaust of the Mass and beat their foreheads against the floor with strident laments, guttural prophecy from the depths of the Andes.

5

The storm strikes over the crags. The dark clouds swoop up like the gray skirts of dancing giantesses. The lightning is a flame of shooting stars. The thunder is the cannonading of invisible hosts. The hail hammers the anvil of the Andes like a ringing symphony of tragedy. *Götterdämmerung!* Twilight of the gods! Storm on the Andes!

The gray dancing skirts swirl high, lift up in golden limbs of lightning, in a white embrace of nude precipices, and a sudden surge of snow from Titanic copulation. The whirl of storm demons makes a rumbling echo, symphonic accompaniment to a dream of Cyclopean love. The uproar bursts into family feud, and the female dancers turn into looping serpents that wrap themselves about the broken pinnacles in a monstrous stranglehold of passion and death. The hail comes rattling in the throat of the coughing world and taps down the valley like a blind giant, heedlessly trampling the cornfields. The uproar subsides and out of the belly of the pregnant storm comes the striped cat of the rainbow, sinuous body curved, claws on the hills, and golden eyes gleaming.

The Indians know what is happening. A poor old widow sent her seven sons, among them an idiot, a blind man, a lame man, and all of them lazy lying tramps, out to till the fields. They merely lay out in the shade all day. Returned home late each evening, "tired and hungry," they told all they had done. When harvest time came, she found herself without a crop and utterly without food.

In her desperation she cut off slices from her flaccid muscles and put them in the pot. When her sons had gluttonously devoured the repast, she flung herself at them in wrath calling them evil names. "You have eaten up everything, even the body of your own mother." Showing them her macerated flesh, she disowned them forever.

Thunder beat upon them; lightning embraced their house in flames, and the mother was converted into a gigantic serpent that looped up, black, into the sky. She hurled down thousands of lightning bolts. In the furious battle with their monstrous mother, they were changed into Hail, the Blind; Ice, the Lame Man; Rain Storm, the Idiot; the rest into Snow, Wind, Thunder and Lightning. In the struggle all the fields were beaten down. To placate their mother the evil sons stripped away all the fruits of the field to lay at her feet in the caves of ice and snow.

Ever since, each year, *Ccatu,* the Mother Serpent, rises up into the sky, and the furious sons sweep down on the fields for the fruits to placate her. Then when the storm subsides the *Ychi ollccos,* who live in the lagoons, come out to sport. From their belly-buttons they throw out at each other streams of light that lift up like the head of a cat and expand in a fan of colors. Let no man point at the rainbow or his index finger will rot away. But sterile girls go down hopefully into the lagoons to bathe; the light leaps over their brown flesh caressingly in a glow of iris colors, and their bodies palpitate with passion and joy. The sun comes out again and the Cuzqueño sings in Quechua:

> "*Puna pisccochos carccani*
> *Mana taitayoc. . . .*"

> "If I had no parents
> I'd be a bird of the crags,
> A bird of the crags!
> I'd have the rain for a little father
> And the snow for a little mother. . . ."

## 6

The door of the wake is open. Any one is welcome to enter. Black-mantled Indian figures, like giant Goya *caprichos*, sit about the coffin of a child who has been visited by Quepque, the dread death spirit. For hours they sit silent, never sobbing, not even the mother, for her child goes to a happier pagan place, a celestial choir, a paradisical nursery, where babes have all they are denied on earth. To weep would prevent their trip to that abode of joy.

Long hours the women mourners sit silent. But in another room, men are drinking, laughing, rattling dice.

Then a stirring. Food comes, *chuño* and barbecued meat and fiery *pisco*, many rounds of *pisco*. The hoarse hilarity moves into the wake beside the coffin. The harp thrums, the flute shrills, tremulous shrill *yaravíes* wail out through the night hours—intertwined music of conquerors and music of the defeated making two races weep together.

At last, mist puffs in through the open door from a world shrill with birds. Dawn comes in gray wraiths; like a kiss of death it comes.

Drunken arms lift the coffin to drunken insecure shoulders; drunken feet stumble through rose dawn to the cemetery.

No one weeps. They go, a slim procession of shuffling fur sandals and hooded figures, like actors in some ancient necromancy; they go silent between two oceans of purple color, the mountains and the sky; they go safely, for God has parted the two oceans that they may tread there.

The Sun! It lifts like a lion above the crest. It flings itself from the mountain into the abyss—a shower of gold and silver, a misty precious rain of light over cupola and tower, over the city of the Incas, the city of the Sun.

# XVIII

## IQUITOS OF THE GREEN HELL

### I

THE Iquitos Malecón, the tree-lined balustrade thorough-fare bordering the wide, dirty, brown Amazón, overlooks thick jungle, sun-spangled water, glaring tin roofs, buzzards, open sewers, strings of launches rocking at rotting wooden steps. A silver world of sun, mist and mirage-like reflections. A green world of massed vegetation.

Dawn. The sun's fire dissolves the river-jungle mist. Half a mile from shore, on verdant Iquitos Island, cattle are bel-lowing, burros braying, and the *chacra* folk are setting forth in flimsy pointed canoes with produce.

The Malecón bustles. The adjacent market buzzes. Eager buyers stream along counters strangely loaded—dried mon-key, fresh turtle meat still quivering, squawking chickens, dead chickens cut into parts, long, fat, fuzzy, black, red-headed tree grubs, *paiche* river fish, fruit, chirimoyas, alli-gator pears, sapotes, pineapples, bananas, melons, mangos.

Outside the market, erect, light-footed cholas expertly balance on their heads, by means of hand-painted rush rings, clay pots or enamel basins or baskets of cooked Pishicayo palm fruit or *aguaje* fruit, red, scaly, egg-shaped—for making soft drinks. They jostle, flash flirtatious black eyes, laugh whole-heartedly at the sallies of white-shirted males perched on the flat concrete balustrade or sprawled on the park benches of the diminutive Plaza de Castilla. Sunshine, noise, chatter. Everyone is gay.

From upstream Belén and Río Itaya comes an increasing hum. The Malecón chatter ceases. Bustling marketers hasten

272

across the plaza to secure a vantage point. The lounge lizards bounce up from their seats. Urchins scale the breast-high balustrade and squat on top gazing expectantly. The market is forgotten. Everything is forgotten. An expectant hush. The San Ramón mail plane roars in—the momentous morning event for this isolated frontier post.

Early morning is the flush part of the day. By ten o'clock the market, deserted, is being scrubbed for the next day. Heat grows. Iquitos declines into hushed dazzling noon hours, oppressive, stifling. The sun blazes over tin roofs and empty thoroughfares. The buzzards sink their heads deep into their soft feathers. Dogs lie panting along the dirty open sewers. People doze behind closed shutters. The prostrate city lies coiled in luxurious dreams.

It will not revive again until late afternoon, not fully until the sun has gone down in a haze of colored jungle mist. Sensation of coolness brings people out to promenade the plaza with its obelisk of War-of-the-Pacific martyrs. White-suited youths with sleek black hair; dusky belles with luscious curves, rounded bosoms; slim, pallid, blue-blood Señoritas of old Castile in shimmering bright organdies, attempt flimsy modishness. Vivid contrast, for on still nights, the jaguar roars in the neighboring jungle; in the street gullies young alligators have been caught; everywhere lurks the menace of malaria, beri beri, bubonic plague, leprosy, and the horrible ulcerous *espundia;* but these dour diseases do not worry the joyous promenaders—the regimental band blares in the kiosk —men one way, women another, round and round; flirtations; sometimes they lead to the altar. . . .

2

Iquitos, Perú's most northern and eastern outpost, western sentinel of the mighty Amazón, is the capital of huge Loreto department, a third of the country's entire area, as large as Spain and Portugal together.

As an Indian fishing village, Iquitos had existed hundreds of years before eighteenth-century white missionaries set foot in the region. Orellano, treacherous companion of Gonzalo Pizarro, passed below here in 1540; a 1555 traveler tells us it already had many people of mixed blood. But the Council of the Indies archives gives the first subduer of the Iquitos Indians as Jesuit father José Bahamonde. In 1730 he founded the "town" Santa María de la Luz de los Iquitos at the Anzo and Amazón river junction; in 1741 Santa Barbara de Iquitos; in 1747, Corazón de Jesús de los Iquitos y de los Huasimoas. The two latter, on the junction with the Nanay River, were probably ancestors of the present city.

The Jesuits continued overlords of the Amazón basin until their expulsion in 1768.

The first bishop of Mainas in 1814 gave the village eighteen inhabitants living in twenty huts, descendants of the aboriginal tribe, now almost vanished through disease and intermarriage. An 1848 census placed the population at 154; by 1851, due to the wiping out by Indian attacks of the important neighbor town San Borja, Iquitos' population jumped to 234.

From 1850 to 1852 Lieutenant William Lewis Herndon and Lardner Gibson of the United States navy explored the Amazón valley and reported: "Iquitos is a fishing village of 227 inhabitants . . . ninety-eight being whites and mestizos of San Borja and other settlements . . . driven from their homes . . . by the Huambisas of the Pastaza and Santiago . . . Iquitos is situated on an elevated plateau . . . different from . . . many towns on the Amazón, most of which are built upon a hill with low swampy country behind . . . coffee and cotton trees growing in the streets . . . no attention . . . paid to either."

By 1859 the population had increased to 500. Iquitos had

begun to grow; October 6, 1853, the *Marajo,* first steamer of the *Compañia Brazilera de Navigación,* had put into the port—a red-letter day. Prior to that navigation had been confined to balsas, canoes and a few sail vessels. In 1854, the Peruvian government placed a 180,000 peso order in England for four steamers; the first, the 500-ton *Pastaza,* arrived February 26, 1864.

But not until the rubber boom and the harrowing "Putumayo atrocities"—brutal exploitation of native rubber gatherers—did Iquitos loom large on South American maps. The first rubber shipment was made in 1892, another in 1898. Soon rubber-gatherers (*caucheros*) flocked into Loreto and surrounding areas. They were bold adventurers, heirs of the Conquistadores, seekers of El Dorado. Between 1898 and 1902, 1,769 tons of rubber were exported. From then on the region exported to Europe and North America via Brazil fabulous quantities of gutta-percha, *jebe* and *caucho.*

Iquitos became one of Latin America's richest cities. Its streets flowed with the gold of the rubber merchants who spent their money as fast as they made it—a diet of cold cash till then never surpassed in South America's history. Venal and other joys flourished. Streets and plazas were laid out. New buildings sprang up. Brick and stone were imported at great cost. The principal hotel, the Malecón Palace, was erected with a marble exterior and other signs of imported splendor. The *nouveaux riches* began bringing in luxuries, acquired snobbishness. Iquitos reigned Queen of the Amazón.

In 1912 the rubber bubble burst. Former millionaire traders became paupers. Europe and the United States turned to other markets. Though the World War temporarily renewed prosperity, soon Iquitos tobaganned rapidly down hill; rubber in 1910-12 worth 560 *soles* per 100 pound quintal, today is worth a bare 40 *soles.* The city's descent was as swift as its earlier rise to extravagance. From its previous golden eminence—though Iquitos still presents evidences of former prosperity—it degenerated into an ordinary dirty river-trading center, depending on inadequately exploited agricultural and tropical products—cotton, tobacco, coffee, rice, hides, lumber, cacao, sisal, kapoc, *tagua* (vegetable ivory), balata, mahogany, dried fish, chicle, and the recently introduced African oil palm (*elæsis guiniensis*).

Today Iquitos' population, approximately 10,000, is composed of the staffs of trading and commercial houses (many are Chinese and Japanese), banks and steamship agencies; officers and men of army, navy, and air-mail service; and cholos—the most numerous—which populate the surrounding river flats and jungle, and cultivate the soil or ship as crews on the small wood-burners which ply the Amazón and its Peruvian tributaries, the Ucayali, Marañón, Placazu, Pachitea, Pichis, Huallaga and Napo rivers.

Aside from the air-mail line to San Ramón in the Chanchamayo valley (established by Leguía and U. S. Commander H. B. Grow in 1927), thence over a hair-raising auto road for a day to Oroyo, then another day's ride by train 16,000 feet over the top of the Andes and down to Lima, the only other feasible communication with the rest of Perú is over the age-old Pichis trail, a journey of many weeks by launch, muleback, then by auto and train.

Iquitos' real outlet is the Amazón. Deep-draft steamers travel every few weeks for Manaos and Para in Brazil. Just below here is the theatre of future imperial struggles as revealed in the near-war scare over Leticia. There Ecuador, Colombia, Brazil and Perú cast jealous eyes on every stream, swamp and jungle plain—a wilderness that some day may mean fabulous wealth. Thus, just as Lima looks away from Perú out upon the seven seas, so Iquitos, a world unto itself, looks down the Amazón.

But unlike Lima, it is closely linked with the activities and spirit of its immediate hinterland. For lonely settlers deep in the virgin forest, it is a longed-for goal, the metropolis that

connects them with the distant world. To it they come to
replenish their supplies, see movies, feel the caress of comfort. The Indian savage drifts down on rafts to trade, then
returns a hero to tell of its strange wonders, its stone buildings, its miraculous bird-machine. To it the missionary, after
months in the wilderness, returns to wonder just where God

is found. To Iquitos come geologists, botanists, zoologists,
ethnologists and other scientists who have searched for
knowledge or wealth. Even the hobo drifts in, searching for
El Dorado, only to be shipped on down to Manaos by general subscription.

### 3

Into Iquitos crowd the primitive influences of the surrounding jungles. Its decaying splendor is hemmed about by cholo
and Indian thatched roofs—the town reveals the constant
race between civilization and jungle.

In the deeper forests, all up and down the little-explored

tributaries, the ancient Indian folk—though some venture half-naked into Iquitos to trade—tranquilly live their ancient ways, except now they collect many tropical products to barter for calicoes, beads, knives, mirrors and other coveted articles.

They range from the most prehistoric primitive to more cultured remnants originally under Inca influences; from the breech-clout to elaborate beautiful costumes, from the guttural limited *inje-inje* language to the complicated *aguaruna-campa* tongues.

The Orejones (inhabiting the lower Napo—a wide, shallow, little-known river—and a small stretch of the Amazón north bank) and the Quechuas (in the small headwater Ecuadorian streams) pierce holes in the earlobes of the young and gradually enlarge them by inserting half-inch thick balsa-wood disks until the openings become three to six inches in diameter—the old Inca practice. Usually naked, for gala wear they use loose lengths of *chambira* fibre of which they also make splendid hammocks and bags. The sub-tribal Tahuas dress themselves entirely in grass costumes, dyed brick-red with *achote*. The women rise immediately after childbirth; the husband takes her place in the hammock and emits piercing cries until his friends bring him gifts. (This custom should be introduced into New York where it really costs something to have a baby.) The Ticuna sub-tribe depilates young girls as soon as they reach puberty.

To other tribes, using the blow-gun (*bobugotarato*) for killing fish, the Orejones trade the famous Ticuna poison—extracts from the *Cocculus toxicoferus* and *Strichnos-castelnau*, Uriari and Ramón plants. They collect sarsaparilla, copal, vegetable oils and waxes, and cut the small Palo de Cruz, a curious, hard, yellowish, black, cross-grained wood which makes fine walking sticks and cabinets, and which they boil to make a blood tonic.

In the middle Napo and on the great Putumayo live about

twenty-five thousand Huitotos, a docile race, users of the *camana* war-club, lance and blow-gun. Some sub-groups are cannibals. Robuchon has described the anthropophagal ceremonies. The victim is killed with an arrow tipped with *curare* poison; the arms and trunk are thrust into a huge terra cotta vat, seasoned with red chile. The heavy beat of the *manjüaré* summons people from far and near to the banquet. Answering beats of the distant *manjüarés* from those accepting the invitation, rolls like an ominous rumbling tide through the deep jungle twilight. Five or six hundred people troop in with discordant shrill cries. The *manjüarés* cease. Silence falls. The head Cacique squats before the vat to pull out the cooked flesh with his hands and tears it into shreds to be passed around. He intones a prayer answered by the sonorous *"heu heu heu"* of the multitude.

Other tribes cut off a piece of the heel of their dead father to wear around their necks as a sacred emblem. They believe in the good spirit Usiñamú and the bad spirit Taifeño. Somewhere on the Igara-Paraná River, they say, large ruins contain much gold. A curse prevents any one's getting to it.

The Muratos, a Jíbaro sub-tribe between the Lower Morona and the Pastaza, are (except for the Macchines, noted for cruelty) docile, industrious and hospitable.

One day a Murato fisherman killed a baby lizard that ate his bait. The furious mother lizard lashed the water with her tail until it overflowed the surrounding region. All the people were drowned except one man who climbed a tall palm tree. Night enveloped the world. The survivor remained on his perch for many moons in continuous darkness. He lived off palm nuts. Now and then he threw one down. From the splash he knew the waters had not yet subsided. Finally, a nut fell on dry earth with a thud. He built himself a house and buried a piece of his own flesh from which a woman grew. Thus was founded the Murato race.

They live in thatched huts in the midst of yuca, banana

and corn fields. The chief food, yuca, also provides their *masato* beer. They also make a refreshing drink from the *tumbo* plant. Their good-looking women wear the *cushma*, a long robe.

The Jíbaros and Zaparos (between the Napo and Pastaza) are a happy crowd who mummify enemies' hands as war-trophies. Despite this slight animosity they are much sought after as servants, are good workmen around the *chacras*.

The Huambisas, another large Jíbaro sub-tribe inhabiting the Morona basin, though some are accustomed to whites, mostly are hostile, especially the deep-jungle dwellers, the Tihuirmas, Juachiguas, Panacheras and Tutunangoras.

The Huambisas and allied tribes, who have ever loved their liberty, destroyed the old towns of Borja and Santiago, and only a few years ago they wiped out a Peruvian frontier post of thirty soldiers. Around Puerto Pardo, the large tribes of Patucas and Chiripaos—which use no canoe and merely roam the forests half-naked in short *cushmas*—are most warlike of all. With spear, lance, blow-gun and huge shield they go forth in cane-crowns of macaw feathers, monkey tails and dyed reed objects to wage war; they strike terror into the hearts of settlers. Prolific, mostly polygamous, many use the *Guayusa* plant to induce sexual desire.

The Aguaranos, on the thickly populated Nieva, collect much gold and silver and barter beads, *achiote*, and *huito*. A wife is sometimes purchased for a goodly chunk of salt. Like all the Jíbaro tribes, they reduce the heads of enemies to a fifth their normal size. The head is placed on a pole in the open air for three days, then a cut is made from the back of the neck to the crown. The bones are carefully re-moved, leaving only the skin. The inside flesh is carbonized away by hot sand. The head is smoked over a special fire of *chonta* and *bucunga* roots, the *alum* in which reduces it to the required size. It is then washed with a strong astringent Renaquilla solution.

Neither features nor hair is lost, though heavier parts become more prominent. The jaws are replaced by *chonta* wood. The lips are sewed shut. Frequently the head of a sloth—symbol of cowardice—is prepared in the same fashion to accompany that of the killed enemy.

This process is carried out by the head-hunter hero in some secluded spot while he abstains from food and drink. As soon as the shrunken head is ready, the hero returns to his tribe, wearing it around his neck by a cord through the crown. A great feast is prepared and much *masato* is drunk. The victor addresses the head with long insulting speeches. Since the lips have been sewed shut the enemy spirit cannot answer back—scarcely sportsmanlike.

The natives even drift down from the far Madre de Dios region. The Conibos, Setebos and Sysibos, when a child reaches the age of ten, have holy old women weave a belt thirty inches long and six inches wide, which is folded in sections like book leaves, on which are inscribed bizarre characters—the *quellca*. From a tree branch are made a cane and a cross which are painted red. These objects are carefully preserved during the individual's lifetime: the *quellca*, wrapped in a white bag, in a basket; the cane and cross in the roof beams or thatch. The body of any dying person is carefully washed and painted black with *hiuto*, dressed in white, and the *quellca* placed on the chest till the last breath. The cross is then put in the corpse's right hand, the cane in the left.

The jungle—strange world of strange people. Yet in Iquitos is many a ferocious head-hunter's son, apparently civilized. Wearing European clothes and packing freight to and from docked steamers, he seems little different, though as yet lower in the economic scale, from his neighbors.

4

In Iquitos two ways of life jostle. Besides a military hospital and good Peruvian and foreign doctors, *curanderos*, or witch-doctors, ply a lucrative trade. Even many "people of reason" think that native *Yerbamora* and *Atopi* leaves for leprosy and other herb knowledge are superior to European science. They even pay proper heed to witchcraft; superstitions are deeply ingrained in the most rational. The cry of the *Tunschis* and the *Urucututos*, owl-like birds, and the fluttering of the *Yan-pippupinta*, a black butterfly, bring inevitable death. The *Ayac-pullitu*, with its sorrowful screech, and the *Puma-garza* also bear evil tidings.

The *Yayay-mamem*, a small swift bird that wails heartbreakingly in the forest, "Aye . . . aye . . . mamá," is an evil spirit enticing children. These are in turn changed into *Yayay-mamemes*, and from then on they cry unavailingly for their mothers. The *ignus fatuus* is the *Caipora*, the wandering soul of an unbaptized one. The *Tunschis* are the shrill whistling souls of those about to die. . . .

The traveler who drinks of the small river Sacachora will never leave Iquitos. . . .

These two antagonistic worlds of reason and superstition find fusion in the cholos, the predominant ethnic ingredient.

Here as elsewhere, the mestizo is a social and economic go-between. Many live by huckstering. They obtain European articles on credit, which they load into *monterías*, large rowboats with roofed cabins. For a small fee they are towed upstream by some launch to the limit of steam navigation, then slowly drift down the current calling in at all small villages, *chacras* and stores on smaller rivers, lakes and streams where regular launches cannot go, trading their wares for cotton, timber, cornmeal, *paiche*, fish-poison, medicinal plants and Indian curios.

On regular freighting routes ply large rafts, about fifty

tree-trunks lashed solidly side by side. The logs, half-awash, are often infested with water-snakes which also hide among the cargo, hence to protect passengers and damageable goods there is a raised platform with thatched roof because of the incessant rains. Another platform serves for the fireplace, pigs, and poultry. Pets of all kinds are carried—dogs, cats, monkeys, ant-eaters, and fleas. Managed by long oars, lashed to either side and manned by half a dozen men, these rafts lazily float downstream, surrounded by a cloud of sandflies by day and a pillar of mosquitoes by night.

Thus there is an ascending hierarchy of traders: gee-string Indian, goods on back and sweating brow; the men of the *monterías* and rafts, sail-boats and launches and little wood-burning steamers; finally native and foreign owners of big Amazón vessels—in such wise do the great industrial nations acquire the many curious raw products necessary for medicine, science, manufacturing and war.

The chola women are never idle. They till the *chacras* and weave fine Panamá hats from the stemless Bombonaje palm; its ten-foot fan-shaped leaves easily split into narrow strips. They make pretty fans from tropical feathers.

The women greatly outnumber the men, which increases natural tropical and mestizan feminine lascivity. Their round luscious forms are scarcely concealed; the heat makes necessary the thinnest garments; and when not chained to toil, they are lively, carefree, and enjoy music, especially the phonograph, accordion and guitar, and risk all for love.

Though very maternal, the Loretian cholas, absorbed in the cultivation of the *chacras,* in weaving and housekeeping, often have to neglect their offspring. Through eating fruits, dirt, and from insect bites, the little children suffer from hookworm, fever, and skin-diseases. Infant mortality is high. The child that survives usually does so through a precocious learning of the laws of the forest, its one inheritance. At

a very early age children skilfully handle canoe, raft, fish-
line and weapons.

"The pure Loretano," remarks one observer, "is a mixture
of Indian, Quechua and European [and he might have added,
Oriental], which in time becomes more homogeneous,
healthier, graceful and determined. Many . . . educated in
the United States [or Europe] . . . speak English and
French with fluency . . . a laughing charming people
whether in town or in the brush."

These are the future citizens, the future race of the upper
Amazón basin.

# PART IV

*LINES OF BATTLE*

# XIX

# LAND BARONS

## I

AGRICULTURE is Perú's most important industry. Four-fifths of the population derive their food, clothing and shelter directly from the soil. Important as is agricultural activity, to obtain precise information about it is difficult. There are few statistics. Most of the farm products which provide Perú's subsistence do not even figure in the export lists. According to trade figures Perú falsely appears to be essentially a mining country. Since 1925—due to decrease in sugar and cotton prices—mining exports have greatly surpassed those of agriculture (petroleum, a new industry, 1916-1926 increased six-fold). Yet mining employs but three percent of all adult male workers—about 30,000.

Nor do even the exported agricultural products provide any clue to real rural activities. Sixty-eight percent comes from the coast, yet three-fourths of Perú's population resides in the Sierra. The leading agricultural products shipped abroad are cotton and derivatives, rice, sugar, wools, hides and gums. Actually these products account for only a small fraction of the working population; cotton requires only 50,000 adult workers, sugar not over 25,000, rice not over 12,000.

Thus the benefit to Perú of these export industries, largely in foreign hands and dependent upon uncontrollable world market prices, has been vastly exaggerated.

Most of Perú's farm products (and these provide food and employment for the mass of the people) are consumed domestically. Agriculture—and precisely that agriculture of

287

which there are little or no statistics, of which the central government has little or no concern—is the real foundation rock of the nation.

## 2

Three types of production exist: the extremely backward feudal serfdom of the Sierra, the semi-modernized coast feudalism, utilizing some scientific methods but with abominably low labor standards, and village communalism.

Large landholding is a Spanish Conquest creation. Its basis was and is usurpation—from the first enormous grant to Pizarro (who in turn granted *encomiendas* to his followers) down to the present. The New Laws (1542-43) abolished the process, but further grants were soon made by Governor Gasca to recompense loyal followers in the struggle against rebellious Gonzalo Pizarro; also by Gasca's successors. These grants were enormous, and though under Viceroy Núñez de Vela and thanks to various protective decrees, Indian rights were at times protected, much of Perú's area was parcelled out.

Legally this spoliation was endorsed by the Crown, subsequently by the Republic governments; morally—through such bulls as that of Alexander VI and by various post-Independence pastorals—it was endorsed by the Church.

Then and since, land has been appropriated usually with violence, the native population being either brutally ejected or absorbed as serfs.

Not an abrupt process, it kept up all during Spanish rule, then was accelerated during and immediately after the Independence wars.

The Bolívar decrees (February, 1824; July, 1825)—motivated by *laissez faire* theories and the equality of all men—provided for distribution of the communal lands as individual possessions not to be freely disposed of until 1850.

A March, 1828, law permitted their disposal if the owner could read and write.

The large landowners, especially as the country was sunk in civil strife, utilized these regulations to expand their possessions. The 1852 Civil Code, antagonistic to the Indian

communities, ostensibly to create small proprietors, gave the *gamonales* still a new weapon. Carlos Valdez de la Torre points out the "astonishing" increase in haciendas in the last century—"in Puno, for example . . . a hundred-fold from 1860-1915."

The spoliation, more slowly now since less land is available and the communes are putting up more resistance, still continues. Wherever there are fertile accessible lands, there the large hacienda has spread its tentacles. Though in Junín in the central Sierra, the indigenous communities have better defended themselves, nevertheless the *gamonales* are lords of the region, all-powerful politically. In other places the age-old abuses continue.

One recent development was the scramble under Leguía, in disregard of native titles, to parcel out all remaining available lands, especially in jungle regions. November 12, 1930, *La Libertad* gave the following list of acquisitions in Loreto and Madre de Dios:

|  | Acres |
|---|---|
| Pres. Augusto Leguía | 37,500 |
| Guillermo A. Leguía | 10,000 |
| Ricardo S. Leguía | 11,260 |
| Lizandro Quesada | 38,517 |
| Enrique Zegarra | 20,310 |
| Juan F. Zegarra | 6,100 |
| Alberto Ayulo | 37,623 |
| Nicolás Salazar Orfila | 38,535, etc. |

Aguilar in *Cuestiones Indígenas* [1] describes how the Indians are dispossessed: "The interested party seeks out a communal landholder, becomes his *compadre* . . . to gain his confidence and induces him to sign to him power of attorney for his defense, for no indigenous property is not being legally contested or in danger of being contested. . . . After some time, the supposed representative presents himself before the judge demanding possession . . . for the . . . power of attorney was no such thing, but a bill of sale, made through a secret deal with the writer of the document, the witnesses and shyster lawyers. Hearings . . . are held; the [supposed] buyer . . . legally established in his right . . . demands the ejection of the usurper of his property. . . . As the Indian's affection for his hut and land cannot be uprooted, he usually . . . from then on remains as a tenant on his own land, the false protector converted into owner and master."

The records of the governmental Patronato of the Indig-

[1] 32 ff.

enous Races are filled with bitter Indian complaints regarding land thefts, seizure of animals and property, kidnapping, abuses by constituted authorities, judges, police, army, and not infrequently by priests.

The Ayacucho Patronato, April 30, 1928, prints the protest of peasants for the manner in which Judge Gerardo Roca, other officials, and the rural guard, seized sections of land, expelled the dwellers en masse, broke up protest meetings and divided the stolen region into five zones with lieutenant governors to hold it.

The investigating commission of the Patronato for Cuzco reported, September 18, 1926: ". . . completely proven . . . the unmentionable abuses of which the Lauramarca Indians are victims . . . ill treatment, exactions and evil procedures . . . in violation of the law and the constitution . . . deported to deadly Ccosñipata Valley regions. . . . Obliged to pay grazing tolls for five years back in a lump sum . . . those unable to make such a large and unaccustomed outlay have had their cattle seized. . . . They have been molested . . . maltreated, respect not even being shown for women; the military forces camp there, live and sustain themselves off . . . the food, domestic animals and cattle of the Indians. . . ."

Further report September 25: "Indigene Melchora Yapuna married to Juan Villagra . . . complains that on the night of Friday, September 17 [during the absence of her husband] twelve mounted soldiers . . . in the midst of the greatest abuses, proceeded to rape her, stifling her desperate cries for aid . . . took with them a cow, horse, five llamas, eleven sheep, domestic animals, food, rope, sacks, wool-shears . . . everything . . . In the same way in her presence they violated her daughter Anastasia Villagra of less than ten years, leaving her unconscious."

By such means, through the centuries, a great feudal landholding system was perfected and extended; the *gamonales* became political dictators, still remain in the saddle, still gouge their spurs deep into the Peruvian nation.

Labor for the haciendas is obtained by contract, land-rental, and semi-serfdom. The wage of supposedly free contracted laborers in Ayacucho, Puno and Cuzco is from 40 to 50 centavos (8 to 10 cents) daily.

The Sierra *gamonales* often shirk personal development of their properties through rentals in return for labor or crop-sharing, rarely money. Francisco Ponce de León has made a detailed study of the rental system in Cuzco.[2]

"In Paucartambo province, the proprietor concedes the use of lands to a group of indigenes on condition that they perform all necessary labor on the hacienda. . . . Generally they work three alternate days a week during the whole year. The renters . . . are also obliged to use their own beasts of burden without remuneration to carry the hacendado's crop to the city, and to serve as *pongos* [personal servants] on the hacienda or more commonly in Cuzco where the proprietors prefer to live. The *pongo* service is done in weekly or monthly turns, either with or without remuneration, according to the area of the rented lands, the number of renters and the generosity of the bosses. Some haciendas are so large they have within their boundaries as many as a dozen indigenous communities, the members of which, though they may own some communal lands, live in large part as renters on surrounding haciendas. . . . Women, widows, and old women unable to pay their share by rude field labor . . . either supply a worker or give their service to the hacienda, being called *mittanes*."

This form of rental has certain advantages, but invariably they get only the poorest land, and frequently the hacendado will let the Indians work their own rented portions only on rainy days or holidays.

3

The resident, non-contracted *yanaconas*, or serfs, in return for a small patch for hut and garden, usually the rockiest poorest soil, must tend the herds and cultivate the hacienda fields at least three days a week without as a rule receiving any remuneration. The *yanacona*, rooted to the hacienda, is held by father-to-son debt; he cannot leave. If the Indian herder loses any animals, the cost is added to his debt, or if he has any animals himself, he must give them up to replace the loss.

Anco, between La Mejorada and Ayacucho, is inhabited by the serfs of two haciendas coming up to the very edge of town. "Everything there," remarks Saenz, "is tinged with the conventional and archaic; the people seem to belong to the same brotherhood . . . a brotherhood of serfs. . . . We asked a young man how he was employed . . . a woman told us in Quechua that he was a lad in the confidence of the master. . . . 'How much do you earn?' we asked him. 'He doesn't earn anything,' she told us, 'for his fathers were also in the service of the master.' . . . We met an old Indian walking with his daughter of about twenty years. She lifted her sombrero, decked with yellow flowers . . . she seemed a pastoress of the Middle Ages. We asked them from what town they came, and they answered, 'We belong to Guillermo Pacheco.' . . . This gentleman, lord of people, is the *gamonal* of Llaccria; his serfs . . . know to whom they belong but not where they live." [3]

"We belong to So-and-so," is a common serf expression. Continues Saenz: "The Sierra hacienda destroys the community and converts the free *comunero* into a serf irremediably lost or throws him into the pathless desert of social inadaptability . . . the tragic struggle between hacienda and community . . . small property lost by the indigenes, won by the hacienda, the slow brutal destruction of men until they are reduced to hunger, converted into pariahs and slaves." [4]

The Fomento *Bulletin* (1926-27): "The recent reclamations which the Indians have been presenting for more than a year . . . produce an impression of horror . . . there is seen the cruelty of the oppressor and the sad situation they suffer. . . . Let us not forget that oppression inevitably produces terrible reactions."

One hacienda, so vast it contains seven villages, reports: "These villages provide us with fourteen *pongos* constantly distributed among the various families of our corporation."

The Indian, thus dragged into household service, loses even his name, is called merely *"Pongo."* He can be rented or loaned to friends; he is an inoffensive but useful beast of burden. In Puno he must wear a special small cap; this indication of his status opens him to abuse wherever he goes. *Pongos* are rarely given clothes or money. I have seen such in wealthy Lima households, cooking, washing, serving table, in stinking rags through which dirty skin showed. The room of one, a girl, was a dark under-stairs cubbyhole, her bed a heap of filthy rags. These families, so proud of their culture,

[3] 172-73.
[4] 185.

their pedigree and titles which they have done nothing to merit, evidently derive such pleasure from brutality they are willing to jeopardize their own hygienic safety. The favorite punishment of one such wealthy dame (which I witnessed and interfered with) was to yank her *ponga* about by one of her eyelids. This poor girl had a child by the eighteen-year-old son of the family, but had to keep the baby in a dirty cloth, for she had no means of getting any clothes for it.

## 4

The Indian suffers any number of abuses. Forced labor for the haciendas is rounded up, if not so openly as some years back, through official pressure, debt liquidation, tax liquidation, what not.

Manuel González Prada translated a native song on the subject:

"My son, I leave;
  Morning reverberates on the volcano;
  Give me my *chonta* cane,
  My jaguar sandals."

  "Father, here are your sandals,
    Here is your cane.
    By why do you look at me and weep,
    Where are you going?"

"The unjust law of the whites
  Tears me from my home;
  I go to toil and starve,
  I go to the deadly mines."

  "You leave us today,
    But when, when do you come back?"

"When the flame of the crags
  Shall love the sandy desert."

"When will the flame of the crags
Love the sandy desert?"

"When the tiger of the forest
Shall drink the waters of the sea."

"When will the tiger of the forest
Drink the water of the sea?"

"When from the condor's egg
A deadly serpent is born."

"When will a deadly serpent
Be born from the condor's egg?"

"When the breast of the whites
Is moved to pity."

"When will the breast of the whites
Be moved to pity?"

"My son, the breast of the whites
Will never be moved to pity."

In 1917 Dr. Augusto A. Belaunde, Health Doctor for Cuzco Department, visited all villages in his jurisdiction: "To enter a rustic hut or a city hovel inhabited by an Indian family is to subject one's sight and olfactory sense to indescribably disagreeable sensations. The family's dwelling is generally small, and always low-roofed, dark, without ventilation. . . . One must stoop to half his natural height, for this tiny door is the only access . . . through which some air or . . . light can enter the place. . . . The eyes, after considerable time, accustomed to that darkness . . . the different objects and animals—in whose company the Indians always live—can be distinguished. . . . Fetid, nauseating odors. . . . Kitchen utensils, plowing implements, vegetables, grain, bits of dried putrid meat, jugs of chicha, chickens, dogs, *cuyes* and pigs; everything scattered about in indescribable confusion. Sprawled on the floor are also ten or twelve members of the same family, the children generally naked, at best, only in ragged bits of cloth. . . . The . . . faces . . . are of a yellowish-gray pallor, eyes frightened, timid, mistrustful. The children run to hide behind the heaps of pots, and shriek with fright if one takes a step toward them. The whole family is suffering from an epidemic. . . . Stretched out on sheep-skins, their bodies still have the clothes they first put on years ago and which will cover them until the cloth falls into shreds. In these clothes they work and sleep. A sick man in feverish condition with that typical glassy look in his eyes, dry lips, feeble voice, and emanating evil odors, will go through his illness lying on the floor, at best permitting himself the luxury of a sheep-skin and some rags as a couch. If the case is a mother suffering from typhus or smallpox, around her are several children lying close up against her body, and a baby nursing at her breast. Some of these children have already caught the disease, the others are inevitably sentenced to prompt contagion. . . ." [5]

The Peruvian laws provide for two to three years military conscription and for annual periods of free labor (also obligatory labor at 60 centavos, *i.e.*, 11 cents) on roads and public works. Either through influences or paying a small fee, every one can evade these obligations except the Indian.

Labor conscription is accompanied by savage abuses. Those handling this forced labor either appropriate the daily pay checks themselves, or force the Indians to sell them at 10 centavos (.016 cents). They also oblige the Indians illegally to work indefinite periods, regardless of family, sowing or harvesting obligations. The Indians are given exemption tickets for three, five or more years in advance, but whenever there is a new labor roundup and the Indian shows his ticket, the officials tear it up, declaring it worthless. What

[5] Delgado, 18-19.

with such army and labor service, the individual's life is so broken up, his chances of bettering his lot so hampered, that the difficult odds against him as compared to mestizos and whites are made even greater.

Often this forced public works labor is illegally appropriated by private haciendas. Often the one who carries out the labor conscription law is the local *gamonal,* who uses the men on his private property; or else he bribes the local official to shunt the labor his way. The official then gets a stipend in addition to the amount already grafted off the Indians.

Nor is there any official effort to check disgraceful vices. The cocaine habit is widespread. The Indian chews coca leaves with a little lime to bring out the drug. As the lime parches his throat, he takes sips of *pisco* alcohol from a little gourd carried for that purpose. In Inca days coca was a government monopoly and used only for religious excitation, for soldiers on campaign or for others undertaking unusually arduous tasks. But the Spaniards soon found it a profitable crop and gradually brought about its widespread popular use, thus perverting and deadening native intelligence and initiative. All Andean Perú is in the coils of this terrible cocaine vice.

Alcoholism has also made its ravages. The Indian, as Valcárcel puts it, is equal to every one in his cups, but not before the law. In Junin, Puno and Cuzco the Indians themselves have tried to put an end to cocainism and alcoholism, but have had no official support.

Thus the government, which should be the first to protect its citizens, not only buttresses up the whole *gamonal* system, but itself commits further terrible abuses against the exploited groups.

5

On the coast, although the labor system follows colonial lines, the large landholders utilize capitalist technology—in short, a semi-feudalism, ranging from the patriarchal charitable system of the Larco brothers in Chiclín to establishments utterly devoid of social vision, practicing exploitation as brutal as that in the highland Sierras. Labor is obtained by the contract *enganche* system, creating debts that hold the *yanaconas* in virtual serfdom—Indians rounded up from the Sierra and paid infamous wages, or Chinese and Japs imported from the Orient.

If wages are seventy-five percent higher than in the highlands (Casa Grande in Chicama Valley pays 90 centavos—22 cents; Batán Grande in Lambayeque one *sol* less 20 centavos to the contractor, *i.e.*, about 19 cents) the proletarianized peon has no cultivable tract allotted him. Wages certainly do not conform to profits. The housing systems are infamous—dark, windowless, dirt-floor rooms without plumbing or sanitation, filthy walls full of vermin.

This modernized coast feudalism is largely foreign—the largest Chicama Valley estate, covering a bigger area than the smaller European nations, is owned by the German Gildermeister; the second largest, Cartavio, by W. R. Grace and Company.

Most great coast companies are independent kingdoms devoid of vital interest in national problems. To them the State has virtually ceded its sovereignty. They appoint the resident government officials, enforce law and order, evade just taxation. In medieval Europe, the cities became the first markets for goods, but in Perú the products of the coast find their market abroad. With tremendous importing advantages, the coast estates also buy necessary supplies abroad. They carry on more commercial intercourse with the outside world than with Perú. Even more than in the Sierra, adjacent towns are strangled, highways cannot be built or properly maintained, the normal economic development of whole regions is shattered. Their local and national influence is negative, corrupting, destructive.

299

The coast haciendas, notes Vásquez, denote imperialism, foreignism, evasion; the highland haciendas denote stagnation, retrogression, colonialism.

Even the coast land-holding class has been largely unable to acquire the Western European liberal bourgeois attitude. As in the South of the United States, where a subject race is exploited and abused, in Perú even more, feudalism has retained all its medieval privileges and organization. Our South, with a stronger injection of industrialism, because part of a larger capitalist mechanism, has at least pretended liberalism. No such necessity has existed in Perú.

Even more, the backward Sierra *gamonales* form a pampered class arrogantly medieval. They are arbitrary, ignorant, bestialized. Few ever open a book; most are as fanatic and superstitious as the Indians they exploit. Absolutely no interest is taken in progressive methods. Absenteeism is common. Many estates are still owned in Spain. Thus from former Jesuit estates in Arequipa (which passed into the hands of the Goyeneche family, relatives of the famous bishop) it is estimated that 300,000 *soles* go annually across the sea.[6] The Peruvian *gamonal*, often residing in Cuzco, Lima or abroad, is not a promoter or manager; his estate is in the hands of crop-renters and mestizo majordomos, ruling like petty kings over Indian *yanaconas*. The hacienda is run on the basis of easy profits rather than efficiency. The *gamonal* has a concept of rent rather than production. Of vast areas, only the very best lands are sowed; the rest, which would require more effort, are neglected or serve for pasturage or other purposes ancillary to hacienda life which obviate the necessity for immediate monetary outlay or the importing of modern goods and appliances. Compared to the 1,463,867 hectares now worked in all Perú, 11,922,209 hectares are cultivable; less than 10 percent is utilized.[7] And most of the

6 Belaunde, 42.
7 Romero, *Decentralismo*, 108.

actual cultivation is quite rudimentary, without technical knowledge.

The measure of *gamonal* patriotism is determined by the manner in which he shoulders taxation. This is ever proportionally heaviest in the lower brackets of income. Properties returning less than 50 *soles* ($12) a year are supposedly tax-free. Yet Encinas has declared [1918] that fully 80 percent of assessed properties should pay no taxes. In addition the Indian must serve on public works and in the army. During the Sánchez Cerro revolt in 1930, the incensed Indians hurled themselves en masse upon the tax offices of Huancayo, as in other places, and destroyed the records.

Though numerous beneficent laws from that of San Martín August 27, 1821, abolishing Indian tribute [it continued to be levied] to that of October 16, 1916, providing a minimum wage of not less than 20 centavos (5 cents) and that of June 28, 1930, which provides a vast plan of Indian political incorporation [never carried out], the Indian still has, through lack of enforcement or other abuses, little legal protection. This general ignoring of the law by *gamonales* and the authorities is well illustrated by the administration of justice. An Indian arrested is an Indian already convicted and sentenced. The judge rarely looks into the case, the state defenders rarely appear in court, merely sign the required form; the Indian is railroaded to jail. Even this steamrolling involves incredible delay. According to the 1926 Memorial of the Cuzco court, there are customarily more than 4,000 annual cases but never more than 300 are examined during the year, although the law stipulates that no one can be held more than 75 days without being duly charged with an offense.[8]

For four centuries, allied with the Church and the militarists, the *gamonales* have run Perú. They have built up a whole hierarchy of functionaries, intermediaries, and para-

[8] Cf. Delgado, 43.

sitic agents mostly mestizos—judges, subprefects, commissars, teachers, tax-collectors, shyster lawyers. All are feudalized. And despite *gamonal* control, agriculture is more deficient—though new European crops have been developed—than under the Incas; communications everywhere are ridiculously inadequate. And the governments provided the country by the *gamonales* have been (and the present one is scarcely an exception) corrupt, inefficient, unpatriotic, unjust and mostly stupidly tyrannical.

The *gamonal* class composes the so-called Civilista party, a clique far more benighted and of less social value than the Díaz Científicos in Mexico—long ago defined by Manuel Prada as a group knowing "the art of eating at all tables and sticking its hands into everybody's pockets." It foregathers in the palatial *Club Nacional* in Lima, which has a magnificent bar, but no library, and determines the fate of the nation. Its outlook, although there are a few notable exceptions, is completely feudal. Honest labor for any one of this caste is considered an ineradicable stain; they maintain, besides having first rights over the women of their workers, numerous mistresses; and they ape the European aristocracy in everything showy, but not at all in real taste or learning.

Mariátegui brings in the following general indictments of Peruvian feudal landholding:

1. It blocks capitalist development.

2. It prevents white immigration except from the lowest groups.

3. Coast feudal estates, linked only with the outside world, prevent any coordinated national economy.

4. They block necessary sanitation in the coast regions.

5. The mountain feudal estates are unable to create national wealth, are chained to primitive methods giving insignificant yield.

For four centuries Perú has been increasingly proving the maxim of Pliny the Younger: "*Latifundia perdidere Ital-*

*iam.*" The Peruvian landlords could well heed the famous words of Tiberius Gracchus:

"Cede part of your wealth if you do not wish to lose all of it. Even the wild beasts have their lairs, but those who shed blood for the fatherland have only the air they breathe. . . . With wives and children they wander without home or shelter. The generals lie when they exhort them to combat for the tombs of their fathers and their homes. . . . They only fight and die to sustain the luxury of others. They are called masters of the world and they have nothing that is theirs, not even a piece of land."

# XX

# TEMPEST IN THE ANDES

I

Every traveler to Perú should visit the ancient Tavern of the Dawn, that mysterious cave of shining stalactites from out of which untold centuries ago the four incestuous Incas, clad in serpent-glistening raiment and carrying the golden staff of empire, came to found the mighty Quechua kingdom.

In this Tavern of the Dawn, among the snow-crags of the "Copper Mountains," beside an immortal fire, now sits the soothsayer of the Andes. Through his fingers flow the knotted records of an ancient race; he utters prophecies few men heed:

"A race is being reborn. The children of the Sun, of the Incas, come out from their dark hovels, once more turn their bleak faces to the sky, hands cupped to recapture the holy fire of their faith and their race. The flame runs along the high crest of the great Andes, from Quito on the Equator through ancient Cuzco to the highlands of Bolivia—beacon light of a new era.

"Rebirth of a race, rebirth of a continent—long centuries roll up like a great tide when a race is born, when a continent is remade.

"Armies will march. Governments will fall. Men—oppressors and oppressed—will be scattered like chaff. Men will die.

"It is a long battle, a struggle not only of centuries, not merely of Perú, but of a whole continent, of the whole New World.

"But the Children of the Sun, despite repeated betrayal, will carry their sacred fire from heights to sea, from jungle to desert plain; they will enter again into the Temples of the Sun.

"Once bronzed men carved an empire out of the crags. Their loins were the color of the earth, the color of the sun-baked adobe walls they built—earth fused with sun and reshaped to power and beauty.

"Tillers of the soil, carvers of mighty stones, worshippers of the Sun, men with big lungs and big hearts able to play and toil ten thousand feet above the sea, they lived as brothers; no man went hungry. . . .

"The boot of the Spanish Conqueror pressed their necks to dust."

The soothsayer sits by his immortal fire in the Tavern of the Dawn above far-flung heights. Winds wail. Snow drives down. The condor wheels with knotted talons. Vicuña herds stamp by.

"Necks bowed, without the sun, the Children of the Sun could only be slaves, Children of Darkness—four centuries in the night of servitude. They closed themselves up in stony silence, in dissimulation, seeming evasion.

"Strong in their sorrow, patiently they have toiled, groping their way slowly toward their birthright, the Sun, source of all life, source of all good, beacon now of a new era, of centuries to come that will be theirs.

"The battle approaches. They will force open the door to their freedom. Blinded by the new light they have discovered, reckless of new power, they will sweep like the hurricane down upon the corrupt cities of civilization; upon Lima, City of Kings. Will half a million white victims be enough to answer five centuries of bloody cruelty?

"The day will come when the Sun of Blood, the Yahuan-Inti, will shine forth again, and all the waters will be turned red: purple will become the yellow waters of Titicaca; purple even the crystalline streams. Blood will rise even to the high snowy crests. Terrible Day of the Sun of Blood. When the Sun of Blood rises, the Incas, still living enchanted, deep in the mysterious land of Antisuyu, will come back once more.

"The people of the Sierra in their raw might, sooner or later will, reforge an empire; they will rule Perú.

"White Creoles will forget their pride and cringe, and bow to new curious laws. The lily-white daughters of wealth will creep to the beds of the new brown rulers disdainfully, to conceal their hauteur and cowardice of caste.

"And thus, out of the rebirth of a race, out of the loins of a people too hardy to be crushed, still a new race will arise, more dexterous, more beautiful, rulers of a new world —the American of the future."

2

The prophecy of our soothsayer need not be dated or taken too literally or even entirely agreed with. Basically the problem is economic and cultural; social, not anthropological; national but also continental. Abelardo Solís has pointed out three antiquated viewpoints: that which wishes to revive Incan glories, reestablish Indian hegemony; that which is purely colonial and feudal; that which is purely bourgeois-democratic.

None of these embraces all of Perú's possibilities and needs. Hope lies, not in the supremacy of the Indian race, poor, backward and superstitious, but in its emancipation, the breaking down of false cultural and caste lines, the creating of a nation through amalgamation of races and customs and the overcoming of terrific geographical handicaps—an eclectic task, depending upon national planning, scientific understanding of social forces, and the ending of human exploitation.

Unfortunately a corrupt minority blindly maintains the

ancient barriers. Thanks to its obstinacy the struggle, sadly enough, will probably be one of battle and fire. But do not think, said González Prada, thirty years ago, that this means "the deluge of barbarism; but rather the fructifying rain of justice." In the case of an uprising of the racially oppressed, the historic rôle of the Indians, allied with the mestizos, will probably be, whatever the dire temporary consequences, to impose their hegemony and people the land "with invincible Spartans" instead of the present corrupt and bland Creoles.

Only through liberation and evolution of the present oppressed groups can the real Perú emerge, the road be cleared for constructive progress. Here is the clue to the future of all Latin America from Mexico to Bolivia and Paraguay.

Undoubtedly the scroll of a great unique mountain-tropic culture—allied with tropical Caribbean culture—ethnically Indian, mestizo, zambo and mulatto—unrolls its record into unpredictable future. Mexico has already lit a beacon in the north. The sparks have spread on the high wind of hope to the furthest peaks of the Andes. In Perú the upsurge of the indigenous and mestizo masses cannot be blocked.

Revolts have occurred. Others will follow. The battle will likely open in war-torn Bolivia. The masses there are resentful at having been led to fruitless death-shambles. But the real cradle of the new movement in South America is Perú. Strange prognostication, for benighted Perú is held to sodden exploitation by ignorant landlords, brutal soldiery, rapacious priests and degenerate politicians.

But Perú must discover itself, will discover itself. The country is intrinsically, inevitably great—great mountains, great jungles, great deserts and plains, great rivers. It is carved in gigantic proportions. Its whole record has been dramatic and momentous.

Land of Inca Cápac and the great Viracocha, land of Pizarro, the bastard swineherd in the shining armour, land of Bolívar and San Martín, soldiers of liberty, land of heroic deed and golden romance, it has been long years since it has produced men to match its natural grandeurs, men able to master the deserts, the crags, the jungles, able to carve out a great nation on the basis of human justice.

Not once during its hundred years of independence has a really noble figure arisen to revindicate the rights of man. Santa Cruz, of early independence times, had a dream of highland unity; it was broken in twain by military jealousies and lowland Creole cunning. Castilla, to promote his political fortunes, liberated the slaves; Piérola tried bourgeois reform and failed. Before that Pizarro, Bolívar, San Martín—all were foreigners. Not since the Incas has Perú had a really important national hero. No Lincoln, no Garibaldi, no Juárez, no Lenin. A sad record, for every people needs the memory of a lofty leader who strikes a path to new freedoms. Perú has no such memory.

Yet for all of its black centuries of unimaginative exploitation, for all its sodden present, of all South America it is today the land of hope. For from the lofty headwaters of the Pauté, the Chambó and the Napo rivers in Ecuador, along the crests, through historic Cajamarca, through Tayabamba and red-stone Huancavelica, to stark and dreary Puno, and on across Lake Titicaca to high La Paz, a race is stirring from its long sleep; ten million people are coming to life again.

As Valcárcel puts it: "It has been an inchoate, a historical, mass. It did not live; it seemed eternal like the mountains, the sky. In its sphinx-like face, the empty hollows told everything; its vacant eyes no longer watched the outline of events. It was a people of stone . . . inert, without words; it had forgotten its history . . . [But] the fields come out of the tomb of their stone dream. There is a gentle whirr of wings; something like the low prelude of a distant symphony. . . . Today there is a spring miracle of the race.

" 'Let us live!' From all sides rises the same cry. The men of the mountain and the plain, the depths and the heights, sound the same cry. . . . It is the strong race, rejuvenated by contact with the soil that reclaims the right to act. Stretched out beneath the crushing weight of an old alien culture, prisoned in the iron band of the conqueror, the driving energy of the aboriginal soul was consumed. The protest bursts forth, and the unanimous cry echoes from crest to crest until it becomes the cosmic clamor of the Andes.

"Culture will again come down from the Andes. . . .

"The Race, in the new cycle visioned, will reappear splendidly, crowned with the eternal values, with firm step toward a future of certain glories: . . . It is the avatar which marks the reappearance of the Andean peoples on the scene of civilization." [1]

"The autochthonous race," states *Antara*, an Ayacucho magazine to promote cultural progress of the mountain regions, "is acquiring wealth and consciousness of its worth, and sooner or later will seize possession of the country."

### 3

Eighty percent of Perú's population revolves largely within the orbit of the Indian culture. According to Wiesse, half of it is pure Indian, a third mixed, only fifteen percent pure white. [2]

Saenz [3] raises the Indian percentage to a possible seventy, insists that certainly this proportion is completely absorbed by the Indian mode of life. Only 11.5 percent of the population, mostly on the coast, is urban. The rest live in small scattered Indian communities, either independent or included in large haciendas or in semi-nomadic state in the jungles. 73 percent of the population resides in the Sierra.

However much exploited, the rural Indian is the backbone of the economic system. For ten thousand years he, plus a

[1] *Tempestad,* 19-22.         [3] 13.
[2] 3rd ed., 155.

few black slaves and Chinese coolies, has been the only worker in Perú. His economic and social rôle is varied. He forms the indigenous communal village in which a large proportion of Perú's farm products is grown; he is the *yanacona* on the large haciendas, where in small settlements he largely follows Indian methods of cultivation. He makes up the rank and file of the conscript army.

A few Indians pass over into the economic status of the mestizos, the group which provides petty officials, rural

school-teachers, the trade-workers, muleteers, petty store-keepers, non-commissioned officers, etc.

Despite their numbers and economic importance, the Quechuas and allied groups are less protected today than during latter Spanish rule. At the bottom of the social heap, they are discriminated against by officials, even of their own race; the courts, which ignore indigenous common law, rarely give them justice; until not so long ago they were actually charged a head-tax for the mere crime of being Indians; they are rounded up like animals for the army and for labor on the large haciendas; they frequently lose their lands; they are mercilessly exploited. Their relation to the Peruvian state is one of onerous obligations, not of rights. They are, as one novelist put it, "birds without nests."

This has meant the non-integration of Perú. "We are,"

states one writer, "the felah peoples, the eternal peasants, Spengler's folk without history. In the capital and small cities lost in the immensity of the country, there is a simulation of occidental culture to justify the varnish of a 'modern' people with which we present ourselves in the concert of the civilized nations? But looking at Perú realistically everything we do to appear civilized results tragically grotesque. Ridiculous is our democratic republicanism, ridiculous our progress, ridiculous beyond all limits those intellectuals and artists who present our people as an imitative aggregation. It is the proper elegant decent gesture to close our eyes to everything disagreeable. What do four million 'lousy' Indians of the Sierra mean to the little gentleman of the *Palais*. To hell with them; they are dirty stupid provincials. These four million men are not utilized, they are quite outside the State, they do not belong to the Peruvian nation."

Yet, for all the darkness of this picture, they are knocking powerfully at the gates of a new era.

4

The Indian ferment, the conflicting duality of the country, the failure to create national unity, has aroused non-Indian intellectuals in behalf of the subjected race. For years more intelligent Peruvians have been awake to the necessity of recognizing the racial and economic bases of Perú. Books and documents on archæology have long aroused interest, but more and more the sociological phases of the race problem attract serious study.

Previously most writers had taken the view of the Conquistadores or "Civilizers," insisting, as such have for four hundred years, on the eradication of Indian customs, the transforming of the Indian communities into European centers, even the complete destruction of the native races—the view of most in the American and English colonies—physicians curing the disease by killing the patient. These heroic suicidal methods are scarcely expedient.

The earliest efforts were made by philanthropists with Franciscan love "for the poor Indian," whom they considered a "minor," an "incompetent," in the eyes of the law, without civil rights, at least unable to exercise them. Protective societies, special public officials, defense leagues, charitable bodies, were instituted similar to societies for the prevention of cruelty to animals. "Guardianship" legislation, a code based on the big-brother idea, was evolved—an altruistic superior spirit. As both colonial and republican governments have been composed precisely of those who exploit the Indian, these laws merely served as convenient hypocrisy.

The most advanced formula at the beginning of this century was education. Schools would soon transform the Andean man into a civilized being. Suppress illiteracy, according to these simplistic sociologists, and the enormous obstacle to the progress of four million serfs would disappear automatically. Compulsory boarding schools to eradicate the last vestiges of Indian customs were advocated.

. For other reformers, obligatory military training was the way out. Take the youth violently out of his environment, convert him into a barracks automaton, and the Indian soldier would become a marvelous creation, a new individual— "civilized." The net result of this procedure, in force now for many years, has been to comb out the most physically fit youths from the villages, thus impoverishing the local stock, and training them to acquire civilized gonorrhea and syphilis to carry back to their villages. Most drift into the ranks of the untrained urban proletariat, dislocated riff-raff.

Another compulsory formula, economic in character, was to create needs for the Indian. Accustom him to use "civilized" objects. Make him consume more, acquire a higher standard of living, and he would be obliged to produce more, would thus become more industrious and ambitious. "The day the Indian sleeps in a brass bed. . . . The day the Indian wears shoes . . ." were phrases of the statesmen of this school. They forgot that during the height of Spanish rule the Indian was forced by the authorities to buy silk stockings, and other luxury articles, which mostly he did not and could not use.

More comprehensive economists favored land-distribution. Each Indian was to become a small proprietor, although as a small individual producer he cannot contribute to national economy or protect himself against the *gamonal*.

Marxian interpreters promptly countered with proposals for land socialization.

Glib formulæ.

5

During the 1879 war with Chile, the Indians—when the rich, many politicians and militarists, had fled to Europe—fought bravely with little equipment or training. Thereafter many conventional prejudices crumbled. The vigorous spirit, González Prada, the first to reëvaluate the Indian, initiated a campaign and for a quarter of a century proclaimed one truth after another, scandalizing colonial-minded Perú, but destroying much hypocrisy. "The nation is constituted by the Indian masses disseminated along the folds of the Cordillera . . . they have been the creators and owners and sustainers of this country." And elsewhere he notes: "And the *inferior races?* When it is remembered that in Perú nearly all men of any intellectual worth have been Indians, cholos or zambos, when the few descendants of the Castilian nobility are seen to engender rachitic sexually perverted types, when no one can find much difference between the facial angle of a gorilla and an ancient Limeñan Marqués, there is no reason to assume inferiority of races." And he counsels the Indians to redeem themselves by their own efforts, for "every white is more or less a Pizarro, a Valverde or an Areche."

Clorinda Matto de Turner, with apostolic fervor, introduced the Indian into the arts in her widely read novel *Birds Without Nests* (1889). In sombre colors, with Russian vigor, she depicts the miserable existence of the former owners of the soil.

A quarter of a century elapsed with only sporadic works by generous souls, while Indian revolts and bloody massacres besmirched Perú's name, still besmirch it.

In 1910, Joaquín Cepedo, Dora Mayer and Pedro S. Zulén —established the "Asociación Pro-Indígena," the first honest effort to defend the native peoples against brutal *gamonalismo*. As it exposed the terrible sore spots of the social structure, the new group was soon silenced by the provincial authorities, defending the interests attacked.

After the Cuzco students' strike, one of the first in all America, which resulted in the founding of an independent university under the presidency of Albert A. Giesecke, the university and its *Revista Universitaria* became a laboratory for Indian investigation. Dr. José Antonio Encinas' notable legal studies of the Indian date from that epoch.

If in general the hope for reform was legal rather than economic, more educational than practical, these activities focused governmental attention, brought the problem into the 1919 constitutional convention. Some salutary clauses were embodied. Shortly after, the official religious *Patronato Nacional de la Raza Indígena* and the Section of Indigenous Affairs in the Ministry of Fomento were created, the latter being empowered to investigate Indian conditions, supervise law enforcement, protect natives from abuse, promote educational, economical and legislative advance. Subsequently, a Bureau of Indian Education (recently suppressed) was established. Unfortunately, the new posts were filled with petty office-seekers.

The governmental Patronato—put under the direct control of the Catholic Church—was mainly significant for its revelation of the surprising new temper of the Indians, who took it far more seriously than was officially intended. They poured into the sessions to air their grievances. The Patronato (suppressed by the troglodyte Sánchez Cerro government) has left valuable records regarding vicious military and political abuses, even includes severe indictments of the clergy itself, found cooperating with large *gamonales* and authorities in dispossessing the Indians.

From 1925 to 1929 intense intellectual pro-Indian agitation was carried on in *Amauta* (Wise Man) and *La Sierra*, the first edited by that rare genius José Carlos Mariátegui. Many other, somewhat short-lived, newspapers and magazines in Cuzco, Arequipa, Cajamarca, Huarás and elsewhere aided the campaign.

Toward the end of 1926 the Grupo Resurgimiento was organized in Cuzco and took the Indian directly into its councils. For the first time in history a Mamaní, a Quispé, or an Aimará sat in an easy chair, hitherto reserved only for "decent" people of a certain social category, and was urged to speak his mind freely. He did so, with exceptional oratory, clarity and knowledge of the world. He opened his soul.

Local society was scandalized by this unprecedented human treatment. Although the promoters were not lynched as would have occurred in our own enlightened South, the conservative landholding class soon persecuted the members. In 1927, one of the Grupo, Luis E. Valcárcel, a prominent archæologist and author, gave a talk on the Indian problem at the University of Arequipa. He was introduced by fellow-member Carlos Manuel Cox, now active in the Aprista movement. A few days later, Valcárcel was sent to the San Lorenzo Island prison; Cox was deported to Mexico. Within twenty-four hours signers of a Lima manifesto demanding Valcárcel's liberty, were arrested.

Several Indians have emerged as literary spokesmen of their race—particularly Alejandro and Arturo Peralta (pseud. Gamaliel Churata), poet and essayist, respectively—participating in the pro-Indian activities of a literary group in southern Perú which published the *Boletín Titikaka*.

J·S·

In 1927 Valcárcel's book, *Tempestad en Los Andes*, was published—a challenge and a gospel. Widely read in the tiniest Indian hamlet and abroad, it became a message to all Indo-America. The book revises the whole Indian problem. "Pro-Indígena, Patronato—always the attitude of the master toward the slave, always the protective air of those who have dominated for five centuries. Never the austere gesture of justice, never the manly word toward the Indian as a man.

316

. . . End once and for all the tearful pitying literature. . . . The peasant of the Andes despises the honied words of condolence. . . . They are fed up with sweet phrases; they are tired of commiseration. The Indian prefers a blow rather than a soft shoulder pat. . . . They know that pity for their oppression has led only to greater contempt for them."

Social and economic investigations now multiply. Since the 'seventies the tradition of scientific investigation had been given enormous stimulus by the great Antonio Raimondi. In the more modern period, already in 1922, Valdizán and Maldonado had published their monumental three-volume work on indigenous medicine. In 1924 Hildebrando Castro Pozo published his comprehensive study of the Indian community, indicating its super-important place in productive and cultural life. In his *Del Ayullu al Imperio* Valcárcel demonstrated that the *ayullu* has been and is the indestructible backbone of Peruvian collectivity. No one in Perú now denies the right of the *ayullu* to survive. It has been re-legalized; it has been accepted.

In 1928 Abelardo Solís published his capable volume *Ante el Problema Agrario Peruano,* in which he argues that, since no one can compete with the political and economic power of the *gamonales,* it is necessary to parcel out the unproductive, unindustrialized estates and socialize the estates already industrialized, which would also bring about the transformation of indigenous communities into large agrarian cooperatives.[4]

That same year José Carlos Mariátegui, Perú's greatest interpreter of economic, social and political problems, turned the searchlight of steel-edge economic analysis upon the whole problem. Valcárcel's book was a call to arms. Mariátegui, even more scathingly, blasted the philanthropic, legal and educational efforts in behalf of the Indian, but also showed by indestructible logic that none of these efforts had

[4] 73, 217, etc.

317

any validity so long as the application of the laws and the educational system remains in the hands of his exploiters.

New official efforts resulted from these activities. Rafael Pareja of Cuzco was commissioned by the government to make a thorough study of Indianism in Mexico—so very far ahead of Perú in economic justice and education. José Angel Escalante, a fervent Indianist, became Minister of Education (1930), but before his comprehensive efforts were well under way, the Sánchez Cerro revolution swallowed up everything constructive in base political turmoil. Save for the brief stay of Dr. Luis E. Galván in the Bureau of Indian Education (his review *Quipus* outlines his plans and hopes), all pro-Indian efforts collapsed. The last official gasp. Since then specialists have been replaced by intriguing bureaucrats interested only in salaries and graft.

In 1930 Uriel García published his powerful *The New Indian*, crowning years of study. In 1931, despite the brutal ignorance of the Sánchez Cerro government, the autonomous San Marcos university named as rector José Antonio Encinas, a man of very broad outlook, who saw Perú's whole problem in terms of Indian regeneration, incorporation into the functioning life of the country. But Sánchez Cerro soon curtailed the university's privileges, blocking Encinas' program. Student strikers protested. The university was closed down, remains closed down.

A stimulating influence was the visit of Moisés Saenz, former Mexican sub-secretary of Education in Mexico—an eminent educator, and international authority on social aspects of the New World Indians—who brought Peruvian students together and promoted Pan-Indian investigation. His book, *Sobre el Indio Peruano y su Incorporación al Medio Nacional* (1933), though weak on the coast and jungle Indians, ties together all the special Peruvian monographs, and enriches their findings by personal investigations, is—despite his over-nationalistic viewpoint—by all odds the best, most, comprehensive work, in the field.[5]

The National-Socialist party, called Apra, has incorporated Indian rights into its creed—"The Indian's cry is the Aprista cry." It commemorated the fourth Centennial of the death of Atahualpa; it brings to the fore the banner of Tahuantinsuyo; it contemplates erecting a monument to Manco Cápac; it lauds Incan socialism as worthy of imitation; it gives the names of the Cuzco emperors to its local organizations; it issues proclamations which terminate with Quechua phrases and expressions of triumph.

The Communists talk, somewhat theoretically, of the autonomous union of the Quechuas and Aimará peoples, and of the federation of the urban masses with the rural Indian.

Only the years can tell how sincere these varied pro-Indian endeavours; Indian development and social justice are necessarily a slow process of evolution, of rebellion, of class and race struggles.

The Indians are both a cultural bloc, i.e., a nationality, and also an oppressed class. When race and class coincide in being oppressed, subjugation is ever more ruthless. Culturally the Indian problem is a race problem. Economically it is more a class problem. Revalidation of Indian culture strikes a blow at class exploitation. Economic liberation forges new weapons

[5] Other trail-blazers include José Angel Escalante and Luis Aguilar. The latter's *Cuestiones Indígenas* synthesizes a certain bitter pessimism—"there is no justice for the Indian." Magistrates, including José Frisancho, the mulatto lawyer Enrique López Albújar and Francisco Mostejo, have opened windows of the Indian's life and hopes. Erasmo Roce, in Ancash, and Manuel A. Quiroga, in Puno, are authors of projected Indian codes. Julian Palacios and Emilio Vásquez have written capably on Indian education. There are numerous song-writers in Quechua, Aimará and Spanish. Though not among the students who have made, or are carrying on, investigations of the Indian problem, all of the Peruvian essayists have written on the subject. Except Mariátegui, mostly they lack sympathy and true understanding. Those who sustain the mestizo (or "new Indian") follow in the footsteps of the transactional doctrines of Ricardo Rojas in his *Eurindia,* and of Vasconcelos in *Raza Cósmica* and *Ideología.* Though inclined to look down on the real Indians with contempt, in general their point of view is sounder than that of the Indianist sentimentalists. All told there is a copious Indianist bibliography. A larger practical and theoretical literature exists in Perú, where little has been done, than in Mexico, where some important strides have been made.

for invigorating native culture. Without such efforts the Peruvian nation cannot be born.

## 6

The Indians themselves, in addition to efforts at communal re-integration and to get legal justice, have often resorted to armed revolt. In many places still survive the *camachicos*, secret indigenous reunions founded during the colonial period to combat the Spanish *encomendero* who robbed their lands.

Indian revolts have featured all Perú's history ever since the great wars of Manco II, of Sayri Tupac and Titu Cusi. Though invariably put down (the hands and legs of those captured were usually hung from the Rimac bridge), toward the end of the colonial period and during the first years of the Republic, such revolts became ever more frequent. Citizenship, the Vote, the Legislation System, were myths of Indian freedom merely disguising the old slavery and providing new tools of Creole class control. In the past fifteen years revolts have again become frequent.

These have not been revolutions to overthrow a system, rather rebellions, collective vengeance, the result of desperation, blind upsurges, reprisals, local not national; they have been anti-urban, anti-Creole, and though the justification has usually been more than sufficient, only too frequently have they been tinged with hate and brutality, *viz.*, the uprisings in Huancané, La Mar, Concepción, Paicona, Puno, and elsewhere.

1661-1668 occurred the fierce Laycacota mine revolts; cries of "Death to King and Pope." Royalist forces finally wiped the town of Laycacota off the map and executed forty-two rebels.

In 1742 the Indians from Pozuzo to Pangoa in the Chanchamayo Valley stormed into revolt under noble Juan Santos, titled Apu-Inca-Atahualpa; but in 1743 General José de

Lamas won the title of Marqués de Menahunoca by suffocating the trouble. In the Lima province rebellion of 1750 the Spaniards hung six Curacas.

Toward the end of the eighteenth century occurred the Catán revolt and the great anti-Creole uprising of José Gabriel Tupac Amarú ("Brilliant Serpent"), an intelligent, learned and valorous Indian; but despite commanding 20,000 men, he was unable to weld them into backing a coördinated plan. At his trial he complained of the continued *repartimientos* of Indians wrenched from their homes to toil in distant zones, with resultant forcing of abandoned womenfolk into prostitution; unjust taxes; forced purchases of luxuries the use of which by Indians was forbidden; slave-like hacienda toil "from two A.M. until the stars came out at night"; wages of only twenty-five centavos a day usually paid in scrip. Such plain talk doomed him to be pulled four ways by four horses; he and his wife had their tongues cut out. He was beheaded and 20,000 of his followers executed. The fight was bravely continued in the Sierra of Puno by his nephew, Andrés Tupac Amarú, allied with General Vilcapasa. At the head of 30,000 native troops they seized Puno, drove the Creole forces, broken, back upon Cuzco, and history might have been altered had not Andrés been killed during a three weeks' battle and Vilcapasa in 1783 been betrayed by two Dominican friars.

Had the 1814-15 revolt of Indian Brigadier Mateo Pumacahua (who in contrast to Tupac Amarú, clearly appreciated civilized technique and almost overthrew Spanish rule) resulted in victory, remarks Basadre, there might have come about a real fusion of Perú, not mere Indian supremacy, nor Creole supremacy such as Independence created and has perpetuated.

In the great 1866 Huancané revolt, the Indians complained of the "oppression and absolutism with which our local authorities have come to exacerbate our patient suffering."

*Pongaje,* work without pay, a forced national loan, unjust taxes, forced levies for building a cathedral, bloody oppressions, were some of the grievances. The revolt was put down by the 1867 "Terror Law" and the brutal tactics of Colonel Caravedo.

In 1885 the Atusparia revolt occurred in Huarás. Prefect Noriego imposed excessive taxes, whipped those not paying, seized Indians for public works, renumbered streets, charging excessively for new plaques. The Indians demanded guarantees, suppression of free labor, lower taxes. Indians refusing to pay taxes were seized, their hair cut off and used to make cinches for horses. Atusparia, the aged Indian *alcalde,* was jailed and tortured because he declined to carry straw to the jail roof. Blamed for the memorial setting forth Indian complaints, he was rearrested. Indians came into Huarás in great numbers to demand the freedom of the prisoners. A fight started. The Indians, reinforced, took the city, sacked Chinese stores and destroyed tax documents and police records. Noriega fled to Lima. The Indian forces occupied Chan Chan, Charhuás and Llanca, won the battle of Yungay. Colonel José Iraola succeeded in retaking Yungay because the Indian leader was drunk, but was promptly besieged by 10,-000 Indians. In the ensuing battle, 1,000 (including those executed) were killed. Government forces entered Huarás after a nine days' siege. Atusparia, wounded, surrendered with guarantees for life, but was apparently murdered. Indian leader Uchcu Pedro then kept the federals busy many months. Finally tricked into a trap, he was taken to Casma and executed. Other revolts occurred in Llave and Huanta, later in Huancané, Azángaro, La Mar, Ayacucho, Puno, Parcona, etc.

This century revolts have again become frequent, arousing real terror in the large landholders and even foreign corporations. They have had only one cause: oppression, abuse, and theft of Indian properties. The bulwark of such revolts has been the communal village; serfs are maltreated without their voice being heard.

Pedro Irigoyen, author of a *gamonal* apologia, declares such uprisings have been directly or indirectly instinct with the desire to refound the Tahuantinsuyo empire. This was one of the slogans of the great Cerro de Pasco mine strike, which swept into its support the surrounding Indian masses. Nevertheless, the basic attack has ever been against the large landholding class. A folder, published by the League of Hacendados, gives an account of revolts between September 24, 1921, and October 18, 1922—thirty-three in all, chiefly in Cuzco and Puno, branding them as purely anti-governmental, seditious, or manifestations of banditry; nevertheless it confesses other aims were involved. When the Indians seized Capachica on November 15, 1921, they obliged the governor to read a proclamation abolishing Republican authority and setting up new Indian control. May 5, 1922, a great crowd of Indians assembled in Azángaro province at the rumor that Protestant missionaries were going to parcel up estates; they were dispersed by force.

These revolts reveal the awakening consciousness of the Indians themselves, their hatred of *gamonalismo,* their faith they can fight their own battles. Where large landholding has been most abusive, there have occurred the most serious uprisings. The hacendados find it harder to maltreat, conscript, or in other ways abuse the individual Indian, who more and more asserts his rights, now by protests, now in the courts, again by organization, and as a last resort, by revolt. The commune is fighting an even better battle; in remote parts of Puno and Cuzco the tide of land seizures by large hacendados is receding, even in turning the other way. In that region, landlordism is bankrupt, technically, economically and morally. The Indian, despite abuse and massacres, increasingly refuses to work for them, he crosses his arms, he sabotages, a continuous general strike of the Andean peasant. In some places there is a definite on-to-the-land movement of dispossessed Indians and communers, which the *gamonales* and the forces of the State have been unable to check except temporarily here and there. There is no definite program. But the indigenous dictatorship of Perú approaches; it is merely waiting its time and leader.

The prophecy of our soothsayer is on the road to fulfillment.

# XXI

# SUN AND SOIL

## I

THE best-nested Indians are those within the communal or *ayullu* system, in origin either pre-Incaic or a continuation of the "reductions"—new communal native towns founded by the Spaniards.

The *ayullu*, which evolved before recorded history, which survived and developed through all the pre-Inca political crises, and which served as the primary unity of social organization in the Tahuantinsuyo empire, persisted, even was protected, down through Spanish colonial days.

Despite centuries of aggressions and reverses and non-legal status, the *ayullu* has survived. Native love for the soil and traditional ways protected it. The national difficulties merely intensified indigenous soil loyalty. Though legally dissolved after Independence, despite political and social confusion, the *ayullu* has persisted.

As late as 1907—declares Dr. Manuel C. Villarán—the communities were not civil persons hence could not be part of any legal suit. By 1920 the law finally reluctantly had to recognize them in other ways, though in ill-defined fashion. This, after a century of complete legal obscurity, attests to the stubbornness of *ayullu* survival. Though the Indians still live in a state of semi-legal twilight, the commune has kept its traditions, has continued to protect its members, has provided refuge in troubled times, has prevented even greater enslavement. The communal dwellers are hardier, display less degeneration than hacienda Indians. Though the aristocratic Lima bosses still fight against a proper codification based upon

325

the facts and customs of *ayullu* life, thus aggravating a duality that can result only in open race and class war, today, along with the large hacienda (for in few places flourishes the individual rancho), the *ayullu* is one of the fundamental cogs in Perú's economic, social and legal system.

The "reductions," the *ayullana* of Spanish origin, are often more mestizo, less rooted in communal psychology. Periodic land-distribution is rarely practiced in either type. Old kinship ties are largely gone. Today the villagers are largely merely neighbor citizens in cooperative pact owning land in common. The *ayullu*, become more commercial, now makes definite attempts to market products rather than supply purely local needs. From such aggregations come the major part of the nationally consumed barley, corn, beans, *oca*, potatoes, *olluco, mashuas, quinúa*, etc., and about a third of Perú's wheat. But otherwise the basic communal customs and psychology remain in force.

The *ayullana* flourish along the spurs and higher rolling hill country of the larger valleys.[1]

[1] Solís (*Problema Agrario Peruano*, 273) laments the lack of statistics, but reports 1,562 *ayulllana* of unknown area distributed as follows:

| Departments | No. |
| --- | --- |
| Piura | 57 |
| Cajamarca | 92 |
| Lambayeque | 5 |
| Libertad | 15 |
| Ancash | 22 |
| Huánuco | 65 |
| Junín | 102 |
| Lima | 60 |
| Huancavelica | 100 |
| Ayacucho | 50 |
| Ica | 11 |
| Apurímac | 113 |
| Cuzco | 350 |
| Arequipa | 85 |
| Puno | 392 |
| Moquegua | 5 |
| Tacna | 38 |
| Total | 1,562 |

He does not include the departments of Tumbes, Amazonas, San Martín, Loreto, or Madre Diós, all vast indigenous regions, which might easily double his figures.

In addition to such farming communities, in the higher Sierras has grown up community ownership of goodly sized herds. Mostly these groups are in a poverty-stricken, superstitious condition, surrounded by the fantastic terror of the crags and evil spirits, such as the gigantesque Lumi-Nuañuc, the death stone, that once a year opens its black jaws with a sound of thunder and music to swallow whoever is near. Through isolation almost sub-normal, their vocabulary reduced to a few guttural words, they sleep with animals on sheep-skins in tiny huts—frightful smelling places, for the inside walls are plastered with fresh cow-dung to dry in order to have winter cooking fuel, the only source of supply. Scarcely able to grow anything at such excessive altitudes, they subsist on a few scrubby potatoes, *oca* and *ollucos*.

They have little conception of values and will trade a grown sheep for a pair of glass earrings, for buttons, mirrors and other gew-gaws, although they use the pre-Spanish *quipu* system of colored cords and knots to keep accurate count of their flocks.

Their principal emotional outlet is the three days of dancing at the time of the branding, when they get drunk on *cañazo*. Even the sheep are given *cañazo*, "so the fox won't get them" and sacrifice is made to Mamá-Pacha with due burial of ears and entrails.

Before the Conquest, herds belonged to the Sun religion, the Inca and noble officials. To be a herder was a great honor; the candidates, carefully chosen from among a few favored families, were educated at an early age; they enjoyed privileges and full imperial protection, a vivid contrast to their present terrible state.

2

The *ayullana*, quite apart from the authorities imposed by national laws, have their own definite system of democratic government. The annual communal assembly, composed of all adults, men and women, determines important undertakings, elects officials; agent, ward treasurers, assessor, secretaries, chapel majordomo, bell ringers, the *ccollana*, who directs cultivation, etc. The villagers, whatever the prior rivalries, are usually extremely loyal to their chosen officials. Trusted older members of the community form a council, the decisions of which are law.

Less formal special reunions—to carry out a given piece of work or gather opinions—are called together by conch-shell trumpet, bamboo cornet, drum, cow-horn, or beating the church bell by the local chief, who accounts to the citizens the results of his mandates, proposes what ought to be done, writes memorials to the central government, sticks constantly by the side of the lawyer defending any particular village case, collects the quotas, pays salaries, contracts for church masses, assists in arranging the patron saint fiesta.

The legal authorities must work through these communal officials—a duality originally fostered by the colonial government, now deep-rooted and valuable. However much outside the law, *ayullu* politics represent the sound functioning of local self-government.

For special communal labors—the building of a home for newlyweds, the cultivating of plots for widows and orphans—the villagers go forth to work to the sound of flute and harp and animated by *aguardiente*, cigarettes and *coca* leaves. If the Inca and sacerdotes no longer augustly break the sod with a golden plow, nevertheless an almost religious solemnity and festive joy reign.

In many places, part of the commons provides revenues to celebrate holy festivals. Many communities have taken on a semi-religious character: the lands, the Indians claim, belong to the various saints, to the convent, or the Church, an attitude partly prompted by need for protection against the *gamonales*. In later years this has permitted the Church to seize many of these lands.

329

But despite all, the *ayullana* more and more re-assert their rights, even acquire new lands, recover old lands.

Thus Chupaca, on the Comas River, wrested back share-worked lands earlier appropriated by the Church. When the Church suddenly rented to favorites who inaugurated the *gamonal* serfdom system the Chupacans became threatening. Soldiers killed seven citizens, threw their bodies into a ditch.

The villagers formed a compact improvement and defense organization, finally obliged the Church to again rent the disputed lands to them rather than to the *gamonales;* later a plan was worked out for purchase and subdivision.

The Church, its hand forced, decently turned half the sales price back to the villagers for community improvement. They invested the funds in a light plant, a flour mill and a twelve-mile irrigation canal fourteen feet wide. Eight acres were donated to the State for a rural school, other plots to the city for a stadium, cattle market and general market.[2]

Chupaca's example is not isolated. Castro Pozo[3] tells how Muquiyauyo, even more effectively, recovered Church lands. Then, instead of spending all funds on religious festivals, the villagers instituted a credit cooperative, later production and consumption cooperatives. From resultant profits Muqui-yauyo then built a magnificent light plant which sells current to seven districts. It has built the best schools in the whole province, and gives the teachers additional pay above that provided by the government. The aptest pupils are sent at community expense to outside preparatory schools and universities. A short time ago Muquiyauyo was an insignificant Indian community; today, concludes Castro Pozo, "not even Jauja, the capital of the province, has more beautiful buildings."

[2] Cf. Saenz, 81-83.
[3] 63-68.

### 3

Visit the home of Indian José Sanguillo in Sapallanga. Pass through a eucalyptus lane, jump across an irrigation ditch, turn the corner past a sky-blue Mary in starred gown against a pink niche background, and knock at a large double door, carved with two sirens and surmounted by a jutting tiled roof.

Little Mercedes in long dust-dragging skirts peeks out with big black eyes, opens the door wider, smiles, and without a word rustles off ahead of you down the brick-paved corridor, her two shiny black pig-tails, interwoven with red ribbon, bobbing on her shawl-covered shoulders.

The buildings sprawl about easily in quiet isolation in the roomy yard. At the end of the corridor is the main room of the adobe tile-roofed house—only one sliding-door window. The roof-tree is graced with a wooden cross and two clay rabbits. Half in the corridor, half on stilts over the patio, is the *tobanco,* or sleeping quarters, under a roof of light bamboo covered with sun-baked clay. Around an "L" is the kitchen. Dangling from the roof of its smoky interior is a cross and blackened Jesus, looking like a chimney-sweep, humped leg on a skull, and holding in his arms and hands the Sun, Moon, a rooster, nails and hammer. Near by hangs jerked meat and a large *mate* or gourd, carved with Inca warriors. Pegged to one side of the house is a large wire-screen chicken-coop.

Near the back, a little garden—white lilies, yellow *sempa-suchiles,* roses, something resembling purple petunias, carnations and violets—clambers bravely against the brown wall. Near by is a reddish-leaved castor-bean tree.

In the second patio beyond a low adobe wall of large rectangular chunks, as if to imitate the huge stones of Cuzco, is the *chacra,* or cultivated field. Corn nods in the light breeze.

There is a corral for burros; in one corner, a dumping ground.

Don José comes out in fur sandals, striped trousers, wide red sash, pleated shirt, leather jacket and felt hat—all made by him, not by his wife. He bids me welcome in prolonged formal phrases—honored he is that I should visit his humble establishment. My reply is equally formal and lengthy. After that everything is simple and jolly.

María, an older daughter, brings us frothy chicha. We discuss the weather, crops, bugs, fiestas, and wool dyes—at odd times, on a primitive loom, José weaves blankets for the local market.

Late afternoon a cloth not too clean is spread over a little home-made table (most families have neither tables, chairs or benches), and we—José, a son Carlos, and myself, none of the women—sat down to what for them was the second meal of the day, the first having been eaten about ten that morning. Terra cotta bowls steamed with soup of toasted barley (*máshica*), potatoes, wheat and *sidça*, a sort of wild mustard. Then stew and rice, highly seasoned with *ají*, or chile—an unusual treat, for meat is rarely eaten—which we washed down with more chicha.

4

Life begins for the Indian child on a straw mat; it continues on the back of the mother in a bright-colored *quipe*, where the babe rides tightly swaddled from neck to toes.

It has been brought into the world precariously. The mother, on beginning birth pains, is made to perspire by hot drinks, massaging, and covering her with all the blankets and clothing in the house. Sometimes, like Sancho Panza, she is bounced up and down in a blanket. Sometimes she is obliged to blow on a bottle or calabash. The umbilical cord is cut with any handy unsterilized knife or scissors, and tied with any chance piece of yarn or sisal fibre; often a thread is extracted from some woven object by the teeth, thus mixing saliva with hand perspiration. If the newly born babe seems sickly, it is doused with cold water to revive it.

Such is the beginning of the individual who later will toil in mine and hacienda, to send out over the world copper and silver, coffee, sugar and other products.

Within a few weeks, for the baptism the father seeks an influential *compadre,* who is rewarded with chickens, sheep, eggs, wood and fruit. The first ceremonies of the cutting of the child's hair, of its nails, and the piercing of the ears (males as well as females) are accompanied by elaborate fiestas which eat up all savings. The presence of the *compadre* again requires generous gifts.

The *quipe* period lasts nearly a year and a half. The baby is not weaned until then, although faulty diet often makes the mother's milk irregular. If so it is carelessly supplemented by cow's or goat's milk from dirty receptacles. Most infants suffer from *enteritas.* Castro Pozo places infant mortality at ninety percent.

Sex life is precocious. Promiscuity introduces the child to intimate sex acts from the day it is born.

Education is scant. "If there is any instruction among the indigenous classes," states an official document, "this is not due to the efforts of the public school or the constitutional mandate . . . providing for free and obligatory education; [but] to the communal system, the economic expansion it permits, prevents enslavement from the age of eight in the mines and haciendas, and permits parents to send their children to school."

According to official 1925 statistics (the situation is worse today) the average school attendance in the vast Puno department, school age population approximately 100,000, was 3,898 children, or less than four percent.[4]

Schools are usually in rented primitive unhygienic quar-

---

[4] Romero, *Monografía del departmento de Puno,* 382.

ters. Modern pedagogical methods are unknown—mere parrot-like repetition of facts, useless or in constant antagonism with the local environment. Occasionally some teacher, in the face of home conditions, obliges the children to observe hygienic rules. Vacations counteract this training; the next teacher will probably take little interest.

But in a few places, Junín particularly, the natives are keenly concerned about schooling. About a decade ago annual Indigenous Congresses began to be held in Lima. Representatives of thirteen departments agreed each of their communities would, without central aid, construct a school. Some were built.

But since 1930 rural education has seriously declined. Trained teachers have been replaced by female relatives of jobholders, mistresses of politicians, and by other unsavory characters. Most schools, except in a few larger centers, have no texts, no blackboards, usually no desks or chairs. The children carry boxes and gasolene cans to sit on; they must write on their knees. Today popular education in Perú, even in larger centers, is in such a disgraceful state that the country can make no claim to belong to the concert of civilized nations.

Indian girls, set to work at domestic duties at the earliest age, are treated worse than boys. From five years on they herd flocks, weave, aid in the fields. Born to misery and toil, they know nothing of the joys of real chilhood, rarely go to school.

In the highlands, parents frequently rent, sell or give them away, advance payment being collected in entirety by the father. In the rare instances in which the victim has escaped or has managed to complain, official intervention has been invoked to stop the practice. More often the owner calls upon the police to restore some runaway girl.

Castro Pozo [5] cites the case in a populous central city of

[5] 89-90.

an Indian girl thus "bought," who tended the cow-stable. Half-nude, she slept in the corral, ate table scraps and worked from dawn till long after dark. Originally "sold" twenty years earlier by her father for thirty *soles* (about seven dollars) at eight percent, she had no idea how much she owed or had earned. Until principle and interest were paid she could not leave; there was no way she could collect the necessary amount.

5

Marriage customs vary widely but certain characteristics pertain to all groups. Matrimony is contracted for girls often at thirteen or fourteen, frequently being arbitrarily arranged between the parents. The marriage request is accompanied with a gift, usually a bottle of *aguardiente* for the father of the desired girl. After vague circumlocutions so characteristic of the Indian—such as the frosts and the inclement anger of *janac-pacha,* the sky—the future parent is invited to drink. Acceptance is consent.

Marriage is preceded by a trial period (the *sirvinacuy*) of six months or a year—Judge Lindsey's companionate marriage idea—in which the bride lives in the house of her future husband's family. Viceroy Toledo tried to destroy this "evil and pernicious custom" by a penalty of fifty lashes; the Catholic Church, from false and childish concepts of morality, has harangued against it for four centuries; but its workability and wisdom have survived all attacks. The trial marriage is rarely abused and rarely dissolved. Later, formal marriage, often long delayed until a priest happens to the village, is effected with great ceremony, though frequently the priest marries everybody en masse. Civil matrimony is very recent.

In more mestizo groups, after the marriage-supper, the godfathers lock the couple in their chamber. The guests dance, voluptuously pantomiming the supposed nuptial pro-

ceedings to the sound of flute, harp and guitar and impro-
vised songs, salaciously recounting what is going on behind
the locked doors.

The newlyweds receive gifts from the community, clothes,
adornments, household utensils, foodstuffs, even money.
Often the community constructs the new house.

Peruvian law largely ignores Indian customs, just as the
Indian ignores the law. His trial, common-law and Church
marriages for instance, on which have been raised enduring
homes involving years of mutual effort and numerous progeny, are not recognized by the State. The law strictly regu-
lates inheritance, indicates precisely what portion goes to
each relative. The Indian follows his own traditions regarding
transmission of his property and his rights in the community.

The law does not permit a married woman to own property—but the Indian communities recognize her pre-
marriage property as still being hers. Often the husband
turns all his own worldly goods, the profits on his sales, etc.,
over to his wife. Children's efforts are also usually fully recognized; the property acquired through their efforts is theirs.

As a male the Indian husband supposedly supplies prestige
and dignity, hence retains privileges of priority and command; for instance the woman on the way to market invariably carries more than does her spouse; he rides, she walks.
But marriage is sufficiently cooperative, based on mutual effort. Economic factors predominate. All members of the
family represent an investment.

If the woman, theoretically considered inferior, shoulders
the major burdens, she thus becomes the majordomo who
knows more about all affairs than her master. She cares for
the house, the children, the meals, the weaving and making
of clothes, some of the field tasks, and most commercial
transactions. When others are asleep she is stripping corn
from the cob, grinding it for the next day's meals. The symbol of feminine activity is the ambulating weaver. Loaded

with her latest baby and her produce, she goes all day, fifteen, twenty miles, over the mountain paths, through villages and wilderness, her distaff ever in motion, her fingers busy. She does the selling in the market. When the man goes off to the haciendas or the mines, his wife arranges the contract, fights for terms. In his absence she remains in exclusive charge of the cultivation of the fields and the sale of products; or if she accompanies him, she also looks after his interests, protests against abuses to the proprietor or officials, despite the fact that usually she is harshly beaten for her pains.

Often women are sent as official village representatives. In 1920 Nicacia Yavar speaking Spanish, Quechua and Aimará perfectly, headed a commission of thirty delegates to protest to President Leguía against the mistreatment of her people.

The worst a Peruvian Indian can say of his wife is that she is sterile or not a good worker. As in the old Tiahuanaco days, fecundity is of major importance. In the older legends, Mamá-Pacha, Goddess of the soil, was ambi-sexual, but she was also a mother—mother of the earth, hence was "wrinkled, elderly as mothers who have given birth to many children." Working ability and fertility in the woman are more important than virginity. A child out of wedlock is often considered an excellent recommendation for marriage, the man taking on any previous children. Once married both are extremely loyal. Morals are high. Women are rarely repudiated. In general they are hard-working, loyal, tender, uncomplaining, valiant, afraid of nothing. More civilized sisters could well imitate at least some of their virtues.

6

Despite lack of trees, the upland valleys—Jauja, Cajamarca, Cuzco—during the rainy season are charming bowers of growing fields and terraced hills. Except for large estates near the cities the picture is wholly indigenous: adobe red-tiled houses perch on every spur; church towers rise slim above the villages; the fields are broken up into plots by stone fences, rows of eucalypti or *cabuyas*.

Despite the centuries of oppression, the *ayullana* breathe simple joy and beauty. They are "pieces of live nature," spontaneous, grown up from life like the trees of the field, without plan, yet with admirable structure. The houses, like little

flocks of sheep, zigzag along cobbled streets, up hill and down dale. At dawn spirals of smoke rise up from adobe and thatch; at night charcoal fires glow valley-across like jaguar eyes in the jungle.

The land is conscientiously worked. Plots are known as *yuntadas, i.e.,* the amount of land an ox-team can plow in a day. The leading crops are corn, potatoes, wheat, barley, *alberjas, quinúa,* beans, *ollucos, ocas, mashua,* onions, cabbage and lettuce. To avoid severe frosts corn is planted in September, harvested in May. Wheat comes later, November to July. Most of the *comuneros* have domestic animals: chickens, pigs, *cuyes,* rabbits, donkeys, often sheep—from five to three hundred head; the more prosperous, a few cows and a yoke of oxen. Each *chacra* has a stable to protect the animals at night, otherwise in this rare cold atmosphere many would perish.

Puno, the highest generally inhabited region, 12,000-15,000 feet, has more cattle-raising than agriculture, though about the huts, more miserable affairs than in the central highlands, they manage to grow a few rachitic potatoes, wheat and *quinúa*.

Fruit trees are rare. Now and then a plum or fig, more rarely a peach. Magueyes and nopales are frequent; some sugar-cane (the altitude requires three years for maturity), more to extract *aguardiente* than sugar.

Work instruments, both on haciendas and in the villages, are primitive—the foot-plow (*chaqui-taclla*); the wooden plow tipped with iron, the short-handled sharp-angled hoe (*racuana*), sickle, *machete*, crow-bar, pick and spade. Nowhere are carts or wagons. The wheel is utterly unknown.

Communal labor is frequent; four or five neighbors often work together, the service loaned being called *aine*, and it is repaid in similar labor (*tulapay*) or in other forms (*muncay*). The work is broken by two rest periods, the *jallapy*—in the morning when food and chicha are taken, and the *coca-matliajcuy*, when coca leaves are masticated. Often the community builds the newlyweds' home. At death ceremonies the bereaved family receive the *huallacc*, a communal contribution of jugs of *aguardiente*, coca, cigarettes, food, even silver, for the requisite accompanying fiesta.

## 7

Ancillary to rural Perú are handicrafts. Around northern Cajamarca weaving and pottery are inferior, not particularly æsthetic, but the further one goes south through the Sierra the finer all handicrafts, although pottery and many other products are inferior to Inca and pre-Inca times.

In the lowlands where in pre-Inca times beautiful cotton

textiles were produced, hand-loom weaving has been driven out by factories, but wool weaving—because of the llama, alpaca, vicuña, domestic and mountain sheep, and other fleece-bearing animals—leads all highland handicraft activities. Specialized categories exist. Some groups merely raise herds or hunt. Merchants sell the freshly skinned skins unsheared. The buyer at once clips off the fleece and washes the hide, the latter to be resold. The wool is carded, made into threads, rolled into balls, and woven on primitive looms, or knitted into sweaters, blankets, ponchos, stockings, and shirts. Pure wool blankets of magnificent quality can be bought for from 4 to 10 *soles* (90 cents to a little over $2). Alpaca rugs, the fluffy wood projecting several inches from the surface, have beautiful somewhat asymmetrical designs.

In tanning, the women buy the hides, prepare the chemical concoctions from native plants, such as the *tuna* and the acacia, and sell the product. The men perform all the rest of the labor; wash the fresh hides, put them in lime to remove all hair; they are tanned, scraped on stone slabs with a knife-shaped bone, washed and dried in the sun—about a fourteen days' treatment. In shoe-making, the man is also the worker, the woman the trader.

Baskets, Panamá hats, mats, rope, hammocks, bags are made from reeds, fibres of various magueys and other plants. Excellent silverwork imitates plants, jewels, filigree, spoons, dishes, ash-trays, elaborate brooches for clasping the richly embroidered *lliclla*, shoulder-shawl—figures of loaded llamas, Indian women weaving, *guacamayos*, turkeys, condors, etc. Gourds and woods are carved with birds, animals, plants or human figures, ancient historical scenes, Inca motifs. Heads, birds and other figures are carved from vegetable ivory, sometimes from stone or marble. Excellent native musical instruments are turned out. Family handicrafts are an integral part of Perú's rural economy.

The distribution hub of such handicraft production is the fair or market. Though not as vivacious as Ecuadorian fairs nor as colorful as those of Guatemala and Mexico, great conglomerations of Indians bring in their wares; others set up eating and drinking booths; the Church also plies a busy trade in candles and offerings. Mostly fairs are held weekly in certain larger centers; Huancayo's market day is Sunday. Great annual fairs are those of Ayacucho, Vilque, Rosaspata, Pucará (Puno). Itinerant fairs advance from town to town throughout an entire region. Some are specialized: grain, wool or some other major product—the great cattle fair of Acuchi for instance.

These fairs have deeper motivation than mere utility. More than mere barter, they are part of the essential communal rhythm, vast social functions. However handsome the price offered, usually the Indian will refuse to sell on the road. He does not care to disassociate the transaction from market social contacts. Camaraderie is more important than profit. For the handicraft tradition ignores time-value. Since the soil provides basic needs, anything gained on handicrafts above prime-material cost represents a profit, regardless of the time or effort consumed in manufacture and sale. The Indian is never in a hurry to sell. The market is never filled with the raucous competitive shouts that greet one in Italy. If not successful at the first market, the vender will cheerfully pack objects hundreds of miles and spend weeks, even months, before disposing of them. The Indian bargains, not to profiteer, but for the pleasurable human relation—"I really want to deal with you." The whole cycle of production and sale is a classic drama, a properly balanced unified fragment of life perfecting an artistic concept.

9

"The mystic and sentimental agrarianism of the aborigines," remarks Saenz, "seems to be diagonally opposed to the juridical agrarian criterion imposed on Perú by European culture." The Indian's relation to the soil in the Andean highlands is unique. He cannot, as can peasants in more favored climes, be separated from it and live; such separation would be like cutting off some vital organ. An Indian without land is a man without lungs. Hence he has never looked upon land as a negotiable property right. It is not something to be bartered but to be exploited.

The Indian approaches the soil with artistic and religious feeling, hence with respect. Animism still a vital force to him, the earth, plants, trees are spiritual entities to be respected, loved or feared.

Unfortunately these pagan beliefs occasionally prevent rational control over resources. A certain village started an irrigation canal, but Pacarma, the spirit of the lake to be drained, came at night in the form of a dwarf to warn them that if the least bit of earth were touched, the waters would flood the whole region. More often animism permits the Indian to live in intimate harmony with his environment. The high peak and the ridge, the rivers, the clouds, outstanding stones, all are divine. When the Indian approaches the *auquillo,* the mound for the *apachita,* the mountain spirit, with great reverence he throws sacred coca leaves upon it with a prayer. Weariness for the traveler or his animal is a sign that he must not proceed until he has paid due reverence to the *apachita.* The seeds of certain plants, the foetus of certain animals because of their potential fecundity, are also personified divinities. On the coast the *colamboa,* snake with a fearsome whip-like tail, is considered holy; these are tamed to guard the house. They swallow rodents and big spiders and other snakes dangerously poisonous. The stories of their loy-

alty and prowess have grown to fantastic proportions—one
for instance held a robber all night in his tail and delivered
the wrong-doer to his master in the morning.

The Indian prays before first breaking the soil with his
plow. Livestock, preferred beings of the Earth Goddess,
Mamá-Pacha, must be treated with reverence. Before taking
chicha some is offered to her, then the lesser *apus* and *auquis*
(divinities of the region and of cultivation) are invoked.
She still rules, a spiritualized conception of the cosmic creator, though most of this earth cult has today been absorbed
in garbled form by the fiestas of San Juan, Santiago, etc.

But there survive special pre-Conquest fiestas related to
the mating period of sheep, the breaking of the soil, the first
sprouts of the year's crop, the bringing of water into irrigation ditches, etc; and the marvellous corn-festival, the
*Calcheo*, when the whole *ayullu*, from the hundred-year-old
elder to the baby *waronucha*, scarcely able to walk, strip off
the corn leaves from the ears, the red, the white, the golden
corn, all to the sound of music, punctuated with dancing—
in joyous thanks to the Sun, the earth, the peaks and the
rivers, with obeisance to a cross of corn-stalks and flowers.
The corn festival is the Te Deum of the *ayullana* in the
temple of the Andes.

10

An integral part of the religious festival is the music and the
dance. Perú is the one New World country with a deep native
musical tradition. The composers are unknown, it is an evolving communal music. The music of one village is often
sharply distinguishable from that of another. Sierra music is
melancholy; coast music is more lively and joyous, luminous
like the shining earth and sky. The themes are short, melody
not especially important, usually restricted to four or five
motifs, giving it monotony but great emotional and hypnotic
force, akin to the ceaseless murmur of the water or the wind.

Dance music has marked rhythm; that accompanying songs
—the native *yaravíes*—is more melodious and sentimental;
the songs are a vital expression of village experiences, and
such verse cycles, with given music as *Lucerito Claro,* are
added to like a long chain of flowers, continued improvisa-
tions that grow gradually into a permanent part of the
cycle. The instruments used are the *tinya,* or tambor, the
*pincullo,* or five-hole flute; the *quena,* seven-hole flute; the
*antara,* a syrinx with from fourteen to twenty bamboo tubes
of varying lengths; spiral conch-shells, bull's horns (*huac-
cla*); the *charangos,* a four-chord guitar-like instrument,
and various adaptations of European instruments. In Cajamarca for fiestas is blown an enormous fifteen-foot bamboo
horn, requiring terrific lung power to sound. Probably in
ancient times its wailing harsh blast served as a signal over
great distances across the Andes. Over the communal
labor ever floats the shrill notes of flutes—*Jújúúúúúúú
Jaicháááááá* . . . as though the very rocks of the crags
were surging, especially when the women come out with the
food. From across the ravine they send back their equally
shrill *Guaaaaaa* . . . *Jaaaaaaa* . . . *Jaaaaa,* high sustained,
and then the singing laughter, *kja* . . . *kju* . . . *kju* . . .
*kju* . . .

And over all presides the solemn ancient temples and spirits
. . . *Apus* . . . *auquis* . . . the imperturbable *Camachi-
cuyi.* . . .

Closely linked with music are five types of communal
dances: bellic, mimic, religious, functional rhythmic and
politico-historical. The first are harsh and stark; the second,
the *tinyapallas,* are comic or formalized mimicking of the
movements of totemic animals or birds—such as the condor,
the turkey, the snake—or other imitative symbolism. Religious dances either celebrate some Biblical anecdote or, as the
dance of the Christians and the Moors, the struggle for survival of the cult; deathwatch dances and others are directly

related to older pagan dances for native gods. The rhythmic dances, mostly Spanish-modified, involve purely voluptuousness of movement; still they have complicated suggestions. The politico-historical dances revive pre-Spanish victories, the Conquest, the Independence Wars and more recent events.

The native peoples of Perú have a rich dance culture, which makes our fox-trots, blues, two-steps seem infantile and barbarous. Our dancing, except on the stage, is merely primitive unimaginative reflex to music, rhythm and sex, without subtlety.

Just a few dances of hundreds:

*War:*

*Cachampa:* Rich dress, derived from tropics, symbolizes entry of armed forces. Sharp guttural cries. Stark music.

*Cachahuaina:* Young warrior dance with symbols of battle and power. Carry young vicuñas on shoulders. Zigzag in pairs. Music rhythmic and undulating.

*Aquilino:* Pre-Spanish dress, simulate bravery, gallantry and generosity. Carry leather flasks and give out *aguardiente* to all passers-by to whom they chant adventures and exploits.

*Caracolito:* Pooched multicolored drawers, blue jacket, red, green or purple shoulder kerchief, cow-skin sandals; fox helmet with plumage or horse-hair. Silver lances, painted wooden shields. Simulates battle. Animals symbolizing valor are imitated. Different groups represent different wards of town and occasionally when ill-feeling exists, the battle becomes real. In the north (Ancash, Libertad, Cajamarca) so-called witches, sometimes devil-negroes, dressed comically, sometimes doused in flour, perform drolleries and maintain order among on-lookers.

*Mimic:*

*Condor:* Black wide-sleeved tunic, caught loosely between legs, fur cap, curved beak mask, white fur around neck. Leaping steps; yawning, picking at soil, wing-like lifting up of black sleeves in Sun invocation. Unmelodious flute and drum music.

*Turkey* (Piura): Women dressed in black, men in ponchos; women, bodies arched, step mincingly like turkey. Men step with bent knees, elbows holding out rainbow poncho like wings. Imitate turkey cries, and strut toward women.

> *Suaz que te pica el pavo!*
> *Suaz que te mete el pi . . . .co!*
> *Suaz, por el . . . espinazo!*

*Ch'uncho* (Forest regions): Dancers wear rich plumed headdress, held by metal diadem. White tunic, feet and ankles painted. Carry two crossed bags, mask, and *chonta* wood arrow. Others imitate black bears; others yellow monkeys. March music. (Probably also a war dance.)

*Religious and Functional:*

*Chuccho Tusuy:* Health dance, leaning on canes.

*Sumaila:* Celebrating departure on or return from a journey. Plumed headdress with long hair tangled with amulets and animal skins. Carry knotted staffs and clubs. Soft march music.

*Jergacunos:* Combination of purely rhythmic and satire of customs. Jokes shouted about conduct of neighbors.

*Canchi:* Celebrates the socially useful and industrious person. Staffs and tasseled banners. Trousers are pooched out at knees. Bells on sandals. Form gymnastic figures, human pyramids, etc., around which rest circle with interlocked arms.

*Arriero:* Muleteer dance. Bronze bell imitates sound of mules. Another dancer carries the lash or guiding staff. Imitate shoeing of mules; flute and bell onomatopoetically imitate the driving in of the nails.

*Avelino:* Rich-poor dance. Satirizes avarice. Some dressed in rich court style, others in rags.

*Quija:* Children dressed as angels. Christmas or Twelfth Night dance.

*Seise:* Records colonial dispute between archbishop and ecclesiastical *Cabildo*. Danced before the Holy Sacrament of the Eucharist with hats on.

*Contra Danza:* Brightly dressed children in Corpus Christi festival.

*Rhythmic:*

*Huayno:* All southern Perú. Harp, violin or *cachimbo* band, often songs. Not merely race melancholy and the sorrowful indifference of the crags, but the vibration of a race and the metallic echo of the stones woven into a bacchanal of summer night.

*Marinela:* The most truly national folk dance.

*Cachaspare:* This monotonous, sad dance of the Sierra to the sound of guitars and syrinxes, or perhaps just the beat of a drum or on a box, evokes inevitably the dismal rain of the solitary peaks, the gray mountains, the far lonely horizons. But the songs are bright enough:

> "Yesterday you looked like a rose;
> Today I see you as a carnation;
> I fell in love with your beauty,

> "When you come into my power
> Like a little lettuce you will 'lettuce'
> Like a little cabbage you will 'cabbage.' "

[In general the rhythmic dances are mestizan, of Spanish, Indian and negro origin in which the pristine symbolism has been subdued and absorbed into a purely art form.]

*Politico-historical:*

*Auquisdanza:* Mass village dance, revives tragedy of Incas killed by Conquistadores. In front go the Spanish captains with an Incan princess, followed by the *Coya* and a chorus of *Ñustas,* or Sun Virgins, rhythmically dancing a sorrowful *cachua.* Other guards follow. The *auquis,* or elders, dressed in short-sleeved *cushma* shirt and short drawers with little bells, come behind, poncho folded over breast and shoulders, and wearing a wide belt of linked coins, mummy masks, ox-skin caps with white ox tail simulating gray hair.

*Pauciña, Wailia, Ccamile:* Monotonous; melancholy downcast heads, white kerchiefs, represent a sorrowful protest at abuses and illnesses.

*Siclla:* Black togas: one carries a book, another a lash, others are court attendants. A bitter satire on lack of justice in the courts.

347

Dates back to the Royal Audiencia established in Cuzco February 25, 1787.

*Ccolla Tusiy:* Victory dance of pre-Spanish conflict.

*Negrillos:* Anti-slavery dance. Black masks, lugubrious rackets. Condemns exploitation of man by man.

*Majiño:* Gaucho sombreros, crossed cavalry symbols, masks, leggings, boots, spurs. Celebrates War of Pacific with Chile.

*Tunantes, Huamanguinos,* etc.: Rich attire. King and Queen of dance. Commemorates Viceregal court.

Dancing in Perú, diffused among all the people, is sophisticated, symbolical and organically social and functional. It has a comprehensive philosophical, æsthetic and utilitarian significance. Our own merchantistic civilization has been unable to create anything comparable in popular importance, in beauty or subtlety.

Another important cultural heritage are the communal legends woven about communal life and great historical events. While coast legends are, though occasionally with Indian notes, largely of European or African origin (such as *Magallenes* "The Treasure"), those of the Sierra (several of which have been repeated in chapters "Roulette" and "Huánuco"), derive directly from group expression. The most extensive Sierra legends are the "Ransom of the Inca," "Death of Atahualpa," "The Treasures of Catalina Huanca," and stories of enchanted Inca towns or palaces, such as Jatunmalco, Aypate and Ayahuaca, or the story of the eleven thousand enchanted llamas loaded with Inca silver in the Paca lagoon.

The Indian world of Perú is, all told, a world of weird beauty and potential greatness. Let not the makers and masters of machines sneer or feel too superior.

# XXII

# GOD OF BATTLES

## I

Popes Alexander VI and Julius II made the Spanish king all powerful in ecclesiastical affairs within his domains. Ever since, Church and State in Perú, which has never known a reform movement, have never been separated. Since the things of Cæsar are the direct concern of the ecclesiastical authorities, the Catholic Church has ever given its blessings to notable official events, has helped shape most of them, has ever helped maintain in power governments which would conserve those feudal institutions based upon mass ignorance, poverty and superstition which during four centuries have failed to provide the population with a well-being comparable to that under the Incas. Christianity, as represented by the Universal Church, has been an active partner in all Perú's evil governments so firmly controlled by the *gamonales,* of whom the ecclesiastical authorities are not among the least important.

Even before 1532, when the first church was founded at Tangaralá, ecclesiasticism has been omnipresent in Perú's political affairs. Priest Father Hernando de Luque—who hoped to garner more souls and money for himself, the Church and the Empire—was one of the original Conquest triumvirate.

Voluble Dominican Friar Vicente de Valverde delivered the ultimatum to the Inca Emperor Atahualpa that his domains had become the property of the Spanish King and the Pope.

Subsequently the "factious and unprincipled" Valverde

349

helped draw up the "badly contrived and worse-written document" which—in foul dishonoring of holy pledge—doomed Atahualpa to official assassination. Later Valverde participated in the killing of Indian General Calcuchimac. In 1534 Valverde performed high Mass in the great Cuzco square in the shadow of the massive Inca palace and the Temple of the Sun at the crowning of Puppet Emperor Inca Manco to befool the subjugated Quechuas.

By 1546 Perú had a priest and councillor of the Inquisition as Supreme Governor. He had Pizarro's youngest brother dragged by mules to his death on the gallows.

For 240 years the Inquisition, an integral part of colonial government, confiscated properties, exiled offenders, lashed them in the public squares, tortured them in dungeons, tore out their tongues, gouged out their eyes, let water drip incessantly on their spines, burned them at the stake.

In 1783 two Dominican friars betrayed the great Indian leader Vilcapasa, causing his beheading and the cutting up of his body into pieces to be impaled in the public plaza.

The first constitutional Independence Congress (September 20, 1882, a date now commemorated by the street which for long blocks now houses Lima's ulcerous open-crib prostitution) was presided over by the estimable priest Javier de Luna Pizarro y Vigil from Arequipa.

The 1823 Congress made the Virgin of Mercedes the patron saint of the revolution. Before the decisive 1825 Ayacucho battle, Generals La Mar, Córdova, and others celebrated solemn Mass and claimed that victory was due to the intercession of Mary, the Immaculate.

The 1834 convention saw Luna Pizarro again in the presiding president's chair. Liberal ecclesiastic Juan Gualberto Valdivia from Arequipa for many years helped make and unmake presidents. Bishop Goyeneche, also of Arequipa, backed General Gamarra and was arrested. Bishop Tomás Diéguez of Trujillo put his weight behind Santa Cruz'

Huaura assembly to deliver northern Perú to the Bolivian Confederation in return for Church guarantees. The bishops of Trujillo, Arequipa and La Paz hastened to form the new constitution.

Under the Republic, ecclesiastics fomented revolutions and riots whenever their privileges were at all menaced.

In honor of a dozen military adventurers who soaked Peruvian soil with blood to seize supreme power, the Church officials sang Te Deum in the cathedral.

In 1923 President Augusto Leguía unsuccessfully attempted to consecrate the country to the Sacred Heart of Jesus.

In 1930 Soldier-dictator Sánchez Cerro temporarily delivered his scepter to a self-created Junta de Notables, presided over by his reverence Monseñor Holguín.

During the 1931 elections, which through false vote-counting put Perú's most fantastic bloody ruler back into the saddle, the Church was his most ardent supporter.


2


Writes a modern ecclesiastic, Father R. Zarate (*El Mundo*, Ed. Ext. No. 6):

"Over the high crest of our history shines radiantly a Cross held in the hands of an apostle: the Cross of the Conquest in the hands of Father Valverde, the first missionary and bishop of Cuzco.

"This cross [still existing in the Temple of Triumph in Cuzco], unjustly forgotten, is the message of Mother Spain . . . sovereign attraction for the Christian Conqueror. Behind it he ascended the age-old Andes. With it he saluted the eternal city of Manco. With the warmth of its divine emanations, he intrepidly subjected the gentle multitude absorbed in the bold advance of the heroes of another God and vassals of another King.

"The Cross advanced, offering the supreme embrace to this God of mankind."

"The Lord's hand," wrote old chronicler Naharro, ". . . led him [Pizarro] and his followers to this remote region for the extension of the holy faith and the salvation of souls."

The Spanish Conquest cannot be conceived of without its ecclesiastical features, an evangelism lacking in English colonizing efforts. Spain, wrapped in the coils of fanatical Counter-Reformation, belligerently girded with a sword, carried the flame of its zeal to the New World.

San Ignacio and Santa Teresa—passionate but steel-edged characters—soon had their sentimental counterparts in Perú. The bigoted Valverde was succeeded by that later fanatical Archbishop who, between 1625 and 1630, burnt down whole Indian villages to induce the inhabitants to abandon their local cults.

Soldiers and priests set out, crossed dark seas as into the bosom of the inscrutable mystery of God. The dusky masses they encountered represented a black void to be filled with spirituality lest the universe itself crumble—the superstitious fear counterpart of their unparalleled valor. Even the gold so zealously sought, for which they risked their lives and plundered and murdered, represented for them, not crass materialism, but a mystic talisman the better to open up the gates of the world for their faith. Is this so different from the modern American who sprays upon his exported dollars, railroads, mines and sanitation, the perfume of self-righteous sponsoring of civilization?

Every Spanish exploit, every violence, every treachery was properly prefaced by Mass and prayer; every victory was attributed to some saint. Pizarro's last expedition set out from Panamá's cathedral with Mass and sermon, banners blessed.

Ere mounting the Andes Pizarro reassured his troops that "in the greatest extremity, God ever fights for his own; . . .

he will humble the pride of the heathen and bring him to the . . . true faith, the great end and aim of the Conquest."

When the little force reached deserted Cajamarca to behold Emperor Atahualpa camped along the hills with his glistening army, Valverde celebrated night Masses, invoked the God of Battles to spread his shield over the despondent soldiers fighting to extend the empire of the Cross; all joined anxiously in the *Esurge Domine* chant: "Rise, O Lord, and judge Thine own cause."

The following day Saint Iago gave them victory. Soon after Valverde helped assassinate Atahualpa.

### 3

Everywhere, the Spaniards tore the old gods from their altars and smashed them. All the native shrines—both for religion's sake and for their gold and jewels, were violated and sacked; new images and the cross, but not new concepts, were substituted for pagan idols.

Even before Pizarro had entered Cuzco, his brother Hernando swept down upon flourishing Pachacámac and burst through the sacred doors expecting to see a hall blazing with gold and precious stones. But only slaughter-house odors steamed up from floor and wall spattered with the blood of llama sacrifice; everything, save for a few gold pieces and some gems scattered on the ground, had been removed from this and adjacent precincts by the cautious native sacerdotes. The deity was "an uncouth monster with human head"— "the god through whose lips Satan had breathed forth the far-famed oracles which had deluded his Indian votaries"— so they hurled it from its place, broke it into a thousand bits. Perhaps to less fanatical eyes it might have been superior to many of the beautiful carvings which have survived the early vandalism of conversion. A stone and plaster cross was planted above the old ruins, and Hernando himself, in eloquent discourse, began the work of proselyting. Especially he taught them the sign of the cross, an invaluable talisman to secure them against devil machinations. To the natives, who already had far more original means of exorcizing dark-

ness, the cross's chief claim to efficacy must have been its novelty.

New churches replaced native shrines. Habit continued the old peregrinations. The two religions linked arms. Is it not significant that the Catholic temple near Lake Titicaca, where the Incan theocracy had its genesis, promptly became one of the most popular in the realm?

In Cuzco, on the ruins of the ancient Temple of the Sun, rose a new church. The dwellings of native priests were converted into monasteries. The House of the Sacred Virgins— the inmates of which were ruthlessly raped by the bearers of the conquering cross and cast into ordinary prostitution—

was made over into a Catholic nunnery where Virginity could be worthily respected.

Yet in some places—especially in Vilcapampa—the resistance to Catholicism was bitter and prolonged. Methods of conversion were correspondingly ruthless. Special punishments were devised for those who refused the Prince of Peace. Villages were razed to the ground; recalcitrants, if not killed outright, were shipped off to the living death of the mines.

## 4

Since Incaic State and Religion were absolutely identified, neither could outlast the other, but the political alliance of Catholic Church and Conquest, substituted for the Quechuas an understandable institutional arrangement.

The collective basis of Incan civilization rested on soil sacredness, more a moral code than a metaphysic. More concerned with rule on earth than in heaven, it was Greek, Chinese, not resembling, except in ritualistic phases, Christianity.

As the Tahuantinsuyo religion—not fabricated from complicated abstractions evolved through centuries of bickering synods, but of a deep life-death philosophy, a portentous animism cloaked in simple allegories—had dominated by artistic concepts and poetic symbolism, the Incans were all the more susceptible to outward Catholic ritual. What survived of the Incaic religion was not a metaphysical concept, but agrarian rites and magical practices, pantheistic sentiment, totemism, tabu, and ritual.

The similarity of native pagan and Catholic practices facilitated conversion. The ritualistic Quechua appurtenances so strongly reminded the conquerors of their own faith, they were convinced that Apostle St. Matthew (so wrote Piedrahita, historian of the Muysacas) must at some earlier period surely have visited those regions introducing Catholic forms. Moved by the great feast of Raymi, Acosta wrote,

"That which is most admirable in the hatred and presumption of Satan is that he not only counterfeited idolatry and sacrifices but also certain ceremonies which Jesus Christ our Lord instituted, and the holy Church uses, especially . . . the sacrament of communion, the most high and divine of all the others." And Herrera said, of rites which probably antedated Christianity: "The Father of Lies would likewise counterfeit the sacrament of Confession." The Sun Virgins were striking counterparts of Christian nuns. Chronicler Cieza de León comments upon the similarity of native concepts of immortality. The Incas had a heaven where the good lived in eternal tranquillity and ease, a hell where the wicked toiled forever, and a devil called Supay. Penance, native use of incense (coca among others), amulets and scapularies made the substitution of Catholic rites and Catholic saints for native gods little more than a change of name. The Virgin of Copacabana inherited an ancient chapel; in many towns Apostle Santiago is merely Llipac, God of Lightning. The old worship followed smoothly, without too great psychological strain, in Catholic grooves.

Today, the further one goes into the remote interior, on down into the eastern jungle country, Christianity is but a loose mould for a vast store of native superstition, idolatry, witchcraft, and false healing. The natives also know something about the art of leaving crutches aside miraculously. All these native superstitions and magical arts are mixed up with Catholic hocus-pocus and saintly invocations. Quaint pagan rites to pacify the souls of the restless dead are invariably jumbled with religious phraseology. In Arequipa, Puno and Cuzco bread stamped with the image of St. Nicholas is dipped in *aguardiente* to keep off sickness and death. The cross has been added to the pagan mountain stone-heap.

The Indian death dances and funeral music, the pantheistic earth cult, the totemic reverence toward certain animals, all require a complex of rites and beliefs centered in the ancient Mamá-Pacha cult but mixed with Catholic verbiage. With their unsold produce, the Indians crowd into the church till it looks like a fair transplanted. Half drunk with chicha, dazed with sweet visions from coca mastication, they wail their devotion of pater-nosters and ave marias; and at the Elevation, they prostrate themselves upon the floor, gluing sweaty brows to the humid tiles; there leaps into their imagination the grandiose spectacle of the Raymi fiestas, when thus bowed to dust they praised the rising Sun over the majestic Andean peaks. Emilio Romero in *Amauta* (December, 1927) imaginatively describes the process and emotions:

"The Indians vibrated with emotion before the solemnity of the Catholic ritual. They saw the image of the sun in the bordered edges of the brocades of the cassocks and in the pluvial capes; and the colors of the rainbow [sacred to them] in the rosettes of fine silk threads on the violet backgrounds. Perhaps they saw the symbol of the *quipus* in the purple tassels and cords of the barefoot abbots . . . the tangible image of their memories and adorations very far from the spirit of monkish thought. The indigenous paganism vibrated in the [new] religious fiestas . . . the elaborate Corpus Christi altars, replete with mirrors in silver frames with grotesque saints; and at the foot of these altars they laid the first fruits of their fields. They toasted the holy images in deep feeling, with the same chicha of the Cápac Raymi libations; and finally amid the exalted cries of their devotion, which for the Spanish priests were shouts of penitence but for the Indian moans of panic, they danced noisy *chachampas* and Quechua gymnastics before the petrified smile of the saints."

The old religion has not died, much of it still lives in the hearts of the people.

Another factor altered Peruvian Catholicism. Imported negro slaves enriched the faith with black sensual fetishism and other obscure superstitions. All along the coast a still darker pagan flavor was imparted to Catholic worship. In

Piura and elsewhere can still be seen the practices Javier Prado, with limited comprehension, bitterly described: "Drunk with liquor, excited by sensual stimulants and libertinage, first the negroes, later the white Creoles, with obscene movements and savage cries, danced in the popular devil and giant festivals, in the battles of Moors and Christians."

The negro was easily converted, remarks González Prada, "because he was not obliged to leap from a vulgar belief to one sublime and diametrically opposed: the doctrine taught by the priest had much resemblance to the superstitions of African tribes. . . ." Negro faith is ever more fervent than the white, and today, he adds, one can almost measure the percentage of African blood in an aristocratic Limeñan dame by the degree of her religiosity.

Peruvian Catholicism is a hybrid product. As in México there are "idols behind altars."

5

The colonial period required less religious zeal and more organization. Ecclesiastical politics became more important than mere conversion. Soon after the Catholic priests installed themselves in the Temple of the Sun, the early evangelizer was replaced by the ecclesiastical official. Not that the evangelical tradition was ever entirely lost. At intervals, note for instance the great 1610 church crusade against paganism, something of the old proselyting zeal reappeared. Successive attempts to dominate and colonize new regions were anticipated by missionary labors—a preparation of the ground for Crown armies and officials. Missionary efforts in eastern Perú kept pushing forward the frontier of Spanish influence, often with great heroism and sagacity.

The Church also brought the Indian communes into line with the Spanish system. Carlos Valdez de la Torre notes

358

how the Church, when population became depleted by forced labor, founded—either through force or persuasion—many new towns by settlements or fused older communities around a common church—"reductions." The Jesuits, when expelled by Charles III in 1617, had 203 haciendas on each of which a "congregation" had been settled.[1]

If the grim Ginés de Sepúlveda sought to make the Church an ally of the feudal landlord class, part of the machinery of colonial oppression, in contrast the somewhat hypocritical Bartolomé de las Casas (to be censored for his active advocacy of negro slavery) saw that the Church's future glory lay in befriending the Indian as the basic rock upon which to erect a great spiritual edifice. Other early ecclesiastics carried the true cross. This conflict in attitude persists today after four centuries.

Father Lope de Atienza's writings abound with honest advice. Pedro de Villagómez, Francisco de Avila, Toribio de Mogrovejo, Bernabé Cobo, Hernando de Avendaño, Pablo José de Amaga, and especially the courageous Rodrigo de Loaysa, showed comprehension, often loftiness of purpose.

In 1542 Las Casas placed his manuscript detailing abuses of the Indians by civil and ecclesiastical authorities and by private *encomenderos* in the hands of the King. A special council in Valladolid put generous new laws upon the books. In Perú the attempt to enforce these precipitated a series of landlord revolts that almost lost the colony for the Crown. Ultimately the humanitarian regulations were politely accepted in official communiques and disregarded in practice.

Las Casas failed and his failure continues to this day. For conservative Victor Andres Belaunde, Catholicism is still the one vital tie between the dominating and dominated races: "Indians, mestizos, whites claim this common mother. The

---

[1] Valdez, 120.

But if the Church founded new towns it was also careful to foment rivalries and jealousies between all communities so as to make native dependence upon the new religious institution more complete. Cf. Saenz, 252-3.

new cult of the old race is Christ-centred; its principal fiesta, Corpus Christi, and the dominant devotion, that of Mary. The *ayullu* survives and the chain-gangs of peonage and contract labor persist; but the gods have definitely gone. In a manner obscure, imperfect, indefinite . . . Christianity has triumphed. This unity of religion is the basis of national unity without which the latter would scarcely exist. The crossing of races gave this unity a biological nexus, but the true spiritual nexus has been given by religion.[2]

This is a naïve confession that the Peruvian nation has not yet been born; a confession that institutionalized religion, not Christianity, has conquered in Perú, that institutionalized religion is an instrument of race and class domination.

The Church, officially allied with the government, still forms part of a clique of medieval landowners and more recently of foreign capital, is an active political and business partner in a land of atrocious exploitation.

6

The great Colonial O.G.P.U. was the Inquisition. Although Atahualpa's execution might be considered the first terroristic act of an officialized Loyola inquisition, not until Viceroy Francisco de Toledo y Figueroa, was the Church, already corrupt, utilized to organize solidly the new colony on the basis of efficient feudal exploitation. November, 1569, in accordance with Philip II's cedula, he instituted the Inquisition with headquarters on the little plaza where now stand the statue of liberator Simón Bolívar and the modern buildings housing the Chamber of Deputies and the Senate, august bodies which convene whenever some dictator permits them to do so.

Sunday, November 15, 1573, the most influential Christian citizens of Lima turned out in gala force to witness the

2 *La Realidad Nacional*, 121.

first *auto-da-fé*, the burning with handclapping and prayers of a French heretic who lived a mysterious hermit life on top of one of the ancient *huacas* which stud Rimac Valley. A second *auto-da-fé* was held in Toledo's presence April 13, 1878. A great procession: the cathedral cross covered by a black veil, priests chanting *"miere mei,"* the Cabildo wearing black capes, *encomenderos* dragging along chained wolves. Sixteen victims, six of them priests, one a merchant, another a lawyer, marched with ropes around their necks, dressed in the green San Benito habit of humiliation, yellow capes, conical hats a yard high painted with devils and flames, and carrying candles of hope. Penalties ranged from 200 lashes to being burned alive and bereft of all worldly possessions.

Through the 240 years' existence of the Peruvian Inquisition, the number of victims, at least in Lima, was relatively small—twenty-nine *autos-da-fé*, some hundreds hanged and but fifty-nine burned at the stake. But in the provinces, the Inquisition had fewer restraints, was far more cruel. Nor do these statistics tell the whole story of general intimidation and dungeon torture, all the tearing out of tongues and eyes, etc.

After all, the worst crime of the Sacred Office was the burning of the books, its stifling of all intellectual freedom. It chained the colonial mind (and thereby the modern Peruvian mind) to backwardness and bigotry, to casuistry and pedantic theogeny. "What science could flourish in Perú?" cried Javier Prado. "Only a vulgar theology, a formal dogmatism . . . a confused and amazing mixture."

But ere the close of his administration, Toledo could send to the King the great golden image of the Sun of Coricancha with the suggestion that it be given to the Pope as a token that Christianity was triumphant over ancient paganism.

7

New wealth weakened all real religious efforts; placed the emphasis ever upon more sumptuous religious festivals, an increasing burden upon the people. The great monasteries became placid refuges of sterile learning, easy living, and of great political and social influence.

Even before the time of Toledo, Church and churchman had become wealthy. As Martel Santoyo said soon after the Conquest: "All the Dominican and Mercederian monasteries have *repartimientos* . . . [this was contrary to the Laws of the Indies]. They try to extract from them [the Indians] as much as they can . . . with this and with alms they grow rich"—everywhere they were setting a bad example. Father Naharro, about the same time, found in all Perú only five Mercederians, four Predicators and three Franciscans to be truly holy and humble.

Most priests became large landowners, part of the landed aristocracy; the Church held vast tracts, as it does to this day. Rodrigo de Loaysa, writing toward the end of the sixteenth century, bemoaned the growing ostentation.

By 1633, the ex-missionary Ribeiro Teixera de Morais openly accused the clergy of not observing the rules of their calling. Christianity for them was but a name, most were more depraved than the heathen. Indiscipline, greed and lax morality had crept in. The clergy had become business men; a slaughter-house monopoly brought them much revenue; they participated in the shady deals of the Corregidores. Out of 1,040 priests with whom Teixera dealt, only five were perfect in the performance of their duties and their mode of life.

Increasingly during the eighteenth century, the clergy sank to its lowest depths. The University of San Marcos, founded by Charles I in 1533, the oldest institution of learning in the New World, had decayed to a second-rate seminary, where bitter physical pummeling between the jealous orders disturbed academic calm. Monks shamelessly kept concubines in rented rooms or their cells, and staged drunken revelries for the gay ladies in sacred precincts. Castel Fuerte describes the rowdy brawls of the nuns, which often obliged prelates or constables to intervene to maintain cloistral peace —for instance the scandal in Santa Clara in 1709, put down by force. Convents, as described by Mauro de Velasco, became petty republics ruthlessly exploiting native labor, showing rich ostentation; the nuns only half withdrew from the mundane world.

## XXIII

## HOLY FLAME

### I

THE colonial Church early showed cleavage along economic and caste lines. The upper clergy almost everywhere, and all the Lima Archbishops, were invariably Spanish. Only fifty-three of 180 bishops and archbishops were not Spanish born —even these were of pure Spanish blood—Creoles—and mostly non-Peruvian. Only late in the colonial period could a Creole reach a high post, a mestizo almost never; the most amazing exception anywhere in the New World was the full-blooded negro who became Archbishop of Panamá. In Perú, as elsewhere, race lines were closely drawn. The lower clergy, made up, not merely of Creoles, but of many mestizos, or cholos, got the poorest assignments, could look for no advancement.

Independence menaced such ecclesiastical privileges. Two Peruvian priests, Chávez de la Rosa and Rodríguez de Mendoza did much to pave the way intellectually for independence. As in Mexico where the poor parish priest Hidalgo struck the first blow for national freedom (only to be promptly excommunicated), the lower Peruvian clergy, hopeful of improving its status, incited their congregations to join liberator San Martín; many poorer priests became agitators, martyrs, and indomitable warriors.

Though the Peruvian Bishops at first had launched furibund pro-Spanish pastorals, they hastened to change color with the growing success of Bolívar's arms. By the close of the wars the churches were chanting:

From You comes all
That is good, O Lord;
You gave us Bolívar,
Glory to You, great God.

Pope Leo XII was sending to "illustrious chief"—Sucre—
"his beloved son, his apostolic greetings and blessings." Bolívar's secretary was writing to the Apostolic Vicar in Chile
that the Peruvian government "for obligations and personal
sentiments" would conform to the "Evangelical maxims" and
"protect the splendor of the Church."

Church influence caused the new Peruvian state to organize itself as a religious feudal entity with Catholicism,
then as now, the official religion. Church officials promptly
seated themselves, as secretaries and advisers, at the right
hand of the Independence marshals, many of whom were
also great landholders. The ecclesiastics framed loquacious
religious legislation. They became cabinet ministers.

Throughout all the Republican period down to the present, Church influence has been paramount both in family
and public affairs. All official documents, however iniquitous,
however much aimed to destroy human rights, are still piously terminated: "May God protect you"—reminiscent of
similar postscripts in Mexico a century ago.

At any threat to their supremacy, the priests, with their
vast hold over the ignorant and fanatical, led revolts and
riots, backed military adventurers and chanted their success.

The clergy undermined the better efforts of Castilla; they
diverted President Piérola, who strove for bourgeois political renovation, from his cause; they blessed the sword
which overthrew the plebeian President Billinghurst. They
were with reactionary Pardo, demagogic Leguía, and bloody
Sánchez Cerro.

One contemporary states (*El Proceso Haya de la Torre*,
XXVII): "The priests have blessed many a semi-savage as
the 'Chosen Son of God,' and from their pulpits have pro-

365

claimed as acts 'pardonable because necessary' the boundless excesses and unmentionable crimes of the most vile and bloody tyrannies [that of Sánchez Cerro] which any country of our Americas has suffered."

Even today numbers of cases can be cited where the priests have incited mob violence or have led mobs to punish those who have criticized the Church; Protestant missionaries everywhere risk their lives.

The high clergy have become Civilistas, part of the reactionary group which has ruled with almost unbroken power from the time of the Chilean war, and thus have participated in nitrate and guano profits.

Though the liberalizing ideas that invariably accompany early industrialization have occasionally threatened to separate Church and political leaders, the bourgeoisie have never really asserted themselves. And Leguía—representative par excellence of foreign capital—who ruled during Perú's greatest modern economic expansion, was hand in glove with the Church; he maintained his tyranny eleven years with direct complicity. He utilized the Archbishop and various bishops in his political campaigns and in his business deals. The Archbishopric Palace, the mansion of the highest dignitary of the Peruvian Church, was converted into a business agency, even engaged in usurious money-lending; and the Church also played in closely with the swarms of foreign adventurers who came to secure valuable concessions. In all official Leguía publications, the Church personalities figure most prominently, and they forced through legislation injurious to the Republic at large, especially with reference to public education, *viz.*, the 1929 laws regarding religious instruction; they blocked all efforts to legalize divorce. Leguía was decorated with the Order of Christ, the oath of which is unconstitutional. His 1923 attempt to consecrate the Republic to the Heart of Jesus, was frustrated only by the threatened strike of United Front of Manual and Intellectual Workers, led by Haya de la Torre. So notorious were the Archbishop Lisson's relations with Leguía that on the dictator's fall, the head of the Church actually had to abandon his office and flee the country. Several bishops and priests also lost their posts—an eleventh-hour attempt of the Church to save its face.

Adventurous Sánchez Cerro, representing the less aristocratic wing of civilismo linked with middle-class job-holders —and who also attracted cholo and Indian elements because of his Spanish-Indian-negro blood and their hatred for Leguía—for a time had a pseudo-anti-clerical tinge. But this was largely to scourge all Leguía partisans, chief among which had been the Episcopate. The Church, soon realizing its real perogatives were not endangered, in the 1931 elections swung behind the candidacy of Sánchez Cerro, as did all the Civilistas, to forestall the victory of Haya de la Torre. As a bitter Apra critic expresses it, the Church "finally surrendered to the soldier of August and kissed and caressed the same boot that had humiliated it."

Yet even the Apristas, considered so radical by conservative Peruvians, no longer oppose the Church, are afraid to tackle the problem. They remind me of González Prada's words, "Every Creole freethinker . . . is a priest turned inside out." In their pamphlets they make much of the fact that prior to the 1932 Trujillo revolt, the rebel Apristas were careful to celebrate a campaign Mass à la Pizarro ere trying to overthrow the government. The God of Battles merely led them to a shambles in which several thousand were slaughtered. The bravest of them, on dying, cried: "Christ saved my soul and Apra will save Perú."

In the meantime, as González Prada said in 1904, "Perú is a nation so Catholic in laws and customs that it merits being called the sub-office of Rome and the future convent of South America."

2

Union of Church and State has confused the educational system. Besides the Patronato of the Indigenous Race—Leguía's organization put entirely into ecclesiastical hands—a large proportion of the government's schools are run by priests, nuns and monks. In Lima the women's normal school, the only complete teacher's college in the country, is managed by nuns—the same ones who became frenzied over the electric cross.

In Cuzco, the intermediary school for girls, with a normal department, is also in nunnish hands. In Ayacucho the Church schools are partially subsidized by the government.

Local teachers often flout government inspectors and take their cases to the bishop or archbishop instead of to the Department of Education.

The June 24, 1929, school law forbids and orders closed all schools and institutions which advocate non-Catholic doctrines. Fathers of non-Catholics can teach their children a different religion only through petition to the Secretariat of Education!

Inevitably during the past century slight modifications of the Church's status have occurred. González Vigil's and González Prada's vigorous writings opened many minds. The 'fifties throughout Latin America were marked by anti-clerical tendencies. In Perú Reformation found echo in the nationalist convention of 1856 where, after tempestuous sessions, some of the special privileges (*fueros*), tithes, primacies and parochial rights were abolished. Even so Article VI specifically safeguarded the canonical tribunals in ecclesiastical matters and forebade "the arrest or the execution of corporal punishment against ecclesiastical persons except in conformity with the canons." Religious tolerance, though discussed, was voted down, not being accepted, and then only in part, until 1907; full tolerance of cults was not implanted until November 11, 1915! Not until 1868 could non-Catholics be buried in a cemetery. Up until 1873, when civil registration was established, the Church kept all birth, marriage and death records. Not until December 23, 1897, was civil marriage granted to non-Catholics, who prior to that had had to live in sin. Not until 1907 was civil marriage made binding, even then was not compulsory for Catholics. Divorce did not appear until 1934!

But Church officials are still named by the government subject to Papal ratification, thus forcing every priest to be a politician. The salaries of all priests and Church officials are paid by the Peruvian government out of taxes collected from all Peruvians whether Catholic or not.

A heavy burden. Thus the town of Ayacucho, with little commerce and no rail communications, is obliged to support a cathedral, twenty-six churches, and five chapels, besides monasteries and convents. The entire department, with a population of 300,000, has 564 religious establishments, one for every 105 heads of families. Besides the salaries and official subsidies to Catholic schools, which are not small, the population must provide money for the upkeep of the Churches and the cult and for the funds which are remitted to Rome. In 1930 one small congregation near Trujillo sent 60,000 *soles* across the seas. What galls many Peruvians is that these salaries are mostly paid to foreigners, who occupy the best posts in the larger centers. In the beautiful and prosperous Jesuit Church in Lima (by special concession granted a parish) I found only one Peruvian father, and he occupied the most menial position; the rest were French, Italian, Spanish and Colombian.

In Iquitos the clergy are entirely foreign, the one native priest having been so shabbily treated that several years ago he became a cashier for a local Jewish firm!

3

The whole Church-State system in Perú rests squarely upon the exploitation of mass ignorance. Birth, registration, baptism, consecration, marriage, death, burial, masses for souls in Purgatory, the blessing of crosses, images and homes, crops, animals, implements—all provide means of extracting juicy fees. In relation to current wage standards and considering that priestly salaries are paid by the government, Church fees are quite exorbitant, especially as they do not cover all the expenses of the various ceremonies. Here are some for the central highlands:

*soles*

| | | |
|---|---|---|
| Chanted Mass | 50 | (Over four months' wages) |
| Ordinary Mass | 12 | |
| Responses | ½ | (Over day's wage) |
| Marriage | 12 | (Thirty days' wages) |
| Burial | 6 | |

A "white" marriage costs 60 *soles* (five months' wages), but often the priest will call an Indian or cholo white to make him pay the higher fee. Even in remote places where there is no cemetery and no priestly ceremony has been held, Church collectors, though they may arrive many months later, inquire who has died, and extract the fee.

For blessing crosses during fiestas, a fee of twenty centavos to five *soles* is charged—according to the size. Holiness is a very dimensional matter in Perú. In Santa María Auxiliadora in Lima donors of building funds were rewarded with marble wall plaques, varying in size according to the sum, which give the generous ones a free ride right into heaven.

"In all the collective manifestations," writes Castro Pozo, "the priest is part and parcel . . . fomenter of all the superstitions and fiestas of the calendar, the blessing of stones, sticks and places where fanaticism imagines the apparition of a Christian divinity"—and all his activities from consecrating the fiesta and exorcizing evil spirits to getting souls out of Purgatory are well paid for. The picture given by Bachman earlier in the book can be duplicated anywhere. Typical of curious fees was that charged—until recently abolished by Bishop Gregorio Castro—for each stirrup in the equestrian Santiago festival in Yanacoa.

Everybody must contribute something to the saintly images, often of gold or silver, carried from chapel to chapel and house to house and through all the throngs of the fiesta. Sometimes the priest leaves the image at a house for a certain number of days, and the efficacy of its presence is so great that the resultant fee must be in accordance.

The Masses for the dead do not have a set day, but are ordered as soon as the interested parties can dispose of the required twenty Peruvian dollars. The priest will go to a village only when he has gotten ten or fifteen persons, whom he classifies according to their ability to pay, though he says but one Mass for all of them.

Chanted Masses required a special class of *cantores*. By Law VI, October 8, 1560, it was ordered that "all pueblos of more than one hundred Indians must have two or three *cantores*," another class of parasites foisted upon native communal life. These *cantores* still exist; they are the long arm and eye of the village priest. They begin as domestics in the parish house to learn to play the organ, sing, and parrot Latin. Today they participate, for a price, in many communal fiestas and events. In addition to the three days of music provided by paid players of the *chirimía*, to which the Pastores are danced, no village watch or funeral is complete without the services of a *cantor*, who naturally charges monopoly rates. If his fees are not paid, he forecloses on property. Many *cantores* have become wealthy hacendados or business men.

The Sierra priests also make use of the blind, considered by the superstitious as supernatural, as witches almost semi-divine. The blind always take part in fiestas and for five or ten centavos give Latin responses (taught them by the priests for a share in the fees) for souls in Purgatory.

The patron saint's rôle is all important; it calls forth elaborate fiestas in which many primitive practices survive. The Indian must also celebrate *alferazgos*, majordomos, and *padrinazgos* (names given to those in charge of the festival). These fiestas are colorful affairs, yet their frequency and their cost keep the Indian in slavery. They not only eat up all the year's savings, but serve as an excuse for getting drunk for from three to five days. As many more are required to recover and get back to work.

Often he will have to go off for six months or a year as a contract laborer in the vain hope of paying back all the expenses; frequently he is caught permanently in the coils of debt slavery; often he loses his property which goes to swell the already vast acreage of adjacent haciendas of the Church. Just to celebrate the annual festival of the patron saint with music and fireworks, natives have to pay the priest from ten to twenty *soles.* The priests promote as many fiestas as possible, for not only do they gladden the native heart but merely the blessing of the crosses as well as the chapels and the various collections and the sale of candles bring in rich returns. Writes Castro Pozo [1]: "There are indigenes who work the whole year to realize these fiestas . . . each one results in the consumption of fifty Peruvian dollars' worth of candles alone. The general expenses run to 250 or 300 Peruvian dollars without counting the workdays lost. . . . It is apparent that the principal object of these annual [priestly] visits is to procure funds to increase the worldly goods of the saint, in the shadow of which flourish the almstaker and many others. The fiesta is, in itself, nothing more . . . than to cause the faithful to congregate and use their faith to extort money."

La Punta near Huancayo celebrates twelve major fiestas a year; Sapallanga celebrates about thirty, to which even the people of relatively advanced Huancayo go out barefoot, on their knees, or otherwise, some four miles. One writer estimates that the Indians lose a third of their working year in religious festivals, with concomitants of exploitation, drunkenness, blessing of crosses, stones, rivers, animals, etc. "There is," remarks Saenz,[2] "a certain relation between the degree of advancement of an indigenous community and its

[1] 244-45.
[2] 249.

liberation from ecclesiastical custom. The more prosperous, the more progressive, cultured and socialized a community, the fewer religious celebrations it has." Thus Sapallanga, over-burdened with fiestas, is poor and miserable; adjacent Huancán, well-to-do and highly developed, celebrates only two.

## 4

Less worthy elements among the clergy have found other more direct ways of dispossessing the Indian. *Libertad* (October 24, 1930) gives an account of how Priest Honorato Chávez of Vacas had stolen the lands of Angamarca, Vivichincha, Tacha, Patmancancha, Yurabrune, Acachica, Mocho and others; how on one occasion, to oust the peasants, he came with the rural guard and four others, all drunk. They attacked the women, robbed homes, stole fifty pigs and other animals.

The same paper (September 27, 1930) printed a complaint of the Indians against Priest Ricardo Rosemberg of Huancayo for stealing the lands in Abancay, Cuzco, with attendant crimes and abuses.

According to the official record of the Patronato of the Raza Indígena of the Department of Ayacucho,[3] when the Judge of First Instance in Castrovirreyna Province was attempting to dispossess Indians of their lands in the Commune of Pauraiya, sixty armed persons arrived in the company of Priest Honorato Chávez with guns and barbed-wire clubs. The Indians were wounded, and Plácido Lauro flogged, nude, and thrown into a well.

In the theft of the Indian lands of San Francisco, armed men appeared, accompanied by the priest Dr. Retamozo.[4]

*El Norte* of Trujillo (April 11, 1934) relates how the Community Romero-Usquiel sent representative Juan En-

---

[3] *Boletín,* June 30, 1928.
[4] *Ibid.*

rique Avila to the departmental capital to protest against the efforts of Priest Heraclío Maunós to dispossess them of lands "owned by them since immemorial times." When I visited Cajamarca I found the nuns of one establishment trying to dispossess Indians of lands.

A survey of the findings of the Patronato and other literature reveals innumerable cases in which priests, whether for their own benefit or for the Church or as accomplices of *gamonales* or officials, have taken direct or indirect part in the spoliation of Indian lands. Sometimes, as in the previously cited example of the Bishop of Trujillo, high officials have been involved.

These continue methods described by González Prada in 1903. The government then and since has provided the monks with arms to "persecute to the death all free-thinkers." In that year the friars of Ocapa near Huancayo were given two large boxes of Manlecher rifles and three "loads" of ammunition. These weapons are often used for evil purposes.

"Clad in a dirty muddy robe, covered by enormous straw sombreros, with large crucifixes (not on the breast but on the stomach), flourishing unusual whips or shouldering a Winchester or Mauser, they go with the menacing air of a conqueror. They speak only vulgar interjections, incitations to hate and of extermination of liberals. They seize crops, appropriate domestic animals, maltreat people, kidnap children, seduce women . . . the friars of Ocapa burned their own church . . . to get fat contributions . . . and blame the crime on the free-thinkers of Huancayo. . . ." [5]

Thus the priests become property owners, and the Church, in its own right, is a great landholder. Besides the vast estates which it owns or in which it has equities, in smaller villages it still retains lands dating from the Conquest when it took over the Inca commons designated for the support of the old

[5] *Horas de Lucha*, 263-65.

religion, or which were specifically allotted by the Crown; these must still be worked free, the income going to the Church. One town in the Sierra has seventeen lay brotherhoods working such lands. Very few villages have recovered the areas appropriated by the Church. Many have, on the other hand, seen additional communal soil pass to the Church. According to Manuel A. Quiroga, in his *La evolución de la propiedad rural en Puno,* the Church in that department owns thirty-three large haciendas in addition to other rural properties secretly held, and much urban property.

For centuries the Peruvian Church has been a ruling institution. At times it has had entire control of the government. On other occasions it has been an active partner in government, and even today it fights bitterly every effort to separate Church and State.

Yet today, after four centuries, the mass of the Peruvian people are ignorant or uneducated, subject to disease and death, vilely exploited; they live in unsanitary miserable homes; their economic lot is worse than it was under the Inca emperors before the coming of the Spaniards. The Church has filled the land with beautiful edifices, but it has not taught the Indians and mestizos who comprise eighty-five percent of the population, how to build decent homes or how to keep their bodies clean. The priest in Perú has catered to native superstition and ignorance, and it is doubtful, given the situation in which the masses live, that he has contributed anything to their real spiritual welfare. One is forced to the reluctant conclusion, despite the many fine priests I have met in Perú, that the Church as an institution is organized for the purpose of mass exploitation and that it is a partner of all the economic classes which foster such exploitation. Thus the Church must bear its share of the blame, after so many centuries of governing responsibility, that today Perú socially and economically is one of the most benighted countries of the western hemisphere.

# XXIV

# EPAULETTES

## I

IMPORTANT political changes in Perú are still made by the army, typically Latin American, but also a unique military machine. Its traditions are not as old as that of the Mexican army, originally a fusion of the feathered bucklers of Moctezuma and the shining helmets of Cortés; yet it is not as modern as the goose-step files of Chile. Perú's army never had to evolve from the European type of knighthood-army. Independence brought it into being as a national army. As a national army—not created as in Mexico by treachery of Crown officials—it has been more orderly, less brutal; but Perú being less a nation than Mexico, its colonial traditions still imperative, its military system is a class system, not primarily to defend the nation but to defend the surviving colonial oligarchy.

The Peruvian army, better controlled than in Mexico, has perpetrated important political changes as the tool of the ruling caste. Merely an instrument for furthering governmental oppression—as when, with the Church, it ousted Billinghurst, who threatened a few popular reforms—its violences have hinged upon petty medieval feuds. The officers are mere sycophants, blind instruments of the wealthy landholding class—honey-jar militarists, obeying *gamonal* orders in return for good salaries, petty privileges and graft.

Despite the aristocratic pretensions of higher officials, they are socially snubbed. They must accept merely patronizing from their aristocratic *gamonal* masters. Except for a few generals, upper social circles and homes are definitely closed

377

to the uniform. Officers are not allowed in the aristocratic Club Nacional, though some exclusive Civilistas condescend to drink with army officers in the public bars.

Because of this army subordination to the Creole, landlord and Church factions, Perú prides itself on definitely

having left its earlier militarism, its lawless *caudillaje*, behind. Vain hope!

The Sánchez Cerro revolt, though it represented merely one wing of Civilismo allied with the middle class, revealed that the old unruly *caudillismo* has not disappeared, and it also revealed other hidden tendencies in army ranks. Though this baby Napoleon from Arequipa was moved merely by the greedy ambitions of less-favored under-officers rather than by patriotism, he based his temporary success on a popular cause. Today the Peruvian army, because of its general mestizo-Indian make-up, which conflicts with the false aristocratic pretensions of its officers, is fertile soil for revolutionary propaganda.

378

2

Immediately following independence, the army was of far greater importance in public affairs than today. It was then in truth the Great Elector.

Independence disintegrated all social groups except the new army and the Church. The Creole landholding aristocracy, attempting to dislodge the favored Spaniards of the same economic group, were temporarily caught between the cogs of the new bourgeoisie and the triumphant independence soldiers.

The mestizo elements were busy hunting their new petty places in the new social scheme. Negro slaves and Indians, dislocated by the wars, offered no social coherence. The army and the Church became, in their respective spheres, all powerful for several decades.

The army came crowned with laurels. As a real Indo-Latin force, inflamed with ideals of liberty, it had provided Perú's most glorious military tradition—the victories of Junín and Ayacucho. But as a ruling institution, it destroyed all liberty in a crass fight for the spoils over the prostrate body of the country, further paralyzing industrial activities already shattered—now also accentuated by severance of Spanish trade and inability to develop new trade routes. Armies could not be properly demobilized. Industry could not absorb them. They could only keep on fighting as their only means of economic survival until gradually the landholding Creoles reorganized their economic and political position.

These early chaotic battles rested on audacity, not scientific skill or proper equipment—no maps, advance parties, exploration, or science. They involved incredible exploits of valor and endurance—Santa Cruz marched an army six hundred miles through the Andes in less than two weeks and went right into battle. Castilla, disembarking in Arica in 1843 with eight men—à la Garibaldi—found no difficulty in whipping together an army that put him into the Presidency. "The battle of Guía (1838) was like that of Tarqui, like that of Injaos, of Alto de la Alianza, and of Chorrillos . . ." writes Basadre.[1] "The men of 1829 resembled those of 1838, 1879, and 1880 [and, he might have added, of 1894, and 1930]: Dissension in plain sight of the enemy, the fatuous hope of winning without organization, preoccupation with petty motives, forgetting the great need of union, struggles between the chiefs of the same band, the decisive moment arriving at an unexpected hour, disorganization in battle, failure to utilize favorable elements, eagerness to throw the blame on any one to save one's own responsibility, self-consolation in defeat by means of loquacity—how familiar, how authentic these things seem!"

The armies were undisciplined, lawless; the officers gay, insolent, reckless and dissipated. Benítez, sent by Salaverry to cut off the enemy, went on a drunken bat, was surprised and put to rout. Salaverry, learning of the disaster from a fleeing sergeant, ordered Benítez shot. But by a brilliant coup, the latter unexpectedly turned defeat into victory and took all his attackers prisoners. Instead of being shot for lack of discipline he was at once promoted.

González Prada describes the militarists of '94 as "hordes of mountaineers captained by bandits, imposers of forced loans, sackers of haciendas, flagellators of recruits, violators of women, executioners of prisoners, in short barbarians . . . defending the laughable legality of the government."[2]

With such lack of discipline and the possibility of such strokes of fortune, the army offered swift personal advancement—also quick disgrace. An army officer in Cabello de Carbonera's novel *El Conspirador* boasts that the militarists go "at once into the Presidency of the Republic and . . .

[1] *Iniciación de la República*, II, 275.
[2] *Horas de Lucha*, 12.

380

without heating their brains or wearing out books, they pass from colonels to presidents." But La Fuente, once a power, in 1831 had to flee across the rooftops, "leaping the highest walls, naked and sick, followed by bullets." Curious concepts of chivalry frequently manifested themselves. Chilean General Blanco Encalada actually proposed to Santa Cruz that each army put up an equal small number of troops to determine the fate of the campaign. Many a quickly made hero was received in Lima under triumphal arches with Viceregal splendor to enjoy the inevitable congratulatory Te Deum in the cathedral.

Greed, vanity, love of power, tinseled popularity were omnipresent motives. Santa Cruz, perhaps Perú's greatest codifier and organizer, began his decrees with an enumeration of his titles: "Andrés Santa Cruz, Great Citizen, Restorer and President of Bolivia, Captain General of the Army, Brigadier General of Colombia, Grand Marshal Pacifier of Perú, Supreme Invictus Protector of the Peruvian North and South States, Chargé of Foreign Relations of the Three States; Supreme Protector of the Perú-Bolivian Confederation; decorated with the medals of the Liberating Army, of the Liberator of Quito, of Pinchincha, of Junín, of Cobija, and with that of Liberator Simón Bolívar, Founder and Chief of the Legion of Honor of Bolivia and of the National Legion of Perú, Grand Official of the Legion of Honor of France, etc. etc. etc."

The leaders loved bombastic empty rhetoric, often in execrable ignorant Spanish full of misspelling and bad grammar, ever with sentimental references to Our Lady of Carmen, Jesus Christ, etc.[3] The proclamations all read—save for names and dates—almost alike, a sort of ritualistic hocuspocus encouraging partisans, damning enemies, and mentioning unselfishness, liberty, constitutional rights.

Generals always considered themselves "Saviors of the

[3] Cf. Nieto a Grau, Oct. 5, 1838.

Fatherland." La Fuente spoke of the "three Peruvian generals [himself, Gamarra, and Santa Cruz] who can and should save the country." In 1838 Perú had seven generals as presidents at one and the same time. Extravagant and absurd edicts were the result of such ignorant power. Gamarra, August 30, 1838, suddenly prohibited all foreign retail commerce and ordered the establishments closed within a week. Salaverry brightly contradicted himself in a proclamation of unparalleled vapidity: "Far be it from me to wade in torrents of blood to arrive at the throne the dazzle of which does not hallucinate a Republican soul. Heaven is witness to the purity of my ideas . . ." This was about as close to a program as most of the generals could get. The worthiest political and social achievements of military rule were the Perú-Bolivian Confederacy of Santa Cruz and the abolition of slavery and suppression of Indian tribute by Castilla.

The early presidential candidates were all generals. They filled cabinets and legislative halls. Militarists such as San Román, Castilla, Echenique, Ibarra, Herencia Zevallos, Prado, Mediburú and La Fuente presided over Congress. They occupied the provincial all-powerful Prefecturas; and generals, as governors of the departments, ruled as local princes, until their teeth were drawn slightly in 1834 and 1839, more effectively by the 1856 constitution. In 1834 it was decreed that the number of officers be limited, deportation of Peruvians without trial was forbidden, also forcible quartering of soldiers on private homes, non-legal tax laws and forced loans; habeas corpus was established, etc. The militarist's exemption from civil law had persisted until that year.

Meanwhile Creole feudalists and the new bourgeoisie merged and bent the militarists to their special interests. This transition period of the bourgeoise-feudal rise to power was featured by a new type of militarist. The purely military *caudillo,* who had to forge his statesmanship entirely from the memory of armed victories, gives way to types, such as

José Galvez, as much politician as militarist—party leader in a Liberal Parliament and active in all the various political jockeyings and conspiracies, or Orbegoso, of illustrious lineage, more a liberal scholar than a militarist.

The new bourgeois-feudal-army group remained in control until their greed and stupidity plunged the country into war with Chile. Cowardice completed their disgrace. Seeing war inevitable, they hastened to dismantle the gunboats and reduce the army to leave more funds available for hurried theft. Frantically they converted their properties into cash and fled, even high army officers, to Europe. No noble names are found among Perú's heroic, ill-equipped defenders. Yet never did a people go down to defeat more gallantly—Dolores, Anagauros, Arica, Tarapacá, Marcavalle, Pucará, San Pablo, Huamachuco, are records any nation could be proud of. But they also reveal the utter stupidity of the war and of the country's rulers—a shameful spectacle of cravenness and corruption.

This gave newer, more popular, militarists, such as Iglesias, Morales, Bermúdez and Cáceres, a brief chance to rule the country. But quite unable to realize that their real power and glory over an extended period could only be maintained by assuming generous leadership of the awakening masses, and equally unable to solve the overwhelming economic problems of defeat, the army elements soon sold out in fright to the Civilistas, under Prado and Piérola, who forged new feudal bourgeoise rule with the aid of British capital.

### 3

Perú's army is a conscript army, an Indian army. It has always been such. During the Independence wars, both sides went into the villages and rounded up Indians to fight. Vagabonds were invariably seized, still are, to fill the ranks. Lavandais, writing of Peruvian conscription in 1851, observed how soldiers came into villages at dawn to drag men out of their homes. Deserters were at once shot. New ones had their heads shaved and their ears marked. Taken to some training center, they were locked up in the Church, being allowed out only to drill.

Deputy Bustamante said in Congress, 1857: "It is impossible to paint in true colors what happens when recruiters appear in a town; cholera, yellow fever and fire cause less fear . . . to evade, they [the villagers] mutilate their own hands and feet, even take out their eyes." Basadre mentions a recent Prefect telegram: "If you want more volunteers, send more ropes."

I myself have seen young men rounded up in villages at the point of the bayonet. The most physically fit are taken off to the larger centers under guard. They go packed into trucks, or in railway freight or cattle cars, like sardines, standing up all day often under the hot sun—to fight for their noble fatherland.

Most of them speak no Spanish, haven't the slightest idea why they fight. When some officer arouses their personal loyalty, they are faithful, dogged and brave, willing to suffer the worst rigors. More generally, they serve half-heartedly, abandon every engagement at the first opportunity. Desertions are always high. "The Indian who whistles the tunes of his home region is sure to desert," remarked Castilla. More recently officers have been taught the Quechua language and make appeals to race sentiments.

In Lima, I heard the head of the national military school, on giving diplomas, declaim: "You are the children of the Sun, our Father. We shall protect the glories of his empire . . ."—a harking back to the old region and race traditions.

The infantry has invariably been made up largely of Indians, the cavalry, of coast zambos and negroes—recently freed slaves. Though brilliantly equipped with magnificent horses, many feathers, gleaming helmets, lances and pennants, since the slave can have no feeling for the fatherland, the cavalry has never given, in either domestic or foreign wars, a good account of itself.

The rank and file are conscripts, the upper officers privileged aristocrats, the average officer, a mestizo bureaucrat who owes job and promotion to petty political intrigue. As such he is not patriotic, is merely hunting for a sinecure which, once obtained, he exploits for his personal benefit. When not grafting with padded army rolls and supply contracts, he is pulling wires to get the softest berth in an agreeable locality, above all in Lima. Hence the army is corrupt. Its notorious inefficiency and lack of equipment were revealed in the War of the Pacific, became worse under Leguía, and although danger of war over Leticia has caused some technical improvement, the terrible inadequacy and corruption was definitely revealed by the needless sacrifices of Peruvian forces in the Loreto jungle combats in 1933. The Peruvian troops were sent into the morasses without proper arms, clothing, food or sanitation; they died like rats.

More than a weapon of national defense, the Peruvian army fills a decorative mission, serves for brilliant parades to give lustre to Archbishop and President. "The Peruvian militarists," remarks the priest in *El Conspirador,* "are good only to execute manœuvres on Corpus Christi day or for the burial of cabinet ministers and Presidents; and in Arequipa the only thing they have been good for is to start revolutions against the governments."

In these public military displays ingenious officials teach their soldiers to form cute stars, circles, triangles and pentagons. Or the soldiers suddenly produce flowers out of their knapsacks and spell out gallant perfumed phrases for the benefit of the applauding multitude—like American college rooters doing stunts between halves, or the Elks on Fourth of July.

4

Explanations have been sought for the curious militarism of
Latin America. For Carlos Octavio Bunge the *deus ex machina* of Creole life are idleness, melancholy and arrogance—
transplanted Spanish characteristics. Among people naturally
indolent, the active militarist leaps into command. Jealousies
soon create battles and tyrannies.

Lucas Ayarragaray finds American militarism a heritage
of Napoleonism. Bolívar fought in the Napoleonic army.
The French revolution, breaking the bonds of authority,
created two traditions, one revolutionary, the other, the military hero ending anarchy. Every Peruvian general—especially
Santa Cruz—thought himself a Napoleon—an imported totemism. Ayarragaray also emphasizes the race motive. Militarism is typically a mestizo product, weapon of men of
mixed blood fighting for a new place in the social scheme.
Arequipa, Perú's mestizo city par excellence, is the seat of
most of the country's armed revolts. In Perú certainly the
most important *caudillos* have ever been mestizos: The white
*caudillos* such as Orbegoso, La Fuente, Salaverry, Torrico,
Nieto, Vivanco, Echenique, if at times more spectacular,
went down to quicker defeat, left less enduring impress on
their country. The mestizan *caudillos*—Gamarra, Santa Cruz,
Castilla, San Román—invariably had more duplicity, audacity, perseverance, and brutal determination. Gamarra, Castilla and San Román were great army organizers. Of all Santa
Cruz was the most messianic; he gave vitality to a vast urge
to reconstruct Bolívar's dream of unity. The most enduring
control in the Republic was forged by Gamarra and Castilla.
The latter provided Perú's most impressive victories.

Perú's most recent, most troglodyte military chieftain,
Sánchez Cerro, was a mestizo and zambo. At the recent com-
memoration of Sánchez Cerro's assassination in Lima, the
majority of the spectators were mulattoes and zambos.

The mestizo, because of the rupturing of his cultural bonds, is the most reckless, restless and astute of New World ethnic elements. His quick fevered imagination, his versatile impressionability, declamatory instincts, social greediness and absence of a logical and solid spirit and of any pragmatic vision of life, contributes to mercurial reactions and messianic illusions. When, in the mestizo, audacity joins hands with cunning, as in Castilla, the *caudillo* par excellence appears.

Francisco García Calderon discovers only political causes of American militarism—the inevitable interreactions of revolution and tyranny, a vicious circle, bitten ever deeper into the habit of a people. Tyranny makes revolution, revolution obliges worse tyranny, then worse revolution—until national exhaustion makes possible a milder form of government through default of the national will. On one hand ideal constitutions, on the other inevitable violators of impractical constitutions, followed by ardent revolutionary defenders of illusory constitutions.

Jorge Basarde in his *Perú* discovers three causes of militarism: National recognition of victorious armies after civil conflict or as a result of political indecision, liquidation of dictatorship, or desperate defense against a social revolution. In general he discerns two types: one after sure victory, one after national defeat.

If regional factors have not been stressed by Peruvian militarists, geography and the failure properly to develop communications are fundamental causes of disturbances. Lack of direct central control has made possible many minor revolts. A regional thesis lurks behind many of the revolts, especially earlier struggles between Gamarra, Santa Cruz and Salaverry—highlands against coast, north highlands against south highlands, all in confusing combinations. The pseudosecession of Loreto, under Piérola, obeyed regional as well as political causes. Even today the Loreto region is a potential

387

independent republic. Cuzco's strong local patriotism has often had armed consequences.

José Ingenieros declares militarism rests basically upon economic injustice. North American colonists could practice democracy because they owned their own lands. Spain practiced empirical exploitation, distributed lands to those who did not wish to work; it never organized production, never promoted intelligent colonization. Exploitation was anarchic and feudal. After Independence, lack of economic organization and maldistribution of wealth resulted in absence of all common aims—aside from a narrow feudal clique, no definite economic groups capable of stabilizing politics. Hence the personal attraction of the military chieftain, the one bond to which distracted people could cling. *Caudillaje* became the tropical adaptation of democracy.

5

Despite the marching and counter-marching of the hordes of Santa Cruz, Gamarra, Salaverry, Echenique, Castilla and others, the Peruvian army rarely displayed Mexican bloodthirstiness. Given the ferocious fighting of those earlier years, the number of executions is singularly small. Captain Rossell was executed in Lima in 1832—he "marched to the gallows as to a parade"; Neigreros, Cosío, Resua and others in 1834; Valle Riestra in 1835; Salaverry and his eight principal followers in 1836; the Bolivian General Armara, taken prisoner, was mysteriously murdered in bed in 1839; Colonel Boza in 1841, Colonel Hercelles in 1842, several minor officials in 1843, General Morán in 1854, President Balta (shot in prison), 1872. Destitution from rank, often restitution soon after, was the customary punishment; Riva-Agüero (ancestor of the recent intolerable cabinet head of Benavides) succeeded in receiving the title "Traitor of the Country," but in general no such violences were committed as the wholesale massacres perpetrated by Sánchez Cerro in 1932 when suppressing the Aprista and Jiménez revolts—Perú's vilest blot.

Past army mildness probably springs from the tradition of Inca and colonial discipline, and from the fact that subsequent internecine wars have never represented any fundamental battle to alter the social system, merely feuds within the governing ranks. Following the example of patriot officers and royalists before the decisive independence battle of Ayacucho, often generals and their staffs advanced to shake hands before opening the battle. All very genteel! Perú, ruled for four hundred years by elements similar to the present Civilistas, will have no sanguinary military tradition till that rule is seriously menaced.

The army feuds of the post-independence were a game, a shifting of balance among governing cliques. In general brutal tactics were not used against the vanquished, for the vanquished were part of the same social group, might any day swing from opposition to support of the victorious government. The battle, on the basis of personalities within a closed governing system, not for principle, had a certain gentility.

But the battle for principles, when and if it comes, will mean real ferocity. Once the right of the present narrow white caste to govern is definitely challenged, war without quarter can be the only result, reprisals on both sides brutal beyond words. For either side to lose will mean to lose everything. Whichever side wins, it will be compelled to destroy its foes ruthlessly to thwart desperate efforts to regain control. Sánchez Cerro has set the pattern.

The army, hitherto never deeply moved by popular currents, is probably—as in Mexico—now on the eve of becoming more definitely a political force in its own rights rather than merely an instrumentality of upper-class ambitions. It will probably pass through a demagogic phase before becoming a patriotic institution; it will shift its allegiance to new races and classes more in accord with its own composition.

For Perú's army, which has ever absorbed mostly mestizan and Indian elements, has often been an escape for oppressed native groups. In Europe, intolerable economic conditions were evaded by emigration to the United States; in Perú the army was often a refuge from starvation, the only channel promising rapid promotion of inferior ethnic elements. Thus its composition, more than are other allied institutions, is more representative of Perú's general population, hence, despite its present rôle, it is potentially Perú's most democratic institution. Though its present leadership is aristocratic and Civilista, it is becoming increasingly sensitive to popular aspirations. Guns have been put in the hands of Indians, who for more than a hundred years have served as cannon fodder; but today the Indians represent the awakening race. Soon they will use their guns in new ways. The Indian soldier has produced types of legendary bravery—Cahuide, José Olaya, Manano de los Santos. Hitherto he has fired his gun unconscious of his power or the reason. But the gun, placed in his hands to defend the life and property of the whites, is the real arbiter of the future. Ultimately, as in Mexico, the army may, however blunderingly, whatever the ensuing evils, contribute to social justice.

The real battle of four centuries approaches. The army sooner or later will abandon the vicious Civilista group it now protects.

# XXV

# WOMEN

I

ONE writer has said, "Liverpool is a commercial city, Florence an artistic city, and Lima a woman city."

Certainly the women of Lima are among the most beautiful and gracious in the world. In them are concentrated all the most charming traditions of viceregal Perú, Europeanism, and tropical seductiveness. They dress smartly, carry themselves with erect independent assurance, affect a sophistication they do not possess. If bravely flirtatious, they are rigidly conservative. With more apparent freedom than in any city between Santiago and Havana, actually they are more hedged about intellectually than their Mexican cousins; they have even less economic freedom than in either Mexico or Havana.

They live by hoary shibboleths of religious and male domination, seldom are well educated (rarely beyond a few grades of grammar school) though usually trained to tinkle the piano, embroider and keep house. They have all the virtues, are fine mothers, but rarely succeed in becoming companions for their husbands. This is partly due to clerical influence. The husband gets the body of the woman, "the minister of the Lord gets her soul . . . when he does not also take possession of her body," and when the man, bored with merely cutaneous delights, finally seeks other diversions, the woman, loving God so much, ends by hating men. The tacit formula is: the woman to the churches and charitable societies; the man to the gambling den and the whore house.

The two extremes of Lima womanhood are represented by

Santa Rosa and by Micaela Villegas, the sinful mestiza known as "Perricholi."

Above all other female characters in Perú, declares Basadre, one must mention Perricholi. In the seventeenth century Terralla characterized the Lima woman as "exaggeratedly dolled up and overdelicate, as empty, candy-sweet, affected affectionate nuisances." But eighteenth-century Perricholi symbolized the new injection of sin and amorous intrigue in their most entrancing aspects. To her the travelers Basil Hall and Max Radiguet dedicated their most exquisite pages. Prosper Merimée, just as he had chosen Carmen from Spain and Córcega from Colombia, found in her a theme for a drama. Thornton Wilder used her in his "Bridge of San Luis Rey" as the *deus ex machina*. The name of the ravishingly beautiful and corrupt Perricholi, who brought a Viceroy to her feet, is celebrated in a dozen poems and volumes. She, above all others, is a symbol of the colony at its highest luxury, when letters flourished and life had developed leisure and sophistication—the most flamboyant epoch just before its imminent dissolution. She was the courtesan of courtesans, an imitator of Pompadour, of the handsome ladies of Avignon and Rome. The drama of her personality, the memory of her amorous abandon, still bring her conquests two centuries after her death. In a conventional epoch, she lived life intensely, impetuously, magnificently, in contrast to contemporary figures mostly austere, illustrious, outstanding, but dry, impenetrable, dignified. In her is all the glamor of Peruvian womanhood created by the lascivity of the conquest and the mixing of bloods.

But even Perricholi finally entered a convent to dedicate herself to God. . . .

In contrast to the venality, cynicism and coldness of foreign Messalinas, a native writer points out that the Peruvian prostitute, at bottom melancholy and superstitious unless completely debased, ever retains an aura of offended dignity, imparts the feeling that no money could adequately pay for what is given. Whereas the foreign prostitute tries to make men believe they are discovering happiness, she makes men feel sinful. The Latin American cabaret is not joyous but sad; life's tragedy persists in such a place. Clandestine joys thus remain a real drama. The Latin America wants no tinsel trappings. He does not fool himself. Latin America is the land of

J.S.

the sensual and sorrowful tango rather than sensual and joyous jazz.

Free love in Perú has never been easy or happy. The sinner, more often than being bold like Perricholi, has been a hypocrite, clandestine or venal. The Peruvian woman does not readily deliver herself outside of matrimony. For her to do so requires a transcendental emotion. All popular music is filled with songs of unhappy or disgraceful loves.

There are many social layers of womanhood in Perú, depending upon racial or economic status. The foregoing conclusions have nothing to do with the Indian woman whom we have already discussed; furthermore they are more true of the criolla than the mestiza, more true even of the provinces than Lima. Perricholi was a mestiza. The mestiza is a passionate troubled soul, seeking vainly to reconcile the violent opposites of romantic love and matrimony. If her sense of personal sacrifice is just as strong as that of the Creole woman, she is less bound by tradition, more apt to break over the traces. No ruling caste status inhibits her.

Yet despite all social and religious barriers, the Peruvian girl of the best society as well as of the mestizo group, once she loves, gives wholly, completely, risking all. Upon the man rests her whole happiness and security. If he debases her, she accepts sorrowingly but determinedly; if he exalts her, she feels her life crowned with mystic and holy beauty. But she lives entirely for love and, if possible, also motherhood, whatever the bond. Her loyalty transcends all disasters and disillusionments.

The Peruvian male, if at times he takes advantage of woman's trust, usually has sharp categories. The long Creole ruling tradition has resulted in a few powerful families to which nearly everybody of any importance is related; it is not wise to break the conventions of this group; resultant ostracism closes all doors.

The conduct of a Peruvian doctor friend of mine is typical. Thursdays and Saturdays he saw his mother punctually at four-thirty; his fiancée of a good family from six to eight; and his chola mistress from eight until dawn—a pre-nuptial arrangement that will continue, with modifications, after marriage, with possibly the accumulation of additional mistresses.

Where family traditions are so strong, where the ruling caste considers honest labor as degrading, where a woman is de-classed if she works, inevitably marriage is the woman's great adventure, her one escape from parental tyranny. If it is merely an escape from one type of tyranny to another, at least her physical and emotional needs are more fully satisfied. If her conduct is closely watched even after marriage, she is at least mistress of her own house and soon has plenty

of children to take her mind off unfulfilled longings which
—since she accepts her husband's desires as unbreakable law
—she would not even admit as existing in her emotional
cosmos.

Thus, more than the romantic hot-blooded mestiza, Perricholi, the archetype of Peruvian womanhood was Rosa, of
Lima, over whom to this day the Limeñans go into holy
frenzy, proud that Perú has contributed a saint to the calendar. The amazing thing is that Rosa's life is utterly dumb
and uneventful—she is merely the apotheosis of almost meaningless good. Fanatically pious from the earliest age, something of a little prig, beautiful though she was, she refused all
suitors, even resisted the beatings of her mother, in order to
dedicate herself to God. Though a sickly rheumatic girl, she
practiced self-flagellation, slept on thorns and sharp stones,
aided the poor and sick, and died uneventfully. She was not
an organizer, had no intellectual flare, as did Teresa or Catalina, the European mystics. The few written records she left
show no originality, merely commonplace platitudes, nothing
comparable to the great poetical and intellectual genius of
Mexico's Sor Juana Inés de la Cruz. She was merely stupid,
generous and pious in a frontier Spanish city over three centuries ago. If there is anything at all striking about her, it is
that ethereal tenderness so characteristic of Peruvian women,
except that in her case, thinned by lack of sexual and mother
experience, it was diverted into an hysterical adoration for
Jesus.

Yet no eulogies of Rosa are too exaggerated for Lima
writers. "She represents the mystic soul of a people, its highest ideal of womanly conduct, and her glory was not merely
Catholic but Peruvian. In her white tunic, she passed lightly
and fragilely, concerned with her work of charity, through
the first years of the colony, and her delicate grace left a
trail of light in the history of her country. After three cen-

turies her name is a symbol of mystic dreams and subjective warmth." Sentimental blah!

## 2

Despite the subordinate rôle of Peruvian women, their integrity of character has served them in good stead in times of national stress. Able to devote themselves to causes with a deep fervor rare in our modern materialistic world, they have played a prominent part in Peruvian history. The Independence struggles called out some of their most noble traits, from the *rabona*, or camp wife, of the marching armies, to the women of the higher classes. Of all cities Ayacucho produced a notable galaxy of women, not only in colonial letters but in bravery—Ventura Ccalamaqui, Phallchamascachi-ttica, María de Bellido. Mother of patriot sons, María de Bellido went to the gallows rather than betray the confidence of the insurgents: After being led a prisoner to the four corners of the public plaza and having her sentence shouted to the world, she said proudly to her executioners, "I am not here to inform but to sacrifice myself."

Not least remarkable was Gamarra's wife, Francisca Zubiaga y Bernales, worthy of a novel and psychological investigation. Though epileptic, she presided over salons, led armies, dismissed cabinet ministers, overturned presidents, acted as President herself, and ever fought for the cause of her husband, until finally exiled to Chile to die in bitterness and defeat, ordering that her heart be sent to her husband. Once she escaped from an Arequipan mob disguised as a priest. Flora Tristán visited her on board the *Guillermo Rourton* where she was held prisoner in Callao preparatory to being deported. "Though prisoner, Doña Pancha was still President. Her expressions showed her consciousness of superiority. . . . Everything in her announced an exceptional woman, as extraordinary for her strength of will as for lofty intelligence.

She was about 34 or 36 years old, of medium height and strongly built, though once very thin. . . . Like Napoleon all her empire of beauty was in her glance—what strength, what pride and penetration! . . . She inspired respect, subdued wills, stimulated admiration."

In general it has been the chola who has shown most independence and initiative in business, love and politics. The Indian woman is barred from active national participation because Indian males are also barred, and the costumes worn by her set her apart, restrict her to her group environment. The Creole woman is super-Catholic and bound by harem traditions. The chola has had to take her place in the ordinary life of the country in a way less trammeled by tradition. And from this vigorous actuation have come forth the famous war-time chola chiefs of Republican Perú; Pacha Anka Huallpacaldo, the blond Melchora, Orko-Asno, and others: women—writes Uriel García—who have been leaders of fanatical multitudes, majordomos of saintly enterprises, fervent political partisans, ready to begin necessary stoning, heads of strong-arm gangs, accomplices of thieves and footpads, and equally their punishers. They are symbols of a new and vigorous, if somewhat lawless, ethnic element.

In the world of modern letters women writers are becoming more common. Matto de Turner was the first to strike the note for Indian liberation in her *Aves sin Nido*; Aurora Cáceres has written some of the most luminous pages regarding Cuzco; Julia Codesido has taken her place as one of Perú's best modern painters; Magda Portal is one of the most valiant leaders of Aprismo.

The accomplishments of such women are doubly significant because of the tremendous obstacles they must overcome even to gain the right for self-expression.

# XXVI

# POUNDS—DOLLARS—YEN

## I

Aꜰᴛᴇʀ Spanish rule, Japan and England dominated Peruvian commerce and investment. Only recently has American capital and trade invaded the field.

Canning of England had a busy finger in breaking up the Spanish empire. If England did not hope too strongly for new colonies, Latin American independence would open up a vast new market and resources for British enterprise. British money financed the independence movements, particularly in Perú.

But it is one thing to finance a revolution, another to keep a new-born republic solvent, especially after the spacious

Spanish viceroyalty. When San Martín entered Lima in 1821, he faced an empty treasury. No organized means existed for garnering revenues. Mining and agriculture shattered, international trade gone, it was not easy to replace Spanish channels. In 1820 Perú's trade, despite internal conflict, was still 14½ million pesos; by 1838 it totalled only slightly more than 7 million, not until 1840 did it reach about 13½ million.

The new independence government, with an army under arms, had to resort to the customary instrument, a forced levy, which increased existing chaos. After so much upheaval, business men were without ready resources. The new English firms planted in Callao, though eager to break up Spanish rule, were far from anxious to shell out hard cash. They protested vigorously.

A compromise provided Perú's first loan, £148,000, without interest, repayable by customs drafts. Further pressing needs were met by creating a bank (February 1, 1822) and issuing fiat money. Lack of confidence and falsification of bills caused the bank to crumple the following year. England came to the rescue with a 6 percent loan of 1,200,000 Peruvian pounds for war materials; and three years later granted the £616,000 War loan, both being redeemed in 1849 by the £1,778,000 conversion loan.

Yet England found Perú remote; activities in the Atlantic coast countries more profitable. Perú turned, at least so far as trade was concerned, to Japan and China. A large Japanese and Chinese immigration current was set in motion. This, since the Orient as yet had developed little modern technique, caused Perú's development to lag behind most of its sister South American republics.

Guano changed the picture. Humboldt's keen eye had appreciated guano possibilities; by 1840 new fertilizer discoveries caused a great scramble to corner the Peruvian deposits. The first guano exports were made in 1830. The deposits were declared common property to be worked by whomsoever desired. Not until 1842 did the Government become fully alive to its great potential wealth; all deposits were then made a State monopoly. Prosperity, if not for Perú, at least for the governing clique and the coast region, may be dated from 1845 when Castilla seized power. The influx of trade and wealth was manna for the war-torn country, manna for the ruling classes. Soon the country plunged into wild speculation. As in all bonanza periods, scandalous abuses occurred. The story of guano in Perú is one of dark corruption, shady contracts, Shylock loans; all the financial manipulations were typically imperialistic trickeries with the irresponsible military political cliques governing a colony by force and fraud —essentially the story of Mexico and oil, Cuba and sugar, Bolivia and tin, Chile and copper. The yard-stick of the Peruvian rulers was ready cash, that of foreign concessionaires quick and fabulous profits. Castilla, for instance, made seventeen contracts, without regard to how rapidly the new resource might be looted, with no concern for the building up of the country, merely to get ready money. Foreign usurers were the real beneficiaries.

In 1853 a small Independence debt of $300,000 to the United States and other independence debts to neighboring countries were cancelled and a new conversion loan, guano-guaranteed, of £2,600,000 at 4½ percent was floated. Some years later a new conversion loan of £5,500,000 at 4½ percent was soon followed by that of 1865 for £10,000,000 at 5 percent. British capital was also drifting into other lines, banking, mining, and business. In 1866, owing to the threat of war with Spain, an additional loan of $5,000,000—actually, only $1,626,000 was issued—for war materials was placed in the United States—our first important entry into the Peruvian loan field.

Rapid financial expansion was heading the country toward the rocks. Revenues had increased from 10 million pesos in

1846 to 62 million in 1869-70. In 1870 a new loan of £12 million at 6 percent provided for railway construction. In 1871 Perú contracted the scandalous Dreyfus loan of £23,-215,000 at 5 percent for public works and irrigations. Financial collapse first manifested itself in a currency crisis that forced the country off the gold standard. Unable to meet its obligations for railway construction, the government was obliged to back the famous "Meiggs Notes," totalling 20 million *soles*. Amid general collapse came the terrible War of the Pacific with Chile. Currency further tobogganed downhill.

Perú did not really begin to emerge from economic collapse until 1893, when as a compromise on the British debt, the bondholders subscribed to the Grace-Donoughmore contract to surrender all claims in exchange for 66 years usufruct on the Peruvian railways, free right of navigation on Lake Titicaca, and other compensations—all under the control of the new Peruvian Corporation. Perú did not emerge from currency disaster until its return to the gold standard in 1900.

From 1879 to the World War marks Britain's most active imperialism, a chaotic expansion of mining development; 1914 to the present is the period of increased American investment. In neither case was there any national planning; both invasions have merely accentuated the vicious contract-labor (*enganche*) system and ruthless exploitation.

2

The World War called in a great deal of British money. This temporary setback was soon offset by increased trade, the rapid development of raw materials, particularly sugar, largely an artificial industry, and in mining: vanadium, gold, silver, coal, and particularly oil. The new American concessions were mostly secured in the customary fashion of our capitalist entrepreneurs in Latin America, with collusion, graft and crooked financial pyramiding. Note the scandalous Brea y Pariñas oil concession. Standard Oil gained a concession to exploit oil for twenty years with a tax of 3 ½ *soles* (now about 75 cents) a ton.

Peruvian exports soared higher and higher, a prosperity that continued until long after the War. 1915 exports totalled 115 million *soles*; in 1920, 350,041,550. By then revenues had reached about 80 million *soles*.

New capital poured in. The United States now sat on the doorstep to loan money. In addition to a $15,000,000 tobacco loan, some $75,000,000 of bonds were floated, only about £2,000,000 being placed in England. The internal debt rose from 58 million *soles* in 1920 to 135 million in 1930.

The sombre history of these American loans, involving the paying of over half a million dollars' commission to Juan Leguía, son of President Leguía, may be read in the U. S. Senate investigations of several years ago. The last loan was foisted upon the American public against the advice of resident American officials, against the advice of the personal representative of the bank itself—high financial manipulations as dark as any in our whole record of foreign-loan activities. Guano graft all over again.

If this by 1930 had given the United States financial predominance in Perú (American investments, $220,000,000; British, $150,000,000) the process, besides terrific loss to naïve American investors, brought corruption and no sound national development.

Perú's indebtedness increased far more rapidly than her trade and powers of production. The last loan was made in the face of declining trade. Collapse was at hand. Finis was suddenly written to Perú's gilded loan period. The country plunged into revolution.

The most superficial study of Perú's economic and financial history would have warned us that the scramble of our bankers to replace England as a loan country would cost both the United States and Perú dearly. One-third of the total of British loans in Perú has been practically always in default. More recently 70 percent has been in default. In relatively prosperous 1910 only 1.8 percent was being paid upon a total investment of £23,004,000. About the same ratio of return exists today. The £9,000,000 of common stock of the Peruvian corporation, controlling over £20,000,-000 of British investments and about 80 percent of the railways in the country, has never paid a dividend, and in recent years not even the £7,500,000 of preferred stock. British capital in the country totals £26,746,006 (that not controlled by the Peruvian Corporation being in breweries, light and power, and the Lobitos Oilfields), on which the average return in 1931 was only 1.9 percent.

Of all countries Perú was the least appropriate for extravagant loans unless for guaranteed productive enterprise.

Perú, since Independence, has ceded to neighboring countries (not including the recent Leticia cession) about 600,-000 square kilometers of territory, more than the area of England, France or Germany. Perú's whole independence record, despite occasional advances, has been largely one of defeat and degeneracy. Population growth has been insignificant. The country was estimated to have 2,800,000 people in 1860. Manuel Jesús Gamarra estimated only 4,500,000 inhabitants in 1923.[1]

Revenues from 1859 to 1923 merely tripled, while those of Argentina increased fifty times, those of Chile twenty times. Though Perú was the first South American country to promote railroad construction, it has only about 2,700 kilometers as compared to 50,000 in Argentina and 8,000 in Chile. Over 18,000 kilometers of roads were supposedly built by Leguía; but this is mostly propaganda; most of them are worthless, narrow, dangerous, unsurfaced; already most have

[1] *Orientación y Organización*, ix.

been washed away, the vast sums spent irretrievably lost. The loan bubble was made possible only by bolstering up a fake reputation for the unjust and illegal government of Leguía.

Trade is a key-index. During the first twenty years of independence Perú's trade had not climbed back to the total for even troubled 1820. If subsequent exploitation of guano increased exports, and President Balta's railroad promotion increased imports, until in 1865 foreign trade totalled 74 million pesos and by 1877, 99 million pesos, by 1891 this had dropped back to 38 millions. In other words in 70 years Perú had not quite doubled her foreign trade. The slowness of Perú's painful economic development is all too patent.

True, the twentieth century has marked a new economic phase. In 1900 Perú's trade totalled about 68 million *soles*, but it was not until 1905 that it totalled 100 million *soles*, and thus had equalled the guano prosperity peak of a quarter of a century earlier. The World War saw trade artificially leap from 125 million *soles* in 1914 to 538 million *soles* in 1920, collapse to 333 million in 1921, rise to 525 million in 1929 and collapse once more to 295 million. In 1933 it totalled 287 million. In other words it is now slightly more than the pre-1914 level—a moral that our noble financiers learned too late. . . . At present rates of exchange Perú's internal and external obligations—if recent internal bank loans of 70 million *soles* are included—will total over 700 million *soles*! [2]

---

[2] On January, 1934, the total external debt of the country was $88,104,440.78 and £3,436,800 plus accumulated interest. The internal debt was £511,300 and 54,671,535 gold *soles* plus interest charges, the floating debt $4,945,929.06, £120,117.13.8 and 57,895,950.58 gold *soles*, plus an accumulated budget deficit from 1908 to 1932 of 11,144,055.53 gold *soles*. Also public works obligations total 10,455,760.99 gold *soles*. A Central Reserve Bank Loan of 3,946,157.07 *soles* and a Callao municipal loan of 1927 of principal and interest of $1,328,707.50 are both guaranteed by the Supreme Government.

3

The new factor in the Peruvian picture is Japanese trade competition. Though not yet appreciable, inroads have been made. A permanent commercial exhibit of Japanese products is maintained; special trade commissions have toured the country; much publicity has been put out, some of it of a sentimental nature, *viz.*, the Inca peoples are of Oriental origin. Owing to low labor costs and inflated currency, the Japanese are able to undersell most competitors in certain classes of cheap goods. They tap the vast low-scale Indian market, largely closed to British and American enterprise. In preparing for the Leticia imbroglio, the government purchased about 80 million *soles* of munitions, much of it from Japan. Japanese citizens enjoy special privileges in the country, not being required to pay the foreign residence fee as are Americans, British and all other nationalities.

4

The whole long story of foreign capital and trade in Perú is a tragedy of colonial exploitation in collusion with a narrow military and aristocratic clique. Nowhere has the falsity of laissez faire and rugged individualism as instruments of sound economic development been better exemplified.

Every development has been determind, not by Peruvian needs, but by international needs. The mainspring has been quick and easy profits. All benefits have been accidental and ancillary. The communications developed, the type of resources tapped, have never been those most essential to the creation of a rounded economy, have never sought to promote the happiness of the Peruvian people as a whole, have never helped knit the country together or develop sound government, or create a stable economic and political situation.

Is it the law of mankind and of nations that peoples with

less advantageous geographical conditions and economic resources must be sacrificed to immediate world needs, must be doomed to debasement even worse than that which the natural resources of their habitat could allow?

Of all countries, the colonial areas demand sound financial and economic planning. Perú, which has never taken a census in sixty years, has never known any such planning, is doing nothing toward that end today, is still in the hands of a narrow military Creole clique merely marking time, hopefully waiting to share in the future spoils of reviving international exploitation of their country, rather than putting their shoulders to the wheel to develop Perú, to increase its real wealth and expand the living standards of its people. Such policies have ever kept Perú either upon the heights of mad speculative prosperity, or in the abyss of poverty and revolution. When foreign credit is good, the Creole clique spends like a drunken sailor but does nothing to better the country economically. In evil times, political stability menaced, revenues scant, each new military *caudillo,* unable to promote more stabilizing activities, obliged to get money by hook or crook, is forced to sell out more of the country's wealth to the foreigner at ruinous terms, merely to get a little ready cash. The old story of the family with the leaky roof. When raining, it was impossible to repair the roof; when not raining, no need to do so.

# XXVII

## LITTLE FATHERLAND:
## REGIONALISM

### I

THE coast-highland conflict has existed since known records, between the proto-Chimu and Chavín folk, between Nazca and Tiahuanaco kingdoms. In the Inca days the feathered warriors of Viracocha and Pachacutec Yupanqui swarmed over the coast and proceeded with real success to integrate the two regions.

The Spaniards destroyed this effort, ruling from the coast and re-creating the old duality.

By the end of the eighteenth century, regional differences culminated, after a series of minor Indian rebellions, in the great Tupac Amarú revolt, which sought the reestablishment of the Inca empire—a hope still vigorous after three centuries of supposed Hispanization.

But paradoxically the Spaniards in a dying struggle to preserve their rule got hold of the highland masses as cannon fodder to oppose the coastland Creole bourgeoisie.

After independence, the military chieftains continued to utilize the Sierra to oppose the Lima trading class which had created the Republic; but soon these early struggles shifted from defense of mere feudal privilege to something more profound. A great mountain Republic, in the process of being formed, found expression in the Perú-Bolivian Confederacy, created October 28, 1836, in accordance with the Orbegoso treaty of the preceding year with Santa Cruz as Supreme Protector. Latent in these blind struggles were unformulated Indian aspirations—a regional kinetics based on divergent race and culture. The balance of political control became Bolivia (then still part of Perú), which allied itself with the other indigenous upland regions.

Against this the "Lowlands" reacted violently. Not merely coastal Lima but lowland Chile and pampas Argentina feared a powerful mountain confederation and resorted to war to break it. Verses were composed ridiculing the snout lips of *Cholo* Santa Cruz—Lima displayed all its white disdain for the Indians and the Sierra, all its race prejudice and ignorance of geography. The eternal duality of coast and highlands broke the country asunder in a series of marches and counter-marches, bloody battles and governmental crises.

The Sierra lost. The mountain chieftains quarreled among themselves. Gamarra, aided by the Chileans and the Argentine battling up from the Chaco to attack Bolivia in the rear, smashed the Confederation, and gave the country a new meaningless constitution with powerful centralist faculties to the Executive, the 1839 Huancayo constitution. Bolivia declared her independence.

The coast recognized this gladly. Native forces thus divided, coastal domination over the Sierra could be assured. And Bolivia, which Santa Cruz dreamed of making the "Macedonia" of South America, remained in backward Indianism, strangled to this day by Perú, Chile, Argentina, Brazil and Paraguay, doomed to economic inferiority until it carves an open road to the sea. The Peruvian Sierra was also doomed, by coastal egotism, to frustrated isolation; and Perú as a whole to the rôle of a backward colonially exploited country.

The hinterland, abandoned as before, to retrogressive feudalism, broke into a series of petty, disjointed, almost independent, principalities and tight cellular Indian communities, all very reminiscent of various political breakdowns prior to the rise of Incan Sierra centralization.

The prosperous guano and saltpetre era affirmed coast con-

trol and colonialism beyond cavil. The new *caudillismo*
turned away from regional aspirations to superficial legal reforms. Coast feuds now determined all national trends—a
struggle between feudalism and the new bourgeoisie, a rivalry
that tore up the whole country anew, but which had little
significance for the hinterland.

When the war with Chile wrenched away Perú's nitrate
fields, and broke her guano monopoly, the coast languished,
and again out of the hardier highlands came a series of military *caudillos*. Temporarily the highlands reasserted political
hegemony. But it was a meaningless interlude, the old prosperity was gone, the country bankrupt, the highland chieftains were too ignorant and vicious to solve Perú's problems.
They delivered the country anew into the hands of the coast
oligarchy—a new amalgamation of bourgeoisie and feudalists.

The rapid influx of foreign capital has accentuated the
ambivalent struggle, has definitely renewed the colonial as
opposed to nationalist or communalistic tendencies, has again
delayed the integration of the Peruvian nation.

But despite this colonialism directed by the coast bourgeoisie, who ally themselves on the one hand with foreign
capital and on the other with the ignorant feudal Sierra landholders and the Church, at the first sign of coast weakness,
highland militarism reasserts itself—hence that recent monster of blood and force, Sánchez Cerro. Undoubtedly these
reversions attest to the existence of powerful if still blind
and unorganized regional forces. The coast-highland antiph-
ony continues to this day, is still the secret of turmoil and
national frustration.

2

If the major division of Perú is between coast and highlands,
closer inspection reveals other details and colors—for instance a definite division exists between north Perú and south
Perú, a difference in geography, climate, customs and psy-

chology. Belaunde, for instance, finds that the Santa Cruz Confederation was popular in the south, not for its principle of integration but for its conformity to historical reality. In northern Perú, the Andes are lower, not so difficult of access. Correspondingly the indigenous population is more influenced by both coast and jungle regions. On the coast this north-south division corresponds to the old Chimú and Nazca separation; in the highlands it springs from the fact that the old Chavín and other cultures were conquered by the Incas and the Quechua language imposed. This fact left an abiding difference in habits and psychology which distinguishes the Cajamarca and Piura regions, for instance, from those of Puno and Cuzco.

Though the broad division is between coast and highlands, some contrary integration, because of centralized government and modern communications, has been achieved between strictly local coastal and highland areas. If there is an antiphonal mountain and coast regionalism, there is also, in certain parts of the country, a welded coast-highland regionalism that spreads broad bands across our picture.

Thus Lima, because of its powerful centripetal force and the building of a very artificial line of communication, the central railroad up the Rimac gorge to Junín province, has created a certain degree of commercial and cultural interchange, which if it is disrupted frequently by cultural and ethnical differences, nevertheless tends to create a region apart from the rest of Perú. The undeveloped Ancash region, largely indigenous in outlook, and pulled on the one hand toward the old Chavín centers and on the other toward the coast to Chimbote, Casma and other points, is also a separate region. Cajamarca forms, with part of the hinterland jungle country and Trujillo and Pacasmayo on the coast another distinct economic zone. Piura and Tumbes form isolated corners. The great Loreto region, of course, has a distinct life, and the central government feared that if the Leticia question were not settled satisfactorily for the inhabitants of Loreto and the Amazonas departments that secession might be declared.

Probably the most distinctly marked regions in Perú are precisely the jungle region and the southern highland region centering in Cuzco. Cuzco, Puno on Lake Titicaca, and Arequipa form a triad of cities which form the triangle of a distinct cultural and economic zone. Arequipa, being lower, more mestizan in population, is often torn between coast and highland influences; but essentially it casts in its lot with Cuzco and Puno; and all three have more bonds, in most ways, with Bolivia than with Lima, a fact which causes the Peruvian government always to keep a wary eye upon any possible efforts of Bolivia to carve a road to the coast.

Thus regionalism in Perú has various aspects. Racially coast and highlands are sharply divided; both form two large separate regions with more or less racial homogeneity. The highlands, speaking for the most part Quechua from end to end, nevertheless have various subtle racial differences between Quechua, Colla, Aimará and other groups, which exercise a formative influence.

Cultural regionalism is further obstructed in many places by geography. The failure to create communications linking the highlands together has created closer connections in some places with the coast than between upland valleys. Nor does economic regionalism entirely coincide with geographical or cultural regionalism. In some places roads and railroads have defeated geographic separatism; in other places economic trends, development of new resources, has broken old cultural and ethnic bonds.

In general there is none of the powerful local patriotism which has at times influenced such regions as those of the Yaquis and Mayas in Mexico, or the Catalans and Basques in Spain; yet deep cultural forces have undoubtedly affected national political events throughout Perú's history, will influence them even more strongly in the near future.

### 3

The Incas solved their distance problem; also the Spaniards —Spanish political organization corresponded to the three-fold necessities of communications, economics, and political control. Numerous rectifications of political divisions were made, e.g., 1717, 1782, 1812.

The Republic did not alter colonial political subdivisions to correspond to its new status. If previous divisions were altered, this was done from a general's tent on the field of battle, not to promote Perú's development but merely to insure military control. Indeed military control was more easily exercised by inhibiting or destroying vital energies and preventing economic development and local prosperity. Perú, because of selfish political and other interests, is ridiculously togged out in the same political clothes of over a century ago.

Tahuantinsuyo, through capable administration, directed a great mass of humanity, something not done today. A colonizing system kept the economic system in balance, eased economic and regional stresses. No such foresight is now exercised.

Today for instance the crowded communities of the Puno, Cuzco and Arequipa region could be easily helped by re-colonization in the ample communal regions of Huánuco.

National failure and ineptitude have given rise to an un-scientific advocacy of regionalism; basically merely a vulgar struggle between the egoism of Lima, city of aristocrats, and provincial frustration, e.g., the federative proposals of 1821 to 1835, merely representing caciquismo, local greed for abusive power. Federalism, based on slavery and peonage, sought the unhampered predominance of the privileged feudalists fearing the new wealthy coast bourgeoisie. As Mariátegui has stated, "Federalism does not appear in our history as a popular revindication, but rather a revindication of *gamonalismo* and its clientele."

Federalism or decentralization have been, more than libertarian movement, ever a thrust of the Sierra landholding class whenever coastal Liberal bourgeoise elements menaced their privileges or sought Church reform. The Departmental Councils of 1873, the Juntas of 1886, the municipal autonomy and regional Congresses of the 1919 Constitution (suppressed in 1922) did not respond to true regional sentiment.

The modern version of federalism is decentralization. But this is purely political and represents less true regionalism than the older federalism. Decentralization, remarks Mariátegui, without the liberation of the peons, merely means the ascendancy of a still more reactionary feudalism—the danger in any regionalism.

Yet at bottom regionalism implies economic, race and cultural emancipation. Probably emphasis upon regionalism blurs the economic struggle, the whole land problem of Perú. Yet the struggle for human emancipation is not a simple lineal affair; certain regional aspirations in Perú are worth fighting for because they involve cultural values which would otherwise be lost with or without economic emancipation. But an examination of the findings of the present-day decentralists and regionalists, such as Gamarra, Romero and Vázquez reveal too great a preoccupation with bureaucratic formulæ, an advocacy of a new geographical hashing up of the departments in some ways as irrational as the present accidental alignment. Regionalism, however obscure, usually has deeper roots than the nation itself. In the end, of course, "true regionalism," as Mariátegui points out, "will only arise through a new social structure."

Luis Alberto Sánchez caustically remarks, "It is rather necessary to unify Perú, which the present centralism prevents. Regionalism as advocated goes back to the spirit of 900 A.D. A real regionalism based on economic emancipation, however, would rectify coast influence. But to obtain this it is necessary to face the unpostponable problem of the Indian and his lands."

Moisés Sáenz points the logic and the moral: "Is Perú condemned to be a country eternally divided? I do not believe so. . . . I do not believe in geographic determinism to the extent of believing it more powerful than the genius of a people. The Incas founded an empire that did not recognize physical barriers; from Ecuador to Chile, over highlands and coast, they extended their dominion and implanted a system. . . . It is foolish to believe in geographic fatalism; it is more worth while to talk of a vigorous nationalism capable of fusing the traditional coexisting ethnic ingredients and of a constructive policy that can overcome physical accidents." [1]

Even this is too narrow a criteria. Ultimately the basic regional, economic and national problems cannot be solved except by a proper Confederation of the Southern States of the Pacific—an idea promoted by Piérola. For the boundaries of Perú, Chile and Bolivia as at present constituted are a defiance of geographical and economic realities. Bolivia with Cuzco, Arequipa and the corresponding coast regions of Perú and Chile form a normal economic, geographic and racial unit, and the proper development of resources and of human progress cannot be realized or South American peace be assured until either Chile and Perú cede the proper areas to Bolivia or until a new confederation provides for free economic functioning of the region indicated. Some such confederation, insists the Peruvian Belaunde, will come inevitably. If not achieved soon, other striking events are likely to occur. They cast their shadows before. The near future offers various possibilities:

[1] 26-27.

(1) A victory of the Aprista reform party introducing adequate regional reorganization, but more likely:

(2) Apra victory followed in southern Perú by an armed agrarian movement (a la Zapata) and a radical labor movement probably leading to at least temporary political secession.

Effects of such a communal agrarian State:

(a) Probable spread of revolution to Bolivia, and creation of a new South Perú-Bolivia State. (b) Possible war with Perú, Chile and Argentina. Peace at any price with Paraguay.

(3) Bolivia, the best-armed nation of Latin America, if losing in the Chaco, may suddenly turn on Perú and strike for ocean outlet through Arequipa.

(4) Defeat in Bolivia may bring fearful revolution, principally hostilized by Chile and Perú. Bolivia would smuggle arms to regional revolutionists in Perú. Revolution and secession in Southern Perú. Alliance with Bolivia. Perhaps the first agrarian Soviet State in the Americas will arise in this region.

# XXVIII

## APRA

I

"A CYCLONE of unrest passes over the aged colonial university and beats upon its weary face and forces it to lift its indifferent eyes to changing reality," wrote Carlos Enrique Paz Soldán in his 1919 book on the students' movement.[1]

Yet nothing is more discouraging than the results of the Peruvian students' movement. Imbued with positivist ideas, small nuclei of students began fighting for university reform as early as 1905; in three years made their voices heard. The clarion call, which really aroused the Peruvian academic world, was the first students' congress in Montevideo in 1908. Yet today, after thirty long years of struggle, although Cuzco University has been somewhat liberalized, San Marcos in Lima, the oldest university on two continents, remains closed for its third year, because the students, refusing to accept its hoary traditions, demand that the government, equally obstinate, modernize the program, cut out ecclesiasticism, and introduce needed scientific changes. In April, 1934, eight students were expelled from the University of Trujillo on its reopening after two years, because they had previously headed a movement to reform its ancient standards. This official persecution is both sad and laughable, because the Trujillo institution is so badly equipped, its standards so medieval, that with all the good-will in the world, it can scarcely become an effective institution of learning.

The first tangible result of the Montevideo Congress was the Cuzco revolt of 1909; in Lima, the inauguration of the

[1] *De la inquietud a la revolución*, 4.

417

University Center, by José Galvez, Riva Agüero, Hermilo Valdizán, Oscar Miró Quesada, etc., which published a stimulating *Revista*—the so-called students' generation of 1910. Though it soon disintegrated over the religious question

through machinations of the Augustinians, some reform was effected especially in the backward medical department.

But the leaders, except for the brilliant Valdizán, now deceased, have since become the most odious and bigoted reactionaries in Perú, Minister Riva Agüero—recently resigning from the cabinet, because opposed to a mutual-consent divorce law—has sought to keep the university closed and throw all education in the hands of the Church. The Miró Quesadas are the owners of Lima's leading daily, *El Comercio*, which distorts news and sneers at every decent effort for reform. As one writer expresses it: "Of that epoch we preserve nothing except a few sentimental airs, a few peripatetic soliloquies and a certain unsupportable farce of erudition . . . [and] a goodly crowd of worn-out actors." Miró Quesada developed such startling themes as how to make cushions and the history and technique of the fan.

Not until 1916 was a bona-fide students' federation formed in Perú, coinciding with the new development of the middle class; Mariano Hurtado de Mendoza has declared, "University Reform is merely the consequence of the general proletarianization of the middle class." The federation at once launched a fight to prevent the militarization of the university. Victorious, the students went on to battle for other university reforms; they demanded independently elected faculties and student participation in the University Council.

The 1918 University of Córdoba strike in Argentina and the influence of Socialistic Alfredo L. Palacios, a great spirit, brought new purposefulness. By 1919 the reactionary academic elements had to gird up their loins to block further reforms. As a result the Lima University remained closed for two years.

A further impulse was given by the International Students' Congress in Mexico. Stimulus, if not a program, was given by the first national students' congress in Cuzco in 1920. Now the students, especially the radical Trujillo group, were gradually winning the support of proletarian elements, were making a new class-conscious bloc.

In May 23, 1923, an enormous student-labor demonstration was led by Haya de la Torre against President Leguía's attempt to dedicate the country to the Sacred Heart of Jesus. San Marcos was converted into a revolutionary barricade. Street-fighting resulted in the deaths of worker Salomón Ponce and student Manuel Alarcón Vidalón.

The government struck back swiftly and harshly, a persecution which lasted throughout Leguía's entire period.

Haya de la Torre, Manuel Seoane, Luis Heysen, Magda Portal, Carlos Manuel Cox, Serafín del Mar were driven into exile; large numbers were thrown into prison, shipped off to the jungles, or killed. But "the generation of 1920," writes a commentator enthusiastically, "leapt over the walls of the Colony and shouted its cry of fraternity to the rest of the youth of the world. . . ."

Some reform was gained in 1928, and reactionary professors eliminated.

The Sánchez Cerro revolution permitted the reactionary elements to seize the University which precipitated a students' general strike, and October 11 the students occupied the buildings militarily. The government tried to arbitrate, but when the students denounced the government for its massacre of workers and peasants in Oyolo and Mal Paso, Sánchez Cerro began to persecute them. January 19, 1931, the students again seized the University and were besieged by force and February 7 they were routed from a meeting with bullets, student Guido Calle being killed; dozens were taken to hospitals and jails, where they declared an eight-day hunger strike. In the face of a general labor strike and horrified public opinion, the government hastened to grant the immediate student demands.

Peace endured a year. Under the pretext that the Communist marine revolt of Callao (May 8, 1932) was backed by the students, the University was invaded by troops and the students arrested. San Marcos, Trujillo and other centers were closed and have remained closed, save for a short time when Sánchez Cerro delivered the Lima institution into the hands of brutal Police Colonel Rospiglosi to be reorganized. He merely kicked out eighty professors and pocketed part of the funds, being applauded by the reactionary daily *El Comercio*.

Benavides' head of Cabinet and Minister of Education Riva Agüero was reported to have said he would never open the institution, that the medieval Catholic University was good enough and the proper place to get a higher education. The University is still closed, its entrances guarded by police.

2

The student generation of 1920 was inevitably obliged to project itself boldly into national politics to change the political system which prevented rational reform. The rebellious nuclei of San Marcos and Trujillo, scattered in exile all over the world, rallied behind the *Alianza Popular Revolucionaria Americana* (APRA), founded by Haya de la Torre, today the most powerful popular political organization in Perú.

Haya, since the death of the great patriot Sandino, is undoubtedly the outstanding popular figure of all Latin America.

I knew him intimately during his exile in Mexico in 1923-4, also that other notable student leader from Cuba, Julio Antonio Mella, subsequently assassinated by the minions of Machado. It was a dramatic moment in Mexican and world affairs. The Mexican revolution, antedating that of Russia, had stumbled through a program of land-distribution, bitter opposition to oil imperialism, was promoting popular education and labor reform; it was in the full swing of accomplishment following the period of years of civil war, before it had become the private monopoly of Calles and a small clique of followers converted into grafting and exploiting landholders, manufacturers, and gamblers. Internationally the situation was equally portentous. The World War had demonstrated the economic and moral bankruptcy of Western Europe. Mussolini had seized power in Italy with a program of revolutionary nationalism. Primo de Rivera had provided an opéra bouffe imitation in Spain. The Social Democrats in Germany were battling the Communists. The Russian revolution was wavering between

Lenin's NEP policy of conciliating the small bourgeoisie and Trotzky's formula of world revolution. China was in uproar. India was simmering. Morocco was in revolt.

The two students, Mella and Haya, both striking personalities, both remarkable orators, both keen minds, both already outstanding figures in Latin America, soon came into sharp conflict. Mella threw in his lot with the Communist Party. Haya was seeking a formula for more realistic immediate political action.

The result was the founding of the Apra movement which brought down on Haya's head a furibund attack from Mella which won for him the undying enmity of the official Communist Third International.

After studying in Oxford, Germany, Geneva, Soviet Russia, Haya toured parts of Latin America, everywhere organizing Apra cells. He was rapidly building up an international following. On the overthrow of Leguía by the 1931 Arequipa revolution, he went back to Perú, it is freely charged backed by large British interests, to become a presidential candidate against Sánchez Cerro.

Undoubtedly Haya won the election. Even with the stealing of ballot boxes, the utilization of military coercion, and the faking of returns, his votes almost equalled those of Sánchez Cerro. Shortly he was thrown into prison by the dictator for a year and a half, mostly incommunicado, with great injury to his health.

While he was in prison occurred the spontaneous Trujillo Aprista revolt, resulting in the cold-blooded massacre of several thousand Apristas, comparable only to the slaughter perpetrated by bloody Martínez some time later in El Salvador.

Haya would probably have been assassinated in prison had it not been for world-wide protests. In New York I helped draft the protest sent out by the American Civil Liberties Union and wrote another one signed by leading American intellectuals and professionals.

After Sánchez Cerro's assassination, Haya at once dedicated himself to the better organization of the Peruvian Apra party. Immediately it swelled to remarkable proportions and achieved astonishing discipline with departments devoted to education, propaganda, defense, discipline, youth, women, cooperatives, economy, etc., all sustained by membership quotas. Workers' schools were opened, war was made on illiteracy, free clinics were started; a workers' restaurant served an excellent meal for twenty-five centavos (six cents), newspapers were founded or reopened: *La Tribuna, Apra, El Norte, El Sol,* etc.

Soon the government and Civilista elements became alarmed. The ridiculous reactionary aristocrat Riva Agüero, put in charge of the cabinet, suppressed the Apra papers in Lima, smashed up headquarters, schools, and restaurants, leaving not a stick of furniture. The Apra leaders went into hiding, dozens of Apristas were jailed. The Apra movement again entered a definite period of official persecution.

## 3

What is the Apra program?

Its literature is copious. I have at hand twoscore books and pamphlets detailing its struggles and program, including the vivid verbatim account of Haya de la Torre's preliminary trial during the time of Sánchez Cerro,[2] which reads like a seminar in political economy rather than the investigation of a political crime.

Haya gives an acount of his exile and the founding of the Apra party and stoutly denies being a Communist.

*Question:* Do you believe that there exists in Perú a struggle between capitalism and the proletariat?

*Answer:* Capitalism among us is incipient, and its devel-

[2] *El Proceso Haya de la Torre,* Guayaquil, 1933.

opment is a necessary stage in social evolution . . . what is necessary to procure is that the capitalistic stage is fulfilled without its . . . abuses and vices . . . and in permanent evolution toward different and better forms. . . .

*Question:* What are the different and better forms?

*Answer:* It is impossible to indicate dogmatically the lines to be followed; rather is it necessary to discover in each social reality, in accordance with its own characteristics, the forms of social betterment. . . .

Perú, Haya declares, is not an industrialized capitalist country, therefore has practically no proletariat, hence any struggle for liberation of the country must for the time being be based on an alliance among peasants, workers and the middle class with a nationalistic program of defense against foreign exploitation.[3]

*Question:* Do you consider that in Perú the basis of indigenous social organization is communist, and should the indigenous communities be the basis of agrarian collectivism? And do you believe that our rural classes are sufficiently oriented in this direction?

Each region, he replied, presented a specific and distinct problem. "The Incaic Empire was communist, not in an industrial sense, but . . . in a primitive or agrarian sense. The 'community' has survived in various regions of the country after four hundred years of struggle with the large landholder implanted by the Conquest. As is well known, there are various types of 'communities.' . . . We propose economic regionalism . . . to endeavor from a nationalistic

---

[3] Trujillo has an agrarian proletariat; Lima has some factory workers, Oroyo and Cerro de Pasco a mining proletariat. But until this century scarcely any factory smoke stained the skies of Lima. In 1858 artisans destroyed the doors and windows imported from Europe for the Lima Chorrillos railway; they burned the cars and routed the troops. The first textile factory was founded in 1847, and was followed by small paper, wax and candle, and glass factories. The first wage strike occurred during the opening of new streets in 1872. A general strike was attempted in 1912 and in 1934.

point of view to promote and strengthen indigenous organization, *i.e.*, protect the 'communities' where they exist and small landholding where it has been established. In general, to increase rural productivity, the Peruvian Aprista Party proposes the establishment of large agrarian cooperatives. . . ."

In his *Política Aprista* Haya presents a comprehensive program, which embraces Perú's whole economic and political scheme.

"We shall investigate the economic reality of the country by means of a new general census . . . the creation of a national department of statistics, and the celebrating of a National Economic Congress, with attendance of all factors of production."

Political boundaries will be modified to conform to economic reality, Congress and all local government to be reorganized on a functional rather than a geographic basis.

The working classes will be guaranteed life, health, moral and material well-being, education, liberty, and economic emancipation; "the gradual and cautious ending of exploitation of man by man." Credit, production and consumption cooperatives are to be fomented. An enlightened modern labor code is outlined, and each Ministry will have special indigenous bureaus.

Church and State will be separated.

In international affairs—a close league between all peoples of Latin America, through commercial treaties, the institution of a Latin American Union, and the creating of Latin American citizenship; peaceful boundary settlements, anti-imperialistic pacts, and a Latin American tribunal of arbitration.

Judicial, tax, public utility rate, customs, tariff and other reforms are advocated.

Basic industries are to be promoted by the State. Transport and insurance are to be progressively nationalized. Currency, banking, and budgetary reforms are promised, the creation of a national bank with industrial, mining and farm branches, control of capital export and special legislation regarding investment and income of foreign capital.

Agriculture, the basic industry, will be given preferential attention, and national agricultural production in all lines, through free informative service regarding markets, production, consumption, national and international statistics will be stimulated. Expropriation of properties, with just recompense, will be carried out where the area is of too great extent, in cases of absenteeism, and where proximity to large cities makes large estates increase the cost of living or prevent urban expansion. Idle lands will be heavily taxed and may be acquired through proper denunciation. Revision of water distribution, immediate attention to irrigation, river flow, etc., are further points.

The mining industry will be overhauled, vanadium and gold will be nationalized, coal production fomented, scandalous concessions to Americans revised or revoked, a national oil refinery will be constructed.

A general program of popular, rural and technical education is proposed and thorough efforts toward sanitation and hygiene. Special steps for the redemption of the Indian to bring about his incorporation in the life of the country, through protective economic measures, fomenting of indigenous industries, art and culture, education, cooperation, use of native tongues in teaching, propaganda against alcohol and cocaine.

Army, police and aviation reforms are also suggested.

The program is comprehensive, too comprehensive. It is opportunistic, bureaucratic, hybrid. It is based on petty bourgeois reforms with slight collectivist tendencies. It is essentially middle-class and national socialist in its trend. Its nationalistic emphasis gives it a Fascist complexion. It is, however, the logical program for its enunciated class basis.

## 4

But Aprismo must be recognized as the most vital popular force in Perú. Its members are imbued with almost mystic fervor; they are the stuff of which martyrs are made. They have been exiled in poverty; they have gone to jail; they have been wounded in battle. They have had their bath of fire and blood. They are fighting for what to them is a sacred cause.

They have a fervent faith in their leadership. Haya is perhaps too much of a God to them. Apra headquarters are plastered down with pictures of Haya in entirely too Mussolini-esque poses.

Their discipline is almost puritanical. They war upon the vices and promote Aprista sports.

It is necessary to recall that Perú has never had a party based upon principles. Previously it has merely had ambitious political and military cliques, greedy for power and privilege. Thus in 1904 González Prada declared that the Peruvian's electoral choice between the Civilistas and Democrats consisted in walking through a narrow alley, both walls smeared with mud and blood so that he was soiled whichever one he touched. Apra is the first party in Perú's history with a concerted body of principles other than that of sustaining a small clique in power.

Past governments have never been rooted in economic facts: no census since 1876, an estimate in 1896, and an even more superficial estimate in 1923, hence no Peruvian government has ever known (except in 1876) how many Peruvians there are, how much Perú produces, or what Perú and its people needed. Hence no government has ever attempted to root itself in the entire Peruvian nationality. Hence the ignorant feudal governments of Perú have always been unstable. Politics have shuttled between anarchy and tyranny, tyranny being but one facet of anarchy. Past governments have been paper democracies, whereas Aprismo, declares Haya, represents "not the old verbal democracy, but a democracy being forged by the people."

Apra principles are not empirical. They have evolved through the trial-and-error method, an ideology gradually developed through prior students' struggles; and though influenced by world trends, are basically related to Peruvian conditions and needs, and to general Latin American needs. More or less Apra is composed of the same social elements (as yet minus the militarists) which made the Mexican 1910-20 revolution, particularly at the Carranza stage. Also, it is similar, though with far deeper roots and broader tactic, to the Cuban A.B.C. movement. It therefore represents a tendency already come to fruition in many places throughout Latin America and probably destined to achieve victory in Perú and elsewhere.

Aprista victory will immediately precipitate new problems. The leaders will be obliged either to make some compromise peace with the feudal Civilistas, which will then precipitate a more radical fundamental revolution, or it will have to deepen its economic program and create a stronger alliance with peasant and Indian forces. The post-revolutionary history of Apra may prove much like that of Madero in Mexico.

Unfortunately, the Apra movement has already compromised its program. It has been trying to conciliate the Church; instead of propagandizing against the militarists, it has advocated justice and efficiency for the army; and it has soft-pedalled its whole anti-imperialistic position, especially with reference to British capital. This opportunism is largely due to Haya de la Torre, now entirely too enmeshed in the intrigues of Lima politics. It is doubtful if this attempt to win the sympathy of the poorer clergy and the army has brought enough effective support to compensate for the loss of mass faith in the Aprista movement itself.

In spite of these opportunistic vacillations, the Apra movement or its counterpart, either with or without Haya's leadership, is apparently destined to be victorious not only in Perú but in nearly all South America. Though Apra has deeper roots in regional consciousness and with far closer alliances with proletariat and peasant than has the official National Revolutionary Party of Mexico, it has a bureaucratic Fascist tinge, like that suggested by the new Mexican Six Year Plan, and the A.B.C. in Cuba.

On the other hand, Perú, unlike Cuba and Mexico, relatively unhampered by the menace of armed intervention, has far more chance to seek a fundamental independent solution of its problems. Hence any prophecy regarding post-revolutionary events in Perú is at present premature. It is difficult, even with intimate knowledge, to plot the political and economic probabilities once a people begins to throw off its centuries-old fetters.

Whatever its defects, whatever its program, whatever future, Aprismo is a great popular movement with remarkable discipline and remarkable leadership. It is the first stirring of a long-oppressed people. It is the beginning of a new Perú.

5

Once we practical northerners smugly believed South America's development would follow conventional capitalist economy—American investments, loans, the Monroe Doctrine, political tutelage, a sphere of influence similar to that of Japan in the Orient—but of course all with humanitarian aims. Our oyster to be eaten nobly.

The writers, publicists, radio announcers and college professors, who served and still serve as semi-official apologists for our bankers, large corporations and diplomats, the academic revindicators of Spanish culture and exploitation—all moved by the Nordic superiority complex—have dis-

torted the picture of the great social and racial tendencies
of the lands of the south. Thanks to the glib misinformation
of these prophets, our citizens have lost billions of dollars,
our future peace in a troubled world was jeopardized.

Now, our loans go into default, our investments are
hedged about by national independence and greater economic

self-sufficiency. One by one we cede our cherished prejudices:
the Platt Amendment, written originally by Root and God;
the Monroe Doctrine, written by Adams and God; the right
of occupation, devised by Big Stick Teddy and perfected in
the name of the self-determination of nations by Woodrow
Wilson.

Warns one native writer: "Come back to reason, men of
Two Worlds. You, white man, hazy mestizo, infected with
European false-superiority—your presumption of 'civilization' is being lost. Don't trust in the inanimate mouths of
your cannon and your other guns. Don't be too proud of

430

your machinery which can fail you. Remember that a short apprenticeship is enough to dominate your mechanisms and manage them with serenity and precision."

Social and material development to the south of us has been delayed by cultural and class conflicts. But the coming epic of South American history will be an organic evolution out of native culture and tradition, the fusing of elements long warring in open contradiction. It involves, especially among the highland tropic peoples, a unique experiment in socialization compounded of modern needs, colonial institutional patterns and ancient indigenous experience—all embraced in theories of democracy, Marxian economics and Fascist force—mass rhythms obeying vital life forces, new social concepts, and determinate æsthetic and ideological forms.

In this effort, Perú and its people will play a leading part.

Then the meaning of the New World in history and our place therein will become intelligible—even to us.

# XXIX

## NEW COLORS

### I

"Perú," remarks Basadre, "is not merely a social and political problem; it is also an artistic problem."

Æsthetics cannot be ignored in the solution of any country's problems; Perú has an architectonic, an æsthetic frame.

In Perú, as in Mexico, æsthetics are interwoven with every national effort. The geographical setting, the quality of the light, the intensity of color, the tones of the landscape, the racial heritages, make æsthetic fulfillment essential to any political fulfillment.

As in all other things, æsthetics in Perú have met, except here and there locally, only frustration. Indian art was aborted as a national expression; it survives in beautiful humble handicrafts despised by the élite. Transplanted Spanish art never had any vital roots. Just as there has been no political, racial or economic fusion, there has been no national art fusion. Merely naïve native art alongside of sophisticated hollow art, but nothing vitally Peruvian, nothing consciously carved into beauty in harmony with national feelings and aspirations, nothing that draws upon the entire energies of a people and also interprets its aspirations.

These statements need qualification. A Peruvian art is now really being born; already that new art is teaching Peruvians to know Perú. Just as in Mexico the first symptom of revolution was rebellion against dead academic standards by the San Carlos academy students, so the first symptom of Perú's approaching birth has come from her artists. But just as the Mexican artists could not produce a mature integrated art Mexican in technique and subject-matter and universal in concept until the revolution created a new environment of social experimentation, so the small group of present Peruvian artists, however nobly striving, still must work in a void. They are painting for an unborn society, hence their work lacks a degree of force, assurance, and fulfillment. They cannot paint effectively for a society they can only surmise.

Like the new political leaders, they have been strongly influenced by Mexico and Russia, particularly by Mexican art. To the disgust of the Lima élite, they have gone forth to find the real Perú. They have painted Indians and mulattoes, coastlanders, highlanders and jungle-dwellers; they have sought to penetrate the inner essence of the landscape, the sky, the people, the psychology of each region. As occurred in the case of the Mexico City aristocracy these paintings, for Lima's upper classes, are horrible; the Lima feudalists bitterly resent their social implications; they resent faithful portrayal of the Indian, because his physical rudeness, his customs, his sorrows, all are a reflection on their centuries of misgovernment. But ere long I predict the new Peruvian school will have nearly as much vogue as the new Mexican school.

The leader is José Sabogal. Revolutionary in technique, social in purpose, he has achieved calm maturity; he does not distort his message by flamboyant experiment. So rooted is Sabogal in his country that his art does not need to be strident, artificially false, nor imbued with the hectic political conflict. Having discovered Perú, he sees clearly the new Perú to arise. Having done all possible in the present benighted social and economic situation, having made his own revolutionary world, to do more would merely lead to fantastic experimentation, ever a symbol of frustration. Sabogal does not feel frustration.

This indicates both the weakness and strength of his work. It is not as violent as the Mexican school, but then Perú is not as violent as Mexico. A more stolid country, from Incan times it has had a tradition of methodical achievement, of calm purposefulness. Indigenous art was ever more sophisticated than that of early Mexico; Lima, too, was always a more sophisticated place than colonial Mexico City; hence Sabogal's art is neither hostile nor effusive; it is healthy without being vulgar, refined without being decadent— balance, fullness, sobriety—also more lyrical and colorful.

More than any one else in politics, literature, or music, Sabogal has discovered Perú in all its historical, geographical and ethnic variations. Some of his xilographs are reminiscent of the pre-Spanish terra-cotta designs. He has reproduced the sumptuousness of the Sun sacerdotes, has caught the whole spirit of the Inca legionaries. And he knows the coast, has captured all the sensual complicated soul of the Lima octaroon. To talk with Sabogal in his atelier in the National School of Fine Arts (of which he is the head) and see his work is to breathe in the essence of Perú's provinces; purple processional robes against the subtle cinnabar color of lofty Huancavelica; the bright swinging rhythm of the Aimará survivors around Huancayo; the colonial mysticism of the arcades of Huanta and Ayacucho; the stark wounded stoniness of Cerro de Pasco under indigo skies; the strange fantasms and mirages of the coast desert, the dreaming quaintness of Moche, the lubricity and holiness of the Corpus Christi processions in Cuzco; the dreary might of Puno.

Now and then he strikes a sardonic note, but none of the poster caricature or anecdotal criticism of Diego, none of the bitter satire, the frenzied straining of José Clemente Orozco, but something more essentially Peruvian, an ironic futility matching Andean majesty, as in his *Procession of our Lord of Miracles*. He feels the dark unearthly beauty of Cuzco's *Taytacha Temblores*—Lord of Earthquakes. In the pagan saint's Procession, the lad with curly wild hair goes mournfully behind the shrilly crying negroes. Various are his versions of Taytacha—the indigenous mass has tragic holy wistfulness, self-abstraction from earthly surroundings; the priests, not so gross as those of Rivera, are stately or epicurean.

He has captured the dancing breeziness of the fiesta of Amancaes, and the elegaic beauty of the Ayacucho canedances—the actors all swing, each in his separate manner, in one communal gyration until the very canvas seems to rotate. And how he loves the llama, its quaint aloofness, its majestic absurdity, its meticulousness, preciseness, its dainty almost deer-like step! Sabogal has caught subtle differences: a canvas of the Cuzco plaza life is different from that of Ayacucho; Cuzco is graver, harsher, stronger; Ayacucho, clearer, more amiable, gayer; both equally sad. "No geographic text," remarks one Peruvian critic, "can reflect so admirably the Peruvian landscape"—the crag where the tragic sky seems still another crag; the singular atmosphere of Mantaro, that gorge of multiple impressions; the opaline atmosphere of the coast in his vision of Cantagallo. What a collection of skies! Sunday market morning skies; noon skies in which the sun falls leaden over empty valleys in forlorn provinces; afternoons with incredible futuristic lights, a bitter vibration from rock to sky and earth and back again; the queer tonalities of stone and baked clay, of portal and roof; light over villages, light on the pampas—truthfulness that swells to mysticism and symbolism, a Bergsonian super-realism that penetrates to the inner essence and embraces all the hierarchical connections.

He presents the horror of provincial languidness, the slow death of the spirit in deserted streets where men have vegetated unimaginatively for centuries, but also the bursting energy of Indian fairs.

However varied his themes, in ensemble his work is unified by a concept of Peruvian importance, of racial freedom, of destruction of exploitation, of hatred of Civilistas and Creoles. But the doctrinaire never distorts his technique. If his greedy-eyed *gamonales* seem to scream protest more vigorous than any propaganda pamphlet, this is merely because of incisive observation. His propaganda value resides in selection, not in purposeful distortion. It is essential, vertical, built up like a Sun temple. His is, rather, a vigilant art which has listened to Perú's long monologue of suffering.

Sabogal not only interprets the new social and political Perú; his art is a racial and cultural blend, revealing the potentialities of the scarcely born mestizo world. Though well-grounded in European art, he has many antecedents in the artifacts of the ancient *huacas* and textiles. Sophisticatedly he revindicates the powerful inspiration, that centuries ago was inspired in the same sort of actuality he has rediscovered. He lifts handicraft skill to world art. The first "modernist" painters lived in Perú twenty centuries ago. Thus he has reestablished a continuity with the only vital art Perú has ever known.

A great fount of inspiration. The surviving artifacts of the earlier world represent perfected technique within a cultural scheme very alien but complete and satisfying—determined by a logic of circumstance for the outsider almost fourth dimensional, yet desirable. What fear, anger, irony, laughter, what reconciling of the terrible and the familiar in the faces of blind beggars, in bearded wrinkled old men, in pregnant women, warriors, judges, musicians—a whole population survives immobile through the centuries. Architectural *huacas* reproduce the ancient fortresses and homes; warrior *huacas* repeat their combats, body to body—flight, mutilation, throwing of enemies from the awful crags, the flush of victory. The religious and sex-act *huacas* are symbolic and esoteric. Zoological *huacas* are inspired in the birds and animals and fishes they knew: pelicans in ludicrous dignity, a wildcat with snarling dripping jaws, a long bird's bill, arched, buried amorously or somnolently on the breast; llamas strutting like roosters; guayavas bursting with juiciness; scorpions sitting up like monkeys; serpents and green worms with red eyes; snails; formalized animals made into blurred batiques with fantastic, shining, white square eyes. All these ornamental *huacas* are unforgettable for their joy and sensuality. Sabogal has inherited this joyousness, irony, and capricious finesse; he purifies this rich vein. He brings a whole submerged stream of culture out into the broad meadows of his comprehension and skill to irrigate the new Peruvian consciousness.

After the Conquest native art almost disappeared, but had moments of powerful revival. It bursts forth, though not often, in colonial art; it is there subtly in the church of Chucuito and of the Compañia in Arequipa; in certain structural designs in Cuzco. It is prolonged somewhat crudely in the carving of Huanta and Ayacucho. Now, after Sabogal, it can never again be ignored.

2

José Sabogal is the dean of an entire new school. Prominent names are Camilo Blas, Julia Codesido, Jorge Viñates Reinoso, Pantigroso, Esquerriloff and others.

Next to Sabogal, the most important is Camilo Blas, Assistant Director of the National School of Fine Arts. He also has travelled to all the most typical and beautiful places of Perú, finding abundant material. In general he is finer, more meticulous than Sabogal, just as Viñates and Codesido are more agile.

Camilo began by interesting himself in provincial Creole and cholo elements. His pictures, such as *Chicha and Toad*, of the *picanterías* (or typical restaurants), shops and scenes of Arequipa and Cuzco are remorseless, not tragic but ironical. Droll and humorous and faithful are his local types with their broad paunches, their excessive love of food, drink, and wild parties.

Subsequently he turned to the Indian in color-rich canvases—*Reaping, Grain Chaffers, Twilight in Namora*—in all a complete panorama of the Andean region. Types, customs, landscapes palpitate in his canvases with deep understanding of the highlands and its people.

At present he is gathering materials and making studies regarding the coast types of Perú, the life of the tropical regions: an airy well-built woman emerges from broad banana leaves—a forceful exact replica of the spirit of the coast, of its intense luxurious sensualism.

Ciro Alegre says of him, "Camilo Blas has definitely conquered a distinguished place in Peruvian and Indo American painting. He has strong character, keen insight and dexterous hands. He is a good seeker and a good achiever, an exponent of his people and of actuality, and therefore intrinsically Peruvian."

3

As in Mexico, Peruvian literature must necessarily lag behind the plastic arts as a form of national and universal expression. Just as painting has been retarded because of the failure to reconcile Indian and Spanish, highland-and-coast duality, and to forge a significant unified collectivity, literature has been even more handicapped. Though the dominant political, commercial and literary language is Spanish, a truly Peruvian literary expression must wait upon the assimilation of the Quechua and other folk for the forging of a more composite tongue which will have warmth, significance, flexibility.

Faulty language medium prevents completely truthful examination of the Peruvian scene. Even more than the painters, the writers must overleap the handicaps of their medium. Even so, a similar revolution has been occurring in literature—writers, too, are forerunners of the new Perú.

The first literature of Perú was colonial, Spanish, imported. The oustanding exception—save for the lost work of Inocencio Mamani and Tucupa Munas-Chan in native Quechua —was the brilliant pro-Indian mestizo historian Garcilazo. But after him—save for the despised Mariano Melgar—a spontaneous sincere romantic who dared to use some of the syntaxes of the street, whose *yaravíes* embrace both the indigenous and the Hispanic spirit—all attempts in literature at cultural synthesis ended; the chain was broken, colonialism dominated. French ideas came in during the independence agitation—Unanue and Baquíjano, the founders of Peruvian sociology, like the modern Marxists, got their ideas and local interpretations from abroad.

Essentially the literature of the Republic remained colonial, even more puerile than before. Witness Luis Benjamín Cisneros' fairly recent elegy to Alfonso XIII! Pre-Independence colonial literature at least had some intrinsic vitality in the very fact of Spanish domination. But Republican literature—the unctuous nostalgia of José Antonio de Lavalle for instance—based upon dead colonial forms and themes, is doubly thin and ludicrous. In general, remarks Mariátegui, "Peruvian literature is a heavy indigestible rhapsody of Spanish literature; all works ignore the living true Perú."

The Lima-Iberian-African influence of early Republican days did impart pageantry; the Limeñan is a colorist. The mountaineer is lyrical and dramatic. But these Andean voices, because of the decay of such cities as Cajamarca, Cuzco and Huancayo, were long mute in Peruvian literature; the writers, even if born in the Andes, all went to Lima for their inspiration and form where, transplanted, cultural roots cut, they wrote with a foreign accent of things not in their blood; they were weaker in theme and treatment than the real neo-colonial Limeños—Ricardo Palma, for instance.

Palma, though he completely excludes the Incaic spirit, wholly ignores the Indian and the Sierra and glorifies Lima and the Colony, his stories and types in his *Tradiciones Peruanas* ring true. He gave the Republic deficient vision concerning its ethnic, psychological and social composition, but at least gave reminiscent vitality by his earthy satire, jest and irreverent fantasy; and as a member of the new middle-class bureaucracy allied with a budding bourgeoisie, he exalted vulgar types and ridiculed Viceregal aristocratic prestige. But the old *mores* bound him; he is bland, sensual, sugary. He couldn't escape or transcend Lima; but he is a real interpreter of Lima.

Not so much a writer as a polemicist, nevertheless Francisco de Paula González Vigil, "the lay clergyman," is undoubtedly the first strong manifestation of free thought in Perú, hence has provided courage and aspiration for subsequent writers. Poverty, jail, exile never daunted him. He struck out valiantly and heroically against militarism and religious ignorance. His successor and commentator Manuel

González Prada describes him as a "lone marble column on the banks of a river of mire."

González Prada (of the second half of the nineteenth century) marks the first break from purely Spanish models to a more general cosmopolitan European influence—consequence of British imperialism and Paris culture. He is Parnassian, Hellenistic, pagan. His *Páginas Libres,* more Occidental and European, less Spanish and colonial, except for his emphatic individualistic and dogmatic tone, breaks with the Viceregal tradition, provides a true metropolitan literature —his philosophical essay *La Vida y La Muerte* is an echo of the famous sonnet *Les Morts* by Lecomte de l'Isle. If he did not furnish a new Peruvian viewpoint, he at least destroyed old walls, letting in new light and air; and he boldly faced his country's problems. His words, "striking sparks and terrible," in an hour of national darkness, after the disgraceful War of the Pacific, are those of a Jeremiah accuser, caustically critical rather than synthetical and creative. He "rises like an affirmative spirit from the field of ruin and misery" in the debacle of the rapacious guano-saltpetre era. *Horas de Lucha* is a challenge unequalled since González Vigil. At the same time he is genial; a sweetened Voltaire; the Anatole France of Perú. He recognized the true Perú to be not that of the Creoles and foreigners inhabiting a narrow strip of coast but of the Indians in the Cordillera. And he adds regretfully, "Perú is a mountain crowned by a cemetery." "Perú is a sick organism; wherever the finger is pressed, pus spurts." He railed against colonialism, Perú's ineffective "childhood," and against the gaseous verbosity of tropical rhetoric and Limeñan pudginess—"Better to be iron than a cloud." He fought conservatism, pseudo-liberalism, evil magistrates, stupid legislators, venal journalists, the aristocracy, the clergy, the militarists—everything poisoning his country. He was a sort of purifying flame, but could not create in accordance with his critical understanding, perhaps

because as D'Ors has stated, "he galloped in two centuries."
He is Perú's second great intellectual prophet.

Abelardo Gamarra, known as "El Tunante," and Seguro,
writers of manners, interpreters of provincial customs, along
with Prada, attempted—though their work, at best, is local,
anecdotal and incidental—to use the language of the street,
to discover the true Peruvian vernacular.

The more modern José Santos Chocano represents a throw-
back to the swashbuckler Conquistadores, to the colonial
spirit, the Spanish rhetoricians, and Limeñan super-exuber-
ance, lacking restraint and discipline. All his fantasies, except
his poems *To the Vicuña* and *The Three Notes*, charmingly
interpretive of the Sierra, are external, alien, modeled on
Spanish literature, on Byron and Victor Hugo, sensitive of
waves of modernity from abroad and not from Perú.

The turn of the century, in Perú, dominated by Rodó the
Cuban, flowed on into the futurist 1910 generation—which
coincided with the great awakening in Mexico. But at bottom frivolous, opportunistic, theatrical, and clever, its
language was rhetorical, vague and verbose, its beliefs skin-
deep, it soon sputtered out, became more colonial than the
colony, merely the voice of the landholding class reestablishing itself after a wave of radical ideas and military dis-
turbance. Its failure is typified by the sterile, aristocratic, and
reactionary José de Riva Agüero y Osma. The promising
1910 generation was really "decadence absorbed in polishing
indolent acrostics," escaping into the soft mooning corruption of Perricholismo.

Something of the Peruvian melting pot simmers in some
of the fine elegiac writing of Ventura García Calderón: a
sensitivity for negro, Indian and white, but far removed
from any organic synthesis: "To my cradle to croon over me
caressingly came women in mourning, and their guttural
songs were of the fields and hot nights in their native Senegal.
Others, pale, timid as slaves still, sighed the complaint of the

oppressed, the *yaraví* hymns. But white women like you, Best Beloved, spoke to me of the witches who came from afar over the paths of the sea to bless me." It is a vague, almost meaningless dream of a Perú that is stirring, coming to life, but which he is unable and unwilling to meet face to face— except in dreams. He frittered out in Paris, more his home than his native land, and wrote nostalgic hopeful books, *The Latin Democracies of South America* and the *Creation of a Continent,* of a new world he would like to see born. To a friend in Montmartre he confessed his Gallic obsession. "I came into the world, my beloved, in your bright city, but I knew a sad infancy in a strange far country."

Another current, despised, less dominant, was born during the same period and gathered force. *Contemporaneos,* founded by Enrique Bustamante y Ballivían and Julio Alfonso Hernández marks new experimentation. Long-forgotten González Prada was even animated to reappear in 1909 among the new young "Independents." Valdelomar, to become a figure of importance, was among the group, also pro-Indian Pedro S. Zulen, who warred on the academists. A still stronger current was started with the publication of Valdelomar's magazine *Colónida*—the so-called "Colónida" revolt against "the conservative taste, eighteen-year-old gallantry and mediocre and wearisome melancholy" of academism and rhetoricalness. Once more a protest, not an affirmation, not an ideology or a method, too soon the group exhausted itself in feeble cries of iconoclasm and snobbishness —a puerile Menckenism. If Valdelomar, Percy Gibson, and Federico More (who vitalized the contrast between Lima and the Sierra) and others stuck a mortal knife into the ribs of vulgar Spanish rhapsody, they also brought in D'Annunzian influences; they were still Parnassian, ivory tower, "Greeks born in a country of zambos," and afraid of political agitation. The movement fizzled out in the romantic Bohemianism of Domingo Martínez Luján, the decadent Manuel

444

Beingolea, a rare and extraordinary Tory, and the iconoclasm of Alberto Guillen, a soured spirit ending up in gymnastical Pirandellianism, and the beautiful "escape" literature of José María Eguren with his child-like reverie, his enchanted infantile sensibility and preciousness, love of Red Kings and medieval trappings in his *El Duque,* his eerie entrancing shadows in his *White Vampires.* He is "a pure echo lost in the American tropics."

The literature of 1917-18 suddenly spouts with Bolshevik echoes. Brusquely it terminates the futile groping of the Colónida period—for instance, Alberto Hidalgo, in his *Panoplia Lírica.* His slogan is "simplicity," he writes hard poems to machines and revolution and Lenin, a fresh but non-Peruvian outside influence.

These various breaks with tradition paved the way for authors earnestly seeking inspiration in the Peruvian scene itself. César Vallejo, a transitionist still in a recondite symbolist cycle, discovers much of the indigenous spirit; *Trilce* has the deep native pessimism and nostalgia.

Enrique López Albújar, a mulatto fiction writer, not only knows the negroes of the coast, as in *Malataché,* but his hard dry sketches of the Sierra bite deep into Indian reality and psychology; he discovers in his *Los Tres Jircos* that the three giant peaks of Huánuco weigh more in local Indian consciousness than all the otherworld of Christianity. He finds the real beat and rhythm of Indian life, discovers the soul and aspiration of the Andean man, as never before in Peruvian literature. Just as López Albújar penetrates critically in fiction form, Luís Valcárcel in his *Los Hombres de Piedra* and *Tempestad en los Andes* gives exact portrayal in fine lyrical prose, and penetrates scientifically in his admirable studies of Incaic evolution—*Del Ayullu al Imperio* is a classic.

The newer writers of Perú are now caught in the current of modern world trends and Peruvian revolutionary activities. Indigenists all of them, their literature corresponds to the pro-*mujik* Tolstoian period. Caught on the horns of the dilemma of communal indigenous experience and the inrush of the machine age, they waver between civilization and primitivism, attempt reconciliation, but too often find the solution in varying shades of colorless Marxian dialectic. All born of the varying schools of decadence, modernism, skepticism, individualism, æstheticism, arduously they are attempting to surmount these approaches, seeking to root themselves in Peruvian realities, to comprehend racial conflict and sociological needs.

Mostly mestizos, they have better insight into both cultures, but are frustrated since their environment denies the amalgamation they biologically embody. Hence mestizo literary frustration now takes refuge in propaganda. Thus Magda Portal, Perú's first important modern woman poet, in her *El derecho de matar, Una esperanza en el mar,* lyrical and human, is driven to action, has been drawn into revolutionary activities, is now one of the Aprista ramrods.

Alcides Spellucín, troubled with dreams of the future, forsook the past, in "a golden boat in search of the good island"—*El Libro de la Nave Dorada.* He sings of the sea, he writes a ballad of the tropics, original but with echoes of Rubén Darío and Herrera y Reissig; then, wounded by existing political inadequacy, like most of his generation, he steps down into the dust and arena of Aprismo to make his golden dream effective.

Perú's best writers are not litterati but social investigators; their work has strong functional vitality—Haya de la Torre, Castro Pozo, Abelardo Solís, César Ugarte, Uriel García, and Basadre. The latter's *Perú: Problema y Posibilidad,* and *La Multitud, la ciudad y el campo* are brilliantly written analyses of Peruvian life and problems; and his two-volume *Iniciación de la República* is the classic interpretive history of the period. All of these authors write for and about the masses, about social forces. They no longer write for the Palais Concert.

Above all must be mentioned the cripple, now dead, José Carlos Mariátegui—by far Perú's most brilliant sociological writer.

His *Seven Essays of Peruvian Reality* are a tour de force of social and economic analysis unequalled in any other South American country; comparable to it are only Molina Enríquez' *Los Grandes Problemas de México* and some of the writing of the notable Argentinian Alberdi.

His work, perhaps because he was a cripple, has something of the inimitable strength of a majestic tree. Fully as incisive and analytical, more relentlessly caustic than González Prada, he is also more creative; his thought grows up cheerfully, and expands organically. Though a Marxist, he has used this philosophical heritage flexibly, realistically; he knows and understands his country as no other writer. He edited the most vital magazine ever published in Perú— *Amauta*, long a thrilling clearing-house of ideas and new literature.

If Perú has never produced a great literature, it has produced three writers great for their independence and originality of thought, their courage, characters forged in a moral substance more enduring than precious metals or stones; they live deep in the hearts of the oppressed Peruvian people. Perú has produced no noble statesmen, no political liberators, no national leaders of masses, until Haya de la Torre; but the potential greatness of Perú as a free country is recorded in the names of its Indian revolters and the three literary figures and thinkers, González Vigil, González Prada and Mariátegui. The colonial period in Peruvian art has definitely ended. It is ended in literature. In music Carlos Sánchez Málaga, Roberto Carpio, Roberto Ojeda and others herald the change. In painting Sabogal and Blas open up the new world.

Only in politics and economics does Perú remain colonial and backward. Soon it will, it must, heed the message of its creative minds. That day Perú will at last be born into the world of valid independent nations. That day it will be reorganized into a definite human aggregation capable of seeking its own destiny and of contributing to the progress and significance of human life both at home and abroad rather than as now supinely bowing to medieval exploitation.

# SELECTED BIBLIOGRAPHY

Acosta, Father José de. The Natural and Moral History of the Indies. Ed. Clemente R. Markham. London, 1880. 2v. (Original Spanish Edition, 1588.)

Aguilar, Luis F. Cuestiones Indígenas. Cuzco, 1922.

Aguirre Morales, Augusto. El Pueblo del Sol. Lima, 1927.

Almanaque Peruano. Anuario Militar. Vol. 12, Lima, 1932.

Alva, Victor Rodrigo. El mito de la revolución de agosto de 1930. Lima, 1933.

Alvarez, Gervacio. Guia de Ayacucho. [?]

Ambrosetti, Juan B. Viaje en la Puna de Atacama de Salta a Caurchari. Buenos Aires, 1904.

Angrand, Leonce. Lettre sur les antiquites de Tiguanaco . . . Paris, 1866.

Armentia, Nicolás. Navegación del Madre de Diós. La Paz, 1887.

Arona, Juan de. Diccionario de Peruanismos. Lima, 1883.

Arriaga, Pablo Joseph de. La extirpación de la idolatría en el Pirú. Lima, 1621. 1920.

Atienza, Lope de. Compendio historial de los Yndios del Pirú. [?] 1585 [?]

Avila, Francisco de. A narrative of the errors, false gods and other super-stitions and diabolical rites which the Indians of Huarochiri lived in ancient times. London, 1873. (In Rites and Laws of Incas. Tr. and ed. by Clemente R. Markham.)

Bachman, Carlos J. Departamento de Lambayeque. Lima, 1921.

Ballón Landa, Alberto. El hombre de la Selva. Lima, 1917.

Bandelier, Adolf Francis. The ruins of Tiahuanaco. Worcester, 1911.

Barranca, José Sebastián. Ollanta (The Quechua Drama). Lima, 1868.

Basadre, Jorge. La Iniciación de la República. Lima, 1929, 1930. 2v.

—— La multitud, la ciudad y el campo en la historia del Perú. Lima, 1929.

—— Perú: Problema y posibilidad. Lima, 1931.

Baudin, Louis. L'empire socialiste des Inkas. Paris, 1928.

—— L'Organisation économique de l'empire des Inkas. Paris, 1929.

Belaunde, Victor Andrés. La realidad nacional. Paris, 1931.

Betanzos, Juan de. Drama y Narración de los Incas. Madrid, 1880.

Bingham, Hiram. Inca Land. Boston, 1922.

*Boletín bimestral de la Junta departamental del patronato de la raza indígena. Departamento de Ayacucho.* Ayacucho, 1928-29.

*Boletín de la Sociedad Geográfica de Lima.* Lima. Vols. V, IX.

Bourman, Isaiah. The Andes of Southern Peru. New York, 1916.

Buchwald, Otto von. Das Reich der Chimus. *Globus* XIV. pp. 149-151.

——— Los Primeros Incas. *Boletín de la Sociedad Ecuatoriana de Estudios históricos americanos.* VII: 115-121. Quito.

Bustamante Cisneros, Ricardo. Condición jurídica de las comunidades de indígenas en el Perú. Lima, 1918.

Cabello de Balboa, Miguel. Miscelánea Antártica. [Ms. 1576-1586?] [Copy 1700-1725?]

Cabello de Carbonera, Mercedes. El Conspirador, Lima, 1892.

——— Historia del Perú. Lima, 1920.

Cáceres, Z. Aurora. La Ciudad del Sol. Pról. by Enrique Gómez Carrillo. Lima, 1927.

Calancha, Antonio de la. Crónica moralizada del orden de San Agustín en el Perú. Barcelona, 1638.

*Cancionero Aprista.* Nos. 1-3. Lima [?]

*Cantos de la revolución.* Lima, 1934.

Casas, Bartolomé de las. De las antiguas gentes del Perú. Madrid, 1892.

Castelnau, Francis de. Expedition dans les parties centrales de l'Amerique du Sud. Paris, 1851. 4v.

Castro, Emilio. El departamento de San Martín. Lima, 1907.

Castro Pozo, Hildebrando. Nuestra Comunidad Indígena. Lima, 1924.

Catolicismo y Aprismo. Ed. Atahualpa. Lima, 1934.

Cavassa, Nicolás. La Chicha como factor del alcoholismo en el Perú. *Reforma Medica,* II, 22. Lima, 1916.

*Censo General de la República del Perú* (1876). Lima, 1878. 7v.

Chantre y Herrera, José. Historia de las misiones del Marañon español. Madrid, 1901.

Chioíno, José (pseud.). El escándalo de Gueppí. Lima, 1934.

Cieza de León, Pedro de. Crónica del Perú. Vol. I, Sevilla, 1553; Vol. II, Madrid, 1880.

Cobo, Bernabé. Historia del Nuevo Mundo. Sevilla, 1890-93.

Córdoba y Urrutia, José María. Estadística histórica, geográfica, industrial y comercial del departamento de Lima. Lima, 1839.

Cosío, Felix. La propiedad colectiva del ayullu. Cuzco, 1916.

Cossío del Pompas, F. Pintura Colonial. Escuela Cuzqueña. Cuzco, 1928.

Cossío P., Felipe. Los buscadores de camino. Lima, 1932.

Cox, Carlos Manuel. En torno al imperialismo. Prol. by Seoane, Manuel. Lima [?]

*Crímenes del Sancho-Civilismo, Las.* La Revolución de Huaraz. Lima, 1933.

Cuentas, Alberto. Puno, sus aborígenes, sus costumbres, usos y diversiones, etc. In *La Crónica,* Lima, July 28, 1920.

Dávila, Francisco. Idolatrías de los indios de Huarochín. Lima, 1918.

Delgado, A. Julio M. Folklore y apuntes para la sociología indígena. Lima, 1931.

Delmar, Serafín. El hombre de estos años. Mexico, 1929.

—— Radiogramas del Pacífico. Lima, 1927.

—— and Portal, Magda. El derecho de matar. La Paz, Bolivia, 1926.

Díaz, Eulogio. Descripción del distrito de San Carlos de Bambamarca. Cajamarca, 1898.

*Dirección General de Enseñanza.* Programas analíticos de instrucción primaria. Lima, 1933.

Eguiguren, Luis Antonio. En la Selva Política. 1930-33. Lima, 1933.

Eguren de Larrea, D. F. El Cusco. Lima, 1929.

Encinas, José Antonio. La educación: su función social en el Perú en el problema de la nacionalización. Lima, 1913.

—— Causas de la criminalidad indígena en el Perú. Lima, 1919.

—— Contribución a una legislación tutelar indigéna. Lima, 1918.

Enock, C. Reginald. Perú. London, 1912. 3d ed.

Escomel, Edmundo. La medicina popular Arequipeña. In *El Pueblo.* Arequipa, Nov. 1921.

Estete, Miguel de. La relación del viage que hizo el señor Hernando Pizarro. . . . Sevilla, 1534. Tr. 1872.

*Facultad de Jurisprudencia. Universidad Mayor de San Marcos.* Causas de la criminalidad indígena en el Perú. Lima, 1919.

Ferrasas, Matías. Informe del médico titular de Iquitos. In Informes y memorias de los médicos titulares; *año,* 1916. Lima, 1918.

Ferrer, David Constantino. Curso de Historia del Perú. Lima, 1932.

Flores, Manuel Benedicto. Pequeños Borrones de Pre-historia Ayacucheña. Ms. Also cf. *Antara,* I, 1, 12-15, Ayacucho, July 28 (November) 1933.

Fowler, Luis R. Monografía histórico-geográfico del departamento de Ayacucho. Lima, 1924.

Frezier, M. Relation du voyage de la Mer du Sud aux cotes du Chily et du Perou. Paris, 1732.

Gamarra, Abelardo. Cf. Tunante.

Gamarra, Manuel Jesús. Orientación y organización. Cuzco, 1926.

Gamarra, Manuel Jesús. La Ciudad de los Incas. Cuzco, 1922.

*Guía histórica artística del Cuzco*, Lima, 1925.

García, J. Uriel. El nuevo indio. Cuzco, 1930.

Garcilazo de la Vega. Los Comentarios Reales de los Incas. New ed. Lima, 1918.

Gavilán, Ramos. Historia del célebre santuario de Nuestra Señora de Copacabana. Lima, 1621.

Geographical and Statistical Synopsis of Perú (1895-98) Lima, 1899.

González de la Rosa, Manuel. Viaje hecho al Partido de Larecaja. . . . In *La Medicina Popular Peruana* by Valdizán and Maldonado, Vol. III. Lima, 1922.

González Prada, Manuel. Horas de Lucha. Lima (?)

Guevara, Tomás. Historia de la civilización araucana. Santiago de Chile, 1898-1922.

Haenke, Tadeo. Descripción del Perú. Lima, 1901.

Harcourt, Raoul y Marie. La Musique des Incas et les Survivances. Paris, 1925. 2v.

Hassel, Jorge M. von. Las tribus salvajes de la región amazónica. In *Boletín geográfico de Lima*. XVII, 64. Lima, 1905.

Haya de la Torre, Victor Raoul. Construyendo el Aprismo. Lima, 1933.

—— Ideario y Acción Aprista. Buenos Aires, 1930.

—— Manifiesto a la Nación. Panamá, 1932.

—— El Plan del Aprismo. Guayaquil, 1932.

—— Política aprista. Lima, 1933.

—— Por la emancipación de América Latina. Buenos Aires, 1927.

—— Teoría y Táctica del Aprismo. 4th ed. Lima, 1931.

Herrera, Genaro G. Leyendas y tradiciones de Loreto. Iquitos, 1918.

Heysen, Luis E. El comandante del Oropesa. Cuzco [?]

—— Presente y Porvenir del Agro Argentino. Pref. by Amadeo, Tomás. Lima, 1933.

Hidalgo, Alberto. Haya de la Torre en su Víspera. Lima, 1931.

—— Actitud de los años. Buenos Aires, 1932.

Holstein, Otto. Chan-Chan: Capital of the great Chimú. *Geographical Review*. Am. Geog. Soc. XVII, 36-61. N. Y. 1927.

Humboldt, Alexander von. Vues de cordilléres et monumens des peuples indigénes de l'Amerique. Paris, 1810.

Ibañez, Francisco. Tradiciones de mi tierra. Arequipa, 1884.

The Indian Problem in Peru. *West Coast Leader*, Lima, Feb. 13, 20, 1934.

Irigoyen, Pedro. El conflicto y el problema indígenas. Lima, 1922.

Izcue, Elena. El arte peruano en la Escuela. Paris, 1927. 2v.

Jenks, James. Tambo. New York, 1928.

Jijón y Caamaño, Jacinto. La religión del imperio de los Incas. Quito, 1919. 2v.

Jiménez: El esfuerzo libertador del comandante. *Anon.* Lima, 1934.

Jumelle, Henri. Les Cultures Coloniales. Paris, 1916.

Karsten, Rafael, 1926. The civilization of South American Indians. New York, 1926.

Lecuanda, José Ignacio de. Descripción geográfica de la ciudad y partido de Trujillo. [?]

Lehmann, Walter, and Doering, Henrich. The Art of Old Peru. London, 1924.

Liga de Hacendados. La Verdad en la Cuestión Indígena. Arequipa, 1922.

López Albujar, Enrique. Cuentos Andinos. Lima, 1924. 2nd ed. 1927.
—— Malataché. Piura [?]

Lorente, Sebastián. Historia Antigua del Perú. Lima, 1860.

Luna H. y Roca, F. Proyecto de Ley Tutelar del Indio. Lima, 1928.

Markham, Clemente Robert. The Incas of Peru. London, New York, 1910.

Málaga Santolalla, Fermín. Departamento de Cajamarca. *Bol. Soc. Geog.* Vol. XX. Lima.

Mariátegui, José Carlos. Siete Ensayos de Interpretación de la Realidad Peruana. Lima, 1928.

Martínez de la Torre. La Teoría del Crecimiento de la Miseria Aplicada a nuestra realidad. Lima, 1929.

Matto de Turner, Clorinda. Aves sin Nido. Valencia, 1889.
—— Tradiciones Cuzqueñas y Leyendas. New ed. Cuzco, 1917.

Mazo, Gabríel del. *La Reforma Universitaria.* Buenos Aires. 6v.

McBride, George McCutchen. The Agrarian Indian Communities of Highland Peru. New York, 1921.

Means, Philip Ainsworth. Ancient Civilizations of the Andes. New York and London, 1931.
—— Fall of the Inca Empire and the Spanish Rule in Peru: 1530-1780. New York and London, 1932.

Mejía Xesape, M. Toribio. Algunas costumbres y creencias de los Indígenas. Prol. by Hermilio Valdizán. Lima, 1923.

Menéndez, Carlos. La ciencia de curar. Arequipa, 1915.

Meneses, Romulo. Nuestra Unidad. La Paz, 1929.
—— Por el Apra. Lima, 1933.

Mesones Muro, Manuel Antonio. La Brujería en el Norte del Perú. In *El Comercio,* Lima, Jan. 24, 1907.
—— Vías al Oriente del Perú. *Bol. Soc. Geog. de Lima,* Vols. V, XIII.

Molina de Cuzco, Cristobal de. The Fables and Rites of the Incas. In Markham, Rites and Laws of the Incas. London, 1873.

Montoya, Arturo. Romancero de las Calles de Lima. Lima, 1932. 5v.

*Mundial.* Lima, Dec. 31, 1928. Special Cuzco and Arequipa edition.

Muñoz, David. Memorias de viaje. Lima, 1901.

Nestarez, Francisco H. Cuentos, tradiciones, leyendas y costumbres quechuas. Lima, 1929.

—— Pisco, su presente, su porvenir. Lima, 1927.

Ogilvie, Alan G. Geography of the Central Andes. New York, 1922.

Oliva, Juan Anello. Historia . . . del Perú y Varones Insignes en Santidad. Lima, 1895.

Olivas Escudero, Bishop Fidel. Apuntes para la historia de Ayacucho. (Huamanga) Ayacucho, 1924.

Ondegardo, Juan Polo de. Los errores y supersticiones de los Indios. Lima, 1916. (In Colección de Libros y documentos referentes a la historia del Perú. Vol. III.)

Orrego, Antenor. El monólogo eterno. Trujillo, 1929.

—— Notas margenales. Trujillo, 1922.

Pacheco, Toribio. Cuestiones Constitucionales. Lima, 1853.

Palma, Ricardo. Tradiciones peruanas. Barcelona, 1893.

—— Neologismos y Americanismos. Lima, 1896.

Pastor, Francisco. El Indígena del Perú. In *Revista de la Universidad de Arequipa.* Arequipa, Nov. 1930.

Paz Soldán, Carlos Enrique. De la revolución a la anarquía universitarias. Lima, 1922.

—— De la inquietud a la revolución. Diez años de rebeldías universitarias, 1909-19. Lima, 1919.

Paz Soldán, Mariano Felipe. Diccionario geográfico estadístico del Perú. Lima, 1877.

Paz Soldán, Mateo. Geografía del Perú. Paris, 1862.

*Partido Aprista Peruano.* Al Pueblo. Lima, 1930.

—— Cuatro aspectos importantes del Aprismo. Lima, 1933.

—— Documentos políticos. Lima, 1932.

Peña Montenegro, Alonso de la. Itinerario para parrochos de Indios. Amberes, 1668.

Peralta, Pedro de. Lima fundado ó Conquista del Perú. Lima, 1732.

Pérez Palma, Ricardo. La evolución mítica en el Imperio del Tahuantin-Suyo. In *Revista Universitaria.* XV. Lima, 1920.

Petrovick, Julian. Naipe adverso. Santiago, 1930.

Pizarro, Pedro. Descubrimiento y Conquista del Perú (c. 1571) Lima, 1917.

—— Relation of the Discovery and Conquest of the Kingdoms of Peru. Tr. P. A. Means, New York, 1921, 2v.

Ponce de León, Francisco. Sistemas de arrendamiento y terrenos de cultivo en el departamento del Cuzco, y el problema de la distribución. Cuzco, 1918.

Portal, Magda. America Latina frente al imperialismo. Lima, 1931.

—— Una Esperanza y el Mar. Lima, 1927.

—— Frente al momento actual. Lima, 1931.

—— El nuevo poema y su orientación hacia una estética económica. Mexico, 1929.

—— and Delmar, Serafín. El Derecho de Matar. La Paz, Bolivia, 1926.

Pounansky, Arthur. Tiahuancu y la civilización prehistórica en el Altiplano Andino. La Paz, 1911.

Pozo, Manuel J. Historia de Huamanga. Ayacucho, 1924.

—— Las Afueras de Huamanga debe ser irrigadas. Ayacucho, 1930.

—— Lo que vió Huamanga por la Independencia. Ayacucho, 1924.

—— El periodismo en Ayacucho. Ayacucho, 1928.

Prescott, Wm. H. History of the Conquest of Peru with a preliminary view of the civilization of the Incas. N. Y. 1848. 2v.

Prince, Carlos (Ed). Lima Antigua. I, Tipos de Antaño. II, Fiestas Religiosas y Profanas. III, La Limeña y mas tipos de antaño. Lima, 1890. 3v.

El Proceso Haya de la Torre. Guayaquil, 1933.

Procter, Robert. Narrative of a journey across the Cordillera of the Andes. . . . (1823-24) London, 1825.

Prado y Ugarteche, Javier. Estado social del Perú bajo la dominación española. Lima, 1894.

Raimondi, Antonio. El Perú. Lima, 1874-1913. 6 vols.

*Revista de Economía y Finanzas.* Lima, 1933-34. Vol. I-II. Nos. 1-5, Vol. III.

*Revista Histórica.* Tomos I-XI. Lima, 1920-34.

Reynolds. Versiones incaicas. Santiago de Chile, 1930.

Riva Agüero, José de la. La historia en el Perú. Lima, 1910.

Rivera, José Eustasio. La Vorágine. New ed. Santiago, 1933.

Robuchón, Eugenio. En el Putumayo y sus afluentes. Lima, 1907.

Romero, Emilio. El decentralismo. Lima, 1932.

—— El departamento de Puno. Lima, 1928.

—— Geografía económica del Perú. Lima, 1930.

Saavedra, Bautista. El Ayullu. La Paz, 1913.

Sabate, Luís. Viaje de los padres misioneros del convento de Cuzco a los tribus salvajes de los Campas, Piros, Conibos y Sipibos. Lima, 1877.

Samañez, Juan Guillermo. Huyhuachu. In *El Comercio,* Feb. 22, Lima, 1914.

Samañez, Juan Guillermo. "Nisun Quichu—Nisunquichu." In *La Crónica*, Aug. 21, Lima, 1921.

Samañez Ocampo, José. Exploración de los ríos peruanos Apurímac, Ene, Tambo, Ucayali y Urubamba. Lima, 1885.

Sánchez, Luis Alberto. Aprismo y religión. Lima, 1933.
—— Carta a una Indoamericana. Quito, 1932.
—— Don Manuel. Lima and Paris, 1930-31.
—— Lima y don Ricardo Palma. Lima, 1927.
—— La literatura peruana. Lima, 1928-29. 2v.
—— Se han sublevado los indios. Lima, 1926.

Sancho de la Hoz, Pedro. An account of the conquest of Peru [c. 1533-48]. N. Y., 1917.

Sarmiento de Gamboa, Pedro. Segunda Parte de la historia general llamada india. Berlin, 1906.

Sievers, Wilhelm. Geografía de Bolivia y Perú. (tr.) Barcelona, 1931.

Schmidt, Max. Kunst und Kultur von Peru. Berlin, 1929.

Solís, Abelardo. Ante el problema agrario peruano. Lima, 1928.

Spruce, Richard. Notes of a botanist on the Amazon Andes. London, 1908.

Squier, E. George. Peru. . . . London, 1864.

Stahl, F. A. En el pais de los Incas. Buenos Aires [n.d.]

Stiglich, Germán. Informe del Jefe de la Comisión Exploradora de las regiones del Ucayali, Fiscarrald y Madre de Dios. Lima, 1907.

Saenz, Moisés. Sobre el indio ecuatoriano. Mexico, 1933.
—— Sobre el indio peruano y su incorporación al medio nacional. Mexico, 1933.

Spelucín, Alcides. El libro de la nave dorada. Lima, 1926.

Seone, Manuel. Las calumnias contra el Aprismo. Buenos Aires, 1932.
—— Comunistas Criollos. 3rd ed. Lima, 1934.
—— La Garra Yanqui. Buenos Aires, 1930.
—— Mirando a Bolivia, con el ojo izquierdo. Buenos Aires, 1926.
—— Nuestros fines. Buenos Aires, 1930, 2nd ed., 1931.
—— Páginas Polémicas. Lima, 1931.

Tello, Julio C. Antiguo Perú. Lima, 1929.

Torre, V. M. La, Informe del Médico titular de Calca y Urubamba, In *Informaciones y memorias de los médicos titulares, Año 1916.* Lima, 1918.

Tovar y R. Enrique D. Ropa Ligera. Anecdotario Nacional. Lima, 1927.

Tudila y Varela, Francisco. Socialismo peruano. Lima, 1905.

Tunante, El (Pseud. Abelardo Gamarra). Lima: Unos cuantos barrios y unos cuantos tipos. Lima, 1907.

Ugarte, César Antonio. Bosquejo de la historia económica del Perú. Lima, 1926.

# SELECTED BIBLIOGRAPHY

Ugaz, Juan. Memoria del Médico Titular de Chiclayo. Lima, 1915. In *Registro Oficial de Fomento*.

Uhle, Max. Las llamitas de piedra del Cuzco. In *Revista Histórica*. Lima, 1906. Vol. I.

Ulloa Cisneros, Abel. Leguía. Apuntes de cartera, 1919-1924. Lima, 1932.
—— Escombros, 1919-1930. Lima, 1934.

Unánue, Hipolito H. Noticia de los trajes, supersticiones, etc. de los indios de la Pampa del Sacramento y montañas de los Andes del Perú. Barcelona, 1914.
—— Guía política, eclesiástica, y militar para el año 1794. Lima, 1794.

Urteaga, Horacio H. El Imperio Incaico. Lima, 1931.
—— Informaciones acerca . . . de los Incas. Lima, 1918.

Valcárcel, Luís E. La cuestión agraria en el Cuzco. Cuzco, 1914.
—— De la Vida Inkaica. Lima, 1925.
—— Del Ayullu al Imperio. Lima, 1925.
—— Tempestad en los Andes. Lima, 1927.

Valdez de la Torre, Carlos. La evolución de las comunidades indígenas. Perú, 1921.

Valdivia, Juan Gualberto. Fragmentos pura la historia de Arequipa. Arequipa, 1846.
—— Las memorias sobre las revoluciones de Arequipa. Arequipa, 1846.

Valdizán, Hermilio and Maldonado, Angel. La Medicina Popular Peruana. Lima, 1922. 3v.

Valera, Blas [c. 1580]. De las costumbres antiguas de los naturales del Perú. Madrid, 1879.

Vasquez, Diógenes. Teoría regionalista y regionalismo peruano. Trujillo, 1932.

Villarán, Manuel Vicente. Condición legal de las comunidades de indígenas. Lima, 1907.

Villagomes, Archbishop Pedro de. Exortaciones é instrucción acerca de las idolatrías de las Indias. Lima, 1919.

Viñas y Mey, Carmelo. El estatuo del obrero indígena en la colonización española. Madrid, 1929.

*West Coast Leader*. Lima. Particularly special numbers on Cuzco, Oriente, Trujillo, Central Railway, etc.

Wiesse, Carlos. Geografía del Perú. (3d ed). Lima, 1921.
—— Historia del Perú. Lima, 1930-31.

Wiesse, María (Myriam). Santa Rosa de Lima. Lima, 1922.

Xerez, Francisco de. [c. 1504-34]. Narrative of the Conquest of Peru. Ed. Clemente K. Markham. London, 1872.

Zárate, Agustín de. Historia del descubrimiento y conquista del Perú. . . . Antwerp, 1555; Madrid, 1853.

# INDEX

459

# INDEX

Ants, 18
  tambocha, 110-11
Anzo River, 274
*Apachita*, 343, 356
*Apamuguaco*, 234
Aphrodisiacs, 203, 280
APRA (Popular Revolutionary Alliance of
    America), 87, 188-91, 197, 316, 319,
    368, 416, 417-29
  and Church, 425, 428
  discipline of, 423
  newspapers, 423
  persecution of, 420, 422, 423, 427
  program, 423-26
  revolt of 1932, 99, 189 ff., 389, 422, cf.
    Trujillo
  schools, 423
*Apra, El*, 423
Aprismo, 397, 417-29, 446
Apristas, 197, 368, 417-29, 446
Apu, 343
Apu-Inca-Atahualpa, cf. Santos, Juan
Apurímac River, 202, 208, 326
Aqueducts, 12, 26, 27, 38, 51, 69, 74, 187
    227
  destruction of, 69
  of Sutucchaca, 227
  Incan festivals for, 41
  Cf. irrigation
*Aquilino*, 345
Aragón, 252
Archælogical remains, 25-29, 187-91, 197,
    202, 228, 256-63, 265-68, 311
Archæology, 105-107, 197-98, 224, 315
Archaic culture, 25, 85
Archbishop of Lima, cf. Lima
Architecture, 254-55, 268
Areche, 314
Arequipa (City), 87, 92, 103-104, 198,
    200, 230, 244-55, 265, 268, 300, 315,
    350, 351, 356, 378, 386, 396, 412,
    438
  and Misti, 244-49
  architecture, 254-55
  cathedral, 245, 252
  character of people, 247-52
  Chucuito, Church of, 437
  Churches, 245-46
  climate, 247
  Compañia, church of, 437
  countryside, 250-51
  diversions, 249-50
  festivals, 251
  Jesuit church, 254
  military leaders, 253-54
  printing press, 253
  revolution of, 422

Arequipa (City) (Cont.)
  Santa Catalina, 246
  superstitions, 245-46
Arequipa (Department), 38, 326, 413,
    415, 416
Argentina, 30, 34, 38, 39, 106, 147, 150,
    403, 408, 416, 419, 447
Arias de Avila, Pedro, 44, 45
Arica, 83, 87, 379, 383
Aristocracy, 77, 82, 83, 175, 302, 313,
    325, 358, 379, 433, 441, 442
Aristocrats, 77, 78, 79, 91-97, 117-27,
    121-22, 166, 237, 378, 413
Armara, General, 388
Army, 14, 79, 87, 113-15, 166-68, 208,
    330, 377-90, 426
  abuses of, 382
  and APRA, 428
  and Church, 377-78
  and democracy, 377, 379
  and Indians, 390
  and landholding class, 377
  and mestizos, 390
  as ruling institution, 379
  cavalry, 384-85
  conscription, 15, 297, 301, 383-85
  conscription, illegal, 182
  corruption of, 385
  depredations of, 379-80
  discipline of, 380
  disorganization of, 379-80
  equipment of, 385
  executions by, 388
  forced loans, 382
  graft in, 385
  independence period, 389
  Indians in, 383, 384
  Indian tradition of, 384
  legal restrictions on, 382
  political intrigues, 385
  popular currents in, 389
  proclamations of, 381
  promotion in, 380-81, 390
  tactics of, 379-80
  Cf. conquest, militarism, militarists,
    Trujillo revolt, assassinations
Arriaga, Pablo Joseph de, 226
Art, 122, 240-41, 255, 426, 432-39
  Chimú, 28
  Church, 199-200
  colonial, 254-55, 268, 437
  indigenous, 432-33, 434, 437
  Mexican school, 199, 432-33
  Mochican, 25-26, 198
  Modern, 193, 198-99, 255, 432-39
  Nazcan, 28
  Spanish, 433

# INDEX

# INDEX

Baptism, 61, 333, 370
Baquijano, 77, 440
Barcelona, 176, 241
Barley, 72, 326, 332, 338
Basadre, Jorge, 74, 182, 321, 380, 384, 387, 392, 432, 446
Basketry, 203, 340
Basques, 74, 412
Batán Grande, 299
Beans, 142, 326, 338
Beingolea, Manuel, 444
*Bejucas*, 18
Belaunde, Augusto A., 296
Belaunde, Victor Andrés, 174, 300, 359, 410, 415
Belen, 272
Belgium, 176
Bellido, María de, 232, 396
Bombonaje Palm, 283
Benalcázar, 63
Benavides, Oscar, 87, 388, 420
Benítez, 380
Berlin, 106
Beri-beri, 16, 111, 273
Bilcas, 62
Billinghurst, 365, 377
Binços, 226
Blankets, 239
Blas, Camilo, 193, 438, 447
Blow-gun, 278, 279, 280
*bobugotarato*, 278
Bocanegro, Edmunod (pseud.), 115-16
*Boletin Titikaka*, 316
Bolívar, Simón, 78, 210, 227, 233, 288, 307, 308, 364-65, 381, 386
statue of, 300
Bolivia, 21, 28, 30, 34, 147, 304, 307, 381, 388, 400, 412, 415, 416
Bolivian Confederation 86, 351, 381, 382, 407, 408, 410
Bolshevism, 85, 109, 445
Bourbons, 77
Bourgeoisie, 22, 77, 79, 80, 82, 87, 367, 379, 382, 383, 407, 410 414, 441
Boza, Colonel, 388
Brazil, 16, 81, 276, 408
Brea y Pariñas concession, 402
Bridges, 28-29, 51, 69, 208, 260
British, cf. English
Brujo, El., 188
Bubonic plague, 273
Bucaneers, 72, 176, 232
Bucunga roots, 280
Buito, 280
Bunge, Carlos Octavio, 386
Bureaucracy, 20, 76, 80, 84, 166-68, 184, 237, 310, 318, 441

Burial practices, 27, 100, 235, 281, 356
Burros, 203, 332, 338
Bustamante y Ballivían, Enrique, 254, 444
Buzzards, 272, 273
Byron, 443

Cabello de Balboa, Miguel, 26, 32
Cabello de Carbonera, Mercedes, 184, 380
Cabello de la Espada, Marqués (pseud.), 95
Cabeza, 142
Cabuyas, 338
Cáceres, Andrés Avelino, 383
Cáceres, Aurora, 256, 397
*Cachahuaina*, 345
*Cachampa*, 345
*Cachaspare*, 347
*Cachimbo*, 347
*Cachua*, 235, 347
*Caciques*, 84, 279
*Caciquismo*, 84, 413
Cactus, 23, 131, 204, 339
Cadiz, 210
Caduy-Rabo, 250
Cahuide, General, 65, 261, 390
Cahuillaca, 262
Caipora, 282
Cairo, 176
Cajabamba, 190
Cajamarca, 34, 51, 53-57, 59, 63, 86, 105, 200, 208, 239, 308, 337, 339, 344, 345, 353, 375, 411, 441
people of, 209
Sierra of, 189, 315
Cajamarca (Department), 326
Cajas, 51, 142
Calasaya portal, 28
Calancha, Father, 187
Calcheo, 343
California, 192
Callacoya, 222
Callahuaya, 133-54, cf. *Curandero*
Callao, 72, 84, 109, 171, 185, 232, 396, 399, 404, 420
Calle, Guido, 420
Calles, Plutarco Elías, 421
*Camachicos*, 320
*Camana*, 279
Camata Valleys, 150
Cannibals, 168, 279
*Canchi*, 346
Candia, Pedro de, 58, 229
Cangonillo, 266
Cangallo, Pampas of, 238
Canning, Minister, 81
Canoes, 272, 275, 280, 284
Canova, 241
Canseco, 253

# INDEX

# INDEX

464

# INDEX

Church (Cont.)
  in Colonial period, 358-63
  legal status of, 369
  miraculous cures of, 356
  monarchical sympathies of, 78
  money-lending by, 367
  property, 359
  rents, 98-100
  ritual, 356, 357
  strike, 127
  tithes, 369
  tribunals, 369
  wealth, 362
  unifying force of, 360
Churriguresque, 77, 254, 263
Chu'uncho, 346
Chuyugal estate, 98-100
Cianaca, Chief Justice, 73
Científicos, 302
Cieza de León, Pedro, 70, 228, 230, 356
Cinnabar, 223, 226, 435
Cintakcaniris, 150
Cisneros, Luis Benjamín, 440
Cium, 26
Civilismo, 378
Civilistas, 87, 302, 366, 368, 378, 383,
  389, 390, 423, 427, 428, 436
Class struggle, 319, 326
Clergy, 237, 315, 364, 365, 374, 391, 428,
  442
Clericalism, 83, 84, 121, 176, 367, cf.
  Church
Climate, 9-14, 16, 18-19, 28, 50, 53, 174,
  184, 199, 247, 410
Coal, 401, 426
Coaque, 50
Coast, 9-12, 20-21, 22, 51, 76, 80, 147,
  236, 246, 298-300, 304, 309, 318,
  339, 387, 407, 408, 411, 412, 414,
  415, 434-36, 438, 440, 445
  area of, 21
  bourgeoisie of, 83
  civilizations of, 25-28, 85-86
  "Eyebrow" of, 10
  industries of, 237
  landholding, 298-300
  proletariat of, 82
  psychology of, 22, 247, 433, 448
  valleys of, 12, 118
  cf. negroes
Cobija, 381
Cobo, Bernabé, 359
Coca, 15, 131, 152, 206, 216, 255, 260,
  329, 339, 356, 357
Cocaine vice, 15, 298, 426
Coca-maliajcuy, 339
Cocculus toxicoferus, 278

Coconuts, 45, 47
Codesido, 397, 438
Coffee, 19, 274, 276, 333
Colamboa, 342
Colca, 202
Colcampata, 260
Collas, 12, 24, 34, 35, 412
Colombia, 23, 30, 44, 147, 276, 381, 392
Colompata, 260, 268
Colonial era, 63-73, 74-79, 86, 254, 320,
  325, 358-63, 391, 398-99, 441, 447
Colonialism, 22, 84, 85, 175-76, 183, 184,
  196, 205-206, 265, 306, 410, 440,
  442, 443
Colónida, 444-45
Colquemarca, 24
Comas River, 330
Comercio, El, 99, 184, 418, 420
Communal lands, cf. Indians
Communications, 20, 34, 36, 74, 79, 183,
  201, 237, 275, 276, 370, 387-88, 411,
  412
Communism, 424
Communist movement, 87
Communist Party, 422
Communist Third International, 422
Communists, 319, 420-24
Compañia Brazilera de Navigación, 275
Concepción, 320
Concessions, 120, 401-402, 426
Concho Pata ruins, 228
Conch-shell trumpet, 19, 329, 344
Concubines, 58, 61
Condesuyne, 38
Condor, 12, 53, 204, 227, 239, 260, 296,
  305, 340, 344
Condor dance, 345
Condorcuna, Mt., battle of, 238
Condorino, Bishop Antonio, 235
Conibos, 281
Conopas, 222
Conquerors, Spanish, 12, 14, 20, 42-65,
  69, 74, 176, 254, 261, 265, 268, 271,
  275, 305, 311, 347, 352, 443
Conquest, Spanish, 44-65, 74-76, 101, 176,
  209, 238, 263, 267, 288, 328, 344,
  349-55, 362, 375, 424, 437
Conquistadores, cf. Conquerors
Conscription, cf. Army
Constitution, 387
  of Independence, 79
  of Huancayo (1839), 408
  of 1919, 414
Constitutional Convention
  of 1823, 350
  of 1834, 350
  of Independence, 350

465

# INDEX

# INDEX

# INDEX

471

# INDEX

Markets, 172, 202-11, 239, 272, 337, 341, 426, 436
  international, 398
Marriage, 370, 394
  customs, 36, 148-49, 217-19, 243, 280, 333, 371
  trial, cf. Sirvinacuy
Martínez Lujan, Domingo, 444
*Masato*, 280, 281
*Mashua*, 326, 332, 338
Masías family, 254
Mass, 269, 329, 350, 352, 353, 368, 370, 371, 372
*Matapalo*, 18
Mateo, 155-66
Matienzo, Bishop, 235
Mauñós, Heraclío, 375
Marx, Karl, 313, 431, 440, 446, 447
Mayas, 412
Mayer, Dora, 314
Means, Philip Ainsworth, 34, 39, 255
Medicine, 18, 40, 102-103, 104-105, 147-154, 213, 266, 278, 317
Medicine men, cf. *Cuaranderos*
Medina, Bishop Cipriano, 235
Meiggs, Henry, 14, 185
Meiggs Notes, 401
Melchora, 397
Melgar, Mariano, 440
Mella, Julio Antonio, 421, 422
Menahunosa, Marqués, cf. Lamas, José de
Mencken, 444
Mercedarians, 362
Mérimée, Prosper, 392
Mestizos, 70, 76, 176, 200, 240, 241, 248-249, 274, 307, 309, 310, 319, 326, 347, 364, 376, 378, 386, 387, 390, 393-94, 395, 430, 436, 440, 446, cf. Cholos
Metal work, 25, 26, 40, 59, 63, 105
Mexicans, 247, 249
Mexico, 22, 23, 40, 69, 76, 81, 176, 183, 192, 199, 205, 232, 261, 302, 391, 395, 400, 412, 434, 443, 447
  army of, 377
  art revolt of, 433
  indigenous art of, 434
  modern art of, 434
  National Revolutionary Party of, 429
  revolution of, 421, 428
  San Carlos academy in, 433
  Six Year Plan of, 429
  university of, 421, 428
Mexico City, 433, 434
Michael Angelo, 268
Middle Ages, 117, 294, 299
Middle Class, 87, 181, 424, 426, 441

Milan, 176
Militarism, 79, 83, 84, 87, 307, 377-90, 413, 441, cf. army
Militarists, 79, 80, 83, 166, 291, 301, 315, 308, 351, 377-90, 400, 410, 428, 442
Mining, 14, 20, 70, 76, 77, 84, 86, 107-108, 175, 238, 287, 320, 323, 333, 352, 399, 400, 401, 424, 426
Miracles, 77, 176-79, 233-37, 251, 267
Miraculous cures, 176-77, 245-46, 356
Miraflores, 117, 124, 171
Miró Quesadas, 184, 418
Miró Quesada, Oscar, 418, 419
Missionaries, 76, 100, 112, 274, 277, 323
Misti, Mt., 244, 249
*Mitmae*, 33, 251
*Mittanes*, 293
Mochicas, 11, 24-26, 39, 85, 187-89, 191, 194, 197-98
Moche, 105, 139, 187, 191-96, 200, 435
  valley of, 184, 188
Mocho, 374
Moctezuma, 40, 377
Mogrovejo, Toribio de, 359
Molina, Alonzo de, 47
Molina, Enríquez, 447
*Molle*, cf. Pepper tree
Mollendo, 10, 244
Money, 74, 76, 91
  circulation of, 76
  lending of, 367
Monkeys, 18, 45, 156, 182, 272, 280, 283, 346, 437
Monroe doctrine, 429, 430
Monteagudo, Mother, 246
*Monterías*, 282, 283
Montesinos de Valverde, Count (pseud.), 92-95
Montevideo Students' Congress, 417
Moon Goddess, 27, 42, 60, 256, 261, 262
Moquegua, 118-19, 326
Mora, Florencia de, 98-99
Mora, José Joaquín de, 80
Morales Bermúdez, Remigio, 253, 383
Morán, General, 388
More, Federico, 444
Moreno, José, Ignacio, 78
Morocco, 422
Morochuchos, 240
Morona River, 279, 280
Mosquitoes, 11, 16, 111, 155, 156
Mostajo, 253
Mostejo, Francisco, 319
Motupe, 51
Mountain sickness, cf. *Saroche*
Moya, José Vicente de la, 233
Moyobamba, 18

474

# INDEX

# INDEX

# INDEX

# INDEX

# INDEX

# INDEX

481

# INDEX